796
GUI

REF

$19.95

DATE			

The Guinness book of
sports records.

© THE BAKER & TAYLOR CO.

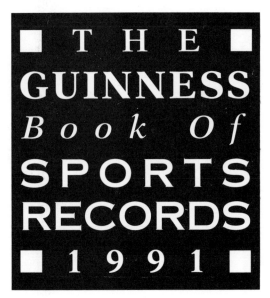

THE
GUINNESS
Book Of
SPORTS
RECORDS
1991

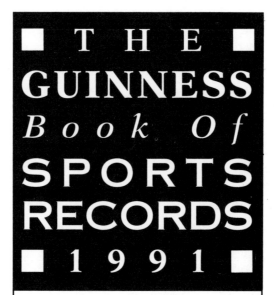

THE GUINNESS Book Of SPORTS RECORDS 1991

EDITOR
Mark Young

CONTRIBUTING EDITORS
Peter J. Matthews
Michelle Dunkley McCarthy
Ian Morrison

56,630

Facts On File
New York • Oxford

THE GUINNESS BOOK OF SPORTS RECORDS 1991

Copyright © 1991 by Guinness Publishing Ltd

Facts On File, Inc.
460 Park Avenue South
New York NY 10016
USA

This book is taken in part from *The Guinness Book of Records* © 1990

Facts On File books are available at special discounts when purchased in bulk quantities for businesses, associations, institutions or sales promotions. Please contact the Special Sales Department of our New York office at 212/683-2244 (dial 800/322-8755 except in NY, AK or HI).

ISBN 0-8160-2649-1 (hardcover)
ISBN 0-8160-2650-5 (paperback)
ISSN 1054-4178

Text design by Ron Monteleone
Jacket design by Ron Monteleone
Composition by Ron Monteleone/Facts On File, Inc.
Production by Michael Braunschweiger
Manufactured by R. R. Donnelley & Sons, Inc.
Printed in the United States of America

10 9 8 7 6 5 4 3 2 1

This book is printed on acid-free paper.

CONTENTS

ACKNOWLEDGMENTS

In order to cover a topic as wide-ranging as the world of sports in a comprehensive manner, the cooperation of a vast number of individuals and organizations is required. I would like to extend my thanks to all the people who have been contacted by our research staff. Regrettably, space prevents me from mentioning everyone. However, I must single out the following individuals whose expertise, patience and consideration have added greatly to this project: Gary K. Johnson, National Collegiate Athletic Association; Ken Park, *Facts On File World News Digest*; Paul Robbins, Eastern editor, *Skiing Magazine*; and Kathy Wydick, LPGA Tour.

Special thanks are given to friends and colleagues who loaned memorabilia to be used for the cover of this book: William S. Romano, Leon J. Battista Jr., John Hansen, Marjorie Bank, Raymond Hill, Peter J. Matthews, Oliver Trager and Tom Drysdale.

Publishing, as with sports, requires the efforts of many people to produce the on-field performance. I would like to thank the talented and professional team of people who have so ably assisted me in producing this book: Gerard Helferich, Olivia McKean, Jo Stein, Ron Monteleone, Dale Williams, Michael Braunschweiger, Grace M. Ferrara, Carole Campbell, Joe Reilly, Gary M. Krebs and Stewart Newport.

Mark Young
New York

INTRODUCTION

"Football [soccer] is not life or death, it's more serious than that."

—Bill Shankly,
Manager, Liverpool F.C., England

Sport incites passion (in 1969 a three-game soccer playoff ignited a war between El Salvador and Honduras). Involvement in sports, both physical and emotional, continues to rise in the United States. On March 11, 1990, the National Football League (NFL) signed a $3.65 billion four-year television pact with the three networks and two cable stations. During the summer 54,871,538 people attended major league baseball games. In the fall 25,012 runners started the New York City Marathon, with 23,774 completing the race. On December 4, 1990 an estimated 41 million viewers, 16.4 percent of the population, watched the San Francisco 49ers v. New York Giants football game.

As Americans' interest in sports grows, so does their thirst for knowledge of each sport's heroes and history. While there are various reference books on sports, none provides a full range of reference material: Fast facts, historical information, and team and individual statistics in all sports. *The Guinness Book of Sports Records 1991*, the first edition published by Facts On File, Inc., fills that gap.

This edition covers 75 sports, providing statistics on winners, losers, all-time individual leaders, championship teams and coaches. For the first time, complete lists of winners are published for every major competition. Also for the first time, records are chronicled at the main levels of each particular sport, e.g., the section on Baseball includes records on the Little League World Series, NCAA Division I, the Olympic Games, the Major Leagues, the League Championship Series and the World Series.

Besides being a complete sports almanac, this edition maintains the Guinness tradition of presenting information in an easy-to-read, entertaining style. A comprehensive index of names, events and sports allows readers to find what they need quickly or sit back and browse at their leisure. As ever, Guinness notes the offbeat. Where else would you find the longest Olympic torch relay within one country? (11,222 miles from Newfoundland to Calgary, Canada. The relay began on November 17, 1987 and ended with the lighting of the Olympic flame on February 13, 1988. The torch traveled 5,088 miles by foot, 4,419 miles by aircraft/ferry, 1,712 miles by snowmobile and 3 miles by dogsled.)

"You can look it up."

—Casey Stengel,
Manager, New York Yankees

ARCHERY

ORIGINS Though the earliest pictorial evidence of the existence of bows is seen in the Mesolithic cave paintings in Spain, archery as an organized sport appears to have developed in the 3rd century A.D. Competitive archery may, however, date back to the 12th century B.C. The National Archery Association of America was established in 1879, and the inaugural National Outdoor Target Championship was held in 1884. The world governing body is the Fédération Internationale de Tir à l'Arc (FITA), founded in 1931.

Highest championship scores The highest scores achieved in either a world or Olympic championship for Double FITA rounds are: men, 2,617 points (possible 2,880) by Darrell Owen Pace (US) and Richard McKinney (US) at Long Beach, CA on 21–22 October 1983; and women, 2,683 points by Kim Soo-nyung (South Korea) at Seoul, South Korea on 27–30 September 1988.

World championships The most titles won by a man is four by Hans Deutgen (Sweden) in 1947–50 and by a woman is seven by Janina Spychajowa-Kurkowska (Poland) in 1931–34, 1936, 1939 and 1947. The United States has a record 14 men's and eight women's team titles.

The most individual world titles won by a US archer is three, by Richard McKinney: 1977, 1983 and 1985. Jean Lee, 1950 and 1952, is the only US woman to win two individual world titles. Luann Ryon was Olympic women's champion in 1976 and also world champion in 1977.

WORLD RECORDS (Single FITA Rounds)

MEN

Event	Archer	Country	Points	Year
FITA	Stanislav Zabrodskiy	USSR	1,342	1989
90 m	Yuriy Leontyev	USSR	329	1988
70 m	Hiroshi Yamamoto	Japan	344	1990
50 m	Richard McKinney	USA	345	1982
30 m	Takayoshi Matsushita	Japan	357	1986
Final	Stanislav Zabrodskiy	USSR	3,963	1989

WOMEN

Event	Archer	Country	Points	Year
FITA	Kim Soo-nyung	S. Korea	1,368	1989
70 m	Kim Soo-nyung	S. Korea	341	1990
60 m	Kim Soo-nyung	S. Korea	347	1989
50 m	Kim Soo-nyung	S. Korea	336	1988
30 m	Joanne Edens	Great Britain	357	1990
Final	Kim Soo-nyung	S. Korea	343	1989

OLYMPIC GAMES Hubert van Innis (Belgium) won a record 9 medals, six gold and three silver medals, at the 1900 and 1920 Olympic Games.

The most successful US archer at the Olympic Games has been Darrell Pace, gold medalist in 1976 and 1984.

FLIGHT SHOOTING

CROSSBOW

2,047 yd 2 in, Harry Drake (US) "Smith Creek" Flight Range near Austin, NV, 30 July 1988.

UNLIMITED FOOTBOW

1 mile 268 yd Harry Drake, Ivanpah Dry Lake, CA, 24 October 1971.

RECURVE BOW

Men: 1,336 yd 1 ft 3 in, Don Brown (US), "Smith Creek" Flight Range, 2 August 1987.

Women: 1,039 yd 1 ft 1 in, April Moon (US), Wendover, UT, 13 September 1981.

CONVENTIONAL FOOTBOW

Men: 1,542 yd 2 ft 10 in, Harry Drake, Ivanpah Dry Lake, 6 October 1979.

Women: 1,113 yd 2 ft 6 in, Arlyne Rhode (US), Wendover, UT, 10 September 1978.

ARCHERY

World Championship Wins (Men)

World Championship Wins (Women)

US CHAMPIONSHIPS The most archery titles won is 17, by Lida Howell (née Scott) between 1883 and 1907.

The most men's titles is nine (3 individual, 6 pairs), by Richard McKinney, 1977, 1979–83, 1985–87. The greatest span of title winning is 29 years, by William Henry Thompson, who was the first US champion in 1879 and won his fifth and last men's title in 1908.

Greatest draw Gary Sentman, of Roseberg, OR drew a longbow weighing a record 176 lb to the maximum draw on the arrow of 28¼ in at Forksville, PA on 20 September 1975.

24 hours—target archery The highest recorded score over 24 hours by a pair of archers is 65,055 during 60 Portsmouth Rounds (60 arrows per round at 20 yd at 2 ft FITA targets) by Mick Brown and Les Powici (both Great Britain) at Guildford, England on 25–26 March 1989.

Paul Peters (US) set an individual record of 31,378 in 56 Portsmouth Rounds at Mukilteo, WA on 11–12 November 1989.

AUSTRALIAN RULES FOOTBALL

ORIGINS A cross between soccer and rugby, Australian Rules football was developed in the mid-19th century by Henry Harrison and Thomas Wills, who helped to form the Melbourne Football Club in 1858. In 1877, the Victorian Football Association was founded, from which eight clubs broke away to form the Victorian Football League (VFL). Four more teams had been admitted by 1925, and in 1987 teams from Queensland and Western Australia joined the league, which has since been renamed the Australian Football League.

VICTORIAN FOOTBALL LEAGUE GRAND FINAL The sport's premier event is the VFL Grand Final, played annually since 1897. Staged at the Melbourne Cricket Ground, the record attendance is 121,696 in 1970. Carlton has won the most championships with 15 titles (1906–08, 1914–15, 1938, 1945, 1947, 1968, 1970, 1972, 1979, 1981–82, 1987).

VFL RECORDS

Highest Score in a Game 345, St. Kilda 204 *v.* Melbourne 141, 6 May 1978.

Highest Team Score 238 by Fitzroy *v.* Melbourne, 28 July 1979.

Most Goals in a Career 2,191, Peter Hudson (Hawthorn, 1963–81).

Most Games 403, Kevin Bartlett (Richmond, 1965–83).

AUTO RACING

ORIGINS The site of the first automobile race is open to debate. There is a claim that the first race was held in the United States in 1878, from Green Bay to Madison, WI, won by an Oshkosh steamer. However, France discounts this, claiming that the La Velocipede, a 19.3-mile race in Paris on 20 April 1887, was the first race. The first organized race did take place in France: 732 miles from Paris to Bordeaux and back, on 11–14 June 1895. The first closed-circuit race was held over five laps of a one-mile dirt track at Narragansett Park, Cranston, RI on 7 September 1896. Grand Prix racing started in 1906, also in France. The Indianapolis 500 was first run on 30 May 1911 (see below).

Fastest circuit The highest average lap speed attained on any closed circuit is 250.958 mph in a time trial by Dr. Hans Liebold (Germany) who lapped the 7.85-mile high-speed track at Nardo, Italy in 1 min 52.67 sec in a Mercedes-Benz C111-IV experimental coupé on 5 May 1979. It was powered by a V8 engine with two KKK turbochargers, with an output of 500 hp at 6,200 rpm.

Fastest pit stop Bobby Unser (US) took 4 seconds to take on fuel on lap 10 of the Indianapolis 500 on 30 May 1976.

Fastest race The fastest race is the Busch Clash at Daytona, FL over 50 miles on a 2 ½-mile 31-degree banked track. In 1987 Bill Elliott (US) averaged 197.802 mph in a Ford Thunderbird. Al Unser Jr. set a world record for a 500-mile race when he won the Michigan 500 on 9 August 1990 at an average speed of 189.727 mph.

INDIANAPOLIS 500

The Indianapolis 500 mile race (200 laps) was inaugurated on 30 May 1911. Two drivers share the record for the most wins (4): A. J. Foyt Jr. (US) in 1961, 1964, 1967 and 1977; and Al Unser (US), in 1970–71, 1978 and 1987. Foyt has also started in 33 Indianapolis 500 races (1959–90). The record time is 2hr 41 min 18.248 sec (185.984 mph) by Arie Luyendyk (Netherlands) driving a 1990 Lola-Chevrolet on 27 May 1990.

The record average speed for four laps qualifying is 225.301 mph by Emerson Fittipaldi (Brazil) in a 1990 Penske-Chevrolet on 13 May 1990. On the same day he set the one-lap record of 225.575 mph. The track record is 228.502 mph by Al Unser Jr. (US) on 11 May 1990. Rick Mears (US) has gained 5 poles in 1979, 1982, 1986, 1988 and 1989. The record prize fund is $6,325,803, and the individual prize record is $1,090,940, by Luyendyk, both in 1990.

INDIANAPOLIS 500 WINNERS

Year	Driver	Speed (mph)
1911	Ray Harroun	74.602
1912	Joe Dawson	78.719
1913	Jules Goux	75.933
1914	Rene Thomas	82.474
1915	Ralph DePalma	89.840
1916	Dario Resta	84.001
1917	(not held)	
1918	(not held)	
1919	Howard Wilcox	88.050
1920	Gaston Chevrolet	88.618
1921	Tommy Milton	89.621
1922	Jimmy Murphy	94.484
1923	Tommy Milton	90.954
1924	L.L. Corum & Joe Boyer	98.234
1925	Peter DePaolo	101.127
1926	Frank Lockhart	95.904
1927	George Souders	97.545
1928	Louis Meyer	99.482
1929	Ray Keech	97.585
1930	Billy Arnold	100.448
1931	Louis Schneider	96.629
1932	Fred Frame	104.144
1933	Louis Meyer	104.162
1934	William Cummings	104.863
1935	Kelly Petillo	106.240
1936	Louis Meyer	109.069
1937	Wilbur Shaw	113.580
1938	Floyd Roberts	117.200
1939	Wilbur Shaw	115.035
1940	Wilbur Shaw	114.277
1941	Floyd Davis & Mauri Rose	115.117
1942	(not held)	
1943	(not held)	
1944	(not held)	

INDIANAPOLIS 500 WINNERS (Continued)

Year	Driver	Speed (mph)
1945	(not held)	
1946	George Robson	114.820
1947	Mauri Rose	116.338
1948	Mauri Rose	119.814
1949	Bill Holland	121.327
1950	Johnnie Parsons	124.002
1951	Lee Wallard	126.244
1952	Troy Ruttman	128.922
1953	Bill Vukovich	128.740
1954	Bill Vukovich	130.840
1955	Bob Sweikert	128.209
1956	Pat Flaherty	128.490
1957	Sam Hanks	135.601
1958	Jim Bryan	133.791
1959	Rodger Ward	135.857
1960	Jim Rathmann	138.767
1961	A. J. Foyt Jr.	139.131
1962	Rodger Ward	140.293
1963	Parnelli Jones	143.137
1964	A. J. Foyt Jr.	147.350
1965	Jim Clark	150.686
1966	Graham Hill	144.317
1967	A. J. Foyt Jr.	151.207
1968	Bobby Unser	152.882
1969	Mario Andretti	156.867
1970	Al Unser	155.749
1971	Al Unser	157.735
1972	Mark Donohue	162.962
1973	Gordon Johncock	159.036
1974	Johnny Rutherford	158.589
1975	Bobby Unser	149.213
1976	Johnny Rutherford	148.725
1977	A. J. Foyt Jr.	161.331
1978	Al Unser	161.363
1979	Rick Mears	158.899
1980	Johnny Rutherford	142.862
1981	Bobby Unser	139.084
1982	Gordon Johncock	162.029
1983	Tom Sneva	162.117
1984	Rick Mears	163.612
1985	Danny Sullivan	152.982
1986	Bobby Rahal	170.722
1987	Al Unser	162.175

INDIANAPOLIS 500 WINNERS (Continued)

Year	Driver	Speed (mph)
1988	Rick Mears	144.809
1989	Emerson Fittipaldi	167.581
1990	Arie Luyendyk	185.984

INDY 500 CAREER MILES (through 1990)

Driver	Races	Miles
A. J. Foyt Jr.	33	11,722.50
Al Unser	25	9,892.50
Gordon Johncock	22	7,275.00
Johnny Rutherford	24	6,980.00
Bobby Unser	19	6,527.50
Mario Andretti	25	6,405.00

INDY 500 CAREER EARNINGS (through 1990)

Driver	Wins	Earnings($)
Rick Mears	3	2,943,285
Al Unser	4	2,814,615
A. J. Foyt Jr.	4	2,294,489
Emerson Fittipaldi	1	2,226,869
Mario Andretti	1	1,954,355
Johnny Rutherford	3	1,691,141

Source: Indianapolis Motor Speedway

BRICKYARD CIRCUIT-BREAKERS ■ ARIE LUYENDYK OF THE NETHERLANDS (BELOW) WON THE 1990 INDIANAPOLIS 500 IN A RECORD TIME OF 2 HR 41 MIN 18.248 SEC (185.984 MPH). EMERSON FITTIPALDI OF BRAZIL (ABOVE) SET THE FOUR LAP QUALIFYING AVERAGE SPEED RECORD AT 225.301 MPH ON 13 MAY 1990.

First woman driver The first and only woman to compete in the Indianapolis 500 is Janet Guthrie. She passed her rookie test in May 1976 and earned the right to compete in the qualifying rounds, but was unable to win a place on the starting line when the Vollstedt-Offenhauser she drove was withdrawn from the race after repeated mechanical failures. In the 61st running of the Indianapolis 500, in 1977, Guthrie became the first woman to compete, although her car developed mechanical problems that forced her to retire after 27 laps. In 1978, she completed the race finishing in 9th place.

Indy Car Championships (CART) The first Indy Car Championship was held in 1909 under the authority of the American Automobile Association (AAA). In 1959 the United States Automobile Club (USAC) took over the running of the Indy series. Since 1979, Championship Auto Racing Teams Inc. (CART) has organized the Indy Championship, which has been called the PPG Indy Car World Series Championship since 1979.

Most Wins The most successful driver in Indy car history is A. J. Foyt Jr., who has won 67 races and seven championships (1960–61, 1963–64, 1967, 1975 and 1979). The record for the most victories in a season is 10 shared by two drivers: A. J. Foyt Jr. (1964) and Al Unser Sr. (1970). Mario Andretti holds the record for the most laps driven in Indy championships at 7,305; he also holds the record for most pole positions at 64.

Through the 1990 season, Rick Mears has the highest career earnings for Indy drivers with $8,268,565. The single season earnings record was set at $2,166,078 in 1989 by Emerson Fittipaldi.

NASCAR (NATIONAL ASSOCIATION FOR STOCK CAR AUTO RACING)

The first NASCAR championship was held in 1949. Since 1971, the championship series has been called the Winston Cup Championship. The championship has been won a record 7 times by Richard Petty (US): 1964, 1967, 1971–72, 1974–75 and 1979.

Petty won 200 NASCAR Winston Cup races in 1,107 starts from 1958 to 1990; his best season was 1967, with 27 wins. Petty, on 1 August 1971, was the first driver to pass $1 million career earnings.

The NASCAR career money record is $12,782,634 through the 1990 season, by Dale Earnhardt; Bill Elliott won a season record $2,383,187 in 1985. Geoff Bodine won 55 races in NASCAR Modified racing in 1978.

Shawna Robinson became the first woman to win a NASCAR race when she won an event in the NASCAR Dash Series at Asheville, NC on 10 June 1988.

WINSTON CUP CHAMPIONSHIP	
Top Five Career Race Winners (1949–90)	
Driver	**Victories**
Richard Petty	200
David Pearson	105
Bobby Allison	86
Cale Yarborough	83
Darrell Waltrip	79

Source: NASCAR

DAYTONA 500

The Daytona 500 has been held at the 2 ½ mile oval Daytona International Speedway in Daytona, FL since 1959. The race is the major event of the NASCAR season. Richard Petty has a record seven wins–1964, 1966, 1971, 1973–74, 1979 and 1981. The record average speed for the race is 177.602 mph by Buddy Baker in an Oldsmobile in 1980. The qualifying speed record is 210.364, by Bill Elliott in a Ford Thunderbird in 1987.

DAYTONA 500 ■ BUDDY BAKER SET AN AVERAGE SPEED MARK OF 177.602 MPH IN WINNING THE 1980 RACE.

DAYTONA 500

Average Winning Speed (mph), 1959-1990

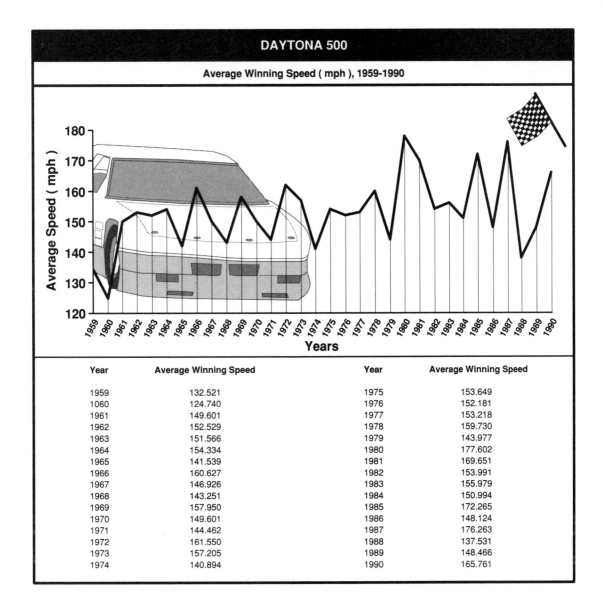

Year	Average Winning Speed	Year	Average Winning Speed
1959	132.521	1975	153.649
1060	124.740	1976	152.181
1961	149.601	1977	153.218
1962	152.529	1978	159.730
1963	151.566	1979	143.977
1964	154.334	1980	177.602
1965	141.539	1981	169.651
1966	160.627	1982	153.991
1967	146.926	1983	155.979
1968	143.251	1984	150.994
1969	157.950	1985	172.265
1970	149.601	1986	148.124
1971	144.462	1987	176.263
1972	161.550	1988	137.531
1973	157.205	1989	148.466
1974	140.894	1990	165.761

WORLD CHAMPIONSHIP GRAND PRIX MOTOR RACING

Most successful drivers The World Drivers' Championship, inaugurated in 1950, has been won a record five times by Juan-Manuel Fangio (Argentina) in 1951 and 1954–57. He retired in 1958, after having won 24 Grand Prix races (two shared) from 51 starts.

Alain Prost (France) holds the records for both the most Grand Prix points in a career, 663.5 and the most Grand Prix victories, 44, from 169 Grand Prix races, 1980–90. The most Grand Prix victories in a year is eight by Ayrton Senna (Brazil) in 1988.

The most Grand Prix starts is 208, by Riccardo Patrese (Italy) from 1977–90.

Two Americans have won the World Drivers' Championship, Phil Hill in 1961 and Mario Andretti, in 1978. Andretti has the most Grand Prix wins by a US driver :12 in 128 races 1968–82.

Oldest and youngest The youngest world champion was Emerson Fittipaldi (Brazil), who won his first World Championship on 10 September 1972 at age 25 yr 273 days. The oldest world champion was Juan-Manuel Fangio, who won his last World Championship on 4 August 1957 at age 46 yr 41 days.

FORMULA ONE CAREER LEADERS ■ ALAIN PROST OF FRANCE HAS THE MOST GRAND PRIX WINS (44 OUT OF 169 RACES) AND THE MOST POINTS (663.5). IN 1990 PROST DROVE FOR THE FERRARI TEAM, WHICH HAS WON A RECORD EIGHT MANUFACTURERS' WORLD TITLES AND A RECORD 103 RACES (1950–90).

Manufacturers Ferrari has won a record eight Manufacturers' World Championships: 1961, 1964, 1975–77, 1979, 1982–83. Ferrari has 103 race wins in 463 Grands Prix 1950–90.

The greatest dominance by one team was by McLaren in 1988, when it won 15 of the 16 Grands Prix. Ayrton Senna had eight wins and three seconds, Alain Prost had seven wins and seven seconds. The McLaren team powered by Honda engines, amassed more than three times the points of their nearest rivals, Ferrari.

Fastest race The fastest overall average speed for a Grand Prix race on a circuit in current use is 146.284 mph by Nigel Mansell (UK) in a Williams-Honda at Zeltweg in the Austrian Grand Prix on 16 August 1987. The qualifying lap record was set by Keke Rosberg (Finland) at 1 min 05.59 sec, an average speed of 160.817 mph, in a Williams-Honda at Silverstone in the British Grand Prix on 20 July 1985.

Closest finish The closest finish to a World Championship race was when Ayrton Senna in a Lotus beat Nigel Mansell in a Williams by 0.014

sec in the Spanish Grand Prix at Jerez de la Frontera on 13 April 1986. In the Italian Grand Prix at Monza on 5 September 1971, 0.61 sec separated winner Peter Gethin (UK) from the 5th-place driver.

LE MANS

The greatest distance ever covered in the 24-hour Grand Prix d'Endurance (first held on 26–27 May 1923) on the old Sarthe circuit at Le Mans, France is 3,314.222 miles, by Dr. Helmut Marko (Austria) and Gijs van Lennep (Netherlands), in a 4907-cc flat-12 Porsche 917K Group 5 sports car, on 12–13 June 1971. The record for the greatest distance ever covered for the current circuit is 3,313.241 miles (average speed 137.718 mph) by Jan Lammers (Holland) Johnny Dumfries and Andy Wallace (both UK) in a Jaguar XJR9 on 11–12 June 1988.

The race lap record (now 8.410-mile lap) is 3 min 21.27 sec (average speed 150.429 mph by Alain Ferté (France) in a Jaguar XRJ9 on 10 June 1989. Hans Stück (West Germany) set the practice lap record of 3 min 14.8 sec (average speed 156.62 mph) on 14 June 1985.

Most wins The race has been won by Porsche cars 12 times in 1970–71, 1976–77, 1979, 1981–87. The most wins by one man is 6 by Jacky Ickx (Belgium), 1969, 1975–77 and 1981–82.

RALLYING

ORIGINS The first long-distance rally was from Beijing, China to Paris, France between 10 June and 10 August 1907. It was won by Prince Scipione Borghese of Italy, driving an Itala. The most famous rally is the Monte Carlo Rally, begun in 1911 (see below).

Longest The longest ever rally was the Singapore Airlines London–Sydney Rally over 19,329 miles from Covent Garden, London, England on 14 August 1977 to Sydney Opera House, Sydney, Australia won on 28 September 1977 by Andrew Cowan, Colin Malkin and Michael Broad in a Mercedes 280E. The longest held annually is the Safari Rally (first run in 1953 as the Coronation Rally, through Kenya, Tanzania and Uganda, but now restricted to Kenya). The race has covered up to 3,874 miles, as in the 17th Safari held from 8–12 April 1971. It has been won a record 5 times by Shekhar Mehta (Kenya), in 1973, 1979–82.

MONTE CARLO The Monte Carlo Rally (first run 1911) has been won a record 4 times by: Sandro Munari (Italy) in 1972, 1975, 1976 and 1977; and Walter Röhrl (West Germany, with codriver Christian Geistdorfer) in 1980, 1982–84, each time in a different car. The smallest car to win was an 851-cc Saab driven by Erik Carlsson (Sweden) and Gunnar Häggbom (Sweden) on 25 January 1962, and by Carlsson and Gunnar Palm on 24 January 1963.

WORLD CHAMPIONSHIP Two World Drivers' Championships (instituted 1979) have been won by Walter Röhrl, 1980 and 1982, Juha Kankkunen (Finland), 1986–87, and by Mikki Biasion (Italy) 1988–89. The most wins in World Championship races is 19, by Hannu Mikkola and Markku Alen (Finland) to April 1990.

DRAG RACING

Piston engined The lowest elapsed time recorded by a piston-engined dragster from a standing start for 440 yd is 4.881 sec by Gary Ormsby (US) with the highest terminal velocity reached at the end of a 440-yd run of 296.05 mph in qualifying for the the NHRA Heartlands Nationals at Topeka, KS on 29 September 1990.

The lowest elapsed time for a woman is 4.962 sec, by Shirley Muldowney (US) at Topeka, KS on 29 September 1989. For a gasoline-powered piston-engined car, the lowest-elapsed time is 7.206 sec by Darrell Alderman (US), driving an Oldsmobile Cutlass at Topeka, KS on 29 September 1990; the highest terminal velocity is 191.32 mph, by Bob Glidden in a Ford Thunderbird at Indianapolis, IN on 4 September 1987.

The lowest elapsed time for a gasoline-powered piston-engined motorcycle is 7.697 sec, by John Myers (US) at Gainesville, FL on 8 March 1990; the highest terminal velocity is 176.47 mph, by John Mafaro (US) at Indianapolis on 4 September 1989.

Most wins The greatest number of wins in National Hot Rod Association national events is 79 by Bob Glidden in Pro Stock, 1973–90.

Rocket or jet-engined The highest terminal velocity recorded by any dragster is 392.54 mph, by Kitty O'Neil (US) at El Mirage Dry Lake, CA on 7 July 1977. The lowest elapsed time is 3.58 sec, by Sammy Miller in a Pontiac "Funny Car" in 1986.

BADMINTON

ORIGINS Badminton is a descendant of the children's game of battledore and shuttlecock. It is believed that a similar game was played in China more than 2,000 years ago. Badminton takes its name from Badminton House in England, where the Duke of Beaufort's family and guests popularized the game in the 19th century. British army officers took the game to India in the 1870s, where the first modern rules were codified in 1876. The world governing body is the International Badminton Federation formed in 1934.

WORLD CHAMPIONSHIPS Three Chinese players have won two individual world titles (instituted 1977): men's singles: Yang Yang 1987 and 1989; women's singles: Li Lingwei 1983 and 1989; Han Aiping 1985 and 1987. Li and Han won the women's doubles in 1985. Three titles have been won by Park Joo-bong (South Korea), men's doubles 1985 and mixed doubles 1985 and 1989, and by Lin Ying (China), women's doubles 1983, 1987 and 1989.

THOMAS CUP An international men's team competition, instituted in 1949. Held every three years until 1982, when it became a biennial event. Indonesia has won the most titles with 8 wins (1958, 1961, 1964, 1970, 1973, 1976, 1979, and 1984). The United States has never won the Thomas Cup.

UBER CUP An international women's team competition modeled after the Thomas Cup. First held in 1957, it was contested triennially until 1984 when it became a biennial event. Japan has won the most titles with five victories (1966, 1969, 1972, 1978 and 1981). The United States has won the Uber Cup three times (1957, 1960 and 1963).

US CHAMPIONSHIPS Judy Hashman has won a record 32 national titles: 12 singles, (1954, 1956–63, 1965–67); 12 doubles, (1953–55, 1957–63, 1966–67); 8 mixed doubles, (1956–62, 1967).

Shortest game In the 1969 Uber Cup in Tokyo, Japan, Noriko Takagi (later Mrs. Nakayama, Japan) beat Poppy Tumengkol (Indonesia) in 9 min.

Longest rallies In the men's singles final of the 1987 All-England Championships between Morten Frost (Denmark) and Icuk Sugiarto (Indonesia), there were two successive rallies of more than 90 strokes.

Most shuttles In the final of the Indian National Badminton Championships 1986, when Syed Modi beat Vimal Kumar 15–12, 15–12, 182 shuttles were used in the 66-min period.

BASEBALL

ORIGINS In 1908, the Spalding Commission, sponsored by Albert G. Spalding, a sporting goods tycoon, concluded that the game of baseball was invented by Abner Doubleday in 1839 at Cooperstown, NY. The legend of Doubleday's efforts has since become deeply embedded in American folklore. Despite this tradition, Spalding's official version of baseball history is disputed by sports historians. They argue that baseball in North America evolved from such English games as cricket, paddleball, trap ball and rounders. Printed references to "base ball" in England date to 1700 and in the United States to the mid-18th century. Uncontested is that Alexander Cartwright Jr. formulated the rules of the modern game in 1845 and the first match under these rules was played on 19 June 1846 when the New York Nine defeated the New York Knickerbockers, 23–1, in four innings. On 17 March 1871 the National Association of Professional Base Ball Players was formed, the first professional league in the United States. Today there are two main professional baseball associations, the National League (organized 1876) and the American League (organized 1901, recognized 1903), that together form the major leagues, along with approximately 20 associations that make up the minor leagues. The champions of the two leagues first played the World Series in 1903 and have played continuously since 1905. (For further details on World Series history see below.)

The first night game was played on 2 June 1883 (M.E. College *v.* professionals from Quincy, IL). The major leagues were slow to adopt this change of program, then considered radical. The Cincinnati Reds were the first big league team to play under lights when they hosted the Philadelphia Phillies on 24 May 1935. President Franklin D. Roosevelt pressed a button at the White House to flick the switch at Crosley Field.

MAJOR LEAGUE RECORDS

Most games played Pete Rose played in a record 3,562 games with a record 14,053 at bats for the Cincinnati Reds (NL), 1963–78 and 1984–86, the Philadelphia Phillies (NL) 1979–83 and the Montreal Expos (NL) 1984. Lou Gehrig played in 2,130 successive games for the New York Yankees (AL) from 1 June 1925 to 30 April 1939.

Most home runs

Career Hank Aaron holds the major league career record with 755 home runs from 12,364 at-bats; 733 for the Milwaukee (1954–65) and Atlanta (1966–74) Braves (NL) and 22 for the Milwaukee Brewers (AL) 1975–76. On 8 April 1974 he bettered the previous record of 714 by Babe Ruth.

Ruth hit his home runs from 8,399 times at bat, earning the highest home run percentage—8.5%. Josh Gibson of the Homestead Grays and Pittsburgh Crawfords, Negro League clubs, achieved a career total of nearly 800 homers, including an unofficial record season's total of 75 in 1931.

Season The major league record for home runs in a season is 61 by Roger Maris for the New York Yankees in 162 games and 590 at-bats in 1961. Babe Ruth hit 60 in 154 games in 1927 for the New York Yankees. The most official home runs in a minor league season is 72 by Joe Bauman of Roswell, NM in 1954.

Game The most home runs in a major league game is four, first achieved by Bobby Lowe for Boston *v.* Cincinnati on 30 May 1894. The feat has been achieved an additional 10 times since then.

Consecutive games The most home runs hit in consecutive games is 8, set by Dale Long for the Pittsburgh Pirates (NL), 19–28 May 1956 and tied

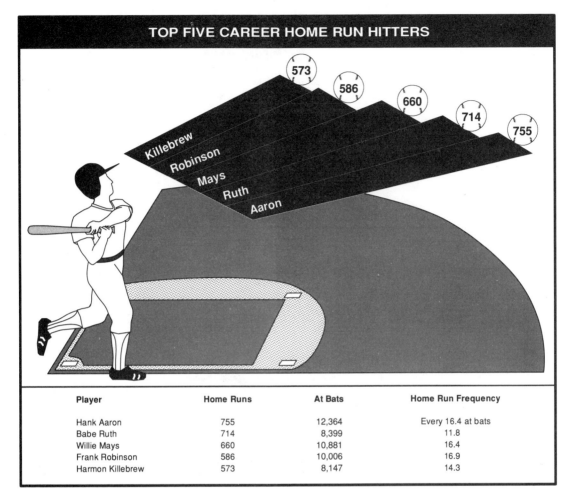

TOP FIVE CAREER HOME RUN HITTERS

Player	Home Runs	At Bats	Home Run Frequency
Hank Aaron	755	12,364	Every 16.4 at bats
Babe Ruth	714	8,399	11.8
Willie Mays	660	10,881	16.4
Frank Robinson	586	10,006	16.9
Harmon Killebrew	573	8,147	14.3

by Don Mattingly for the New York Yankees (AL) on 18 July 1987.

Grand Slams Seven players have hit two grand slams in a single game. They are: Tony Lazzeri for the New York Yankees (AL) on 24 May 1936; James R. Tabor for the Boston Red Sox (AL) on 4 July 1939; Rudolph York for the Boston Red Sox (AL) on 27 July 1946; Jim Gentile for the Baltimore Orioles (AL) on 9 May 1961; Tony Cloninger for the Atlanta Braves (NL) on 3 July 1966; James T. Northrup for the Detroit Tigers (AL) on 24 June 1968; and Frank Robinson for the Baltimore Orioles (AL) on 26 June 1970.

Don Mattingly of the New York Yankees (AL) hit six grand slams in 1987. Lou Gehrig hit 23 grand slams during his 17 seasons with the New York Yankees (AL), 1923–39.

Most career hits The career record for most hits is 4,256, by Pete Rose. He played 24 seasons with three teams: the Cincinnati Reds (NL) 1963–78, the Philadelphia Phillies (NL) 1979–83, the Montreal Expos (NL) 1984 and the Cincinnati Reds (NL) 1984–86. Rose's record hits total came from a record 14,053 at-bats, which gave him a career average of .303

Most consecutive hits Pinky Higgins had 12 consecutive hits for the Boston Red Sox (AL) in a 4-game span, 19–21 June 1938. This was equaled by Moose Droppo for the Detroit Tigers (AL) 14–15 July 1952. Joe DiMaggio hit in a record 56 consecutive games for the New York Yankees (AL) in 1941; he went to bat 223 times, with 91 hits, totaling 56 singles, 16 doubles, 4 triples and 15 home runs.

Home runs and stolen bases The first player to hit 40 or more home runs and have 40 stolen bases in a season was Jose Canseco for the Oakland Athletics (AL) in 1988. His tallies were 42 and 40 respectively.

Walks Babe Ruth holds the records for career walks, 2,056, and the single season record, 170 in 1923.

Two players share a record six walks for a single game: Jimmie Foxx of the Boston Red Sox (AL) set the mark on 16 June 1938 and Andre Thornton of the Cleveland Indians (AL) tied the record on 2 May 1984 in a game that went 18 innings.

Strikeouts The batter with the career strikeout record is Reggie Jackson, with 2,597 in 21 seasons with four teams. The season record is 180, by Bobby Bonds, right fielder for the San Francisco Giants (NL) in 1970. The longest run of games without striking out is by Joe Sewell, while playing third base for the Cleveland Indians (AL), who went to bat 437 times in 115 consecutive games in 1929. He had a record seven seasons batting at least 500 times yet with fewer than 10 strikeouts and struck out only 114 times in his 14-year career.

Most games won by a pitcher Cy Young had a record 511 wins and a record 750 complete games from a total of 906 games and 815 starts in his career for the Cleveland Spiders (NL) 1890–98, the St. Louis Cardinals (NL) 1899–1900, the Boston

BASEBALL MAJOR LEAGUE RECORDS

CAREER BATTING RECORDS

Batting average:	.367, Ty Cobb (Detroit-AL), Philadelphia-AL), 1905–28
Runs scored:	2,245, Ty Cobb, 1905–28
Runs Batted in (RBIs):	2,297, Hank Aaron (Milwaukee, Atlanta- NL Milwaukee-AL), 1954–76
Base hits:	4,256 Pete Rose (Cincinnati-NL, Philadelphia-NL , Montreal-NL), 1963–86
Total bases:	6,856, Hank Aaron (Milwaukee Atlanta-NL, Milwaukee-AL), 1954–76

SEASON BATTING RECORDS

Batting average:	.440, Hugh Duffy (Boston-NL; 236 hits in 529 at bats), 1894
modern record (1900-present):	.426, Nap Lajoie (Philadelphia-AL; 232 hits in 544 at bats), 1901
Runs scored:	192, Billy Hamilton (Philadelphia-NL; in 131 games), 1894
modern record (1900-present):	177, Babe Ruth (New York-AL; in 152 games), 1921
Runs batted in (RBIs):	190, Hack Wilson (Chicago-NL; in 155 games), 1930
Base hits:	257, George Sisler (St. Louis-AL; 631 times at bat, 143 games), 1920
Singles:	202, Wee Willie Keeler (Baltimore-NL; in 128 games), 1898
modern record (1900-present):	198, Lloyd Waner (Pittsburgh-NL), 1927
Doubles:	67, Earl Webb (Boston-AL; in 151 games), 1931
Triples:	36, Owen Wilson (Pittsburgh-NL; in 152 games), 1912
Total bases:	457, Babe Ruth (New York-AL; 85 singles, 44 doubles, 16 triples, 59 home runs), 1921

SINGLE GAME BATTING RECORDS

Runs batted in (RBIs):	12, Jim Bottomley (St. Louis-NL v. Brooklyn), 16 September 1924
Base hits:	9, John Henderson Burnett (Cleveland-AL; in 18 innings), 10 July 1932
Total bases:	18, Joe Adcock (Milwaukee-AL; 1 double, 4 home runs), 31 July 1954

BASEBALL MAJOR LEAGUE RECORDS (Continued)

CAREER PITCHING RECORDS

Games won: 511, Cy Young (in 906 games Cleveland, St. Louis, Boston-NL and Cleveland, Boston-AL), 1890–1911

Shutouts: 113, Walter Johnson (Washington-AL; in 802 games), 1907–27

Strikeouts: 5,308, Nolan Ryan (New York-NL, California-AL, Houston-NL, Texas-AL), 1968–90

SEASON PITCHING RECORDS

Games won: 60, Old Hoss Radbourn (Providence-NL; and 12 losses), 1884

modern record (1900-present): 41, Jack Chesbro (New York-AL), 1904

Shutouts: 16, George Bradley (St. Louis-NL; in 64 games), 1876

modern record (1900-present): 16, Grover Alexander (Philadelphia-NL; 48 games), 1916

Strikeouts: 513, Matt Kilroy (Baltimore-AL), 1886

modern record (1900-present): 383, Nolan Ryan (California-AL), 1973

SINGLE GAME PITCHING RECORDS

Strikeouts (9 innings): 20, Roger Clemens (Boston-AL) v. Seattle, 29 April 1986

Strikeouts in extra innings: 21, Tom Cheney (Washington-AL) v. Baltimore (16 innings), 12 September 1962

AL American League   NL National League

Red Sox (AL) 1901–08, the Cleveland Indians (AL) 1909–11 and the Boston Braves (NL) 1911. He pitched a record total of 7,357 innings. The career record for most pitching appearances is 1,070 by Hoyt Wilhelm for a total of nine teams between 1952 and 1969; he set the career record with 143 wins by a relief pitcher. The season's record is 106 appearances, by Michael Marshall for the Los Angeles Dodgers (NL) in 1974.

Most consecutive games won by a pitcher Carl Hubbell New York Giants (NL) won 24 consecutive games, 16 in 1936 and 8 in 1937.

Strikeouts Nolan Ryan struck out a record 383 batters for the California Angels (AL) in 1973. He also holds the career strikeout record, with 5,308 strikeouts.

Shutouts The record for the most shutouts in a career is 113, pitched by Walter Johnson in his 21-season career with the Washington Senators (AL), 1907–27. Don Drysdale pitched 6 consecu-

tive shutouts for the Los Angeles Dodgers (NL) between 14 May and 4 June 1968. Orel Hershiser pitched a record 59 consecutive shutout innings for the Los Angeles Dodgers (NL) from 30 August to 28 September 1988.

No-hitters Nolan Ryan, playing for the Texas Rangers (AL) against the Oakland Athletics (AL), pitched his 6th no-hitter on 11 June 1990. Johnny Vander Meer of the Cincinnati Reds (NL) is the only player in baseball history to have pitched consecutive no-hitters 11–15 June 1938.

Perfect game A perfect nine-inning game, in which the pitcher allows the opposition no hits, no runs and does not allow a man to reach first base, was first achieved by John Lee Richmond for Worcester against Cleveland in the NL on 12 June 1880. There have been 13 subsequent perfect games, including one World Series game, over nine innings, but no pitcher has achieved this feat more than once.

1990, THE YEAR OF THE NO-HITTER

The procession of hunched hitless batters trudging back to the dugout became a familiar sight in baseball during the 1990 season, the year of the no-hitter. Nine no-hitters (see box) were thrown by ten pitchers (California Angels starter Mark Langston and reliever Mike Witt combined for the first of them), breaking the modern major league record of seven, pitched in 1908 and 1917.

Several individual records were set: Randy Johnson, Seattle Mariners, became the tallest pitcher (6 ft 10 in) to throw a no-hitter; Nolan Ryan, Texas Rangers, became the oldest (43), extending his all-time no-hitter record to six; Dave Stewart, Oakland A's, and Fernando Valenzuela, Los Angeles Dodgers, pitched no-hitters on the same day, June 29—the first time it happened this century; Andy Hawkins, New York Yankees, became only the second player in history to lose a nine-inning no-hitter.

Although hitters may blame no-hitters on umpires, night games, bad luck, voodoo and even artificial turf, they cannot claim that the ball was doctored . . . Dwight (Doc) Gooden didn't throw one!

NOLAN RYAN

TERRY MULHOLLAND

MIKE WITT

DAVE STEWART

DAVE STIEB

FERNANDO VALENZUELA

ANDY HAWKINS

MARK LANGSTON

RANDY JOHNSON

MELIDO PEREZ

NO-HITTERS IN 1990

Date	Pitcher	Game (Home team listed first)	Result
April 11	Mark Langston (7) Mike Witt (2)	California Angels (v. Seattle Mariners)	Won 1–0
June 2	Randy Johnson	Seattle Mariners (v. Detroit Tigers)	Won 1–0
June 11	Nolan Ryan	(Oakland A's v.) Texas Rangers	Won 5–0
June 29	Dave Stewart	(Toronto Blue Jays v.) Oakland A's	Won 5–0
June 29	Fernando Valenzuela	Los Angeles Dodgers (v. St. Louis Cardinals)	Won 6–0
July 1	Andy Hawkins	(Chicago White Sox v.) New York Yankees	Lost 4–0
July 12	Melido Perez	Chicago White Sox (v. New York Yankees)	Won 8–0*
August 15	Terry Mulholland	Philadelphia Phillies (v. San Francisco Giants)	Won 6–0
September 2	Dave Stieb	(Cleveland Indians v.) Toronto Blue Jays	Won 3–0

* 6 innings, rain

SOX THERAPY ■ CHICAGO WHITE SOX RELIEVER
BOBBY THIGPEN NOTCHED 57 SAVES IN 1990 TO
SET A NEW MAJOR LEAGUE RECORD.

On 26 May 1959, Harvey Haddix Jr. pitched a perfect game for 12 innings for the Pittsburgh Pirates against the Milwaukee Braves in the National League, but lost in the 13th.

Saves Bobby Thigpen saved a record 57 games for the Chicago White Sox (AL) in 1990. The career record for saves is 341, by Rollie Fingers in his 18 seasons playing for the Oakland Athletics (AL), the San Diego Padres (NL) and the Milwaukee Brewers (AL), 1968–85. Fingers completed his record save total in 907 relief appearances.

Fielding Pitcher Paul Lindblad (Kansas City/Oakland A's [AL]) played 385 consecutive games without committing an error over a period of nine seasons, 1966–74, to set the major league mark. The consecutive games errorless streaks at each position are held by the following: first base: 193, Steve Garvey, San Diego Padres (NL), 1983–85; second base: 91, Joe Morgan, Cincinnati Reds (NL), 1977–78; third base: 97, James Davenport, San Francisco Giants (NL), 1966–68; shortstop: 95, Cal Ripken, Jr., Baltimore Orioles (AL), 1990; outfield: 266, Donald Demeter, Philadelphia Phillies (NL) and Detroit Tigers (AL), 1962–65; catcher:

159, Rick Cerone, New York Yankees (AL) and Boston Red Sox (AL), 1987–89.

Triple plays On July 17, 1990 the Minnesota Twins became the first major league team to turn 2 triple plays in one game. Their victims were the Boston Red Sox, who, nevertheless, overcame this milestone to win the game 1–0. The game was played in Boston's Fenway Park. The hapless batters were Tom Brunansky (4th inning) and Jody Reed (8th inning). Both plays were scored 5–4–3.

Youngest player The youngest major league player of all time was the Cincinnati Reds (AL) pitcher Joe Nuxhall, who played one game in June 1944, at age 15 yr 314 days. He did not play again in the National League until 1952. The youngest player to play in a minor league game was Joe Louis Reliford who played for the Fitzgerald Pioneers against Statesboro in the Georgia State League, at age 12 yr 234 days on 19 July 1952.

Oldest player Satchel Paige pitched for the Kansas City A's (AL) at age 59 yr 80 days on 25 September 1965.

Shortest and tallest players The shortest major league player was Eddie Gaedel, a 3 ft 7 in, 65 lb midget, who pinch-hit for the St. Louis Browns (AL) v. the Detroit Tigers (AL) on 19 August 1951. Wearing number 1/8, the batter with the smallest ever major league strike zone walked on four pitches. Following the game, major league rules were hastily rewritten to prevent any recurrence. The tallest major leaguer of all time is Randy Johnson, Seattle Mariners (AL), a 6 ft 10 in pitcher, who played in his first game for the Montreal Expos (NL) on 15 September 1988.

Most Valuable Player Award There have been three different Most Valuable Player (MVP) Awards in baseball: the Chalmers Award (1911-14), the League Awards (1922-29) and the Baseball Writers' Association of America Awards (1931-present). Frank Robinson is the only player who has won the award in both leagues: 1961, Cincinnati Reds (NL), and 1966, Baltimore Orioles (AL). The most selections in the annual vote of the Baseball Writers' Association is three, won by: National League: Stan Musial (St. Louis), 1943, 1946, 1948; Roy Campanella (Brooklyn), 1951, 1953, 1955; Mike Schmidt (Philadelphia), 1980–81, 1986. American League: Jimmie Foxx (Philadelphia), 1932–33, 1938; Joe DiMaggio (New York), 1939, 1941, 1947; Yogi Berra (New York), 1951, 1954–55; Mickey Mantle (New York), 1956–57, 1962.

CHALMERS AWARD (1911-14)

NATIONAL LEAGUE

Year	Player	Team	Position
1911	Wildfire Schulte	Chicago Cubs	OF
1912	Larry Doyle	New York Giants	2B
1913	Jake Daubert	Brooklyn Dodgers	1B
1914	Johnny Evers	Boston Braves	2B

AMERICAN LEAGUE

Year	Player	Team	Position
1911	Ty Cobb	Detriot Tigers	OF
1912	Tris Speaker	Boston Red Sox	OF
1913	Walter Johnson	Washington Senators	P
1914	Eddie Collins	Philadelphia A's	2B

LEAGUE AWARD (1922-29)

NATIONAL LEAGUE

Year	Player	Team	Position
1922	no selection		
1923	no selection		
1924	Dazzy Vance	Brooklyn Dodgers	P
1925	Rogers Hornsby	St. Louis Cardinals	2B
1926	Bob O'Farrell	St. Louis Cardinals	C
1927	Paul Waner	Pittsburgh Pirates	OF
1928	Jim Bottomley	Chicago Cubs	2B
1929	Rogers Hornsby	St. Louis Cardinals	2B

AMERICAN LEAGUE

Year	Player	Team	Position
1922	George Sisler	St. Louis Browns	1B
1923	Babe Ruth	New York Yankees	OF
1924	Walter Johnson	Washington Senators	P
1925	Roger Peckinpaugh	Washington Senators	SS
1926	George Burns	Chicago White Sox	1B
1927	Lou Gehrig	New York Yankees	1B
1928	Mickey Cochrane	Philadelphia A's	C
1929	no selection		

BASEBALL WRITERS AWARD (1931-1990)

NATIONAL LEAGUE

Year	Player	Team	Position
1931	Frankie Frisch	St. Louis Cardinals	2B
1932	Chuck Klein	Philadelphia Phillies	OF
1933	Carl Hubbell	New York Giants	P
1934	Dizzy Dean	St. Louis Cardinals	P
1935	Gabby Hartnett	Chicago Cubs	C
1936	Carl Hubbell	New York Giants	P
1937	Joe Medwick	St. Louis Cardinals	OF
1938	Ernie Lombardi	Cincinnati Reds	C
1939	Bucky Walters	Cincinnati Reds	P
1940	Frank McCormick	Cincinnati Reds	1B
1941	Dolf Camilli	Brooklyn Dodgers	1B
1942	Mort Cooper	St. Louis Cardinals	P

BASEBALL WRITERS AWARD (1931-1990)
(Continued)

NATIONAL LEAGUE (Continued)

Year	Player	Team	Position
1943	Stan Musial	St. Louis Cardinals	OF
1944	Marty Marion	St. Louis Cardinals	SS
1945	Phil Cavarretta	Chicago Cubs	1B
1946	Stan Musial	St. Louis Cardinals	1B–OF
1947	Bob Elliott	Boston Braves	3B
1948	Stan Musial	St. Louis Cardinals	OF
1949	Jackie Robinson	Brooklyn Dodgers	2B
1950	Jim Konstanty	Philadelphia Phillies	P
1951	Roy Campanella	Brooklyn Dodgers	C
1952	Hank Sauer	Chicago Cubs	OF
1953	Roy Campanella	Brooklyn Dodgers	C
1954	Willie Mays	New York Giants	OF
1955	Roy Campanella	Brooklyn Dodgers	C
1956	Don Newcombe	Brooklyn Dodgers	P
1957	Hank Aaron	Milwaukee Braves	OF
1958	Ernie Banks	Chicago Cubs	SS
1959	Ernie Banks	Chicago Cubs	SS
1960	Dick Groat	Pittsburgh Pirates	SS
1961	Frank Robinson	Cincinnati Reds	OF
1962	Maury Wills	Los Angeles Dodgers	SS
1963	Sandy Koufax	Los Angeles Dodgers	P
1964	Ken Boyer	St. Louis Cardinals	3B
1965	Willie Mays	San Francisco Giants	OF
1966	Roberto Clemente	Pittsburgh Pirates	OF
1967	Orlando Cepeda	St. Louis Cardinals	1B
1968	Bob Gibson	St. Louis Cardinals	P
1969	Willie McCovey	San Francisco Giants	1B
1970	Johnny Bench	Cincinnati Reds	C
1971	Joe Torre	St. Louis Cardinals	3B
1972	Johnny Bench	Cincinnati Reds	C
1973	Pete Rose	Cincinnati Reds	OF
1974	Steve Garvey	Los Angeles Dodgers	1B
1975	Joe Morgan	Cincinnati Reds	2B
1976	Joe Morgan	Cincinnati Reds	2B
1977	George Foster	Cincinnati Reds	OF
1978	Dave Parker	Pittsburgh Pirates	OF
1979	Willie Stargell	Pittsburgh Pirates	1B
	Keith Hernandez	St. Louis Cardinals	1B
1980	Mike Schmidt	Philadelphia Phillies	3B
1981	Mike Schmidt	Philadelphia Phillies	3B
1982	Dale Murphy	Atlanta Braves	OF
1983	Dale Murphy	Atlanta Braves	OF

NATIONAL LEAGUE (Continued)

Year	Player	Team	Position
1984	Ryne Sandberg	Chicago Cubs	2B
1985	Willie McGee	St. Louis Cardinals	OF
1986	Mike Schmidt	Philadelphia Phillies	3B
1987	Andre Dawson	Chicago Cubs	OF
1988	Kirk Gibson	Los Angeles Dodgers	OF
1989	Kevin Mitchell	San Francisco Giants	OF
1990	Barry Bonds	Pittsburgh Pirates	OF

AMERICAN LEAGUE

Year	Player	Team	Position
1931	Lefty Grove	Philadelphia A's	P
1932	Jimmie Foxx	Philadelphia A's	1B
1933	Jimmie Foxx	Philadelphia A's	1B
1934	Mickey Cochrane	Detroit Tigers	C
1935	Hank Greenberg	Detroit Tigers	1B
1936	Lou Gehrig	New York Yankees	1B
1937	Charlie Gehringer	Detroit Tigers	2B
1938	Jimmie Foxx	Boston Red Sox	1B
1939	Joe DiMaggio	New York Yankees	OF
1940	Hank Greenberg	Detroit Tigers	OF
1941	Joe DiMaggio	New York Yankees	OF
1942	Joe Gordon	New York Yankees	2B
1943	Spud Chandler	New York Yankees	P
1944	Hal Newhouser	Detroit Tigers	P
1945	Hal Newhouser	Detroit Tigers	P
1946	Ted Williams	Boston Red Sox	OF
1947	Joe DiMaggio	New York Yankees	OF
1948	Lou Boudreau	Cleveland Indians	SS
1949	Ted Williams	Boston Red Sox	OF
1950	Phil Rizzuto	New York Yankees	SS
1951	Yogi Berra	New York Yankees	C
1952	Bobby Shantz	Philadelphia A's	P
1953	Al Rosen	Cleveland Indians	3B
1954	Yogi Berra	New York Yankees	C
1955	Yogi Berra	New York Yankees	C
1956	Mickey Mantle	New York Yankees	OF
1957	Mickey Mantle	New York Yankees	OF
1958	Jackie Jensen	Boston Red Sox	OF
1959	Nellie Fox	Chicago White Sox	2B
1960	Roger Maris	New York Yankees	OF
1961	Roger Maris	New York Yankees	OF
1962	Mickey Mantle	New York Yankees	OF
1963	Elston Howard	New York Yankees	C

AMERICAN LEAGUE (Continued)

Year	Player	Team	Position
1964	Brooks Robinson	Baltimore Orioles	3B
1965	Zoilo Versalles	Minnesota Twins	SS
1966	Frank Robinson	Baltimore Orioles	OF
1967	Carl Yastrzemski	Boston Red Sox	OF
1968	Denny McLain	Detroit Tigers	P
1969	Harmon Killebrew	Minnesota Twins	3–1B
1970	Boog Powell	Baltimore Orioles	1B
1971	Vida Blue	Oakland A's	P
1972	Dick Allen	Chicago White Sox	1B
1973	Reggie Jackson	Oakland A's	OF
1974	Jeff Burroughs	Texas Rangers	OF
1975	Fred Lynn	Boston Red Sox	OF
1976	Thurman Munson	New York Yankees	C
1977	Rod Carew	Minnesota Twins	1B
1978	Jim Rice	Boston Red Sox	OF-DH
1979	Don Baylor	California Angels	OF-DH
1980	George Brett	Kansas City Royals	3B
1981	Rollie Fingers	Milwaukee Brewers	P
1982	Robin Yount	Milwaukee Brewers	SS
1983	Cal Ripken Jr.	Baltimore Orioles	SS

FAMILY AFFAIR ■ ON 31 AUGUST 1990, KEN GRIFFEY, SR. AND KEN GRIFFEY, JR., OF THE SEATTLE MARINERS, BECAME THE FIRST FATHER AND SON TO PLAY ON THE SAME MAJOR LEAGUE TEAM IN BASEBALL HISTORY.

AMERICAN LEAGUE (Continued)

Year	Player	Team	Position
1984	Willie Hernandez	Detroit Tigers	P
1985	Don Mattingly	New York Yankees	1B
1986	Roger Clemens	Boston Red Sox	P
1987	George Bell	Toronto Blue Jays	OF
1988	Jose Canseco	Oakland A's	OF
1989	Robin Yount	Milwaukee Brewers	OF
1990	Rickey Henderson	Oakland A's	OF

Cy Young Award Awarded since 1956 to the outstanding pitcher in each major league, the most wins is three: National League: Tom Seaver (New York Mets), 1969, 1973, 1975; Steve Carlton (Philadelphia Phillies), 1977, 1980, 1982; Sandy Koufax (Los Angeles Dodgers), 1963, 1965–66: American League: Jim Palmer (Baltimore Orioles), 1973, 1975–76.

Dwight Gooden (New York Mets) at 21 yrs old became the youngest pitcher to win the Cy Young Award in 1985 by unanimous vote of the 24 sportswriters who make the selection.

Father and son On August 31, 1990, Ken Griffey Sr. and Ken Griffey Jr., of the Seattle Mariners (AL), became the first father and son to play for the same major league team at the same time. Griffey Sr., an 18-year veteran, was signed by Seattle on August 29. Griffey Jr. established himself as an "All- Star" in his second season with the Mariners. In 1989 the Griffeys became the first father/son combination to play in the major leagues at the same time. Griffey Sr. played for the Cincinnati Reds (NL) during that season.

Shortest games The New York Giants (NL) beat the Philadelphia Phillies (NL), 6–1, in nine innings in 51 min on 28 September 1919.

Longest games The Brooklyn Dodgers (NL) and the Boston Braves (NL) played to a 1–1 tie after 26 innings on 1 May 1920. The Chicago White Sox (AL) played the longest ballgame in elapsed time—8 hr 6 min—before beating the Milwaukee Brewers, 7–6, in the 25th inning on 9 May 1984 in Chicago. The game started on Tuesday night and was tied at 3–3 when the 1 A.M. curfew caused suspension until Wednesday night.

The actual longest game was a minor league game in 1981 that lasted 33 innings. At the end of 9 innings the score was tied, 1–1, with the Rochester (NY) Red Wings battling the home team Pawtucket (RI) Red Sox. At the end of 21 innings it was tied, 2–2, and at the end of 32 innings the score was still 2–2, when the game was suspended. Two months later, play was resumed and 18 minutes later, Pawtucket scored one run and won. The winning pitcher was the Red Sox Bob Ojeda.

Record Attendances The all-time season record for attendances for both leagues is 55,173,597 in 1989 (29,848,634 for the 14-team American League, and 25,324,963 for the 12-team National League). The American League record is 30,331,417 set in 1990, the National League record was set in 1989 (see above). The record for home-team attendance is held by the Toronto Blue Jays (AL) at 3,885,284 in 1990.

"The Star-Spangled Banner" The traditional singing of the national anthem before the playing of the national pastime became the source of a record itself this season. Helen Hudson, an entertainer from New York, sang the "The Star-Spangled Banner" at every major league ballpark in 1990. Beginning on April 19 in Atlanta, GA, "the home of the brave(s)," her tour of the 26 arenas ended in San Diego, CA, on September 3.

Managers Connie Mack managed in the major leagues for a record 53 seasons, and he achieved a record 3,776 regular season victories (and a record 4,025 losses), 139 wins and 134 losses for the Pittsburgh Pirates (NL) 1894–96 and 3,627 wins and 3,891 losses for Philadelphia Athletics (AL), a team he later owned, 1901–50. The most successful in the World Series has been Casey Stengel who managed the New York Yankees (AL) to seven wins in 10 World Series, winning in 1949–53, 1956 and 1958, and losing in 1955, 1957 and 1960.

Joe McCarthy also managed the New York Yankees to seven wins, 1932, 1936–39, 1941 and 1942,

OH SAY, DID YOU SEE? ■ **ENTERTAINER HELEN HUDSON SANG THE NATIONAL ANTHEM AT EVERY BALLPARK IN 1990.**

and his teams lost in 1929 (Chicago) and 1942 (New York). Of managers to have achieved at least 1,500 regular season wins, he has the highest winning percentage with 0.614%, 2,126 wins and 1,335 losses in his 24-year career, with the Chicago Cubs (NL) 1926–30, the New York Yankees (AL) 1931–46, the Boston Red Sox (AL) 1948–50. He never had an overall losing season.

MANAGERS

TOP FIVE REGULAR SEASON WINNERS

Manager	Won	Lost	Percentage
Connie Mack	3,776	4,025	.484
John McGraw	2,840	1,984	.589
Bucky Harris	2,159	2,219	.493
Joe McCarthy	2,126	1,335	.614
Walter Alston	2,040	1,613	.558

WORLD SERIES

ORIGINS Played annually between the winners of the National League and the American League, the World Series was first staged unofficially in 1903, and officially from 1905. The most wins is 22, by the New York Yankees between 1923 and 1978 from a record 33 series appearances for winning the American League titles between 1921 and 1981. The most National League titles is 19, by the Dodgers—Brooklyn 1890–1957, Los Angeles 1958–88.

WORLD SERIES 1903–90

Year	Winner	Loser	Series
1903	Boston Red Sox (AL)	Pittsburgh Pirates (NL)	5–3
1904	no series		
1905	New York Giants (NL)	Philadelphia A's (AL)	4–1
1906	Chicago White Sox (AL)	Chicago Cubs (NL)	4–2
1907	Chicago Cubs (NL)	Detroit Tigers (AL)	4–0–1*
1908	Chicago Cubs (NL)	Detroit Tigers (AL)	4–1
1909	Pittsburgh Pirates (NL)	Detroit Tigers (AL)	4–3
1910	Philadelphia A's (AL)	Chicago Cubs (NL)	4–1
1911	Philadelphia A's (AL)	New York Giants (NL)	4–2
1912	Boston Red Sox (AL)	New York Giants (NL)	4–3–1*
1913	Philadelphia A's (AL)	New York Giants (NL)	4–1
1914	Boston Braves (NL)	Philadelphia A's (AL)	4–0
1915	Boston Red Sox (AL)	Philadelphia Phillies (NL)	4–1
1916	Boston Red Sox (AL)	Brooklyn Dodgers (NL)	4–1
1917	Chicago White Sox (AL)	New York Giants (NL)	4–2
1918	Boston Red Sox (AL)	Chicago Cubs (NL)	4–2
1919	Cincinnati Reds (NL)	Chicago White Sox (AL)	5–3

WORLD SERIES 1903–90 (Contined)

Year	Winner	Loser	Series
1920	Cleveland Indians (AL)	Brooklyn Dodgers (NL)	4–3
1921	New York Giants (NL)	New York Yankees (AL)	5–3
1922	New York Giants (NL)	New York Yankees (AL)	4–0–1*
1923	New York Yankees (AL)	New York Giants (NL)	4–2
1924	Washington Senators (AL)	New York Giants (NL)	4–3
1925	Pittsburgh Pirates (NL)	Washington Senators (AL)	4–3
1926	St. Louis Cardinals(NL)	New York Yankees (AL)	4–3
1927	New York Yankees (AL)	Pittsburgh Pirates (NL)	4–0
1928	New York Yankees (AL)	St. Louis Cardinals (NL)	4–0
1929	Philadelphia A's (AL)	Chicago Cubs (NL)	4–1
1930	Philadelphia A's (AL)	St. Louis Cardinals (NL)	4–2
1931	St. Louis Cardinals (NL)	Philadelphia A's (AL)	4–3
1932	New York Yankees (AL)	Chicago Cubs (NL)	4–0
1933	New York Giants (NL)	Washington Senators (AL)	4–1
1934	St. Louis Cardinals (NL)	Detroit Tigers (AL)	4–3
1935	Detroit Tigers (AL)	Chicago Cubs (NL)	4–2
1936	New York Yankees (AL)	New York Giants (NL)	4–2
1937	New York Yankees (AL)	New York Giants (NL)	4–1
1938	New York Yankees (AL)	Chicago Cubs (NL)	4–0
1939	New York Yankees (AL)	Cincinnati Reds (NL)	4–0
1940	Cincinnati Reds (NL)	Detroit Tigers (AL)	4–3
1941	New York Yankees (AL)	Brooklyn Dodgers (NL)	4–1
1942	St. Louis Cardinals (NL)	New York Yankees (AL)	4–1
1943	New York Yankees (AL)	St. Louis Cardinals (NL)	4–1
1944	St. Louis Cardinals (NL)	St. Louis Browns (AL)	4–2
1945	Detroit Tigers (AL)	Chicago Cubs (NL)	4–3
1946	St. Louis Cardinals (NL)	Boston Red Sox (AL)	4–3
1947	New York Yankees (AL)	Brooklyn Dodgers (NL)	4–3
1948	Cleveland Indians (AL)	Boston Braves (NL)	4–2
1949	New York Yankees (AL)	Brooklyn Dodgers (NL)	4–1
1950	New York Yankees (AL)	Philadelphia Phillies (NL)	4–0
1951	New York Yankees (AL)	New York Giants (NL)	4–2
1952	New York Yankees (AL)	Brooklyn Dodgers (NL)	4–3
1953	New York Yankees (AL)	Brooklyn Dodgers (NL)	4–2
1954	New York Giants (NL)	Cleveland Indians (AL)	4–0
1955	Brooklyn Dodgers (NL)	New York Yankees (AL)	4–3
1956	New York Yankees (AL)	Brooklyn Dodgers (NL)	4–3
1957	Milwaukee Braves (NL)	New York Yankees (AL)	4–3
1958	New York Yankees (AL)	Milwaukee Braves (NL)	4–3
1959	Los Angeles Dodgers (NL)	Chicago White Sox (AL)	4–2
1960	Pittsburgh Pirates (NL)	New York Yankees (AL)	4–3
1961	New York Yankees (AL)	Cincinnati Reds (NL)	4–1
1962	New York Yankees (AL)	San Francisco Giants (NL)	4–3
1963	Los Angeles Dodgers (NL)	New York Yankees (AL)	4–0
1964	St. Louis Cardinals (NL)	New York Yankees (AL)	4–3

WORLD SERIES 1903–90 (Contined)

Year	Winner	Loser	Series
1965	Los Angeles Dodgers (NL)	Minnesota Twins (AL)	4–3
1966	Baltimore Orioles (AL)	Los Angeles Dodgers (NL)	4–0
1967	St. Louis Cardinals (NL)	Boston Red Sox (AL)	4–3
1968	Detroit Tigers (AL)	St. Louis Cardinals (NL)	4–3
1969	New York Mets (NL)	Baltimore Orioles (AL)	4–1
1970	Baltimore Orioles (AL)	Cincinnati Reds (NL)	4–1

WORLD SERIES 1903–90 (Contined)

Year	Winner	Loser	Series
1971	Pittsburgh Pirates (NL)	Baltimore Orioles (AL)	4–3
1972	Oakland A's (AL)	Cincinnati Reds (NL)	4–3
1973	Oakland A's (AL)	New York Mets (NL)	4–3
1974	Oakland A's (AL)	Los Angeles Dodgers (NL)	4–1
1975	Cincinnati Reds (NL)	Boston Red Sox (AL)	4–3
1976	Cincinnati Reds (NL)	New York Yankees (AL)	4–0

THE NATIONAL PASTIME

The Distribution of World Series Championships by State

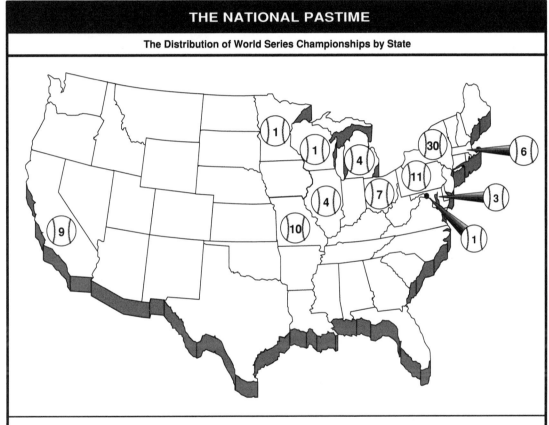

State	Wins	Teams
New York	30	New York Yankees 22, New York Giants 5, New York Mets 2, Brooklyn Dodgers 1
Pennsylvania	11	Pittsburgh Pirates 5, Philadelphia A's 5, Philadelphia Phillies 1
Missouri	10	St. Louis Cardinals 9, Kansas City Royals 1
California	9	Los Angeles Dodgers 5, Oakland A's 4
Ohio	7	Cincinnati Reds 5, Cleveland Indians 2
Massachusetts	6	Boston Red Sox 5, Boston Braves 1
Illinois	4	Chicago White Sox 2, Chicago Cubs 2
Michigan	4	Detroit Tigers
Maryland	3	Baltimore Orioles
Wisconsin	1	Milwaukee Braves
Minnesota	1	Minnesota Twins
Washington D.C.	1	Washington Senators

WORLD SERIES 1903–90 (Contined)

Year	Winner	Loser	Series
1977	New York Yankees (AL)	Los Angeles Dodgers (NL)	4–2
1978	New York Yankees (AL)	Los Angeles Dodgers (NL)	4–2
1979	Pittsburgh Pirates(NL)	Baltimore Orioles (AL)	4–3
1980	Philadelphia Phillies (NL)	Kansas City Royals (AL)	4–2
1981	Los Angeles Dodgers (NL)	New York Yankees (AL)	4–2
1982	St. Louis Cardinals (NL)	Milwaukee Brewers (AL)	4–3
1983	Baltimore Orioles (AL)	Philadelphia Phillies (NL)	4–1
1984	Detroit Tigers (AL)	San Diego Padres (NL)	4–1
1985	Kansas City Royals (AL)	St. Louis Cardinals (NL)	4–3
1986	New York Mets (NL)	Boston Red Sox (AL)	4–3
1987	Minnesota Twins (AL)	St. Louis Cardinals (NL)	4–3
1988	Los Angeles Dodgers (NL)	Oakland A's (AL)	4–1
1989	Oakland A's (AL)	San Francisco Giants (NL)	4–0
1990	Cincinnati Reds (NL)	Oakland A's	4–0

* Tied Game

Most valuable player The only men to have won the award twice are: Sandy Koufax, Los Angeles Dodgers (NL), 1963, 1965; Bob Gibson, St. Louis Cardinals (NL), 1964, 1967; and Reggie Jackson, Oakland A's (AL), 1973, New York Yankees (AL), 1977.

DEJA VU ALL OVER AGAIN ■ NEW YORK YANKEES WHITEY FORD (OPPOSITE PAGE) AND YOGI BERRA (ABOVE) BOTH HOLD WORLD SERIES APPEARANCES MARKS. FORD PITCHED IN 11 SERIES, THE MOST FOR A PITCHER, AND BERRA PLAYED IN 14, A RECORD FOR ALL PLAYERS.

WORLD SERIES RECORDS

Most wins: 22, New York Yankees AL , 1923–78

Most series played: 14, Yogi Berra (New York Yankees-AL), 1947–63

Most series played by pitcher: 11, Whitey Ford (New York Yankees-AL), 1950–64

WORLD SERIES CAREER RECORDS

Batting average (min. 75 at bats): .391, Lou Brock (St. Louis Cardinals—NL; 34 hits in 87 at bats, 3 series), 1964–68

Runs scored: 42, Mickey Mantle (New York Yankees-AL), 1951–64

Runs batted in (RBIs): 40, Mickey Mantle (New York Yankees-AL), 1951–64

Base hits: 71, Yogi Berra (New York Yankees-AL), 1947–63

Home runs: 18, Mickey Mantle (New York Yankees-AL), 1951–64

Victories pitching: 10, Whitey Ford (New York Yankees-AL), 1950–64

Strikeouts: 94, Whitey Ford (New York Yankees-AL) , 1950–64

WORLD SERIES RECORDS (Continued)

WORLD SERIES SINGLE SERIES RECORDS

**Batting average
(4 or more games)** .750, Billy Hatcher (Cincinnati Reds-NL; 9 hits in 12 at-bats), 1990

Runs scored: 10, Reggie Jackson (New York Yankees-AL), 1977

**Runs batted in
(RBI's):** 12, Bobby Richardson (New York Yankees-AL), 1960

**Base hits
(7-game series):** 13, Bobby Richardson (New York Yankees-AL), 1960
Lou Brock (St. Louis Cardinals-NL), 1968
Marty Barrett (Boston Red Sox-AL), 1986

WORLD SERIES RECORDS (Continued)

WORLD SERIES SINGLE SERIES RECORDS (Continued)

Home runs: 5, Reggie Jackson (New York Yankees-AL; in 20 at-bats), 1977

Victories pitching: 3, Christy Matthewson (New York Yankees-AL; in 5-game series), 1905
Jack Coombs (Philadelphia A's-AL; in 5-game series), 1910
Ten other pitchers have won three games in more than five games

Strikeouts: 35, Bob Gibson (St. Louis Cardinals-NL; in 7 games), 1968

23, Sandy Koufax (Los Angeles Dodgers-NL; in 4 games), 1963

WORLD SERIES SINGLE GAME RECORDS

Home runs: 3, Babe Ruth (New York Yankees-AL) v. St. Louis Cardinals, 6 October 1926
Babe Ruth (New York Yankees-AL) v. St. Louis Cardinals, 9 October 1928
Reggie Jackson (New York Yankees-AL) v. Los Angeles Dodgers, 18 October 1977

Runs batted in (RBI's) in a game: 6, Bobby Richardson (New York Yankees-AL) v. Pittsburgh Pirates, 8 October 1960

Strikeouts by pitcher in a game: 17, Bob Gibson (St. Louis Cardinals-NL) v. Detroit Tigers, 2 October 1968

Perfect game (9 innings): Don Larson (New York Yankees-AL) v. Brooklyn Dodgers, 8 October 1956

AL American League, NL National League

RED MACHINE ■ BILLY HATCHER, CINCINNATI REDS, BROKE BABE RUTH'S 72-YEAR-OLD WORLD SERIES BATTING AVERAGE RECORD OF .625, HITTING .750 (9 FOR 12), IN THE REDS' 1990 SERIES TRIUMPH.

Attendance The record attendance for a series is 420,784 for the six games when the Los Angeles Dodgers beat the Chicago White Sox 4–2 between 1 and 8 October 1959. The single-game record is 92,706 for the 5*th* game of this series at the Memorial Coliseum, Los Angeles on 6 October 1959.

LEAGUE CHAMPIONSHIP SERIES 1969-90

League Championship Series (LCS) playoffs began in 1969 when the American and National Leagues expanded to 12 teams each and created two divisions, East and West. To determine the respective league pennant winners, the division winners played a best-of-five-game series, which was expanded to best-of-seven in 1985.

NATIONAL LEAGUE

Year	Winner	Loser	Series
1969	New York Mets (East)	Atlanta Braves (West)	3–0
1970	Cincinnati Reds (West)	Pittsburgh Pirates (East)	3–0
1971	Pittsburgh Pirates (East)	San Francisco Giants (West)	3–1
1972	Cincinnati Reds (West)	Pittsburgh Pirates (East)	3–2
1973	New York Mets (East)	Cincinnati Reds (West)	3–2
1974	Los Angeles Dodgers (West)	Pittsburgh Pirates (East)	3–1
1975	Cincinnati Reds (West)	Pittsburgh Pirates (East)	3–0
1976	Cincinnati Reds (West)	Philadelphia Phillies (East)	3–0
1977	Los Angeles Dodgers (West)	Philadelphia Phillies (East)	3–1
1978	Los Angeles Dodgers (West)	Philadelphia Phillies (East)	3–1
1979	Pittsburgh Pirates (East)	Cincinnati Reds (West)	3–0
1980	Philadelphia Phillies (East)	Houston Astros (West)	3–2
1981	Los Angeles Dodgers (West)	Montreal Expos (East)	3–2
1982	St. Louis Cardinals (East)	Atlanta Braves (West)	3–0
1983	Philadelphia Phillies (East)	Los Angeles Dodgers (West)	3–1
1984	San Diego Padres (West)	Chicago Cubs (East)	3–2
1985	St. Louis Cardinals (East)	Los Angeles Dodgers (West)	4–2
1986	New York Mets (East)	Houston Astros (West)	4–2
1987	St. Louis Cardinals (East)	San Francisco Giants (West)	4–3
1988	Los Angeles Dodgers (West)	New York Mets (East)	4–3
1989	San Francisco Giants (West)	Chicago Cubs (East)	4–1
1990	Cincinnati Reds (West)	Pittsburgh Pirates (East)	4–2

AMERICAN LEAGUE

Year	Winner	Loser	Series
1969	Baltimore Orioles (East)	Minnesota Twins (West)	3–0
1970	Baltimore Orioles (East)	Minnesota Twins (West)	3–0
1971	Baltimore Orioles (East)	Oakland A's (West)	3–0
1972	Oakland A's (West)	Detroit Tigers (East)	3–2
1973	Oakland A's (West)	Baltimore Orioles (East)	3–2
1974	Oakland A's (West)	Baltimore Orioles (East)	3–1
1975	Boston Red Sox (East)	Oakland A's (West)	3–0

LEAGUE CHAMPIONSHIP SERIES 1969-90 (Continued)

AMERICAN LEAGUE (Continued)

Year	Winner	Loser	Series
1976	New York Yankees (East)	Kansas City Royals (West)	3–2
1977	New York Yankees (East)	Kansas City Royals (West)	3–2
1978	New York Yankees (East)	Kansas City Royals (West)	3–1
1979	Baltimore Orioles (East)	California Angels (West)	3–1
1980	Kansas City Royals (West)	New York Yankees (East)	3–0
1981	New York Yankees (East)	Oakland A's (West)	3–0
1982	Milwaukee Brewers (East)	California Angels (West)	3–2
1983	Baltimore Orioles (East)	Chicago White Sox (West)	3–1
1984	Detroit Tigers (East)	Kansas City Royals (West)	3–0
1985	Kansas City Royals (West)	Toronto Blue Jays (East)	4–3
1986	Boston Red Sox (East)	California Angels (West)	4–3
1987	Minnesota Twins (West)	Detroit Tigers (East)	4–1
1988	Oakland A's (West)	Boston Red Sox (East)	4–0
1989	Oakland A's (West)	Toronto Blue Jays (East)	4–1
1990	Oakland A's (West)	Boston Red Sox (East)	4–0

COLLEGE BASEBALL

Various forms of college baseball have been played throughout the 20th century, however, the NCAA did not organize a championship until 1947 and did not begin to keep statistical records until 1957.

NCAA DIVISION I REGULAR SEASON

Hitting records The most career home runs was 100, by Pete Incaviglia for Oklahoma State in three seasons, 1983–85. The most career hits was 118, by Phil Stephenson for Wichita State in four seasons, 1979–82.

Pitching records Don Heinkel won 51 games for Wichita State in four seasons, 1979–82. Derek Patsumo struck out 541 batters for the University of Hawaii in three seasons, 1977–79.

COLLEGE WORLD SERIES The first College World Series was played in 1947 at Kalamazoo, MI. The University of California at Berkeley defeated Yale University 8–7. Since 1950 the College World Series has been played continuously at Rosenblatt Stadium, Omaha, NE.

Most championships The most wins in division one is 11 by the University of Southern California (USC) in 1948, 1958, 1961, 1963, 1968, 1970–74 and 1978.

Hitting records The record for most home runs in a College World Series is four shared by three players: Bud Hollowell (University of Southern

California), 1963; Pete Incaviglia (Oklahoma State), 1983–85; Ed Sprague (Stanford University), 1987–88. Keith Moreland of the University of Texas holds the record for the most hits in a College World Series career with 23 hits in three series 1973–75.

Pitching records The record for most wins in the College World Series is four games shared by nine players: Bruce Gardner (University of Southern California), 1958, 1960; Steve Arlin (Ohio State), 1965–66; Bert Hooton (University of Texas at Austin), 1969–70; Steve Rogers (University of Tulsa), 1969, 1971; Russ McQueen (University of Southern California), 1972–73; Mark Bull (University of Southern California), 1973–74; Greg Swindell (University of Texas), 1984–85; Kevin Sheary (University of Miami of Florida), 1984, 1985; Greg Brummett (Wichita State), 1988–89.

Carl Thomas of the University of Arizona struck out 64 batters in three College World Series, 1954–56.

LITTLE LEAGUE WORLD SERIES

Little League Baseball was founded in 1939 in Williamsport, PA, by Carl Stotz and George and Bert Bebble. In 1947, the inaugural Little League World Series was played—Maynard, PA defeating Lock Haven, PA 16–7. At this time there were 12 leagues throughout Pennsylvania, and Little League had expanded beyond the state borders to Hammonton, NJ. By 1950, there were 307 leagues throughout the United States, and Little League Baseball was quickly establishing itself as an American institution. In 1957 Monterrey, Mexico became the first international team to win the title. In 1989 Carl Yastrzemski became the first Little League graduate to be inducted into the Baseball Hall of Fame.

Most Championships Taiwan (Chinese Taipei), 14 (1969, 1971–74, 1977–81, 1986–88, 1990).

Most Championships (US-State) Pennsylvania 4 (Maynard–1947, Lock Haven–1948, Morrisville–1955, Levittown–1960) and Connecticut 4 (Stamford–1951, Norwalk–1952, Windsor Locks–1965, Trumbull–1989).

Baseball Hall of Fame Little League Inductees Only two graduates of Little League Baseball have been inducted into the Baseball Hall of Fame: Carl Yastrzemski (1989) and Jim Palmer (1990).

World Series/Little League World Series Players Three players have participated in both the Little League World Series and the Major League World Series: Jim Barbieri (Schenectady, NY–1954 and Los Angeles Dodgers–1966), Boog Powell (Lakeland, FL–1954 and Baltimore Orioles–1966, 1969–71), Carney Lansford (Santa Clara, CA–1969 and Oakland A's–1988–90).

Baseball Holding: Travis S. Johnson, age 16, of Elsberry, MO, held nine regulation baseballs in one hand without any adhesives on 14 September 1989.

BASKETBALL

ORIGINS The game of "Pok-ta-Pok" was played in the 10th century B.C., by the Olmecs in Mexico and closely resembled basketball in its concept. "Ollamalitzli" was a variation of this game played by the Aztecs in Mexico as late as the 16th century A.D.. If the solid rubber ball was put through a fixed stone ring the player was entitled to the clothing of all the spectators. Modern basketball was devised by the Canadian-born Dr. James A. Naismith at the Training School of the International YMCA College at Springfield, MA in mid-December 1891. The first game played under modified rules was on

---

NBA RECORDS (through 1989-90)

POINTS

Game: 100, Wilt Chamberlain, Philadelphia Warriors v. New York Knicks, 2 March 1962

Season: 4,029, Wilt Chamberlain, Philadelphia Warriors, 1962

Career: 38,387, Kareem Abdul-Jabbar, Milwaukee Bucks; Los Angeles Lakers, 1970–89

FIELD GOALS

Game: 36, Wilt Chamberlain, Philadelphia Warriors v. New York Knicks, 2 March 1962

Season: 1,597, Wilt Chamberlain, Philadelphia Warriors, 1962

Career: 15,837, Kareem Abdul-Jabbar, Milwaukee Bucks; Los Angeles Lakers, 1970–89

NBA RECORDS (through 1989–90) (Continued)

FIELD GOALS (Continued)
Highest Percentage

Season: .727, Wilt Chamberlain, Los Angeles Lakers (426 out of 586), 1972

Career:
(min. 2,000) .599, Artis Gilmore, Chicago Bulls; San Antonio Spurs; Boston Celtics, 1977–88

ASSISTS

Game: 29, Kevin Porter, New Jersey Nets v. Houston Rockets, 24 February 1978

Season: 1,134, John Stockton, Utah Jazz, 1989-90

Career: 9,887, Oscar Robertson, Cincinnati Royals; Milwaukee Bucks, 1960–74

REBOUNDS

Game: 55, Wilt Chamberlain, Philadelphia Warriors v. Boston Celtics, 24 November 1960

Season: 2,149, Wilt Chamberlain, Philadelphia Warriors, 1961

Career: 23,924, Wilt Chamberlain, Philadelphia/San Francisco Warriors; Philadelphia 76ers; Los Angeles Lakers, 1959–73

ASSISTS ■ JOHN STOCKTON, UTAH JAZZ, SET AN NBA SINGLE SEASON ASSIST MARK OF 1,134 IN 1989–90.

STOP THIEF! ■ MAURICE CHEEKS, NEW YORK KNICKS, HOLDS THE NBA ALL-TIME STEAL RECORD AT 2,066 THROUGH 1989–90.

20 January 1892. The International Amateur Basketball Federation (FIBA) was founded in 1932; it has now dropped the word Amateur from its title.

NATIONAL BASKETBALL ASSOCIATION (NBA)

ORIGINS The Amateur Athletic Union (AAU) organized the first national tournament in the United States in 1897. The first professional league was the National Basketball League (NBL), founded in 1898, but this league only lasted two seasons. The American Basketball League was formed in 1925, but declined and the NBL was refounded in 1937. This organization merged with the Basketball Association of America in 1949 to form the National Basketball Association (NBA).

Individual scoring Wilt Chamberlain set an NBA record with 100 points for the Philadelphia Warriors v. New York Knicks. The final result was 169 points to 147 at Hershey, PA on 2 March 1962. In this game, witnessed by 4,124 people, Chamberlain made 36 field goals and 28 free throws (in 32 attempts) and a record 59 points in a half (the second). The free throws game record was equaled by Adrian Dantley for the Utah Jazz v. the Houston Rockets at Las Vegas, NV on 5 January 1984 (in 31 attempts). The most points scored in an NBA game in one quarter is 33, by George Gervin for San Antonio v. New Orleans on 9 April 1978 (2nd quarter).

Most games Kareem Abdul-Jabbar took part in a record 1,560 NBA regular season games over 20 seasons, totaling 57,446 minutes played, for the Milwaukee Bucks (1969–75) and the Los Angeles Lakers (1975–89). He also played a record 237 play-off games.

The most successive games is 906, by Randy Smith for the Buffalo/San Diego Clippers, the Cleveland Cavaliers, the New York Knicks and the San Diego Clippers from 18 February 1972 to 13 March 1983. The record for playing complete games in one season is 79, by Wilt Chamberlain for the Philadelphia Warriors in 1962, when he was on court for a record 3,882 minutes. Chamberlain went through his entire career of 1,945 games without fouling out.

Most points Kareem Abdul-Jabbar set NBA career records with 38,387 points, including 15,837 field goals in regular season games, and 5,762 points, including 2,356 field goals in play-off games. The previous record holder, Wilt Chamberlain, had an average of 30.1 points per game for his total of 31,419 for the Philadelphia Warriors (1959–62), the San Francisco Warriors (1962–65), the Philadelphia 76ers (1964–68) and the Los Angeles Lakers (1968–73). He scored 50 or more points in 118 games, including 45 in 1961/2 and 30 in 1962/3 to the next best career total of 17, held by Elgin Baylor and Michael Jordan. Wilt Chamberlain set season's records for points and scoring average with 4,029 at 50.1 per game and also for field goals, 1,597, for Philadelphia in 1961/2.

The highest career average for players exceeding 10,000 points is 32.8 by Michael Jordan 14,106 points in 427 games for the Chicago Bulls, 1984–90. Jordan also holds the career scoring average record for play-offs at 35.4 for 1,309 points in 37 games 1984–90.

Steals The most steals in an NBA game is 11, by Larry Kenon for the San Antonio Spurs at Kansas

City on 26 December 1976. Alvin Robertson set season's records for the San Antonio Spurs in 1985/6 with 301 at a record average of 3.67 per game

Blocked shots The record for most blocked shots in an NBA game is 17, by Elmore Smith for the Los Angeles Lakers *v*. the Portland Trail Blazers at Los Angeles on 28 October 1973.

Most Valuable Player Kareem Abdul-Jabbar was elected the NBA most valuable player a record six times, 1971–72, 1974, 1976–77 and 1980.

Youngest and oldest player The youngest NBA player was Bill Willoughby who made his debut for the Atlanta Hawks on 23 October 1975 at 18 yr 156 days. The oldest NBA regular player was Kareem Abdul-Jabbar, who made his last appearance for the Los Angeles Lakers at age 42 yr 59 days in 1989.

Tallest player Tallest in NBA history was Manute Bol of the Washington Bullets, Golden State Warriors and Philadelphia 76ers, at 7 ft 6¾ in, who made his pro debut in 1985.

Highest score The highest aggregate score in an NBA game is 370, when the Detroit Pistons (186) beat the Denver Nuggets (184) at Denver, CO on 13 December 1983. Overtime was played after a 145–145 tie in regulation time. The record in regulation time is 318, when the Denver Nuggets beat the San Antonio Spurs 163–155 at Denver on 11 January 1984. The most points in a half is 97, by Atlanta in the 2nd half at San Diego on 11 February 1970. The most points in a quarter is 58, by Buffalo at Boston (4th quarter) on 20 October 1972.

Winning margin The greatest winning margin in an NBA game was the 63 points, by which the Los Angeles Lakers, 162, beat the Golden State Warriors, 99, on 19 March 1972.

Coaches The most successful coach in NBA history is Red Auerbach with 1,037 career wins (938 regular season, 99 playoffs). Auerbach coached three teams, the Washington Capitols 1946–49, the Tri-Cities Blackhawks 1949–50 and the Boston Celtics 1950–66. He led the Celtics to a record nine NBA championships, including eight consecutive titles 1959–66.

In his nine seasons with the Los Angeles Lakers (1981–90), coach Pat Riley won 102 playoff games to set the NBA all-time mark. Riley also compiled a league record .733 (533–194) regular season winning percentage.

NBA CHAMPIONSHIP The Boston Celtics have won a record 16 NBA titles, in 1957, 1959–66, 1968–69, 1974, 1976, 1981, 1984, 1986.

NBA CHAMPIONSHIP FINALS (1947–90)

Year	Winner	Loser	Series
1947	Philadelphia Warriors	Chicago Stags	4–1
1948	Baltimore Bullets	Philadelphia Warriors	4–2
1949	Minneapolis Lakers	Washington Capitols	4–2
1950	Minneapolis Lakers	Syracuse Nationals	4–2
1951	Rochester Royals	New York Knicks	4–3
1952	Minneapolis Lakers	New York Knicks	4–3
1953	Minneapolis Lakers	New York Knicks	4–1
1954	Minneapolis Lakers	Syracuse Nationals	4–3
1955	Syracuse Nationals	Fort Wayne Pistons	4–3
1956	Philadelphia Warriors	Fort Wayne Pistons	4–1
1957	Boston Celtics	St. Louis Hawks	4–3
1958	St. Louis Hawks	Boston Celtics	4–2
1959	Boston Celtics	Minneapolis Lakers	4–0
1960	Boston Celtics	St. Louis Hawks	4–3
1961	Boston Celtics	St. Louis Hawks	4–1
1962	Boston Celtics	Los Angeles Lakers	4–3

NBA HEAD COACHES

ALL-TIME WINNING PERCENTAGE* (Regular Season)

Coach	Won	Lost	Percentage	Teams
Pat Riley	533	194	.733	Los Angeles Lakers (1981–90)
K. C. Jones	463	193	.706	Washington Bullets (1973–76) Boston Celtics (1983–88)
Billy Cunningham	454	196	.698	Philadelphia 76ers (1977–85)
Red Auerbach	938	479	.662	Washington Capitols (1946–49) Tri-Cities Blackhawks (1949–50) Boston Celtics (1950–66)
Tom Heinsohn	427	263	.619	Boston Celtics (1969–77)

* Minimum 400 wins

Year	Winner	Loser	Series
1963	Boston Celtics	Los Angeles Lakers	4–2
1964	Boston Celtics	San Francisco Warriors	4–1
1965	Boston Celtics	Los Angeles Lakers	4–1
1966	Boston Celtics	Los Angeles Lakers	4–3
1967	Philadelphia 76ers	San Francisco Warriors	4–2
1968	Boston Celtics	Los Angeles Lakers	4–2
1969	Boston Celtics	Los Angeles Lakers	4–3
1970	New York Knicks	Los Angeles Lakers	4–3
1971	Milwaukee Bucks	Baltimore Bullets	4–0
1972	Los Angeles Lakers	New York Knicks	4–1
1973	New York Knicks	Los Angeles Lakers	4–1
1974	Boston Celtics	Milwaukee Bucks	4–3
1975	Golden State Warriors	Washington Bullets	4–0
1976	Boston Celtics	Phoenix Suns	4–2
1977	Portland Trailblazers	Philadelphia 76ers	4–2
1978	Washington Bullets	Seattle SuperSonics	4–3
1979	Seattle SuperSonics	Washington Bullets	4–1
1980	Los Angeles Lakers	Philadelphia 76ers	4–2
1981	Boston Celtics	Houston Rockets	4–2
1982	Los Angeles Lakers	Philadelphia 76ers	4–2
1983	Philadelphia 76ers	Los Angeles Lakers	4–0
1984	Boston Celtics	Los Angeles Lakers	4–3
1985	Los Angeles Lakers	Boston Celtics	4–2
1986	Boston Celtics	Houston Rockets	4–2
1987	Los Angeles Lakers	Boston Celtics	4–2

Year	Winner	Loser	Series
1988	Los Angeles Lakers	Detroit Pistons	4–3
1989	Detroit Pistons	Los Angeles Lakers	4–0
1990	Detroit Pistons	Portland Trailblazers	4–1

MOST POINTS ■ MICHAEL JORDAN, CHICAGO BULLS, SCORED 63 POINTS AGAINST THE BOSTON CELTICS ON 20 APRIL 1986 TO SET AN NBA PLAYOFF GAME POINTS RECORD.

NBA PLAYOFF RECORDS

POINTS

Game: 63, Michael Jordan, Chicago Bulls (v. Boston Celtics) (incl. two overtime periods), 20 April 1986
61, Elgin Baylor, Los Angeles Lakers (v. Boston Celtics) (regulation play), 14 April 1962

Series: 284, Elgin Baylor, Los Angeles Lakers (v. Boston Celtics); in 7 games, 1962

Career: 5,762, Kareem Abdul-Jabbar, Milwaukee Bucks, Los Angeles Lakers; in 237 games, 1970–89

FIELD GOALS

Game: 24, Wilt Chamberlain, Philadelphia 76ers (v. Syracuse Nationals); in 42 attempts, 14 March 1960
John Havlicek, Boston Celtics (v. Atlanta Hawks); in 36 attempts, 1 April 1973
Michael Jordan, Chicago Bulls (v. Cleveland Cavaliers); in 45 attempts, 1 May 1988

Series: 113, Wilt Chamberlain, San Francisco Warriors (v. St. Louis); in 6 games, 1964

Career: 2,356, Kareem Abdul-Jabbar, Milwaukee Bucks, Los Angeles Lakers; in 237 games, 1970–89

NBA PLAYOFF RECORDS (Continued)

ASSISTS

Game: 24, Magic Johnson, Los Angeles Lakers (v. Phoenix Suns), 15 May 1984
John Stockton, Utah Jazz (v. Los Angeles Lakers), 17 May 1988

Series: 115, John Stockton, Utah Jazz (v. Los Angeles Lakers); in 7 games, 1988

Career: 2,080, Magic Johnson, Los Angeles Lakers, 1980–90

REBOUNDS

Game: 41, Wilt Chamberlain, Philadelphia 76ers (v. Boston Celtics), 5 April 1967

Series: 220, Wilt Chamberlain, Philadelphia 76ers (v. Boston Celtics); in 7 games, 1965

Career: 4,104, Bill Russell, Boston Celtics, 1957–69

FREE THROWS MADE

Game: 30, Bob Cousy, Boston Celtics (v. Syracuse Nationals); in 32 attempts, (incl. four overtimes), 21 March 1953
23, Michael Jordan, Chiacgo Bulls (v. New York Knicks); in 28 attempts, (regulation play), 14 May 1989

Series: 86, Jerry West, Los Angeles Lakers (v. Baltimore Bullets); in 6 games, 1965

Career: 1,213, Jerry West, Los Angeles Lakers (1,507 attempts), 1961–74

SHOWTIME! ■ MAGIC JOHNSON(ABOVE), LOS ANGELES LAKERS, HOLDS THE NBA PLAYOFF ASSIST RECORDS FOR A GAME (24) AND A CAREER (2,080). PAT RILEY (LEFT) LED THE LAKERS TO 102 PLAYOFF WINS, THE MOST BY ANY COACH IN NBA HISTORY.

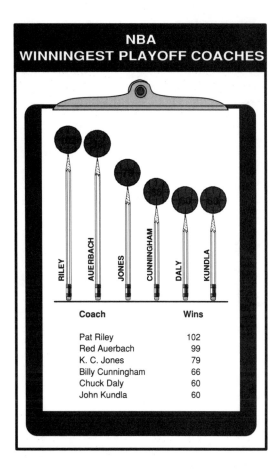

NBA WINNINGEST PLAYOFF COACHES

Coach	Wins
Pat Riley	102
Red Auerbach	99
K. C. Jones	79
Billy Cunningham	66
Chuck Daly	60
John Kundla	60

NCAA RECORDS

CHAMPIONSHIPS First contested in 1939, the record for most Division One titles is 10, by the University of California at Los Angeles (UCLA), 1964–65, 1967–73, 1975. The only player to have been voted the most valuable player in the NCAA final three times was Lew Alcindor of UCLA in 1967–69. He subsequently changed his name to Kareem Abdul-Jabbar.

Coaches The man to have coached the most victories in NCAA Division I competition is Adolph Rupp at Kentucky, with 875 wins (and 190 losses), 1931–72. John Wooden coached UCLA to all 10 of its NCAA titles.

NCAA CHAMPIONSHIP

The NCAA finals were first contested in 1939 at Northwestern University, Evanston, IL. The University of Oregon, University of Oklahoma, Villanova University and Ohio State University were the first "final four." Oregon defeated Ohio State 46–33 to win the first NCAA title. The University of California at Los Angeles (UCLA) has won the most championships with 10 victories, 1964–65, 1967–73, 1975.

NCAA CHAMPIONSHIP GAME (1939–90)

Year	Winner	Loser	Score
1939	Oregon	Ohio State	46–33
1940	Indiana	Kansas	60–42
1941	Wisconsin	Washington State	39–34
1942	Stanford	Dartmouth	53–38
1943	Wyoming	Georgetown	46–34
1944	Utah	Dartmouth	42–40
1945	Oklahoma A&M	NYU	49–45
1946	Oklahoma A&M	North Carolina	43–40
1947	Holy Cross	Oklahoma	58–47
1948	Kentucky	Baylor	58–42
1949	Kentucky	Oklahoma A&M	46–36
1950	CCNY	Bradley	71–68
1951	Kentucky	Kansas State	68–58
1952	Kansas	St. John's	80–63
1953	Indiana	Kansas	69–68
1954	LaSalle	Bradley	92–76
1955	San Francisco	LaSalle	77–63
1956	San Francisco	Iowa	83–71
1957	North Carolina	Kansas	54–53
1958	Kentucky	Seattle	84–72
1959	California	West Virginia	71–70
1960	Ohio State	California	75–55
1961	Cincinnati	Ohio State	70–65
1962	Cincinnati	Ohio State	71–59
1963	Loyola (IL)	Cincinnati	60–58
1964	UCLA	Duke	98–83
1965	UCLA	Michigan	91–80
1966	Texas Western	Kentucky	72–65
1967	UCLA	Dayton	79–64
1968	UCLA	North Carolina	78–55
1969	UCLA	Purdue	92–72
1970	UCLA	Jacksonville	80–69
1971	UCLA	Villanova	68–62
1972	UCLA	Florida State	81–76
1973	UCLA	Memphis State	87–66
1974	N. Carolina State	Marquette	76–64
1975	UCLA	Kentucky	92–85
1976	Indiana	Michigan	86–68
1977	Marquette	North Carolina	67–59
1978	Kentucky	Duke	94–88

Year	Winner	Loser	Score
1979	Michigan State	Indiana State	75–64
1980	Louisville	UCLA	59–54

NCAA CHAMPIONSHIP GAME (1939–90)
(Continued)

Year	Winner	Loser	Score
1981	Indiana	North Carolina	63–50
1982	North Carolina	Georgetown	63–62

NCAA CHAMPIONSHIP GAME (1939–90)
(Continued)

MARCH MADNESS

The Distribution of NCAA Division I Men's Basketball Champions by State

State	Wins	Teams
California	14	UCLA 10, San Francisco 2, Stanford 1, California 1
Kentucky	7	Kentucky 5, Louisville 2
Indiana	5	Indiana 5
North Carolina	4	North Carolina 2, North Carolina State 2
Ohio	3	Cincinnati 2, Ohio State 1
Pennsylvania	2	La Salle 1, Villanova 1
Michigan	2	Michigan 1, Michigan State 1
Oklahoma	2	Oklahoma A&M 2
Kansas	2	Kansas 2
Wisconsin	2	Marquette 1, Wisconsin 1
Massachusetts	1	Holy Cross 1
New York	1	CCNY 1
Oregon	1	Oregon 1
Wyoming	1	Wyoming 1
Utah	1	Utah 1
Illinois	1	Loyola, Illinois 1
Texas	1	Texas Western 1
Nevada	1	UNLV 1
Washington, D.C.	1	Georgetown 1

NCAA CHAMPIONSHIP GAME (1939–90)
(Continued)

Year	Winner	Loser	Score
1983	N. Carolina State	Houston	54–52
1984	Georgetown	Houston	84–75
1985	Villanova	Georgetown	66–64
1986	Louisville	Duke	72–69

NCAA CHAMPIONSHIP GAME (1939–90)
(Continued)

Year	Winner	Loser	Score
1987	Indiana	Syracuse	74–73
1988	Kansas	Oklahoma	83–79
1989	Michigan	Seton Hall	80–79
1990	UNLV	Duke	103–73

NCAA MEN'S CHAMPIONSHIP GAME RECORDS

TEAM RECORDS

Most championships: 10, UCLA, 1964–65, 1967–73, 1975

First championships: Oregon defeated Ohio State 46–33, 1939

Most points: 103, UNLV (v. Duke), 1990

Most field goals: 41, UNLV (v. Duke), 1990

Highest field goal percentage: 78.6%, Villanova (v. Georgetown) (22–28), 1985

Most 3-point field goals: 10, Oklahoma (v. Kansas), 1988

Rebounds: 61, UCLA (v. Purdue), 1969.

Assists: 24, UNLV (v. Duke), 1990.

Blocked shots: 7, Louisville (v. Duke), 1986
Syracuse (v. Indiana), 1987

Steals: 16, UNLV (v. Duke), 1990

INDIVIDUAL RECORDS

Most points: 44, Bill Walton, UCLA (v. Memphis State), 1973

Most field goals: 21, Bill Walton, UCLA (v. Memphis State), 1973

Highest field goal percentage: 95.5%, Bill Walton, UCLA (v. Memphis State) (21–22), 1973

3-point field goals: 7, Steve Alford, Indiana (v. Syracuse), 1987
Dave Sieger, Oklahoma (v. Kansas), 1988

Rebounds: 21, Bill Spivey, Kentucky (v. Kansas State), 1951

Assists: 9, Alvin Franklin, Houston (v. Georgetown), 1984
Michael Jackson, Georgetown (v. Villanova), 1985

Blocked shots: 3, Rony Seikaly, Syracuse (v. Indiana), 1987
Derrick Coleman, Syracuse (v. Indiana), 1987
Dean Garrett, Indiana (v. Syracuse), 1987

Steals: 7, Tommy Amaker, Duke (v. Louisville), 1986
Mookie Blaylock, Oklahoma (v. Kansas), 1988

NCAA CHAMPIONSHIP TOURNAMENT RECORDS (INDIVIDUAL)

POINTS

Most Scored

Game:	61, Austin Carr, Notre Dame v. Ohio State, 7 March 1970
Tournament:	184, Glen Rice, Michigan (6 games), 1989
Career:	358, Elvin Hayes, Houston (13 games), 1966–68

FIELD GOALS

Most Scored

Game:	25, Austin Carr, Notre Dame v. Ohio State, 7 March 1970
Tournament:	75, Glen Rice, Michigan (6 games), 1989
Career:	152, Elvin Hayes, Houston (13 games), 1966–68

Highest Percentage

Game: (Min. 10 made)	100, Kenny Walker, Kentucky v. Western Kentucky (11–11), 1976 Marvin Barnes, Providence v. Pennsylvania (10–10), 1973
Tournament: (Min. 5 games)	78.8, Christian Laettner, Duke (26–33 in 5 games), 1989
Career: (Min. 60 made)	68.6, Bill Walton, UCLA (109–159), 1972–74

POINTS AND FIELD GOALS ■ AUSTIN CARR, NOTRE DAME, SANK 25 FIELD GOALS AND SCORED 61 POINTS AGAINST OHIO STATE ON 7 MARCH 1970 TO SET NCAA TOURNAMENT MARKS.

POINTS, FIELD GOALS AND REBOUNDS ■ ELVIN HAYES, HOUSTON, HOLDS CAREER NCAA TOURNAMENT MARKS FOR POINTS (358), FIELD GOALS (152) AND REBOUNDS (222).

NCAA CHAMPIONSHIP TOURNAMENT RECORDS (INDIVIDUAL) (Continued)

FIELD GOALS (Continued)

Three-Point Field Goals

Game:	11, Jeff Fryer, Loyola-Marymount v. Michigan, 18 March 1990
Tournament:	27, Glen Rice, Michigan (6 games), 1989
Career:	38, Jeff Fryer, Loyola-Marymount, 1988–90

FREE THROWS

Most Scored

Game:	23, Bob Carney, Bradley v. Colorado, 1954
Tournament:	55, Bob Carney, Bradley (5 games), 1954
Career:	90, Oscar Robertson, Cincinnati, 1958–60

Highest Percentage

Game: **(Min 10 made)**	100, 17 players have accomplished this feat.
Tournament: **(Min. 10 made)**	100, 12 players have attained perfect postseason precision.
Career:	91.7, Bill Bradley, Princeton (88–96), 1963–65

HIGHEST SCORING AVERAGE (NCAA TOURNAMENT)

Top Five (Minimum 7 Games)

	Player	Team	Average	Totals
1.	Austin Carr	Notre Dame	41.3	289 points in 7 games
2.	Bill Bradley	Princeton	33.7	303 points in 9 games
3.	Oscar Robertson	Cincinnati	32.4	324 points in 10 games
4.	Jerry West	West Virginia	30.6	275 points in 9 games
5.	Bo Kimble	Loyola-Marymount	29.1	204 points in 7 games

NCAA CHAMPIONSHIP TOURNAMENT RECORDS (INDIVIDUAL) (Continued)

REBOUNDS

Game: 31, Nate Thurmond, Bowling Green v. Mississippi State, 1963

Tournament: 97, Elvin Hayes, Houston (5 games), 1968

Career: 222, Elvin Hayes, Houston (13 games) , 1966–68

ASSISTS

Game: 18, Mark Wade, UNLV, 1987

Tournament: 61, Mark Wade, UNLV (5 games), 1987

Career: 106, Sherman Douglas, Syracuse (14 games), 1986–89

NCAA CHAMPIONSHIP TOURNAMENT RECORDS (TEAM)

GAME

Most Points: 149, Loyola-Marymount (v. Michigan), 1990

Fewest Points: 20, North Carolina (v. Pittsburgh), 1941

Most Field Goals: 52, Iowa (v. Notre Dame), 1970

Fewest Field Goals: 8, Springfield (v. Indiana), 1940

Highest Field Goal Percentage: 79%, North Carolina (v. Loyola-Marymount) (49–62), 1988

Lowest Field Goal Percentage: 19.4, Creighton (v. Cincinnati) (14–72), 1962

Most 3-point field goals: 21, Loyola-Marymount (v. Michigan), 1990

Free Throws: 41, Utah (v. Santa Clara), 1960

Rebounds: 86, Notre Dame (v. Tennessee), 1958

Assists (since 1984): 36, North Carolina (v. Loyola-Marymount), 1988

Blocked Shots (since 1986): 13, Louisville (v. Illinois), 1989

Steals: 19, Providence (v. Austin Peay), 1987

TOURNAMENT

Most Points: 571, UNLV (6 games), 1990

Most Field Goals: 218, UNLV (5 games), 1977

3-point Field Goals: 56, Loyola-Marymount (4 games), 1990

Free Throws: 146, Bradley (5 games), 1954

SHARPSHOOTER ■ PISTOL PETE MARAVICH, LSU, SET NCAA RECORDS FOR MOST POINTS (SEASON, CAREER) AND MOST FIELD GOALS (SEASON, CAREER), 1968–70.

PASSIN' REBEL ■ MARK WADE, UNLV, SET AN NCAA SINGLE SEASON ASSIST MARK OF 406 IN 1987.

NCAA DIVISION I REGULAR SEASON RECORDS (through 1989–90) (Continued)

FIELD GOALS

Game: 41, Frank Selvy, Furman v. Newberry, 13 February 1954

Season: 522, Pete Maravich, LSU, 1970

Career: 1,387, Pete Maravich, LSU, 1968–70

ASSISTS

Game: 22, Tony Fairly, Baptist v. Armstrong State, 9 February 1987
Avery Johnson, Southern-B.R. v. Texas Southern, 25 January 1988
Sherman Douglas, Syracuse v. Providence, 28 January 1989

Season: 406, Mark Wade, UNLV, 1987

Career: 960, Sherman Douglas, Syracuse, 1986–89

REBOUNDS

Game: 51, Bill Chambers, William & Mary v. Virginia, 14 February 1953

Season: 734, Walt Dukes, Seton Hall, 1953

Career: 2,243, Tom Gola, La Salle, 1952-55

GENERAL SHERMAN ■ SYRACUSE GUARD SHERMAN DOUGLAS TIED THE NCAA ASSISTS RECORDS FOR A GAME (22) AND SET THE RECORD FOR A CAREER (960), 1986–89.

COACHES

NCAA DIVISION 1 ALL-TIME VICTORIES

Coach	Teams	Wins
Adolph Rupp	Kentucky (1931–72)	875
Phog Allen	Kansas & Baker (1908–09) Kansas & Haskell (1909) Central Missouri State (1913–19) Kansas (1920–56)	770
Henry Iba	NW Missouri State (1930–33) Colorado (1934) Oklahoma State (1935–70)	767
Ed Diddle	Western Kentucky (1923–64)	759
Ray Meyer	DePaul (1943–84)	724

WOMEN'S CHAMPIONSHIPS

First contested in 1982, the record for most Division One titles is two by the University of Southern California, 1983–84, Tennessee, 1987 and 1989 and Louisiana Tech University, 1982 and 1988.

The regular season match aggregate record is 261, when St. Joseph's (Indiana) beat North Kentucky 131–130 on 27 February 1988. The most points by a woman in a college career is 4,061 by Pearl Moore of Francis Marion College. Florence, SC, 1975–79.

NCAA WOMEN'S CHAMPIONSHIP GAME RECORDS

TEAM RECORDS

Most championships: 2, Louisiana Tech (1982, 1988), USC (1983–84), Tennessee (1987, 1989)

First championships: Louisiana Tech defeated Cheyney State 76–62, 1982

Most points: 97, Texas (v. USC), 1986

Most field goals: 40, Texas (v. USC), 1986

Highest field goal percentage: 58.8%, Texas (v. USC) (40–68), 1986

Most 3-point field goals: 11, Stanford (v. Auburn), 1990

Rebounds: 57, Old Dominion (v. Georgia), 1985

Assists (since 1985): 22, Texas (v. USC), 1986

Blocked shots (since 1988): 7, Tennessee (v. Auburn) 1989

Steals (since 1988): 12, Louisiana Tech (v. Auburn), 1988

INDIVIDUAL RECORDS

Most points: 27, Cheryl Miller, USC (v. Louisiana Tech), 1983
Cynthia Cooper, USC (v. Texas), 1987
Bridgette Gordon, Tennessee (v. Auburn), 1989

Most field goals: 12, Erica Westbrooks, Louisiana Tech (v. Auburn), 1988

Highest field goal percentage: 88.9%, Jennifer White, Louisiana Tech (v. USC) (8–9), 1983

Most 3-point field goals: (since 1988) 6, Katy Steding, Stanford (v. Auburn), 1990

Rebounds: 20, Tracy Claxton, Old Dominion (v. Georgia), 1985

Assists: (since 1985) 10, Kamie Ethridge, Texas (v. USC), 1986
Melissa McCray, Tennessee (v. Auburn), 1989

Blocked shots: (since 1988) 5, Sheila Frost, Tennessee (v. Auburn), 1989

Steals: (since 1988) 6, Erica Westbrooks, Louisiana Tech (v. Auburn), 1988

NCAA WOMEN'S REGULAR SEASON RECORDS

SEASON

Points:	904, Cindy Brown, Long Beach State, 1987
Field Goals:	392, Barbara Kennedy, Clemson, 1982
Rebounds:	534, Wanda Ford, Drake, 1985
Assists:	355, Suzie McConnell, Penn State, 1987
Free Throws:	275, Lorri Bauman, Drake, 1982

CAREER

Points:	3,122, Patricia Hoskins, Mississippi Valley State, 1985–89
Field Goals:	1,259, Joyce Walker, Louisiana State, 1981–84
Rebounds:	1,887, Wanda Ford, Drake, 1983–86
Assists:	1,307, Suzie McConnell, Penn State, 1984–88
Free Throws:	907, Lorri Bauman, Drake, 1981–84

OUTSTANDING IN HER FIELD GOALS ■ BARBARA KENNEDY, CLEMSON, HOLDS THE NCAA WOMEN'S SEASON RECORD FOR MOST FIELD GOALS (392), SET IN 1982.

TOP COACH ■ JODY CONRADT, TEXAS, HOLDS THE NCAA WOMEN'S COACHING RECORD FOR MOST VICTORIES. THROUGH 1989–90, CONRADT HAD STEERED THE LONGHORNS TO 556 WINS.

Coaches Jody Conradt of the University of Texas has won the most games in Womens NCAA Division I competition with 556 victories through the 1989–90 season.

OLYMPIC GAMES The men's basketball competition was introduced at the Berlin Olympiad in 1936. The US has won a record nine titles. From 1936 through 1972, the US compiled a 63-game winning streak, which was snapped by the Soviet Union in the championship game in Munich, West Germany.

The women's basketball competition was introduced at the Montreal Olympiad in 1976. Both the Soviet Union (1976 and 1980) and the US (1984 and 1988) have won two gold medals.

OLYMPIC GAMES
MEN

Year	Gold	Silver	Bronze
1936	USA	Canada	Mexico
1948	USA	France	Brazil
1952	USA	USSR	Uruguay
1956	USA	USSR	Uruguay
1960	USA	USSR	Brazil
1964	USA	USSR	Brazil
1968	USA	Yugoslavia	USSR
1972	USSR	USA	Cuba
1976	USA	Yugoslavia	USSR
1980	Yugoslavia	Italy	USSR
1984	USA	Spain	Yugoslavia
1988	USSR	Yugoslavia	USA

World Championships The USSR has won the most titles at both the men's World Championships (instituted 1950) with three (1967, 1974 and 1982) and women's (instituted 1953), with six (1959, 1964, 1967, 1971, 1975 and 1983).

WORLD CHAMPIONSHIPS

Year	Men	Women
1950	Argentina	—
1953	—	USA
1954	USA	—
1957	—	USA
1959	Brazil	USSR
1963	Brazil	—
1964	—	USSR
1967	USSR	USSR
1970	Yugoslavia	—
1971	—	USSR
1974	USSR	—
1975	—	USSR

WORLD CHAMPIONSHIPS (Continued)

Year	Men	Women
1978	Yugoslavia	—
1979	—	USA
1982	USSR	—
1983	—	USSR
1986	USA	USA
1990	Yugoslavia	USA

Longest field goal Christopher Eddy scored a field goal, measured at 90 ft 2¼ in, for Fairview High School v Iroquois High School at Erie, PA on 25 Feb 1989. The shot was made as time expired in overtime and won the game for Fairview, 51-50.

BIATHLON

The biathlon, which combines cross-country skiing and rifle shooting, was first included in the Olympic Games in 1960; World Championships were first held in 1958. Since 1984 there has been a women's World Championship; a women's biathlon will be contested at the 1992 Olympics.

OLYMPIC GAMES Two Olympic individual titles have been won by: Magnar Solberg (Norway), in 1968 and 1972; and by Franz-Peter Rötsch (East Germany) at both 10 km and 20 km in 1988. The USSR has won all six 4 x 7.5 km relay titles, from 1968 to 1988. Aleksandr Tikhonov, who was a member of the first four teams, also won a silver in the 1968 20 km.

WORLD CHAMPIONSHIPS Frank Ullrich (East Germany) has won a record six individual world titles, four at 10 km, 1978–81, including the 1980 Olympics, and two at 20 km, 1982–83. Aleksandr Tikhonov was in 10 winning USSR relay teams, 1968–80, and won four individual titles.

The Biathlon World Cup (instituted 1979) was won four times by Frank Ullrich, in 1978 and 1980–82.

BILLIARDS

ORIGINS The earliest recorded mention of billiards was in France in 1429, and Louis XI, King of France 1461–83, is reported to have had a billiard table.

WORLD CHAMPIONSHIPS The greatest number of World Championships (instituted 1870) won by one player is eight, by John Roberts Jr. (UK), in

1870 (twice), 1871, 1875 (twice), 1877 and 1885 (twice). The record for world amateur titles is four, by Robert James Percival Marshall (Australia), in 1936, 1938, 1951 and 1962.

Youngest champion The youngest winner of the world professional title is Mike Russell, aged 20 yr 49 days, when he won at Leura, Australia on 23 July 1989.

Highest breaks The highest certified break made by the anchor cannon is 42,746 by William Cook (England) from 29 May to 7 June 1907.

The official world record under the then balkline rule is 1,784, by Joe Davis in the United Kingdom Championship on 29 May 1936.

Walter Albert Lindrum (Australia) made an official break of 4,137 in 2 hr 55 min against Joe Davis at Thurston's on 19–20 January 1932, before the balkline rule was in force.

The highest break recorded in amateur competition is 1,149, by Michael Ferreira (India) at Calcutta, India on 15 December 1978.

Under the more stringent "two pot" rule, restored on 1 January 1983, the highest break is Ferreira's 962 unfinished, in a tournament at Bombay, India on 29 April 1986.

3 CUSHION

ORIGINS This pocketless variation dates back to 1878. The world governing body, the Union Mondiale de Billiard (UMB), was formed in 1928.

Most titles Willie F. Hoppe (US) won 51 billiards championships in all forms, spanning the pre- and postinternational era from 1906 to 1952.

UMB Raymond Ceulemans (Belgium) has won 19 world 3-cushion championships (1963–73, 1975–80, 1983, 1985).

BOBSLED AND LUGE

BOBSLED

ORIGINS The oldest known sled is dated *c.* 6500 B.C. and came from Heinola, Finland. The first known bobsled race took place at Davos, Switzerland in 1889. The International Federation of Bobsleigh and Tobogganing was formed in 1923, followed by the International Bobsleigh Federation in 1957.

MOST OLYMPIC TITLES The Olympic four-man bob title (instituted 1924) has been won five times by Switzerland (1924, 1936, 1956, 1972 and 1988).

The United States (1932, 1936), Switzerland (1948, 1980), Italy (1956, 1968), West Germany (1952, 1972) and East Germany (GDR) (1976, 1984) have each won the Olympic two-man bob (instituted 1932) event twice.

The most gold medals won by an individual is three, by Meinhard Nehmer (GDR) and Bernhard Germeshausen (GDR) in the 1976 two-man, and 1976 and 1980 four-man events.

WORLD CHAMPIONSHIPS The world four-man bob title (instituted 1924) has been won 19 times by Switzerland (1924, 1936, 1939, 1947, 1954–57, 1971–73, 1975, 1982–83, 1986–90), including five Olympic victories.

Italy won the two-man title 14 times (1954, 1956–63, 1966, 1968–69, 1971 and 1975).

UNITED STATES Two American bobsledders have won two gold medals: driver Billy Fiske III and crewman Clifford Barton Grey in 1928 and 1932. At age 16 yr 260 days in 1928, Fiske was America's youngest ever Winter Games gold medalist.

Oldest gold medalist The oldest age at which a gold medal has been won at any sport at the Winter Olympics is 49 yr 7 days, by James Jay O'Brien (US) at four-man bob.

LAID BACK ■ HANS RINN, EAST GERMANY, HAS WON THE OLYMPIC TWO-SEATER LUGE GOLD MEDAL A RECORD TWO TIMES.

LUGE

In Luge the rider adopts a supine as opposed to a sitting position. Official international competition began at Klosters, Switzerland in 1881. The first European championships were held at Reichenberg, Germany in 1914 and the first World Championships at Oslo, Norway in 1953. The International Luge Federation was formed in 1957. Luge became an Olympic sport in 1964.

WORLD/OLYMPIC CHAMPIONSHIPS The most successful riders in the World Championships have been Thomas Köhler (GDR), who won the single-seater title in 1962, 1964 (Olympic). 1966 and 1967 and shared the two-seater title in 1967 and 1968 (Olympic), and Hans Rinn (GDR), Olympic champion two-seater 1976 and 1980 and world champion at single-seater 1973 and 1977, two-seater 1977 and 1980.

Margit Schumann (GDR) has won five women's titles, 1973-6, 1976 (Olympic) and 1977.

Steffi Walter (née Martin [GDR]) became the first rider to win two Olympic single-seater luge titles, with victories at the women's event in 1984 and 1988.

Fastest speed The highest recorded, photo-timed speed is 85.38 mph, by Asle Strand (Norway) at Tandådalens Linbana, Sälen, Sweden on 1 May 1982.

BOWLING

ORIGINS The ancient German game of nine-pins (*Heidenwerfen*—"knock down pagans") was exported to the United States in the early 17th century. In 1841, the Connecticut State Legislature prohibited the game and other states followed. Eventually a 10th pin was added to evade the ban. The first body to standardize rules was the American Bowling Congress (ABC), established in New York City on 9 September 1895.

PROFESSIONAL BOWLERS ASSOCIATION (PBA)

Most titles Earl Anthony of Dublin, CA has won a lifetime total of 41 PBA titles through 1986. The record number of titles won in one PBA season is eight by Mark Roth of North Arlington, NJ, in 1978.

TRIPLE CROWN The United States Open, PBA National Championship and the Firestone Tournament of Champions comprise the Triple Crown of men's professional bowling. No bowler has won each title in the same year, and only three have managed to win all three during a career. The first bowler to accumulate the three legs of the triple crown was Billy Hardwick: National Championship (1963); Firestone Tournament of Champions (1965); US Open (1969). Hardwick's feat was matched by Johnny Petraglia: Firestone (1971); US Open (1977); National (1980); and Pete Weber; Firestone (1987); US Open (1988); National (1989).

US OPEN Inaugurated in 1942, the most wins is four by two bowlers: Don Carter in 1953–54 and 1957–58 and Dick Weber in 1962–63 and 1965–66.

PBA NATIONAL CHAMPIONSHIP Inaugurated in 1960, the most wins is six by Earl Anthony in 1973–75 and 1981–83.

FIRESTONE TOURNAMENT OF CHAMPIONS Inaugurated in 1965, the most wins is three by Mike Durbin in 1972, 1982 and 84.

Perfect games A total of 141 perfect (300 score) games were bowled in PBA tournaments in 1990, the most ever for one year. Dick Weber rolled three perfect games in one tournament (Houston, TX) in 1965, as did Billy Hardwick of Louisville, KY (in the Japan Gold Cup competition) in 1968, John Wilcox (at Detroit, MI) in 1979, Norm Meyers of

KINGPIN ■ EARL ANTHONY HAS WON A CAREER RECORD 41 PBA TITLES.

TRIPLE CROWN ■ THREE BOWLERS HAVE WON ALL THREE LEGS OF THE PBA TRIPLE CROWN: BILLY HARDWICK (ABOVE, UPPER LEFT), JOHNNY PETRAGLIA (ABOVE) AND PETE WEBER (ABOVE, UPPER RIGHT).

St. Louis (at Peoria, IL). In 1979, Ray Shackelford of Hartwood, VA (at St. Louis, MO) in 1982, Shawn Christensen of Denver (at Denver, CO) in 1984, and Amleto Monacelli of Venezuela (at Tuscon, AZ) in 1989.

Amleto Monacelli rolled seven perfect games on the 1989 tour and Guppy Troup of Savannah, GA, rolled six perfect games on the 1979 tour.

Highest earners Marshall Holman won a record $1,925,957 in Professional Bowlers Association (PBA) competitions through 1990.

Mike Aulby of Indianapolis, IN set a single season earnings mark of $298,237 in 1989.

AMERICAN BOWLING CONGRESS (ABC)

Highest score The highest individual score for three games is 899 by Thomas Jordan at Union, NJ on 7 March 1989. He followed with a 299, setting a 4- game series record of 1,198 pins. Glenn Allison rolled a perfect 900 in a 3-game series in league play on 1 July 1982, at La Habra Bowl, Los Angeles, CA but the ABC could not recognize the record when an ABC inspector determined the lanes were improperly dressed. Highest 3-game team score is 3,858 by Budweisers of St. Louis on 12 March 1958.

The highest season average attained in sanctioned competition is 245.63 by Doug Vergouven of Harrisonville, MO in the 1989–90 season.

Juniors Brentt Arcement, at age 16, bowled a 3-game bowling series of 888, the highest ever bowled in a league or tournament sanctioned by the Young American Bowling Alliance, which is the national organization serving junior bowlers age 21 and under.

Consecutive strikes The record for consecutive strikes in sanctioned match play is 33 by John Pezzin at Toledo, OH on 4 March 1976.

Perfect scores (individual) The highest number of sanctioned 300 games is 40 by Bob Learn Jr. of Erie, PA.

Two perfect games were rolled back-to-back *twice* by Al Spotts of West Reading, PA on 14 March 1982 and again on 1 February 1985.

Highest doubles The ABC national tournament record of 561 was set in 1989 by Rick McCardy and Steve Mesmer of Redford, MI. The record score in a doubles series is 1,499 set in 1989 by Gus Yannaras (757) and Gary Daroszewski (742) of Milwaukee, WI.

Perfect scores (team) Les Schissler of Denver was the first bowler to score 300, in the Classic team event in 1967. Through 1990, 20 perfect games have been bowled in team play. In all, there have been 98 perfect games in the ABC tournament through 1990.

Strikes and spares in a row In the greatest finish to an ABC title, Ed Shay set a record of 12 strikes in a row in 1958, when he scored a perfect game for a total of 733 in singles. Most strikes in a row is 20 by Lou Viet of Milwaukee, WI in 1977. The most spares in a row is 23 by Lieutenant Hazen Sweet of Battle Creek, MI in 1950.

WOMEN'S INTERNATIONAL BOWLING CONGRESS (WIBC)

Highest score Patty Ann of Appleton, WI, had a record 5 year composite average of 222.5 through the 1985–90 season. She also had the best one-season average, 232, in the 1983–84 season.

Jeanne Maiden of Solon, OH, has rolled 17 perfect games to set the WIBC career record. She also set a record of 40 consecutive strikes in 1986 and rolled an 864 on games of 300–300–264.

The highest 5-woman team score for a 3-game series is 3,493 by Lisa's Flowers and Gift Shop, Franklin, WI, in the 1989-90 season. The highest game score by a 5-woman team is 1,244 by Chamberlain Wholesale, of Detroit, MI in the 1987–88 season.

CHAMPIONSHIP TOURNAMENTS The highest score for a 3-game series in the annual WIBC Championship Tournament is 746 by Linda Kelly of Huber Heights, OH in the 1987 doubles event.

The record for one game is 300 by Lori Gensch of Milwaukee, WI in the 1979 doubles event; by Rose Walsh of Pomona, CA in the 1986 singles event; and by Linda Kelly of Huber Heights, OH in the 1987 singles event.

Dorothy Miller of Chicago, IL has won 10 WIBC Championship Tournament events, the most by an individual. Millie Ignizo is the only one to have won three WIBC Queen Tournaments—1967, 1970 and 1971.

The highest WIBC Championship Tournament lifetime average is 199.17 by Dorothy Fothergill of Lincoln, RI, who had bowled for 10 years, but is now inactive.

HIGHEST SCORE ■ LINDA KELLY ROLLED A RECORD **746** IN A THREE-GAME SERIES IN THE **1987** WIBC CHAMPIONSHIP TOURNAMENT.

QUEENPIN ■ DOROTHY MILLER HAS WON A CAREER RECORD 10 WIBC CHAMPIONSHIP TOURNAMENT TITLES.

Perfect games The most 300 games rolled in a career is 17 by Jeanne Maiden of Solon, OH. The oldest woman to bowl a perfect game (12 strikes in a row) was Helen Duval of Berkeley, CA, at age 65 in 1982. Of all the women who rolled a perfect game, the one with the lowest average was Diane Ponza of Santa Cruz, CA who had a 112 average in the 1977–78 season.

Consecutive strikes, spares and splits The record for most consecutive strikes is 40 by Jeanne Maiden (see above). Mabel Henry of Winchester, KY had 30 consecutive spares in the 1986–87 season. Shirley Tophigh of Las Vegas, NV holds the unenviable record of rolling 14 consecutive splits.

BOXING

ORIGINS Boxing with gloves is depicted on a fresco from the Isle of Thera, Greece that has been dated to 1520 B.C. The earliest prize-ring code of rules was formulated in England on 16 August 1743 by the champion pugilist Jack Broughton, who reigned from 1734 to 1750. Boxing, in 1867, came under the Queensberry Rules formulated for John Sholto Douglas, 8th Marquess of Queensberry. New York was the first state to legalize boxing in the United States in 1896. Today professional boxing is regulated in each state by athletic or boxing commissions.

Longest fights The longest recorded fight with gloves was between Andy Bowen and Jack Burke at New Orleans, LA on 6–7 April 1893. It lasted 110 rounds, 7 hr 19 min (9:15 P.M.–4:34 A.M.) and was declared a no contest (later changed to a draw). Bowen won an 85-round bout on 31 May 1893. The longest bare-knuckle fight was 6 hr 15 min between James Kelly and Jack Smith at Fiery Creek, Dalesford, Victoria, Australia on 3 December 1855.

The greatest number of rounds was 276 in 4 hr 30 min when Jack Jones beat Patsy Tunney in Cheshire, England in 1825.

Shortest fights The shortest fight on record appears to be one in a Golden Gloves tournament at Minneapolis, MN on 4 November 1947, when Mike Collins floored Pat Brownson with the first punch and the contest was stopped, without a count, 4 sec after the bell.

The shortest world title fight was 45 sec, when Lloyd Honeyghan (UK) beat Gene Hatcher (US) in an IBF welterweight bout at Marbella, Spain on 30 August 1987. Some sources also quote the Al McCoy 1st round knockout of George Chip in a middleweight contest on 7 April 1914 as being in 45 sec.

Most fights without loss Of boxers with complete records, Packey McFarland (US) had 97 fights (5 draws) in 1905–15 without a defeat.

Pedro Carrasco (Spain) won 83 consecutive fights from 22 April 1964 to 3 September 1970, drew once and had a further nine wins before his loss to Armando Ramos in a WBC lightweight contest on 18 February 1972.

Most knockouts The greatest number of finishes classified as "knockouts" in a career is 145 (129 in professional bouts), by Archie Moore (US).

The record for consecutive KOs is 44, by Lamar Clark (US) from 1958 to 11 January 1960.

HEAVYWEIGHT DIVISION

HEAVYWEIGHT CHAMPIONS	
Undisputed Champions	**Reign**
James J. Corbett	1892–97
Bob Fitzsimmons	1897–99
James J. Jeffries	1899–1904

HEAVYWEIGHT CHAMPIONS (Continued)

Undisputed Champions	Reign
Marvin Hart	1905–06
Tommy Burns	1906–08
Jack Johnson	1908–15
Jess Willard	1915–19
Jack Dempsey	1919–26
Gene Tunney	1926–28
Max Schmeling	1930–32
Jack Sharkey	1932–33
Primo Carnera	1933–34
Max Baer	1934–35
James J. Braddock	1935–37
Joe Louis	1937–49
Ezzard Charles	1949–51
Jersey Joe Walcott	1951–52
Rocky Marciano	1952–55
Floyd Patterson	1956–59
Ingemar Johansson	1959–60
Floyd Patterson	1960–62
Sonny Liston	1962–64

HEAVYWEIGHT CHAMPIONS (Continued)

Undisputed Champions	Reign
Cassius Clay (Muhammad Ali)	1964–67
Joe Frazier	1968–73
George Foreman	1973–74
Muhammad Ali	1974–78
Leon Spinks	1978
Mike Tyson	1987–90
James "Buster" Douglas	1990
Evander Holyfield	1990–
WBC Champions	**Reign**
Ken Norton	1978
Larry Holmes	1978–84
Tim Witherspoon	1984
Pinklon Thomas	1984–86
Trevor Berbick	1986
Mike Tyson	1986–87*
WBA Champions	**Reign**
Ernie Terrell	1965–67
Jimmy Ellis	1968–70
Muhammad Ali	1978

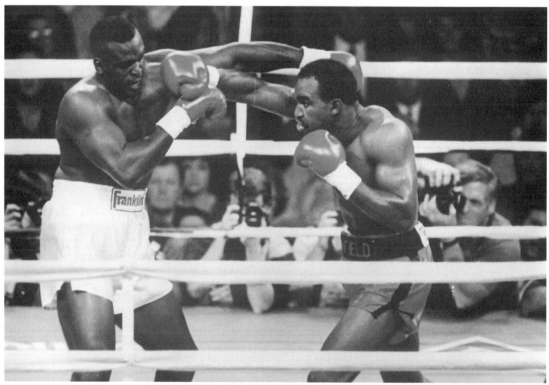

HEAVYWEIGHT CHAMPION ■ EVANDER HOLYFIELD WON THE UNDISPUTED WORLD HEAVYWEIGHT CROWN WITH A THIRD-ROUND KNOCKOUT OF BUSTER DOUGLAS ON 25 OCTOBER 1990 IN LAS VEGAS, NV.

HEAVYWEIGHT CHAMPIONS (Continued)

WBA Champions	Reign
John Tate	1979–80
Mike Weaver	1980–82
Michael Dokes	1982–83
Gerrie Coetzee	1983–84
Greg Page	1984–85
Tony Tubbs	1985–86
Tim Witherspoon	1986
James "Bonecrusher" Smith	1986–87
Mike Tyson	1987*

IBF Champions	Reign
Larry Holmes	1984–85
Michael Spinks	1985–87
Tony Tucker	1987
Mike Tyson	1987*

* Reunified Title

Earliest title fight Long accepted as the first world heavyweight title fight, with gloves and 3-min rounds, was that between John L. Sullivan and "Gentlemen" James J. Corbett in New Orleans, LA on 7 September 1892. Corbett won in 21 rounds. The fight between Sullivan, then the world bare-knuckle champion, and Dominick F. McCafferey in Chester Park, Cincinnati, OH on 29 August 1885 was staged under Queensberry Rules with the boxers wearing gloves over six rounds. The referee, Billy Tait, left the ring without giving a verdict, but when asked two days later said that Sullivan had won.

Reign

Longest Joe Louis (US) was champion for 11 years 252 days, from 22 June 1937, when he knocked out James J. Braddock in the 8th round at Chicago, IL, until announcing his retirement on 1 March 1949. During his reign, Louis defended his title a record 25 times.

Shortest 83 days for WBA champion James "Bonecrusher" Smith (US), 13 December 1986 to 7 March 1987, and for Ken Norton (US), recognized by the WBC as champion from 18 March–9 June 1978. Tony Tucker (US) was IBF champion for 64 days, 30 May–2 August 1987.

Most recaptures Muhammad Ali is the only man to regain the heavyweight championship twice. Ali first won the title on 25 Februrary 1964, defeating Sonny Liston. He defeated George Foreman on 30 October 1974, having been stripped of the title by the world boxing authorities on 28 April 1967. He won the WBA title from Leon Spinks on 15 Sep-

tember 1978, having previously lost to him on 15 Februrary 1978.

Undefeated Rocky Marciano is the only world champion at any weight to have won every fight of his entire professional career (1947–56); 43 of his 49 fights were by knockouts or stoppages.

Oldest successful challenger Jersey Joe Walcott (US) was 37 yr 168 days when he knocked out Ezzard Charles on 18 July 1951 in Pittsburgh, PA. He was also the oldest holder, at 38 yr 236 days, losing his title to Rocky Marciano on 23 September 1952.

Youngest Mike Tyson (US) was 20 yr 144 days when he beat Trevor Berbick (US) to win the WBC version at Las Vegas, NV on 22 November 1986. He added the WBA title when he beat James "Bonecrusher" Smith on 7 March 1987 at 20 yr 249 days. He became universal champion on 2 August 1987 when he beat Tony Tucker (US) for the IBF title.

Lightest Bob Fitzsimmons (UK) weighed 167 lb when he won the title by knocking out James J. Corbett at Carson City, NV on 17 March 1897.

WORLD CHAMPIONS (ANY WEIGHT)

Reign

Longest Joe Louis's heavyweight duration record of 11 yr 252 days stands for all divisions.

Shortest Tony Canzaneri (US) was world light welterweight champion for 33 days, 21 May to 23 June 1933, the shortest period for a boxer to have won and lost the world title in the ring.

Youngest Wilfred Benitez (Puerto Rico) was 17 yr 176 days when he won the WBA light welterweight title in San Juan, Puerto Rico on 6 March 1976.

Oldest Archie Moore, who was recognized as a light heavyweight champion up to 10 February 1962 when his title was removed, was then believed to be between 45 and 48.

Most recaptures The only boxer to win a world title five times at one weight is Sugar Ray Robinson (US), who beat Carmen Basilio (US) in Chicago Stadium, IL on 25 March 1958 to regain the world middleweight title for the fourth time.

AMATEUR

Most Olympic Titles Only two boxers have won three Olympic gold medals: southpaw László Papp (Hungary), middleweight winner in 1948, light middleweight winner in 1952 and 1956; and

OLYMPIAN EFFORT ■ TEOFILO STEVENSON, CUBA, WON THREE OLYMPIC HEAVYWEIGHT CHAMPIONSHIPS, IN 1972, 1976 AND 1980. THE ONLY OTHER BOXER TO WIN THREE TITLES WAS LÁZLÓ PAPP, HUNGARY: MIDDLEWEIGHT, 1948, AND LIGHT MIDDLEWEIGHT, 1952, 1956.

Teofilo Stevenson (Cuba), heavyweight winner in 1972, 1976 and 1980.

The only man to win two titles in one celebration was Oliver L. Kirk (US), who won both bantam and featherweight titles in St. Louis, MO in 1904, but he needed only one bout in each class.

A record that will stand forever is that of the youngest Olympic boxing champion: Jackie Fields (né Finkelstein [US]), who won the 1924 featherweight title at 16 yrs 162 days. The minimum age for Olympic boxing competitors is now 17.

Oldest Gold Medalist Richard Kenneth Gunn (UK) won the Olympic featherweight gold medal on 27 October 1908 in London, England, at age 37 yr 254 days.

WORLD CHAMPIONSHIPS Two boxers have won three world championships (instituted 1974): Teofilo Stevenson (Cuba) heavyweight winner in 1974, 1978 and super-heavyweight winner in 1986, and Adolfo Horta (Cuba), bantamweight winner in

1978, featherweight winner in 1982 and lightweight winner in 1986.

US CHAMPIONSHIPS US Amateur Championships were first staged in 1888. The most titles won is five by middleweight W. Rodenbach, 1900–04.

CANOEING

ORIGINS The most influential pioneer of canoeing as a sport was John MacGregor, a British attorney, who founded the Canoe Club in Surrey, England in 1866. The sport's world governing body is the International Canoe Federation, founded in 1924.

The New York Canoe Club, founded in Staten Island, NY, in 1871, is the oldest in the United States. The American Canoe Association was formed on 3 August 1880.

OLYMPIC GAMES Gert Fredriksson (Sweden) won a record six Olympic gold medals, 1948–60. He also won a silver and a bronze medal—for a record medals total of eight. The most gold medals won by a woman is three by two canoeists: Lyudmila Pinayeva (née Khvedosyuk [USSR], 1964–72; Birgit Schmidt (née Fischer [East Germany]), 1980–88. The most gold medals won at one Olympics is three, by Vladimir Parfenovich (USSR) in 1988, and by Ian Ferguson (New Zealand) in 1984.

UNITED STATES The only American canoeist to have won two Olympic gold medals is Gregory Mark Barton who won at K1 and K2 1,000 m events in 1988. He also has a US record three medals, as he took bronze at K1 1,000 m in 1984.

WORLD CHAMPIONSHIPS (in Olympic years, the Games also act as the World Championship). Birgit Schmidt (East Germany) has won a record 22 titles, 1978–88. The men's record is 13 by Gert Fredriksson (Sweden), 1948–60; Rudiger Helm (East Germany), 1976–83; Ivan Patzaichin (Romania), 1968–84.

UNITED STATES NATIONAL CHAMPIONSHIP Marcia Ingram Jones Smoke won 35 national titles from 1962–81. The men's record is 33 by Ernest Riedel from 1930–48.

Highest speed The Hungarian 4 man kayak Olympic champions in 1988 at Seoul, South Korea covered 1,000 m in 2 min 58.54 sec in a heat. This represents an average speed of 12.53 mph.

In this same race, the Norwegian four achieved a 250 m split of 42.08 sec between 500 m and 750 m for a speed of 13.29 mph.

Longest race The Canadian Government Centennial Voyageur Canoe Pageant and Race from Rocky Mountain House, Alberta to the Expo 67 site at Montreal, Quebec covered 3,283 miles. Ten canoes represented Canadian provinces and territories. The winner of the race, which took from 24 May to 4 September 1967, was the Province of Manitoba canoe *Radisson*.

24 hours Men Zdzislaw Szubski paddled 157.1 miles in a Jaguar K1 canoe on the Vistula River, Wlocklawek to Gdansk, Poland, on 11–12 September 1987.

24 hours Women Lydia Formentin paddled 97.2 miles on the Swan River, Western Australia in 1979.

Flat water Thomas J. Mazuzan paddled, without benefit of current, 123.98 miles on the Barge Canal in NY on 24–25 September 1986.

Open sea Randy Fine (US) paddled 120.6 miles along the Florida coast on 26–27 June 1986.

Eskimo rolls with paddle Ray Hudspith (UK) achieved 1,000 rolls in 34 min 43 sec at the Elswick Pool, Newcastle-upon-Tyne, England on 20 March 1987.

Colin Hill (UK) completed 1,712 continuous rolls at Alsager Leisure Centre, Staffordshire, England on 28 February 1990.

"Hand rolls" Colin Hill achieved 1,000 rolls in 31 min 55.62 sec at Consett, England on 12 March 1987. He also achieved 100 rolls in 2 min 39.2 sec at Crystal Palace, London, England on 22 February 1987. He completed 3,700 continuous rolls at Durham City Swimming Baths, County Durham, England on 1 May 1989.

Canoe raft A raft of 376 kayaks and canoes, held together by hands only, while free floating for 30 seconds, was established on the Johor Strait at Sembawang, Singapore on 26 June 1990.

CRICKET

ORIGINS Cricket originated in England in the Middle Ages. It is impossible to pinpoint its exact origin; however, historians believe that the modern game developed in the mid-16th century. The earliest surviving scorecard is from a match played between England and Kent on 18 June 1744. The Marylebone Cricket Club (MCC) was founded in 1787 and, until 1968, was the world governing body for the sport. The International Cricket Conference (ICC) is responsible for international (Test) cricket, while the MCC remains responsible for the laws of cricket.

INTERNATIONAL (TEST) CRICKET

Test match cricket is the highest level of the sport. The Test playing nations are Australia, England, India, New Zealand, Pakistan, Sri Lanka and the West Indies. South Africa was a founding member of the ICC, but ceased to be a member in 1961. Test matches are generally played over five days. The result is decided by which team scores the most runs in two full innings (one inning sees all 11 members of a team come to bat; their opponents must achieve 10 outs to end the inning). If, at the end of the allotted time period, one or either team has not completed two full innings then the game is declared a tie. The first Test match was played at Melbourne, Australia on 15–19 March 1877 between Australia and England.

NATIONAL CRICKET CHAMPIONSHIPS

Australia The premier event in Australia is the Sheffield Shield, an interstate competition contested since 1891–92. New South Wales has won the title a record 40 times.

TEST MATCH CRICKET RECORDS (1877–June 1990)

TEAM

Most Wins:	231, England
Most Played:	661, England
Highest Score:	903, England v. Australia (Surrey, England), 20–23 August 1938
Lowest Score:	26, New Zealand v. England (Auckland, New Zealand), 28 March 1955

TEST MATCH CRICKET RECORDS (1877–June 1990) (Continued)

INDIVIDUAL

Most Tests:	125, Sunil Gavaskar (India), 1971–87
Most Runs (Innings):	365, Garfield Sobers (West Indies v. Pakistan), 27 February–1 March 1958
Most Runs (Series):	974, Don Bradman (Australia v. England), 1930
Most Runs (Career):	10,122, Sunil Gavaskar (India) , 1971–87
Most Wickets (Innings):	10, Jim Laker (England v. Australia), 30–31 July 1956
Most Wickets (Game):	19, Jim Laker (England v. Australia), 26–31 July 1956
Most Wickets (Series):	49, Sydney Barnes (England v. South Africa), 1913–14
Most Wickets (Career):	415, Richard Hadlee (New Zealand), 1973–90

BATSMAN SUPREME ■ SUNIL GAVASKAR, INDIA, HAS SCORED A RECORD 10,122 RUNS IN A RECORD 125 CRICKET TEST MATCH APPEARANCES.

England The major championship in England is the County Championship, an intercounty competition officially recognized since 1890. Yorkshire has won the title a record 30 times.

India The Ranji Trophy is India's premier cricket competition. Established in 1934 in memory of K. S. Ranjitsinhji, it is contested on a zonal basis, culminating in a playoff competition. Bombay has won the tournament a record 30 times.

New Zealand Since 1975, the major championship in New Zealand has been the Shell Trophy. Otago and Wellington have each won the competition four times.

Pakistan Pakistan's national championship is the Quaid-e-Azam Trophy, established in 1953. Karachi has won the trophy a record six times.

South Africa The Currie Cup, donated by Sir Donald Currie, was first contested in 1889. Transvaal has won the competition a record 28 times.

West Indies The Red Stripe Cup, established in 1966, is the premier prize played for by the association of Caribbean islands (plus Guyana) that form the West Indies Cricket League. Barbados has won the competition a record 12 times.

CROQUET

ORIGINS Its exact beginnings are unknown, however, it is believed that croquet developed from the French game *jeu de mail*. A game resembling croquet was played in Ireland in the 1830s and introduced to England 20 years later. Although played in the United States for a number of years, a national body was not established until the formation of the United States Croquet Association (USCA) in 1976. The first United States Championship was played in 1977.

USCA NATIONAL CHAMPIONSHIPS J. Archie Peck has won the singles title a record four times (1977, 1979–80, 1982). Ted Prentis has won the doubles title four times with three different partners (1978, 1980–81, 1988). The teams of Ted Prentis and Ned Prentis (1980–81) and Dana Dribben and Ray Bell (1985–86) have each won the doubles title twice. The New York Croquet Club has won a record six National Club Championships (1980–83, 1986, 1988).

CURLING

ORIGINS The traditional home of curling is Scotland; some historians, however, believe that the sport originated in the Netherlands in the 15th century. There is evidence of a curling club in Kilsyth, Scotland in 1716, but the earliest recorded club is the Muthill Curling Club, Tayside, Scotland, formed in 1739, which produced the first known written rules of the game on 17 November 1739. The Grand (later Royal) Caledonian Curling Club was founded in 1838 and was the international governing body of the sport until 1966, when the International Curling Federation was formed.

CLEAN SWEEP ■ BUD SOMERVILLE (KNEELING) HAS BEEN SKIP ON FIVE US NATIONAL AND TWO WORLD CHAMPIONSHIP CURLING TEAMS.

Scottish immigrants introduced curling to North America in the 18th century. The earliest known club was the Royal Montreal Curling club, founded in 1807. The first international game was between Canada and the United States in 1884, the inaugural Gordon International Medal series. In 1832, Orchard Lake Curling Club, MI, was founded, the first in the United States. The oldest club in continuous existence in the US is Milwaukee Curling Club, WI, formed circa 1850. Regional curling associations governed the sport in the US until 1947, when the United States Women's Curling Association was formed, followed in 1958 by the Men's Curling Association. In 1986, the United States Curling Association was formed and is the current governing body for the sport. In Canada, the Dominion Curling Association was formed in 1935, renamed the Canadian Curling Association in 1968.

Curling has been a demonstration sport at the Olympic Games of 1924, 1932, 1964 and 1988.

WORLD CHAMPIONSHIPS

Most titles Canada has won the men's World Championships (instituted 1959) 20 times, 1959–64, 1966, 1968–72, 1980, 1982–83, 1985–87, 1989–90.

The most women's World Championships (instituted 1979) is six, by Canada (1980, 1984–87, 1989).

The US has won the men's world title four times, with Bud Somerville skip on the first two winning teams, 1965 and 1974.

UNITED STATES NATIONAL CHAMPIONSHIP

Men First held in 1957, two curlers have been skips on five championship teams: Bud Somerville (Superior Curling Club, WI in 1965, 1968–69, 1974, 1981), and Bruce Roberts (Hibbing Curling Club, MN—1966–67, 1976–77, 1984). Bill Strum of the Superior Curling Club has been a member of five title teams in 1965, 1967, 1969, 1974 and 1978).

Women First held in 1977, Nancy Langley, Seattle, WA has been the skip of a record four championship teams, 1979, 1981, 1983 and 1988.

THE LABATT BRIER (FORMERLY THE MACDONALD BRIER 1927–79) Canada's premier curling competition, the Brier was first held at the Granite Club, Toronto in 1927. Sponsored by Macdonald Tobacco Inc., it had been known as the Macdonald Brier; since 1980 Labatt Brewery has sponsored the event. The most wins is 22 by Manitoba (1928–32, 1934, 1936, 1938, 1940, 1942, 1947, 1949, 1952–53, 1956, 1965, 1970–72, 1979 1981, 1984). Ernie Richardson (Saskatchewan) has been winning skip a record four times (1959–60, 1962–63).

His brothers Arnold and Sam Richardson were also members of each championship team.

Perfect Game Stu Beagle, of Calgary, Alberta, Canada, played a perfect game (48 points) against Nova Scotia in the Canadian Championships (Brier) at Fort William (now Thunder Bay), Ontario on 8 March 1960.

Bernice Fekete, of Edmonton, Alberta, Canada, skipped her rink to two consecutive eight-enders on the same ice at the Derrick Club, Edmonton on 10 January and 6 February 1973.

Two eight-enders in one bonspiel were scored at the Parry Sound Curling Club, Ontario, Canada from 6–8 January 1983.

Fastest game Eight curlers from the Burlington Gold and Country Club curled an eight-end game in 47 min 24 sec, with time penalties of 5 min 30 sec, at Burlington, Ontario, Canada on 4 April 1986, following rules agreed with the Ontario Curling Association. The time is taken from when the first rock crosses the near hogline until the game's last rock comes to a complete stop.

Longest throw The longest throw of a curling stone was a distance of 576 ft 4 in, by Eddie Kulbacki (Canada) at Park Lake, Neepawa, Manitoba, Canada on 29 January 1989. The attempt took place on a specially prepared sheet of curling ice on frozen Park Lake, which is a record 1,200 ft long.

Largest bonspiel The largest bonspiel (curling tournament) in the world is the Manitoba Curling Association Bonspiel, held annually in Winnipeg, Canada. In 1988, there were 1,424 teams of four men, a total of 5,696 curlers, using 187 sheets of curling ice.

Largest rink The world's largest curling rink is the Big Four Curling Rink, Calgary, Alberta, Canada, opened in 1959. Ninety-six teams and 384 players are accommodated on two floors, each with 24 sheets of ice.

CYCLING

Origins The forerunner of the bicycle, the celerifere was demonstrated in the garden of the Palais Royale, Paris, France in 1791. The velocipede, the first practical pedal-propelled vehicle, was built in March 1861 by Pierre Michaux and his son Ernest and demonstrated in Paris. The first velocipede race occurred on 31 May 1868 at the Parc St. Cloud, Paris, over a distance of 1.24 miles. The first international organization was the International Cyclist Association (ICA), founded in 1892, which launched the first world championships in 1893. The current governing body, the Union Cycliste International (ICI), was founded in 1900.

OLYMPIC GAMES The most gold medals won is three, by Paul Masson (France in 1896); Francisco Verri (Italy in 1906); and Robert Charpentier (France in 1936). Daniel Morelon (France) won two in 1968 and a third in 1972; he also won a silver in 1976 and a bronze medal in 1964.

The only US woman to win a cycling gold medal is Connie Carpenter-Phinney, who won the individual road race in 1984. She became the first woman to compete in the winter and summer Olympics—she had competed as a speed skater in 1972.

WORLD CHAMPIONSHIPS World Championships are contested annually. They were first staged for amateurs in 1893 and for professionals in 1895.

The most wins in a particular event is 10, by Koichi Nakano (Japan), professional sprint 1977–86.

The most wins in a men's amateur event is seven, by Daniel Morelon (France), sprint 1966–67, 1969–71, 1973, 1975; and Leon Meredith (UK), 100 km motor paced 1904–05, 1907–09, 1911, 1913.

The most women's titles is eight, by Jeannie Longo (France), pursuit 1986 and 1988–89 and road 1985–87 and 1989–90.

The most world titles won by a US cyclist is four, in women's 3 kilometers pursuit by Rebecca Twigg, 1982, 1984–85 and 1987. The most successful man has been Greg LeMond, winner of the individual road race in 1983 and 1989.

TOUR DE FRANCE

First staged in 1903, the Tour meanders throughout France and sometimes neighboring countries over a four-week period. Three riders have each won the event five times: Jacques Anquetil (France; 1957, 1961–64), Eddy Merckx (Belgium; 1969–72, 1974), Bernard Hinault (France; 1978–79, 1981–82, 1985).

Longest Race 3,569 miles in 1926

TOUR DE FRANCE CHAMPIONS		
Year	Winner	Country
1903	Maurice Garin	France
1904	Henri Cornet	France
1905	Louis Trousselier	France
1906	Rene Pottier	France
1907	Lucien Petit-Breton	France
1908	Lucien Petit-Breton	France

Year	Winner	Country
1909	Francois Faber	Luxembourg
1910	Octave Lapize	France
1911	Gustave Garrigou	France
1912	Odile Defraye	Belgium
1913	Philippe Thys	Belgium
1914	Philippe Thys	Belgium
1915	not held	
1916	not held	
1917	not held	
1918	not held	
1919	Firmin Labot	Belgium
1920	Philippe Thys	Belgium
1921	Leon Scieur	Belgium
1922	Firmin Labot	Belgium
1923	Henri Pelissier	France
1924	Ottavio Bottecchia	Italy
1925	Ottavio Bottecchia	Italy
1926	Lucien Buysse	Belgium
1927	Nicholas Frantz	Luxembourg
1928	Nicholas Frantz	Luxembourg
1929	Maurice Dewaele	Belgium
1930	Andre Leducq	France
1931	Antonin Magne	France
1932	Andre Leducq	France
1933	Georges Speicher	France
1934	Antonin Magne	France
1935	Romain Maes	Belgium
1936	Sylvere Maes	Belgium
1937	Roger Lapebie	France
1938	Gino Bartali	Italy
1939	Sylvere Maes	Belgium
1940	not held	
1941	not held	
1942	not held	
1943	not held	
1944	not held	
1945	not held	
1946	Jean Lazarides	France
1947	Jean Robic	France
1948	Gino Bartali	Italy
1949	Fausto Coppi	Italy
1950	Ferdinand Kubler	Switzerland
1951	Hugo Koblet	Switzerland

Year	Winner	Country
1952	Fausto Coppi	Italy
1953	Louison Bobet	France
1954	Louison Bobet	France
1955	Louison Bobet	France
1956	Roger Walkowiak	France
1957	Jacques Anquetil	France
1958	Charly Gaul	Luxembourg
1959	Federico Bahamontes	Spain
1960	Gastone Nencini	Italy
1961	Jacques Anquetil	France
1962	Jacques Anquetil	France
1963	Jacques Anquetil	France
1964	Jacques Anquetil	France
1965	Felice Gimondi	Italy
1966	Lucien Aimar	France
1967	Roger Pingeon	France
1968	Jan Janssen	Netherlands
1969	Eddy Merckx	Belgium
1970	Eddy Merckx	Belgium
1971	Eddy Merckx	Belgium
1972	Eddy Merckx	Belgium
1973	Luis Ocana	Spain
1974	Eddy Merckx	Belgium
1975	Bernard Thevenet	France
1976	Lucien van Impe	Belgium
1977	Bernard Thevenet	France
1978	Bernard Hinault	France
1979	Bernard Hinault	France
1980	Joop Zoetemilk	Netherlands
1981	Bernard Hinault	France
1982	Bernard Hinault	France
1983	Laurent Fignon	France
1984	Laurent Fignon	France
1985	Bernard Hinault	France
1986	Greg LeMond	USA
1987	Stephen Roche	Ireland
1988	Pedro Delgado	Spain
1989	Greg LeMond	USA
1990	Greg LeMond	USA

The closest race ever was in 1989 when after 2,030 miles over 23 days (1–23 July) Greg LeMond (US), who completed the Tour in 87 hr 38 min 35 sec, beat Laurent Fignon (France) in Paris by only 8 sec.

AN AMERICAN IN PARIS ■ GREG LEMOND IS THE ONLY US CYCLIST TO HAVE WON THE TOUR DE FRANCE. IN 1990 LEMOND CAPTURED HIS THIRD TOUR TITLE.

The fastest average speed was 24.16 mph by Pedro Delgado (Spain) in 1988.

The longest ever stage was the 486 km from Les Sables d'Olonne to Bayonne in 1919. The most participants was 204 starters in 1987.

Greg LeMond became the first American winner in 1986; returned from serious injury to win in 1989 and 1990.

Women The inaugural women's Tour de France was staged in 1984. Jeannie Longo (France) has won the event a record four times, 1987–90.

Longest one-day race The longest single-day "massed start" road race is the 342–385 miles Bordeaux-Paris, France, event. Paced over all or part of the route, the highest average speed was 29.32 mph, by Herman van Springel (Belgium) for 363.1 miles in 13 hr 35 min 18 sec, in 1981.

TRANSCONTINENTAL CYCLING RECORDS

UNITED STATES

Fastest Time (Men) Michael Secrest, Flint, MI, completed the 2,915-mile 1990 Race Across AMerica course in a record 7 days 23 hr 16 min on 24 June 1990. Secrest's average speed was 15.24 mph.

Fastest Time (Women) Susan Notorangelo, Harvard IL, completed the 2,910 mile 1989 Race

TOUR DE FORCE ■ BERNARD HINAULT, FRANCE, HAS WON THE TOUR DE FRANCE FIVE TIMES, A RECORD HE SHARES WITH JACQUES ANGUETIL, FRANCE, AND EDDY MERCKX, BELGIUM.

TRANSCONTINENTAL CYCLING RECORDS

MEN

Category	Name	Start-Finish	Days:Hr:Min	Mileage	Date
US (West to East) (Solo/unpaced)	Michael Secrest	HB-AC	07:23:16	2,915	6/90
US (East to West) (Solo/unpaced)	Michael Coles	SAV-SD	11:08:15		5/84
US (Double) (Solo/unpaced)	Bob Breedlove	AL-CM-NYC-AL	22:13:36	5,823	8/89
US (West to East) (Tandem/unpaced)	Lon Haldeman & Pete Penseyres	HB-AC	07:14:55		5/87
US (West Coast) (Solo/unpaced)	Michael Shermer	SE-SD	03:23:49		6/84
US (East Coast) (Solo/unpaced)	Victor Gallo	MI-PO	05:19:56		6/89
Canada (Solo/unpaced)	Ron Dossenbach	VA-NS	13:15:04	3,698	8/88

WOMEN

Category	Name	Start-Finish	Days:Hr:Min	Mileage	Date
US (West to East) (Solo/unpaced)	Susan Notorangelo	CM-NYC	09:09:09	2,910	8/89
US (West to East) Tandem/unpaced)	Estelle Grey & Cheryl Marek	SM-NYC	10:22:48		7/84
US (West (Coast) (Solo/unpaced)	Elaine Mariolle	SE-SD	04:22:01		5/84

AC—Atlantic City, NJ
AL—Alton, IL
CM—Costa Mesa, CA
HB—Huntington Beach, CA
MI—Miami, FL
NS—Nova Scotia
NYC—New York City
PO—Portland, ME
SAV—Savannah, GA
SD—San Diego, CA
SE—Seattle, WA
SM—Santa Monica, CA
VA—Vancouver, BC
Credit: Ultra-Marathon
Cycling Association

TRANSCONTINENTAL ■ IN 1989 SUSAN NOTORAN-GELO SET WOMEN'S RECORDS FOR FASTEST TIME (9 DAYS 9 HRS 9 MIN) AND FASTEST AVERAGE SPEED (12.92 MPH) FOR CYCLING ACROSS THE US.

Across AMerica course in a record 9 days 9 hr 9 min on 22 August 1989.

Fastest Average Speed (Men) Pete Penseyres, Fallbrook, CA, rode at an average speed of 15.4 mph in his 1986 Race Across AMerica victory. Penseyres completed the 3,107.3 mile course in 8 days 9 hr 47 min, which averages out to 369.55 miles per day.

Fastest Average Speed (Women) In 1989, Susan Notorangelo attained the fastest average speed of 12.92 mph.

CANADA The trans-Canada record is 13 days 15 hr 4 min by Ronald J. Dossenbach, Windsor, Ontario, from Vancouver, BC to Halifax, Nova Scotia on 30 July–12 August 1988

Highest speed The highest speed ever achieved on a bicycle is 152.284 mph, by John Howard (US) behind a windshield at Bonneville Salt Flats, UT on 20 July 1985. It should be noted that considerable help was provided by the slipstreaming effect of the lead vehicle.

The 24 hr record behind pace is 860 miles 367 yd by Hubert Ferdinand Opperman in Melbourne, Australia on 23 May 1932.

Highest Mark Merrony of Tenby cycled at an altitude of 21,030 ft close to the relatively flat south summit of Mera Peak, Nepal on 7 May 1989.

CYCLO-CROSS

The greatest number of World Championships (instituted 1950) has been won by Eric de Vlaeminck (Belgium) with the Amateur and Open in 1966 and six Professional titles in 1968–73.

ROLLER CYCLING

James Baker (US) achieved a record speed of 153.2 mph at El Con Mall, Tucson, AZ on 28 January 1989.

DARTS

ORIGINS Darts, or Dartes (heavily weighted 10-in throwing arrows), were first used in Ireland in the 16th century, as a weapon for self-defense. The Pilgrims played darts for recreation aboard the Mayflower in 1620. The modern game dates to 1896 when Brian Gamlin of Bury, England devised the present board numbering system. The first recorded score of 180, the maximum with three darts, was by John Reader at the Highbury Tavern, Sussex, England in 1902.

WORLD CHAMPIONSHIP Instituted in 1978, it is the leading tournament in the professional players' calendar. Eric Bristow of England has won the title a record five times (1980–81, 84–86). In addition to the world championship, three other tournaments make up the "big four." They are the World Masters Championship (instituted 1974), the News of the World Championship (instituted 1928) and the World Cup Singles (instituted 1978). No player has won all four events in one year, however Bristow and John Lowe (England) have won all four titles. In addition to his world championships (see above), Bristow has won five World Masters Championships (1977, 1979, 1981, 1983–84); two News of the World Titles (1983–84); and four World Cup titles (1983, 1985, 1987, 1989). Lowe won the World Masters in 1976 and 1980; World Professional in 1979 and 1987; the News of the World in 1981; and the World Cup singles in 1981.

Least darts: Scores of 201 in four darts, 301 in six darts, 401 in 7 darts and 501 in 9 darts have been achieved on various occasions.

Roy Edwin Blowes (Canada) was the first person to achieve a 501 in nine darts, "double-on, double-off," at the Widgeons Pub, Calgary, Canada on 9 March 1987. His scores were: Bull, treble 20, treble 17, five treble 20s and a double 20 to finish.

The lowest number of darts thrown for a score of 1,001 is 19, by Cliff Inglis (160, 180, 140, 180, 121, 180, 40) at the Bromfield Men's Club, Devon England on 11 November 1975 and Jocky Wilson (140, 140, 180, 180, 180, 131, Bull) at The London Pride, Bletchley, England on 23 March 1989.

A score of 2,001 in 52 darts was achieved by Alan Evans at Ferndale, Wales on 3 September 1976.

A score of 3,001 in 73 darts was thrown by Tony Benson at the Plough Inn, Gorton, England on 12 July 1986.

Linda Batten set a women's 3,001 record of 117 darts at the Old Wheatsheaf, Enfield, England on 2 April 1986.

A score of 100,001 was achieved in 3,732 darts by Alan Downie of Stornoway, Scotland on 21 November 1986.

EQUESTRIAN SPORTS

ORIGINS Evidence of horseback riding dates from a Persian engraving dated c. 3000 B.C. The three seperate equestrian competitions recognized at the Olympic level are show jumping, dressage and the three-day event. The earliest known show jumping competition was in Ireland when the Royal Dublin Society held its first "Horse Show" on 15 April 1864. Dressage competition derived from the exercises taught at 16th century Italian and French horsemanship academies, while the three-day event developed from cavalry endurance rides. The world governing body for all three disciplines is the Federation Equestre Internationale (FEI), founded in Brussels, Belgium in 1921.

SHOW JUMPING

OLYMPIC GAMES Show Jumping was introduced at the Paris Olympiad in 1900, but was not included again until 1912 at Stockholm, when both team and individual competitions were staged. The most Olympic gold medals won by a rider is five by Hans-Gunther Winkler (West Germany), 1956, 1960, 1964 and 1972 in the team competition, and in 1956 the individual championship. In addition, he won silver and bronze medals in the team competition in 1976 and 1968 respectively, for a record seven medals overall. Pierre Jonquères

GOLD MEDALIST ■ JOE FARGIS (SEEN RIDING TOUCH OF CLASS) WON TWO GOLD MEDALS AT THE 1984 OLYMPICS, INDIVIDUAL AND TEAM EVENTS, SETTING THE MARK FOR MOST GOLD MEDALS BY A US RIDER.

THREE-DAY EVENT ■ J. MICHAEL PLUMB (SEEN RIDING BLUE STONE) HOLDS THE RECORD FOR MOST OLYMPIC MEDALS WON BY A US RIDER WITH SIX: GOLD, 1976, 1984; SILVER, 1964, 1968, 1972, 1976.

d'Oriola (France) is the only person to have won the individual gold medal twice, 1952 and 1964.

UNITED STATES Two US riders have won individual gold medals: Bill Steinkraus won in 1968 and also won two silver and one bronze medal in 1952–68; Joe Fargis won both individual and team gold medals in 1984 as well as team silver in 1988.

The most team wins is six by Germany in 1936, 1956, 1960, 1964 and as West Germany in 1972 and 1988. The lowest score obtained by a winner is no faults, by Frantisek Ventura (Czechoslovakia) on Eliot, 1928, and Alwin Schockemöhle (West Germany) on Warwick Rex, 1976.

OLYMPIC CHAMPIONS			
Year	Rider	Country	Horse
1900	Aime Haegeman	Belgium	Benton II
1912	Jean Cariou	France	Mignon
1920	Tommaso Lequio	Italy	Trebecco
1924	Alphonse Gemuseus	Switzerland	Lucette
1928	Frantisek Ventura	Czechoslovakia	Eliot
1932	Takeichi Nishi	Japan	Uranus

OLYMPIC CHAMPIONS (Continued)
Individual Competition

1936	Kurt Hasse	Germany	Tora
1948	Humberto Mariles Cortes	Mexico	Arete
1952	Pierre Jonqueres d'Oriola	France	Ali Baba
1956	Hans-Gunter Winkler	Germany	Halla
1960	Raimondo d'Inzeo	Italy	Posillipo
1964	Pierre Jonqueres d'Oriola	France	Lutteur B
1968	Bill Steinkraus	USA	Snowbound
1972	Graziano Mancinelli	Italy	Ambassador
1976	Alwin Schockemohle	West Germany	Warwick Rex
1980	Jan Kowalczyk	Poland	Artemor
1984	Joe Fargis	USA	Touch of Class
1988	Pierre Durand	France	Jappeloup

WORLD CHAMPIONSHIPS The men's World Championship was inaugurated in 1953. In 1965, 1970 and 1974 seperate women's championships were held. The first integrated championship was held in 1978 and is now held every four years. Two riders share the record for most men's championships with two victories: Hans-Gunter Winkler (West Germany; 1954–55) and Raimondo d'Inzeo (Italy; 1956, 1960). The women's title was won twice by Janou Tissot (née Lefebvre) of France, in 1970 and 1974. No rider has won the integrated competition more than once.

WORLD CHAMPIONS

Year	Rider	Country	Horse
1953	Francisco Goyoago	Spain	Quorum
1954	Hans-Gunter Winkler	West Germany	Halla
1955	Hans-Gunter Winkler	West Germany	Halla
1956	Raimondo d'Inzeo	Italy	Merano
1960	Raimondo d'Inzeo	Italy	Gowran Girl
1965	Marion Coakes*	Great Britain	Stroller
1966	Pierre Jonqueres d'Oriola	France	Pomone
1970	David Broome	Great Britain	Beethoven
1970	Janou Lefebvre*	France	Rocket
1974	Hartwig Steenken	West Germany	Simona
1974	Janou Tissot (née Lefebvre)*	France	Rocket
1978	Gerd Wiltfang	West Germany	Roman
1982	Norbert Koof	West Germany	Fire II
1986	Gail Greenhough	Canada	Mr. T
1990	Eric Navet	France	Malesan Quito de Baussy

*Women's Champion

Jumping records The official Fédération Equestre Internationale records are: high jump, 8 ft 1¼ in, by Huasó, ridden by Captain Alberto Larraguibel Morales (Chile) at Viña del Mar, Santiago, Chile on 5 February 1949; long jump over water, 27 ft 6¾ in, by Something, ridden by André Ferreira (South Africa) at Johannesburg, South Africa on 25 April 1975.

THREE-DAY EVENT

OLYMPIC GAMES & WORLD CHAMPIONSHIPS Charles Ferdinand Pahud de Mortanges (Netherlands), won a record four Olympic gold medals, team 1924 and 1928, individual (riding Marcroix) 1928 and 1932. He also won a team silver medal in 1932.

Bruce Davidson (US) is the only rider to have won two world titles (instituted 1966), on Irish Cap in 1974 and Might Tango in 1978.

UNITED STATES The most medals won for the US is six by J. Michael Plumb; team gold 1976 and 1984, and four silver medals, team 1964, 1968 and 1972, and individual 1976. Tad Coffin is the one US rider to have won both team and individual gold medals, in 1976.

DRESSAGE

OLYMPIC GAMES & WORLD CHAMPIONSHIPS Germany (West Germany post-1968) has won a record seven team gold medals, 1928, 1936, 1964, 1968, 1976, 1984 and 1988, and has most team wins, 6, at the World Championships (instituted 1966). Dr. Reiner Klimke (West Germany) has won a record six Olympic golds (team 1964–88, individual, 1984) and won an individual bronze in 1976, for a record seven medals overall. He is the only rider to win two world titles, on Mehmed in 1974 and Ahlerich in 1982. Henri St. Cyr (Sweden) won a record two individual Olympic gold medals, 1952 and 1956.

FENCING

ORIGINS Evidence of swordsmanship can be traced back to Egypt as early as *circa* 1360 B.C., where it was demonstrated during religious ceremonies. The development of the sword as a weapon accelerated during the Middle Ages, when the invention of gunpowder made armor obsolete. Fencing, "fighting with sticks," gained popularity as a sport in Europe in the 16th century. The modern foil, a light court sword, was introduced in France in the mid-17th century, in the late 19th century the fencing "arsenal" was expanded to include the épée, a heavier dueling weapon, and the sabre, a light cutting sword.

Fencing was included in the first Olympic Games of the modern era at Athens in 1896, and is one of only six sports to be featured in every Olympiad. The Federation Internationale d'Escrime (FIE), the world governing body, was founded in Paris, France in 1913. The first European Championships were held in 1921 and were expanded into World Championships in 1935.

In the US, the Amateur Fencers League of America (AFLA) was founded on 22 April 1891 in New York City. This group assumed supervision of the sport in the US, staging the first national championship in 1892. In June 1981, the AFLA changed its name to the United States Fencing Association (USFA).

OLYMPIC GAMES The most individual Olympic gold medals won is three by Ramón Fonst (Cuba), in 1900 and 1904 (2) and by Nedo Nadi (Italy), in 1912 and 1920 (2). Nadi also won three team gold medals in 1920, making five gold medals at one celebration, the record for fencing.

Edoardo Mangiarotti (Italy), with six gold, five silver and two bronze, holds the record of 13 Olympic medals. He won them for foil and épée from 1936 to 1960.

The most gold medals won by a woman is four (1 individual, 3 team), by Yelena Dmitryevna Novikova (née Byelova, [USSR]), from 1968 to 1976, and the record for all medals is seven (2 gold, 3 silver, 2 bronze), by Ildikó Sági (formerly Ujlaki, née Retjö, [Hungary]), from 1960 to 1976.

UNITED STATES The only US Olympic champion was Albertson Van Zo Post who won the men's single sticks and team foil (with two Cubans) at the 1904 Games.

WORLD CHAMPIONSHIP The greatest number of individual world titles won is five, by Aleksandr Romankov (USSR), at foil 1974, 1977, 1979, 1982 and 1983.

Four women foilists have won three world titles: Hélène Mayer (Germany), 1929, 1931, 1937; Ilona Schacherer-Elek (Hungary), 1934–5, 1951; Ellen Müller-Preis (Austria), 1947, 1949–50; and Cornelia Hanisch (West Germany), 1979, 1981, 1985.

UNITED STATES NATIONAL CHAMPIONSHIPS The most US titles won at one weapon is 12 at sabre, by Peter J. Westbrook, in 1974, 1975, 1979–86, 1988 and 1989. The women's record is 10 at foil,

ON GUARD ■ PETER J. WESTBROOK (KNEELING) HAS WON A RECORD 12 U.S. NATIONAL FENCING CHAMPIONSHIPS AT SABRE.

by Janice Lee York Romany in 1950–51, 1956–57, 1960–61, 1964–66 and 1968.

The most individual épée championships won is seven, by Michael Marx in 1977. 1979, 1982, 1985–87 and 1990. L. G. Nunes won the most foil championships, with six—1917, 1922, 1924, 1926, 1928 and 1932. Vincent Bradford won a record number of women's épée championships with 4 in 1982–84 and 1986.

NCAA CHAMPIONSHIP DIVISION I (MEN) Inaugurated in 1941, New York University has won the most titles: 12 (1947, 1954, 1957, 1960–61, 1966–67, 1970–71, 1973–74, 1976). The longest consecutive title streak is 4 wins by Wayne State (MI), 1982–85.

Michael Lofton, New York University, has won the most titles in a career with four victories in the sabre, 1984–87. Abraham Balk, New York University, is the only man to win 2 individual titles in one year, 1947 (foil and épée).

NCAA CHAMPIONSHIP DIVISION I (WOMEN) Inaugurated in 1982, Wayne State (MI) has won the most titles: 3 (1982, 1988–89).

Caitlin Bilodeaux (Columbia-Barnard) and Molly Sullivan (Notre Dame) have both won the individual title twice; Bilodeaux (1985, 1987), Sullivan (1986, 1988).

In 1990, the NCAA team competition was combined for the first time, with Penn State taking the title.

FIELD HOCKEY

ORIGINS Hitting a ball with a stick is a game that dates back to the origins of man. Bas-reliefs and frescoes discovered in Egypt and Greece depict hockey-like games. A drawing of a "bully-off" on the walls of a tomb at Beni Hassan in the Nile Valley has been dated to *circa.* 2050 B.C. The birthplace of modern hockey is the United Kingdom, where the first definitive code of rules was established in 1886. The Federation Internationale de Hockey (FIH), the world governing body, was founded on 7 January 1924. Field Hockey was added to the Olympic Games program in 1908 and became a permanent feature in 1928. The sport was introduced to the US in 1921 by a British teacher, Constance M. K. Applebee. The Field Hockey Association of America (FHAA) was founded in 1928 by Henry Greer. The first game was staged between the Germantown Cricket Club and the Westchester Field Hockey Club, also in 1928.

OLYMPIC GAMES India's team was Olympic champion from the reintroduction of Olympic hockey in 1928 until 1960, when Pakistan beat them 1–0 at Rome, Italy. India had its 8th win in 1980.

A women's tournament was added in 1980, when Zimbabwe was the winner. The Netherlands won in 1984 and Australia in 1988.

United States The US men won the bronze medal in 1932, but only three teams played that year; the US women won the bronze in 1984.

MEN

The first international match was the Wales v. Ireland match at Rhyl, Wales on 26 January 1895. Ireland won 3–0.

Highest international score The highest score was when India defeated the United States 24–1 at Los Angeles, CA in the 1932 Olympic Games.

Most international appearances Heiner Dopp represented West Germany 283 times between 1975 and 1990, indoors and out.

Greatest scoring feats The greatest number of goals scored in international hockey is 267, by Paul Litjens (Netherlands) in 177 games.

Fastest goal in an international John French scored 7 sec after the bully-off for England v. West Germany at Nottingham, England on 25 April 1971.

Greatest goalkeeping Richard James Allen (India) did not concede a goal during the 1928 Olympic tournament and conceded a total of only three in the following two Olympics of 1932 and 1936. In these three Games, India scored a total of 102 goals.

MOST APPEARANCES ■ SHERYL JOHNSON HAS MADE A RECORD 137 APPEARANCES FOR THE US FIELD HOCKEY TEAM, FROM 1978–90.

Longest game The longest international game on record was one of 145 min (into the 6th period of extra time), when the Netherlands beat Spain 1–0 in the Olympic Games at Mexico City, Mexico on 25 October 1968.

WOMEN

The first national association was the Irish Ladies' Hockey Union founded in 1894. The first international match was an England v. Ireland game in Dublin in 1896. Ireland won 2–0.

Most international appearances Valerie Robinson made a record 144 appearances for England from 1963 to 1984. Sheryl Johnson has made a record 137 appearances for the US from 1978 to 1990.

Highest scores The highest score in an international match was when England beat France 23–0 at Merton, England on 3 February 1923.

Highest attendance The highest attendance was 65,165 for the match between England and the US at Wembley, England on 11 March 1978.

NCAA DIVISION I (WOMEN) Inaugurated in 1981, Old Dominion has won the most championships with 4 titles: 1982–84 and 1988.

FISHING

Oldest existing club The Ellem fishing club was formed by a number of Edinburgh and Berwickshire gentlemen in Scotland in 1829. Its first annual general meeting was held on 29 April 1830.

Largest single catch The largest officially ratified fish ever caught on a rod was a man-eating great white shark (*Carcharodon carcharias*) weighing 2,664 lb and measuring 16 ft 10 in long, caught on a 130-lb test line by Alf Dean at Denial Bay, near Ceduna, South Australia on 21 April 1959. A great white shark weighing 3,388 lb was caught by Clive Green off Albany, Western Australia on 26 April 1976 but will remain unratified as whale meat was used as bait.

In June 1978, a great white shark measuring 20 ft 4 in in length and weighing more than 5,000 lb was harpooned and landed by fishermen in the harbor of San Miguel, Azores.

The largest marine animal killed by hand harpoon was a blue whale 97 ft in length, by Archer Davidson in Twofold Bay, New South Wales, Australia in 1910. Its tail flukes measured 20 ft across and its jaw bone 23 ft 4 in.

INTERNATIONAL GAME FISH ASSOCIATION (IGFA) WORLD RECORDS The International Game Fish Association (IGFA) recognizes world records for game fish—both freshwater and saltwater—for a large number of species. Its thousands of categories include all-tackle, various line classes and tippet classes for fly fishing. New records recognized by the IGFA reached an annual peak of 1,074 in 1984.

Longest fight The longest recorded individual fight with a fish is 32 hr 5 min by Donal Heatley (New Zealand) with a black marlin (estimated length 20 ft and weight 1,500 lb) off Mayor Island off Tauranga, North Island, New Zealand on 21–22 January 1968. It towed the 13.2-ton launch 50 miles before breaking the line.

Casting The longest freshwater cast ratified under ICF (International Casting Federation) rules is 574 ft 2 in, by Walter Kummerow (West

FRESHWATER & SALT WATER ALL-TACKLE CLASS WORLD RECORDS

A selection of records ratified by the International Game Fish Association to September 1990.

Species	Weight		Angler	Location	Date
Arawana	10 lb	2 oz	Gilberto Fernandes	Puraquequara Lake, Amazon, Brazil	3 Febuary 1990
Barracuda, Mexican	21 lb	0 oz	E. Greg Kent	Phantom Isle, Costa Rica	27 March 1987
Barracuda, Blackfin	15 lb	0 oz	Alejandro Caniz	Puerto Quetzal, Guatemala	29 October 1988
Barracuda, Great	83 lb	0 oz	K.J.W. Hackett	Lagos, Nigeria	13 January 1952
Bass, Giant Sea	536 lb	8 oz	James D. McAdam Jr.	Anacapa Island, California	20 August 1968
Bass, Striped	78 lb	8 oz	Albert McReynolds	Atlantic City, NJ	21 September 1982
Bass, Striped (Landlocked)	66 lb	0 oz	Theodore Furnish	O'Neill Forebay, Los Ramos, CA	29 June 1988
Bass, White	6 lb	13 oz	Ronald L. Sprouse	Lake Orange Orange, VA	31 July 1989
Bass, Whiterock	24 lb	3 oz	David N. Lambert	Leesville Lake, Virginia	12 May 1989
Bluefish	31 lb	12 oz	James M. Hussey	Hatteras, NC	30 January 1972

FRESHWATER & SALT WATER ALL-TACKLE CLASS WORLD RECORDS (Continued)

A selection of records ratified by the International Game Fish Association to September 1990.

Species	Weight	Angler	Location	Date
Carp	75 lb 11 oz	Leo van der Gugten	Lac de St. Cassien, France	21 May 1987
Carp, Grass	29 lb 0 oz	Jerry G. Sardone	Lake Thoreau, Reston, VA	20 May 1990
Catfish, Blue	97 lb 0 oz	Edward B. Elliott	Missouri River, SD	16 September 1959
Chub	5 lb 12 oz	Luis Rasmussen	Helige, Sweden	26 July 1987
Cod, Atlantic	98 lb 12 oz	Alphonse Bielevich	Isle of Shoals, NH	8 June 1969
Conger	102 lb 8 oz	Raymond E. Stewart	Plymouth, England	18 July 1983
Eel, American	4 lb 7 oz	William Cummings	Lake Ronkonkoma, NY	15 November 1986
Flounder, Summer	22 lb 7 oz	Charles Nappi	Montauk, NY	15 September 1975
Flounder, Winter	7 lb 0 oz	Einar F. Grell	Fire Island, NY	8 May 1986
Grouper, Black	112 lb 6 oz	Donald W. Bone	Dry Tortugas, FL	27 January 1990
Haddock	9 lb 15 oz	Jim Donohue	Perkins Cove, Ogunquit, ME	24 May 1988
Halibut, Pacific	356 lb 8 oz	Gregory C. Olsen	Castineau Channel, Juneau, AK	8 November 1986
Marlin, Black	1,560 lb 0 oz	Alfred Glassell Jr.	Cabo Blanco, Peru	4 August 1953
Marlin, Blue (Atlantic)	1,282 lb 0 oz	Larry Martin	St. Thomas, Virgin Islands	6 August 1977
Marlin, Blue (Pacific)	1,376 lb 0 oz	Jay de Beaubien	Kaaiwi Point, Kona Coast, HI	31 May 1982
Marlin, Striped	494 lb 0 oz	Bill Boniface	Tutukaka, New Zealand	16 January 1986
Marlin, White	181 lb 14 oz	Evandro Luiz Coser	Vitoria, Brazil	8 December 1979
Pike, Northern	55 lb 1 oz	Lothar Louis	Lake of Grefeern, West Germany	16 October 1986
Perch, Nile	152 lb 1 oz	Kurt M. Fenster	Tende Bay, Entebbe, Uganda	4 June 1989
Salmon, Chinook	97 lb 4 oz	Les Anderson	Kenai River, AK	17 May 1985
Salmon, Coho	33 lb 4 oz	Jerry Lifton	Salmon River, Pulaski, NY	27 September 1989
Shark, Blue	437 lb 0 oz	Peter Hyde	Catherine Bay, NSW, Australia	2 October 1976
Shark, Greenland	1,708 lb 9 oz	Terje Nordtvedt	Trondheimsfjord, Norway	18 October 1987
Shark, Hammerhead	991 lb 0 oz	Allen Ogle	Sarasota, FL	30 May 1982
Shark, Mako	1,115 lb 0 oz	Patrick Guillanton	Black River, Mauritius	16 November 1988
Shark, Tiger	1,780 lb 0 oz	Walter Maxwell	Cherry Grove, SC	14 June 1964
Shark, White	2,664 lb 0 oz	Alfred Dean	Ceduna, Australia	21 April 1959
Snapper, Red	461 lb 8 oz	E. Lane Nicholls	Destin, FL	1 October 1985
Stingray	294 lb 0 oz	Iain Foulger	River Gambia, The Gambia	4 November 1988
Sturgeon, White	468 lb 0 oz	Joey Pallotta III	Benicia, CA	9 July 1983

FRESHWATER & SALT WATER ALL-TACKLE CLASS WORLD RECORDS (Continued)

A selection of records ratified by the International Game Fish Association to September 1990.

Species	Weight		Angler	Location	Date
Swordfish	1,182 lb	0 oz	L. Marron	Iquique, Chile	17 May 1953
Tarpon	283 lb	0 oz	M. Salazar	Lake Maracaibo, Venezuela	19 March 1956
Trout, Brown	35 lb	15 oz	Eugenio Cavaglia	Nahuel Huapi, Argentina	16 December 1952
Trout, Lake	65 lb	0 oz	Larry Daunis	Great Bear Lake, NWT, Canada	8 August 1970
Trout, Rainbow	42 lb	2 oz	David White	Bell Island, AK	22 November 1970
Tuna, Bigeye (Atlantic)	375 lb	8 oz	Cecil Browne	Ocean City, MD	26 April 1977
Tuna, Bigeye (Pacific)	435 lb	0 oz	Russel Lee	Cabo Blanco, Peru	17 April 1957
Tuna, Bluefin	1,496 lb	0 oz	Ken Fraser	Aulds Cove, Nova Scotia, Canada	26 October 1979
Wahoo	149 lb	0 oz	John Pirovano	Cat Cay, Bahamas	15 June 1962
Walleye	25 lb	0 oz	Mabry Harper	Old Hickory Lake, Tennessee	1 April 1960
Zander	25 lb	2 oz	Harry Tennison	Trosa, Sweden	12 June 1986

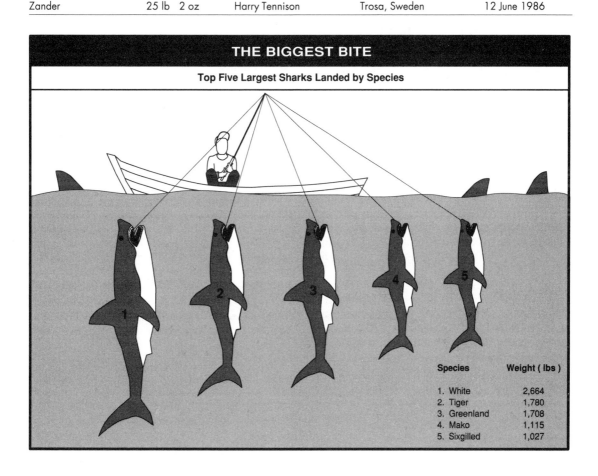

THE BIGGEST BITE

Top Five Largest Sharks Landed by Species

Species	Weight (lbs)
1. White	2,664
2. Tiger	1,780
3. Greenland	1,708
4. Mako	1,115
5. Sixgilled	1,027

Germany), for the Bait Distance Double-Handed 30 g event held at Lenzerheide, Switzerland in the 1968 Championships.

At the currently contested weight of 17.7 g, the longest Double-Handed cast is 457 ft ½ in by Kevin Carriero (US) at Toronto, Canada on 24 July 1984.

The longest Fly Distance Double-Handed cast is 319 ft 1 in by Wolfgang Feige (West Germany) at Toronto, Canada on 23 July 1984.

FOOTBALL

ORIGINS On 6 November 1869 the universities of Princeton and Rutgers staged what is generally regarded as the first intercollegiate football game at New Brunswick, NJ. In October 1873 the Intercollegiate Football Association was formed (Columbia, Princeton, Rutgers and Yale), with the purpose of standardizing rules. At this point football was a modified version of soccer. The first significant move toward today's style of play came when Harvard accepted an invitation to play McGill University (Montreal, Canada) in a series of three challenge matches, the first being in May 1874, under modified rugby rules. Walter Camp is credited with organizing the basic format of the current game. Between 1880–1906, Camp sponsored the concepts of scrimmage lines, 11-man teams, reduction in field size, "downs" and "yards to gain" and a new scoring system. In 1902, the first Rose Bowl game was played at Pasadena, CA; it has been played continuously since 1916.

William (Pudge) Heffelfinger became the first professional player on 12 November 1892, when he was paid $500 by the Allegheny Athletic Association (AAA) to play for them against the Pittsburgh Athletic Club (PAC). In 1893, PAC signed one of its players, believed to be Grant Dibert, to the first known professional contract. The first game to be played with admitted professionals participating was played at Latrobe, PA, on 31 August 1895, Latrobe YMCA defeating the Jeanette Athletic Club 12–0. Professional leagues existed in Pennsylvania and Ohio at the turn of the 20th century; however, the major breakthrough for professional football was the formation of the American Professional Football Association (APFA), founded in Canton, OH on September 17, 1920. Reorganized a number of times, the APFA was renamed the National Football League (NFL) on 24 June 1922. Since 1922, several rival leagues have challenged the NFL, the most significant being the All-America Football Conference (AAFL) and the American Football League (AFL). The AAFL began play in 1946 but after four seasons merged with the NFL for the 1950 season. The AFL challenge was stronger and more acrimonius. Formed in 1959, the inaugural season was 1960. The AFL-NFL "war" was halted on June 4, 1966, when an agreement to merge the leagues was announced. The leagues finally merged for the 1970 season, but an AFL-NFL Championship game, the Super Bowl, was first played in January 1967.

Most games played George Blanda played in a record 340 games in a record 26 seasons in the NFL, for the Chicago Bears (1949, 1950–58), Baltimore Colts (1950), Houston Oilers (1960–66), Oakland Raiders (1967–75). The most seasons service for one club is 19 by Jim Marshall, Minnesota Vikings (1961–79).

THE LONGEST PLAYS

Run from scrimmage Tony Dorsett (Dallas Cowboys) ran through the Minnesota Vikings defense for a 99-yard touchdown on 3 January 1983.

Field Goal 63 yards by Tom Dempsey, (New Orleans Saints) v. Detroit Lions, on 8 November 1970.

Pass Completion The longest pass completion, all for touchdowns, is 99 yards performed by six quarterbacks: Frank Filchok (to Andy Farkas), (Washington Redskins) v. Pittsburgh Steelers, 15 October 1939; George Izo (to Bobby Mitchell), (Washington Redskins) v. Cleveland Browns, 15 September 1963; Karl Sweetan (to Pat Studstill), (Detroit Lions) v. Baltimore Colts, 16 October 1966; Sonny Jurgensen (to Gerry Allen), (Washington Redskins) v. Chicago Bears, 15 September 1968; Jim Plunkett (to Cliff Branch), (Los Angeles Raiders) v. Washington Redskins, 2 October 1983; Ron Jaworski (to Mike Quick), (Philadelphia Eagles) v. Atlanta Falcons, 10 November 1985.

Punt Steve O'Neal (New York Jets) booted a 98-yard punt on 21 September 1969 v. Denver Broncos.

HAPPY RETURNS

Interception Return Venice Glenn (San Diego Chargers) intercepted a Denver Broncos pass and returned it 103 yards for a touchdown on 29 November 1987.

Kickoff Return Three players share the record for a kickoff return at 106 yards: Al Carmichael (Green Bay Packers) v. Chicago Bears, 7 October

NATIONAL FOOTBALL LEAGUE RECORDS

POINTS

Game: 40, Ernie Nevers, Chicago Cardinals *v.* Chicago Bears (6 TDs, 4 PATs), 28 November 1929

Season: 176, Paul Hornung, Green Bay Packers (15 TDs, 41 PATs, 15 FGs), 1960

Career: 2,002 George Blanda, Chicago Bears; Baltimore Colts; Houston Oilers; Oakland Raiders (9 TDs, 943 PATs, 335 FGs), 1949–75

TOUCHDOWNS

Scored

Game: 6, Ernie Nevers, Chicago Cardinals *v.* Chicago Bears, 28 November 1929
"Dub" Jones, Cleveland Browns *v.* Chicago Bears, 25 November 1951
Gale Sayers, Chicago Bears *v.* San Francisco 49ers, 12 December 1965

Season: 24, John Riggins, Washington Redskins, 1983

Career: 126, Jim Brown, Cleveland Browns, 1957–65

Passing

Game: 7, Sid Luckman, Chicago Bears *v.* New York Giants, 14 November 1943
Adrian Burk, Philadelphia Eagles *v.* Washington Redskins, 17 October 1954
George Blanda, Houston Oilers *v.* New York Titans, 19 November 1961
Y. A. Title, New York Giants *v.* Washington Redskins, 28 October 1962
Joe Kapp, Minnesota Vikings *v.* Baltimore Colts, 28 September 1969

Season: 48, Dan Marino, Miami Dolphins, 1984

Career: 342, Fran Tarkenton, Minnesota Vikings;

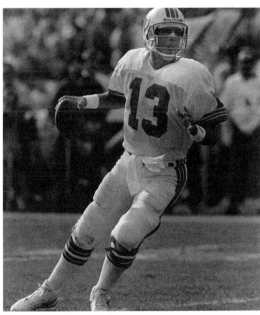

MIAMI ASTOUND MACHINE ■ DOLPHINS QUARTERBACK DAN MARINO HAS SET NFL SEASON PASSING RECORDS FOR MOST YARDS GAINED (5,084), COMPLETIONS (378) AND ATTEMPTS (623).

CATCH THIS! ■ ON 26 NOVEMBER 1989, WILLIE "FLIPPER" ANDERSON, LOS ANGELES RAMS, SET AN NFL SINGLE-GAME RECORD FOR RECEIVING YARDAGE WHEN HE CAUGHT 15 PASSES FOR 336 YARDS. NOW THAT'S A RECORD THAT WILL TAKE SOME CATCHING UP TO!

TOUCHDOWNS (Continued)

Receptions

Game: 5, Bob Shaw, Chicago Cardinals v. Baltimore Colts, 2 October 1950
Kellen Winslow, San Diego Chargers v. Oakland Raiders, 22 November 1981
Jerry Rice, San Francisco 49ers v. Atlanta Falcons, 14 October 1990

Season: 22, Jerry Rice, San Francisco 49ers, 1987

Career: 100, Steve Largent, Seattle Seahawks, 1976–89

Rushing

Game: 6, Ernie Nevers, Chicago Cardinals v. Chicago Bears, 28 November 1929

Season: 24, John Riggins, Washington Redskins, 1983

Career: 110, Walter Payton, Chicago Bears, 1975–87

Punt Returns

Game: 2, Jack Christiansen, Detroit Lions v. Los Angeles Rams, 14 October 1951
Jack Christiansen, Detroit Lions v. Green Bay Packers, 22 November 1951
Dick Christy, New York Titans v. Denver Broncos, 24 September 1961
Rick Upchurch, Denver Broncos v. Cleveland Browns, 26 September 1976
LeRoy Irvin, Los Angeles Rams v. Atlanta Falcons, 11 October 1981
Vai Sikahema, St. Louis Cardinals v. Tampa Bay Buccaneers, 21 December 1986

Season: 4, Jack Christiansen, Detroit Lions, 1951
Rick Upchurch, Denver Broncos, 1976

Career: 8, Jack Christiansen, Detroit Lions, 1951–58
Rick Upchurch, Denver Broncos, 1975–83

Kickoff Returns

Game: 2, Timmy Brown, Philadelphia Eagles v. Dallas Cowboys, 6 November 1966
Travis Williams, Green Bay Packers v. Cleveland Browns, 12 November 1967
Ron Brown, Los Angeles Rams v. Green Bay Packers, 24 November 1985

Season: 4, Travis Williams, Green Bay Packers, 1967
Cecil Turner, Chicago Bears, 1970

Career: 6, Ollie Matson, Chicago Cardinals; Los Angeles Rams; Detroit Lions; Philadelphia Eagles, 1952–64

PASSING

Yards Gained

Game: 554, Norm Van Brocklin, Los Angeles Rams v. New York Yankees, 28 September 1951

Season: 5,084, Dan Marino, Miami Dolphins, 1984

Career: 47,003, Fran Tarkenton, Minnesota Vikings; New York Giants, 1961–78

Completions

Game: 42, Richard Todd, New York Jets v. San Francisco 49ers, 21 September 1980

Season: 378, Dan Marino, Miami Dolphins, 1986

Career: 3,686, Fran Tarkenton, Minnesota Vikings; New York Giants, 1961–78

NATIONAL FOOTBALL LEAGUE RECORDS (Continued)

PASSING (Continued)
Attempts

Game: 68, George Blanda, Houston Oilers v. Buffalo Bills, 1 November 1964

Season: 623, Dan Marino, Miami Dolphins, 1986

Career: 6,467, Fran Tarkenton, Minnesota Vikings; New York Giants, 1961–78

Average Yards Gained

Game:
(Min. 20 attempts) 18.58, Sammy Baugh, Washington Redskins v. Boston Yanks (24–446), 31 October 1948

Season
(Qualifiers): 11.17, Tommy O'Connell, Cleveland Browns (110–1,229), 1957

Career
(Min. 1,500 attempts): 8.63, Otto Graham, Cleveland Browns (1,565–13,499), 1950–55

Intercepted

Game: 8, Jim Hardy, Chicago Cardinals v. Philadelphia Eagles, 24 September 1950

Season: 42, George Blanda, Houston Oilers, 1962

Career: 277, George Blanda, Chicago Bears; Baltimore Colts; Houston Oilers; Oakland Raiders, 1949–75

PASS RECEIVING
Receptions

Game: 18, Tom Fears, Los Angeles Rams v. Green Bay Packers, 3 December 1950

Season: 106, Art Monk, Washington Redskins, 1984

Career: 819, Steve Largent, Seattle Seahawks, 1976–89

Yards Gained

Game: 336, Willie Anderson, Los Angeles Rams v. New Orleans Saints, 26 November 1989

Season: 1,746, Charley Hennigan, Houston Oilers, 1961

Career: 13,089, Steve Largent, Seattle Seahawks, 1976–89

Average Yards Gained

Game
(3 catches): 60.67, Bill Gorman, Houston Oilers v. Denver Broncos (3–182), 20 November 1960
Homer Jones, New York Giants v. Washington Redskins, 12 December 1965(3–182)

Season
(24 catches): 32.58, Don Currivan, Boston Yanks (24–782), 1947

Career
(200 catches): 22.26, Homer Jones, New York Giants; Cleveland Browns (224–4,986), 1964–70

NATIONAL FOOTBALL LEAGUE RECORDS (Continued)

RUSHING
Yards Gained

Game: 275, Walter Payton, Chicago Bears v. Minnesota Vikings, November 20 1977

Season: 2,105, Eric Dickerson, Los Angeles Rams, 1984

Career: 16,726, Walter Payton, Chicago Bears, 1975–87

Attempts

Game: 45, Jamie Morris, Washington Redskins v. Cincinnati Bengals, 17 December 1988

Season: 407, James Wilder, Tampa Bay Buccaneers, 1984

Career: 3,838, Walter Payton, Chicago Bears, 1975–87

Average Yards Gained

**Game
(10 attempts):** 17.09, Marion Mottley, Cleveland Browns v. Pittsburgh Steelers (11–188), 9 October 1950

**Season
(Qualifiers):** 9.94, Beattie Feathers, Chicago Bears (101–1,004), 1934

**Career
(700 attempts):** 5.22, Jim Brown, Cleveland Browns (2,359–12,312), 1957–65

INTERCEPTIONS

Game: 4, 16 players have achieved this feat.

Season: 14, Dick "Night Train" Lane, Los Angeles Rams, 1952

Career: 81, Paul Krause, Washington Redskins; Minnesota Vikings, 1964–79

KICKING
Field Goals
Most

Game: 7, Jim Bakken, St. Louis Cardinals v. Pittsburgh Steelers, 24 September 1967
Rich Karlis, Minnesota Vikings v. Los Angeles Rams, 5 November 1989

Season: 35, Ali Haji-Sheikh, New York Giants, 1983

Career: 373, Jan Stenerud, Kansas City Chiefs; Green Bay Packers; Minnesota Vikings, 1967–85

Attempts

Game: 9, Jim Bakken, St. Louis Cardinals v. Pittsburgh Steelers, 24 September 1967

Season: 49, Bruce Gossett, Los Angeles Rams, 1966
Curt Knight, Washington Redskins, 1971

Career: 638, George Blanda, Chicago Bears; Baltimore Colts; Houston Oilers; Oakland Raiders, 1949–75

KICKING/Field Goals (Continued)

50 or More Yards

Game: 2, This record has been achieved 19 times; Nick Lowery, Kansas City Chiefs, is the only kicker to have matched this record 3 times.

Season: 6, Dean Biasucci, Indianapolis Colts, 1988

Career: 18, Nick Lowery, New England Patriots; Kansas City Chiefs, 1978, 80–89

POINTS AFTER TOUCHDOWN (PATs)

Most

Game: 9, Pat Harder, Chicago Cardinals *v.* New York Giants, 17 October 1948
Bob Waterfield, Los Angeles Rams *v.* Baltimore Colts, 22 October 1950
Charlie Gogolak, Washington Redskins *v.* New York Giants, 27 November 1966

Season: 66, Uwe von Schamann, Miami Dolphins, 1984

Career: 943, George Blanda, Chicago Bears; Baltimore Colts; Houston Oilers; Oakland Raiders, 1949–75

PUNTING

Most

Game: 15, John Teltschik, Philadelphia Eagles *v.* New York Giants, 6 December 1987

Season: 114, Bob Parsons, Chicago Bears, 1981

Career: 1,154, Dave Jennings, New York Giants; New York Jets, 1974–87

Average Yards Gained

**Game
(Min. 4 punts)** 61.75, Bob Cifers, Detroit Lions *v.* Chicago Bears (4–247), 4 November 1946

**Season
(Qualifiers):** 51.40, Sammy Baugh, Washington Redskins (35–1,799), 1940

**Career
(Min. 300 punts):** 45.10, Sammy Baugh, Washington Redskins (338–15,245), 1937–52

SACKS

Compiled since 1982

Game: 7, Derrick Thomas, Kansas City *v.* Seattle Seahawks, 11 November 1990

Season: 22, Mark Gastineau, New York Jets, 1984

Career: 114.5, Lawrence Taylor, New York Giants, 1982–90

Most times sacked (compiled since 1963)

Game: 12, Bert Jones, Baltimore Colts *v.* St. Louis Cardinals, 26 October 1980
Warren Moon, Houston Oilers *v.* Dallas Cowboys, 29 September 1985

Season: 72, Randall Cunningham, Philadelphia Eagles, 1986

Career: 483, Fran Tarkenton, Minnesota Vikings; New York Giants, 1961–78

Source: NFL

1956; Noland Smith (Kansas City Chiefs) *v.* Denver Broncos, 17 December 1967; Roy Green (St. Louis Cardinals) *v.* Dallas Cowboys, 21 October 1979. All three players scored touchdowns.

Missed Field Goal Return Al Nelson (Philadelphia Eagles) returned a Dallas Cowboys' missed field goal 101 yards for a touchdown on 26 September 1971.

Fumble Return Jack Tatum (Oakland Raiders) returned a Green Bay Packers' fumble 104 yards for a touchdown on 24 September 1972.

STREAKS

REGULAR SEASON (TEAM)

Wins 17, Chicago Bears, 1933–34.

Wins (Regular Season and Playoffs) 18: Chicago Bears, 1933–34; Chicago Bears, 1941–42; Miami Dolphins, 1972–73; San Francisco 49ers, 1989–90.

Games Without Defeat 25, Canton Bulldogs, 1921–23 (22 wins, 3 ties).

Losses 26, Tampa Bay Buccaneers, 1976–77.

REGULAR SEASON (INDIVIDUAL)

Games, Played 282, Jim Marshall, Cleveland Browns, 1960; Minnesota Vikings, 1961–79.

Games, Scoring 151, Fred Cox, Minnesota Vikings, 1963–73.

Games, Scoring Touchdowns 18, Lenny Moore, Baltimore Colts, 1963–65.

Points After Touchdown (PATs) 234, Tommy Davis, San Francisco 49ers, 1959–65.

Field Goals 24, Kevin Butler, Chicago Bears, 1988–89.

TOUCHDOWN STREAK ■ JOHNNY UNITAS, BALTIMORE COLTS, THREW TOUCHDOWN PASSES IN 47 CONSECUTIVE GAMES.

SACK LEADER ■ NEW YORK GIANTS LINEBACKER LAWRENCE TAYLOR HOLDS THE NFL ALL-TIME SACK RECORD WITH 114.5.

KICKING STREAK ■ KEVIN BUTLER, CHICAGO BEARS, BOOTED 24 CONSECUTIVE FIELD GOALS, 1988–89.

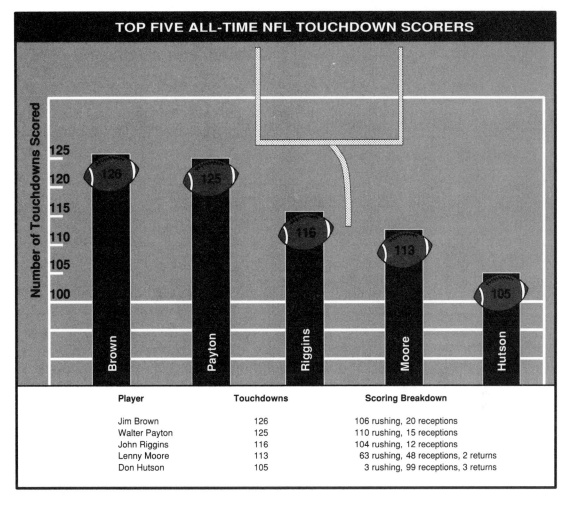

TOP FIVE ALL-TIME NFL TOUCHDOWN SCORERS

Player	Touchdowns	Scoring Breakdown
Jim Brown	126	106 rushing, 20 receptions
Walter Payton	125	110 rushing, 15 receptions
John Riggins	116	104 rushing, 12 receptions
Lenny Moore	113	63 rushing, 48 receptions, 2 returns
Don Hutson	105	3 rushing, 99 receptions, 3 returns

Games, 100 or more yards rushing 11, Marcus Allen, Los Angeles Raiders, 1985–86

Games, Touchdowns (Rushing) 13, John Riggins, Washington Redskins, 1982–83. George Rogers, Washington Redskins, 1985–86.

Passes Completed 22, Joe Montana, San Francisco 49ers v. Cleveland Browns, 29 November 1987 (5); v. Green Bay Packers, 6 December 1987 (17).

Games, Touchdown Passes 47, Johnny Unitas, Baltimore Colts, 1956–60.

Games, Four or more Touchdown Passes 4, Dan Marino, Miami Dolphins, 1984.

Games, Touchdown Receptions 13, Jerry Rice, San Francisco 49ers, 1986–87.

Games, Pass Receptions 177, Steve Largent, Seattle Seahawks, 1977–89.

Highest Aggregate Score in an NFL game On 27 November 1966, the Washington Redskins defeated the New York Giants 72–41 in Washington D.C. The Redskins 72 points also set the mark for most points scored by a team in a regular season game. In the 1940 NFL Championship Game, the Chicago Bears defeated the Washington Redskins, 73–0, to set the all-time team score.

Greatest Comeback in NFL history On December 7, 1980, the San Francisco 49ers, playing at home, trailed the New Orleans Saints 35–7 at half-time. In the 2nd half, the 49ers, led by Joe Montana, scored 31 unanswered points to win the game 38–35. The 49ers had overcome a deficit of 28 points, the largest in NFL history.

Largest Trade in NFL history Based on the number of players and/or draft choices involved, the largest trade in NFL history is 15, which has happened twice. On 26 March 1953 the Baltimore Colts and Cleveland Browns exchanged 15 players; and on 28 January 1971, the Washington Redskins and Los Angeles Rams completed the transfer of seven players and eight draft choices.

COACHES

Most seasons 40, George Halas, Decatur/Chicago Staleys/Chicago Bears (1920–29, 1933–42, 1946–55, 1958–67).

TOP TEN NFL ALL-TIME WINS, INCLUDING PLAYOFFS

Coach	Teams	Wins
George Halas	Decatur/Chicago Staleys/Chicago Bears (1920–29, 1933–42, 1946–55, 1958–67)	325
Don Shula	Baltimore Colts (1963–69); Miami Dolphins (1970—)	300
Tom Landry	Dallas Cowboys (1960–88)	271
Curly Lambeau	Green Bay Packers (1921–49); Chicago Cardinals (1950–51); Washington Redskins (1952–53)	229
Chuck Noll	Pittsburgh Steelers (1969–)	202
Chuck Knox	Los Angeles Rams (1973–77); Buffalo Bills (1978–82); Seattle Seahawks (1983–)	171
Paul Brown	Cleveland Browns (1950–62); Cincinnati Bengals (1968–75)	170
Bud Grant	Minnesota Vikings (1967–83, 1985)	168
Steve Owen	New York Giants (1931–53)	153
Hank Stram	Dallas Texans/Kansas City Chiefs (1960–74); New Orleans Saints (1976–77)	136

Source: NFL

NFL CHAMPIONSHIP

The first NFL championship was awarded in 1920 to the Akron Pros, as the team with the best record. From 1920–31, the championship was based on regular season records. The first championship game was played in 1932. In January 1967, the first Super Bowl was played, the Green Bay Packers (NFL) defeating the Kansas City Chiefs (AFL), 35–10. This game concluded the 1966 NFL and AFL seasons. The NFL and AFL merged for the 1970 season. The first NFL Super Bowl was played in January 1971 between the Baltimore Colts (AFC) and the Dallas Cowboys (NFC), with the Colts winning to become the 1970 NFL champions.

The Green Bay Packers have won a record 11 NFL titles, 1929–31, 1936, 1939, 1944, 1961–62, 1965–67.

NFL CHAMPIONS

Season	Winner	Loser	Score
1920	Akron Pros	——	——
1921	Chicago Staleys	——	——
1922	Canton Bulldogs	——	——
1923	Canton Bulldogs	——	——
1924	Cleveland Bulldogs	——	——
1925	Chicago Cardinals	——	——
1926	Frankford Yellowjackets	——	——
1927	New York Giants	——	——
1928	Providence Steam Roller	——	——
1929	Green Bay Packers	——	——
1930	Green Bay Packers	——	——
1931	Green Bay Packers	——	——
1932	Chicago Bears	Portsmouth Spartans	9–0
1933	Chicago Bears	New York Giants	23–21
1934	New York Giants	Chicago Bears	30–13
1935	Detroit Lions	New York Giants	26–7
1936	Green Bay Packers	Boston Redskins	21–6
1937	Washington Redskins	Chicago Bears	28–21
1938	New York Giants	Green Bay Packers	23–17
1939	Green Bay Packers	New York Giants	27–0
1940	Chicago Bears	Washington Redskins	73–0
1941	Chicago Bears	New York Giants	37–9
1942	Washington Redskins	Chicago Bears	14–6
1943	Chicago Bears	Washington Redskins	41–21
1944	Green Bay Packers	New York Giants	14–7
1945	Cleveland Rams	Washington Redskins	15–14
1946	Chicago Bears	New York Giants	24–14
1947	Chicago Cardinals	Philadelphia Eagles	28–21
1948	Philadelphia Eagles	Chicago Cardinals	7–0
1949	Philadelphia Eagles	Los Angeles Rams	14–0
1950	Cleveland Browns	Los Angeles Rams	30–28
1951	Los Angeles Rams	Cleveland Browns	24–17
1952	Detroit Lions	Cleveland Browns	17–7
1953	Detroit Lions	Cleveland Browns	17–16
1954	Cleveland Browns	Detroit Lions	56–10
1955	Cleveland Browns	Los Angeles Rams	38–14
1956	New York Giants	Chicago Bears	47–7
1957	Detroit Lions	Cleveland Browns	59–14
1958	Baltimroe Colts	New York Giants	23–17
1959	Baltimore Colts	New York Giants	31–16
1960	Philadelphia Eagles	Green Bay Packers	17–13
1961	Green Bay Packers	New York Giants	37–0
1962	Green Bay Packers	New York Giants	16–7
1963	Chicago Bears	New York Giants	14–10
1964	Cleveland Browns	Baltimore Colts	27–0
1965	Green Bay Packers	Cleveland Browns	23–12

SUPER BOWL

No.	Season	Winner	Loser	Score
I	1966	Green Bay Packers	Kansas City Chiefs	35–10
II	1967	Green Bay Packers	Oakland Raiders	33–14
III	1968	New York Jets	Baltimore Colts	16–7
IV	1969	Kansas City Chiefs	Minnesota Vikings	23–7
V	1970	Baltimore Colts	Dallas Cowboys	16–13
VI	1971	Dallas Cowboys	Miami Dolphins	24–3
VII	1972	Miami Dolphins	Washington Redskins	14–7
VIII	1973	Miami Dolphins	Minnesota Vikings	24–7
IX	1974	Pittsburgh Steelers	Minnesota Vikings	16–6
X	1975	Pittsburgh Steelers	Dallas Cowboys	21–17
XI	1976	Oakland Raiders	Minnesota Vikings	32–14
XII	1977	Dallas Cowboys	Denver Broncos	27–10
XIII	1978	Pittsburgh Steelers	Dallas Cowboys	35–31
XIV	1979	Pittsburgh Steelers	Los Angeles Rams	31–19
XV	1980	Oakland Raiders	Philadelphia Eagles	27–10
XVI	1981	San Francisco 49ers	Cincinnati Bengals	26–21
XVII	1982	Washington Redskins	Miami Dolphins	27–17
XVIII	1983	Los Angeles Raiders	Washington Redskins	38–9
XIX	1984	San Francisco 49ers	Miami Dolphins	38–16
XX	1985	Chicago Bears	New England Patriots	46–10
XXI	1986	New York Giants	Denver Broncos	39–20
XXII	1987	Washington Redskins	Denver Broncos	42–10
XXIII	1988	San Francisco 49ers	Cincinnati Bengals	20–16
XXIV	1989	San Francisco 49ers	Denver Broncos	55–10
XXV	1990	New York Giants	Buffalo Bills	20–19

THE SUPER BOWL

(Years in this section refer to the NFL season, not the year of the game.) First held in January 1967 between the winners of the NFL and the AFL. Since 1970 it has been contested by the winners of the National and American Conferences of the NFL. The most wins is four, by the Pittsburgh Steelers in 1974–75, 1978–79, coached by Chuck Noll on each occasion, and by the San Francisco 49ers in 1981, 1984, 1988 and 1989, coached by Bill Walsh (1981, 1984, 1988) and George Seifert (1989).

Most appearances The most Super Bowl appearances is five by the Dallas Cowboys (2 wins, 3 losses), 1970–71, 1975, 1977–78 and by the Miami Dolphins (2 wins, 3 losses), 1971–73, 1982, 1984.

The most appearances by a player is also five shared by seven players: Marv Fleming (Green Bay Packers 1966–67; Miami Dolphins 1971–73); Larry Cole (Dallas Cowboys 1970–71, 1975, 1977–78);

SUPER BOWL RECORD ■ DON SHULA HAS BEEN HEAD COACH OF SIX SUPER BOWL TEAMS: BALTIMORE COLTS, 1968; MIAMI DOLPHINS, 1971–73, 1982, 1984. HE HAS WON TWO GAMES AND LOST FOUR.

Cliff Harris (Dallas Cowboys 1970–71, 1975, 1977–78); D. D. Lewis (Dallas Cowboys 1970–71, 1975, 1977–78); Preston Pearson (Baltimore Colts 1968; Pittsburgh Steelers 1974; Dallas Cowboys 1975, 1977–78); Charlie Waters (Dallas Cowboys 1970–71, 1975, 1977–78); Rayfield Wright (Dallas Cowboys 1970–71, 1975, 1977–78).

Don Shula has coached six Super Bowls to set the all-time mark: Baltimore Colts, 1968; Miami Dolphins, 1971–73, 1982, 1984. He won 2 games and lost 4.

Highest scores The highest aggregate score was 66 points when the Pittsburgh Steelers beat the Dallas Cowboys 35–31 on 21 January 1979. The highest team score and record victory margin was when the San Francisco 49ers beat the Denver Broncos 55–10 at New Orleans, LA on 28 January 1990. In their 42–10 victory over the Denver Broncos on 31 January 1988, the Washington Redskins scored a record 35 points in the 2nd quarter.

Most valuable player Joe Montana quarterback of the San Francisco 49ers, has been voted the Super Bowl MVP on a record three occasions, 1981, 1984 and 1989.

SUPER BOWL MVPs

Game	Player	Team	Position
I	Bart Starr	Green Bay Packers	Quarterback
II	Bart Starr	Green Bay Packers	Quarterback
III	Joe Namath	New York Jets	Quarterback
IV	Len Dawson	Kansas City Chiefs	Quarterback
V	Chuck Howley	Dallas Cowboys	Linebacker
VI	Roger Staubach	Dallas Cowboys	Quarterback
VII	Jake Scott	Miami Dolphins	Safety
VIII	Larry Csonka	Miami Dolphins	Running Back
IX	Franco Harris	Pittsburgh Steelers	Running Back
X	Lynn Swann	Pittsburgh Steelers	Wide Receiver
XI	Fred Biletnikoff	Oakland Raiders	Wide Receiver
XII	Randy White	Dallas Cowboys	Defensive Tackle
XIII	Terry Bradshaw	Pittsburgh Steelers	Quarterback

SUPER BOWL MVPs (Continued)

Game	Player	Team	Position
XIV	Terry Bradshaw	Pittsburgh Steelers	Quarterback
XV	Jim Plunkett	Oakland Raiders	Quarterback
XVI	Joe Montana	San Francisco 49ers	Quarterback
XVII	John Riggins	Washington Redskins	Running Back
XVIII	Marcus Allen	Los Angeles Raiders	Running Back
XIX	Joe Montana	San Francisco 49ers	Quarterback
XX	Richard Dent	Chicago Bears	Defensive End
XXI	Phil Simms	New York Giants	Quarterback
XXII	Doug Williams	Washington Redskins	Quarterback
XXIII	Jerry Rice	San Francisco 49ers	Wide Receiver
XXIV	Joe Montana	San Francisco 49ers	Quarterback
XXV	O.J. Anderson	New York Giants	Running Back

SUPER BOWL RECORDS

POINTS

Game: 18, Roger Craig, San Francisco 49ers, XIX
Jerry Rice, San Francisco 49ers, XXIV

Career: 24, Franco Harris, Pittsburgh Steelers, IX, X, XIII, XIV
Roger Craig, San Francisco 49ers, XIX, XXIII, XXIV
Jerry Rice, San Francisco 49ers, XXIII, XXIV

TOUCHDOWNS

Scored

Game: 3, Roger Craig, San Francisco 49ers, XIX
Jerry Rice, San Francisco 49ers, XXIV

Career: 4, Franco Harris, Pittsburgh Steelers, IX, X, XIII, XIV
Roger Craig, San Francisco 49ers, XIX, XXIII, XXIV
Jerry Rice, San Francisco 49ers, XXIII, XXIV

Passing

Game: 5, Joe Montana, San Francisco 49ers, XXIV

Career: 11, Joe Montana, San Francisco 49ers, XVI, XIX, XXIII, XXIV

PASSING

Yards Gained

Game: 357, Joe Montana, San Francisco 49ers, XXIII

Career: 1,142, Joe Montana, San Francisco 49ers, XVI, XIX, XXIII, XXIV

Completions

Game: 29, Dan Marino, Miami Dolphins, XIX

Career: 83, Joe Montana, San Francisco 49ers, XVI, XIX, XXIII, XXIV

SUPER BOWL RECORDS (Continued)

PASSING (Continued)

Highest Completion Percentage

Game
(20 attempts): 88.0, Phil Simms, New York Giants (22–25), XXI

Career
(40 attempts): 68.0, Joe Montana, San Francisco 49ers (83–122), XVI, XIX, XXIII, XXIV

PASS RECEIVING

Receptions

Game: 11, Dan Ross, Cincinnati Bengals, XVI
Jerry Rice, San Francisco 49ers, XXIII

Career: 20, Roger Craig, San Francisco 49ers, XIX, XXIII, XXIV

Yards Gained

Game: 215, Jerry Rice, San Francisco 49ers, XXIII

Career: 364, Lynn Swann, Pittsburgh Steelers, IX, X, XIII, XIV

RUSHING

Yards Gained

Game: 204, Timmy Smith, Washington Redskins, XXII

Career: 354, Franco Harris, Pittsburgh Steelers, IX, X, XIII, XIV

INTERCEPTIONS

Game: 3, Rod Martin, Oakland Raiders, XV

Career: 3, Chuck Howley, Dallas Cowboys, V, VI
Rod Martin, Oakland/Los Angeles Raiders, XV, XVIII

FIELD GOALS

Game: 4, Don Chandler, Green Bay Packers, II
Ray Wersching, San Francisco 49ers, XVI

Career: 5, Ray Wersching, San Francisco 49ers, XVI, XIX

LONGEST PLAYS

**Run from
Scrimmage:** 74 yards, Marcus Allen, Los Angeles Raiders, XVIII

**Pass
Completion:** 80 yards, Jim Plunkett, (to Kenny King) Oakland Raiders, XV
Doug Williams, (to Ricky Sanders) Washington Redskins, XXII

Field Goal: 48 yards, Jan Stenerud, Kansas City Chiefs, IV
Rich Karlis, Denver Broncos, XXI

Punt: 63 yards, Lee Johnson, Cincinnati Bengals, XXIII

Source NFL

SUPER PLAY ■ MARCUS ALLEN, LOS ANGELES RAIDERS, RAN **74** YARDS ON ONE PLAY IN SUPER BOWL XVIII TO SET THE SUPER BOWL RECORD FOR A RUN FROM SCRIMMAGE.

COLLEGE FOOTBALL (NCAA)

The oldest collegiate series still contested is that between Yale and Princeton, first played in November 1873, three years before the formation of the Intercollegiate Football Association. The first Rose Bowl game was held at Pasadena, CA on 1 January 1902, when Michigan beat Stanford 49–0. The National Collegiate Athletic Association began classifying college teams into divisions I, II and III in 1973. Five years later division I was subdivided into 1–A and 1–AA.

NCAA OVERALL CAREER RECORDS (DIVISIONS 1-A, 1-AA, II AND III)

Points Scored 474, Joe Dudek, Plymouth State (Div. III), 1982–85.

Rushing (yards) 6,320, Johnny Bailey, Texas A&I (Div. II), 1986–89.

Passing (yards) 13,220, Neil Lomax, Portland State (Div II; 1–AA), 1977; 1978–80.

Receptions (yards) 4,693, Jerry Rice, Mississippi Valley (Div. 1–AA), 1981–84.

Receptions (most) 301, Jerry Rice, Mississippi Valley (Div. 1–AA), 1981–84.

Field Goals (Game) 8, Goran Lingmerth, Northern Arizona (Div. 1–AA). Booting 8 out of 8 kicks, Lingmerth set the record on 25 October 1986 v. Idaho.

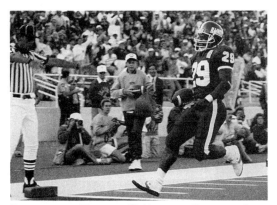

TOUCHDOWN RECORD ■ HOWARD GRIFFITH, ILLINOIS, SCORES ONE OF HIS NCAA-RECORD EIGHT TOUCHDOWNS AGAINST SOUTHERN ILLINOIS ON 22 SEPTEMBER 1990.

NCAA DIVISION 1–A RECORDS

POINTS

Game: 48, Howard Griffith, Illinois v. Southern Illinois (8 TDs), 22 September 1990

Season: 234, Barry Sanders, Oklahoma State, (39 TDs), 1988

Career: 394, Anthony Thompson, Indiana, (65 TDs, 4 PATs), 1986–89

TOUCHDOWNS
Scored

Game: 8, Howard Griffith, Illinois v. Southern Illinois, 22 September 1990

Season: 39, Barry Sanders, Oklahoma State, 1988

Career: 65, Anthony Thompson, Indiana, 1986–89

NCAA DIVISION 1-A RECORDS (Continued)

TOUCHDOWNS (Continued)

Passing

Game: 11, David Klinger, Houston v. Eastern Washington, 17 November 1990

Season: 54, David Klinger, Houston, 1990

Career: 86, Ty Detmer, BYU, 1988–90

Receptions

Game: 6, Tim Delaney, San Diego State v. New Mexico State, 15 November 1969

Season: 22, Emmanuel Hazard, Houston, 1989

Career: 38, Clarkston Hines, Duke, 1986–89

Rushing

Game: 8, Howard Griffith, Illinois v. Southern Illinois, 22 September 1990

Season: 37, Barry Sanders, Oklahoma State, 1988

Career: 64, Anthony Thompson, Indiana, 1986–89

Punt Returns

Game: 2, By many players.

Season: 4, Golden Richards, BYU, 1971
Cliff Branch, Colorado, 1971
James Henry, Southern Mississippi, 1987

Career: 7, Jack Mitchell, Oklahoma, 1946–48
Johnny Rodgers, Nebraska, 1970–72

Kickoff Returns

Game: 2, This record has been achieved 7 times. Raghib Ismail, Notre Dame, is the only player to do it twice: v. Rice, 5 November 1988, v. Michigan, 16 September 1989.

ROCKET MAN ■ RAGHIB "ROCKET" ISMAIL, NOTRE DAME, IS THE ONLY PLAYER TO HAVE COMPLETED A KICKOFF RETURN FOR A TOUCHDOWN TWICE IN ONE GAME ON TWO OCCASIONS.

TOUCHDOWNS (Continued)
Kickoff Returns (Continued)

Season: 3, Forrest Hall, San Francisco, 1946
Stan Brown, Purdue, 1970
Anthony Davis, Southern Cal, 1974
Willie Gault, Tennessee, 1980
Terance Mathis, New Mexico, 1989

Career: 6, Anthony Davis, Southern Cal, 1972–74

PASSING
Yards Gained

Game: 716, David Klinger, Houston v. Arizona State, 1 December 1990

Season: 5,188, Ty Detmer, BYU, 1990

Career: 11,425, Todd Santos, San Diego State, 1984–87

Completions

Game: 48, David Klinger, Houston v. SMU, 20 October 1990

Season: 374, David Klinger, Houston, 1990

Career: 910, Todd Santos, San Diego State, 1984–87

Attempts

Game: 79, Matt Vogler, TCU v. Houston, 3 November 1990

Season: 643, David Klinger, Houston, 1990

Career: 1,484, Todd Santos, San Diego State, 1984–87

Average Yards Gained

**Game
(Min. 40 attempts):** 13.93, Marc Wilson, BYU v. Utah (41 for 571 yards), 5 Nov 1977

**Season
(Min. 200 attempts):** 1.31, Chuck Long, Iowa (236 for 2,434 yards), 1983

**Career
(Min. 750 attempts):** 9.00, Jim McMahon, BYU (1,060 for 9,536 yards) 1977–78, 80–81

PASS RECEIVING
Receptions

Game: 22, Jay Miller, BYU v. New Mexico, 3 November 1973

Season: 142, Emmanuel Hazard, Houston, 1989

Career: 263, Terance Mathis, New Mexico, 1985–87, 89

NCAA DIVISION 1-A RECORDS (Continued)

PASS RECEIVING (Continued)

Yards Gained

Game: 349, Chuck Hughes, UTEP v. North Texas, 18 September 1965

Season: 1,779, Howard Tilley, Tulsa, 1965

Career: 4,254, Terance Mathis, New Mexico, 1985–87, 89

Average Yards Gained

**Game
(Min. 5 catches):** 52.6, Alex Wright, Auburn v. Pacific (5 for 263 yds), 9 September 1989

**Season
(Min. 50 catches):** 24.4, Henry Ellard, Fresno State (62 for 1,510 yds), 1982

**Career
(Min. 100 catches):** 21.9, Elmo Wright, Houston (153 for 3,347 yds), 1968–70

RUSHING

Yards Gained

Game: 377, Anthony Thompson, Indiana v. Wisconsin, 11 November 1989

Season: 2,628, Barry Sanders, Oklahoma State, 1980–82

Career: 6,082, Tony Dorsett, Pittsburgh, 1973–76

Attempts

Game: 57, Kent Kitzmann, Minnesota v. Illinois, 12 November 1977

Season: 403, Marcus Allen, Southern Cal, 1981

Career: 1,215, Steve Bartalo, Colorado State, 1983–86

Average Yards Gained

**Game
(Min. 15 rushes):** 21.40, Tony Jeffrey, TCU v. Tulane (16 for 343 yards), 13 September 1986

**Season
(Min. 225 rushes):** 7.81, Mike Rozier, Nebraska (275 for 2,148 yards), 1983

**Career
(Min. 275 rushes):** 7.61, Mike Rozier, Nebraska, (668 for 4,780 yards), 1981–83

INTERCEPTIONS

Game: 5, Lee Cook, Oklahoma State v. Detroit, 28 November 1942
Walt Pastuszak, Brown v. Rhode Island, 8 October 1949
Byron Beaver, Houston v. Baylor, 22 September 1962
Dan Rebsch, Miami (Ohio) v. Western Michigan, 4 November 1972

Season: 14, Al Worley, Washington, 1968

Career: 29, Al Brosky, Illinois, 1950–52

NCAA DIVISION 1–A RECORDS (Continued)

FIELD GOALS

Most Conversions

Game: 7, Mike Prindle, Western Michigan v. Marshall, 29 September 1984
Dale Klein, Nebraska v. Missouri, 19 October 1985

Season: 29, John Lee, UCLA, 1984

Career: 80, Jeff Jaeger, Washington, 1983–86

Most Points

Game: 24, Mike Prindle, Western Michigan v. Marshall (7 FGs, 3 PATSs), 29 September 1984

Season: 131, Roman Anderson, Houston (22 FGs, 65 PATs), 1989

Career: 393, Derek Schmidt, Florida State (73 FGs, 174 PATs), 1984–87

POINTS AFTER TOUCHDOWN (PATs)

Most Conversions

Game: 13, Terry Leiweke, Houston v. Tulsa, 23 November 1968

Season: 67, Cary Blanchard, Oklahoma State, 1988

Career: 174, Derek Schmidt, Florida State, 1984–87

PUNTING

Most Punts

Game: 36, Charlie Calhoun, Texas Tech v. Centenary, 11 November 1939

Season: 101, Jim Bailey, Virginia Military, 1969

Career: 320, Cameron Young, Texas Christian, 1976–79

Average Yards Gained

Game
(Min. 5 punts): 60.4, Lee Johnson, BYU v. Wyoming (5 for 302 yds), 8 Oct 1983

Season
(Min. 50 punts): 48.2, Ricky Anderson, Vanderbilt (58 for 2,793), 1984

Career
(Min. 200 punts): 44.7, Ray Guy, Southern Mississippi (200 for 8,934), 1970–72

2-POINT ATTEMPTS MADE

Game: 6, Jim Pilot, New Mexico State v. Hardin-Simmons, 25 Nov 1961

Season: 6, Pat McCarthy, Holy Cross, 1960
Jim Pilot, New Mexico State, 1961
Howard Twilley, Tulsa, 1964

Career: 13, Pat McCarthy, Holy Cross, 1960–62

Source: NCAA

LONGEST PLAYS

Run from scrimmage 99 yards by four players: Gale Sayers (Kansas *v.* Nebraska), 1963; Max Anderson (Arizona State *v.* Wyoming), 1967; Ralph Thompson (West Texas State *v.* Wichita State), 1970; Kelsey Finch (Tennessee *v.* Florida), 1977.

Field Goal 67 yards by three players: Russell Erxleben (Texas *v.* Rice), 1977; Steve Little (Arkansas *v.* Texas), 1977; Joe Williams (Wichita State *v.* Southern Illinois), 1978.

Pass Completion 99 yards by seven players: Fred Owens (to Jack Ford), Portland *v.* St. Mary's, CA, 1947; Bo Burris (to Warren McVea), Houston *v.* Washington State, 1966; Colin Clapton (to Eddie Jenkins), Holy Cross *v.* Boston U, 1970; Terry Peel (to Robert Ford), Houston *v.* Syracuse, 1970; Terry Peel (to Robert Ford), Houston *v.* San Diego State, 1972; Cris Collingsworth (to Derrick Gaffney), Florida *v.* Rice, 1977; Scott Ankrom (to James Maness), TCU *v.* Rice, 1984.

Punt 99 yards by Pat Brady, Nevada-Reno *v.* Loyola, CA in 1950.

Biggest Boot On 16 October 1976, Ove Johannson, Abilene Christian, kicked the longest field goal in football history. With a tail wind of 18-20 mph the ball traveled an amazing 69 yards for the score.

CONSECUTIVE RECORDS

REGULAR SEASON (TEAM-DIV I-A)

Wins 47, Oklahoma, 1953–57.

Undefeated (including Bowl Games) 63, Washington (59 wins, 4 ties), 1907–17.

Losses 34, Northwestern. This undesirable streak started on 22 September 1979 and was finally snapped three years later on 25 September 1982 when Northern Illinois succumbed to the Wildcats 31–6.

REGULAR SEASON (INDIVIDUAL-DIV I-A)

Scoring Touchdowns (Games) 23, Bill Burnett, Arkansas. Burnett amassed 47 touchdowns during his 23-game streak, which ran from 5 October 1968–31 October 1970.

Point After Touchdown Attempts (PATs) 135 shared by two players: Van Tiffin, Alabama (1983–86); Tim Leshar, Oklahoma (1984–86).

Field Goals 30, Chuck Nelson, Washington, 1981–82.

Field Goals (Games) 19 shared by two players: Larry Roach, Oklahoma State (1983–84); Gary Gussman, Miami (Ohio) (1986–87).

100 yards + rushing (Games) 31, Archie Griffin, Ohio State, 15 September 1973–22 November 1975.

200 yards + rushing (Games) 5, Barry Sanders, Oklahoma State, 1988.

Passes Completed 22 shared by two players: Steve Young, BYU *v.* Utah State, 30 October 1982, *v.* Wyoming, 6 November 1982; Chuck Long, Iowa *v.* Indiana, 27 October 1984.

Touchdown Passes (Games) 22, Steve Young, BYU, 1982–83.

Touchdown Passes (Consecutive) 6, Brooks Dawson, UTEP *v.* New Mexico, 28 October 1967. Dawson completed his first 6 passes for touchdowns, which must rank as the greatest start to a game ever.

Touchdown Receptions (Games) 10, Mike Chronister, BYU, 1976–77.

Pass Receptions (Games) 44, Gary Williams, Ohio State, 1979–82.

NATIONAL CHAMPIONS 1924–1990

In 1924 Professor Frank G. Dickinson devised a mathematical point system, the Dickinson System to calculate the national college football champion. In 1936 the Associated Press introduced the AP poll, a ranking of college teams per a vote of sportswriters and broadcasters. In 1950 United Press, now UPI, introduced a coaches' poll. The Dickinson System was abandoned in 1940, but the AP and UPI polls are still used as the basis for declaring the national college football champion. AP and UPI have chosen different champions on eight occasions; 1954, 1957, 1965, 1970, 1973, 1974, 1978, 1990.

Year	Team	Record
1924	Notre Dame	10–0–0
1925	Dartmouth	10–0–0
1926	Stanford	10–0–1
1927	Illinois	7–0–1
1928	Southern Cal	9–0–1
1929	Notre Dame	9–0–0
1930	Notre Dame	10–0–0
1931	Southern Cal	10–1–0
1932	Michigan	8–0–0
1933	Michigan	7–0–1
1934	Minnesota	8–0–0
1935	SMU	12–1–0
1936	Minnesota	7–1–0
1937	Pittsburgh	9–0–1
1938	TCU	11–0–0
1939	Texas A&M	11–0–0
1940	Minnesota	8–0–0
1941	Minnesota	8–0–0
1942	Ohio State	9–1–0
1943	Notre Dame	9–1–0
1944	Army	9–0–0
1945	Army	9–0–0
1946	Notre Dame	8–0–1
1947	Notre Dame	9–0–0
1948	Michigan	9–0–0
1949	Notre Dame	10–0–0
1950	Oklahoma	10–0–0
1951	Tennessee	10–0–0
1952	Michigan State	9–0–0
1953	Maryland	10–1–0
1954	Ohio State (AP)	10–0–0
	UCLA (UPI)	9–0–0
1955	Oklahoma	11–0–0
1956	Oklahoma	10–0–0
1957	Auburn (AP)	10–0–0
	Ohio State (UPI)	9–1–0

NATIONAL CHAMPIONS 1924–1990 (Continued)

Year	Team	Record
1958	LSU	11–0–0
1959	Syracuse	11–0–0
1960	Minnesota	8–2–0
1961	Alabama	11–0–0
1962	Southern Cal	11–0–0
1963	Texas	11–0–0
1964	Alabama	10–1–0
1965	Alabama (AP)	9–1–1
	Michigan State (UPI)	10–1–0
1966	Notre Dame	9–0–1
1967	Southern Cal	10–1–0
1968	Ohio State	10–0–0
1969	Texas	11–0–0
1970	Nebraska (AP)	11–0–1
	Texas (UPI)	10–1–0
1972	Southern Cal	12–0–0
1973	Notre Dame (AP)	11–0–0
	Alabama (UPI)	11–1–0
1974	Oklahoma (AP)	11–0–0
	Southern Cal (UPI)	10–1–0
1975	Oklahoma	11–1–0
1976	Pittsburgh	12–0–0
1977	Notre Dame	11–1–0
1978	Alabama (AP)	11–1–0
	Southern Cal (UPI)	12–1–0
1980	Georgia	12–0–0
1981	Clemson	12–0–0
1982	Penn State	11–1–0
1983	Miami, FL	11–1–0
1984	BYU	13–0–0
1985	Oklahoma	11–1–0
1986	Penn State	12–0–0
1987	Miami, FL	12–0–0
1988	Notre Dame	12–0–0
1989	Miami, FL	10–1–0
1990	Colorado (AP)	11–1–1
	Georgia Tech (UPI)	11–0–1

Most Wins (1924–90) 11, Notre Dame (1924, 1929–30, 1943, 1946–47, 1949, 1966, 1973, 1977, 1988).

BOWL GAMES

The oldest college bowl game is the Rose Bowl. First played on 1 January 1902 at Tournament

WHO'S NUMBER 1?

The Distribution of the National College Football Champions by State

State	Wins	Teams
Indiana	11	Notre Dame 11
California	9	Southern Cal 7, UCLA 1, Stanford 1
Texas	6	Texas 3, SMU 1, TCU 1, Texas A&M 1
Oklahoma	6	Oklahoma 6
Alabama	6	Alabama 5, Auburn 1
Michigan	5	Michigan 3, Michigan State 2
Minnesota	5	Minnesota 5
Pennsylvania	4	Pittsburgh 2, Penn State 2
Ohio	4	Ohio State 4
Florida	3	Miami 3
New York	3	Army 2, Syracuse 1
Georgia	2	Georgia 1, Georgia Tech 1
New Hampshire	1	Dartmouth 1
Illinois	1	Illinois 1
Tennessee	1	Tennessee 1
Maryland	1	Maryland 1
Louisiana	1	LSU 1
Nebraska	1	Nebraska 1
South Carolina	1	Clemson 1
Utah	1	BYU 1
Colorado	1	Colorado 1

Park, Pasadena, CA, where Michigan, defeated Stanford 49–0. The second game did not take place until 1916, but has been played continuously since.

The other three bowl games that make up the "big four" are the Orange Bowl, initiated in 1935, the Sugar Bowl, 1935 and the Cotton Bowl, 1937.

THUD! ■ ON 16 OCTOBER 1976, OVE JOHANN-SON, ABILENE CHRISTIAN, KICKED THE LONGEST FIELD GOAL IN FOOTBALL HISTORY. WITH A TAIL WIND OF 18-20 MPH THE BALL TRAVELED AN AMAZ-ING 69 YARDS FOR THE SCORE.

MOST WINS

Rose Bowl 19, Southern Cal.

Orange Bowl 11, Oklahoma.

Sugar Bowl 7, Alabama.

Cotton Bowl 9, Texas.

Alabama, Georgia and Notre Dame are the only three teams to have won each of the "big four" bowl games. Alabama has played in the most bowl games, 43, and won the most bowl games, 23.

HEISMAN TROPHY

Awarded annually since 1935 by the Downtown Athletic Club of New York to the top college football player as determined by a poll of journalists, it was originally called the D.A.C. Trophy but the name was changed in 1936. Its full title is the John W. Heisman Memorial Trophy and is named after the first athletic director of the Downtown Athletic Club. The only double winner has been Archie Griffin of Ohio State, 1974–75. Notre Dame, with seven, has had more Heisman Trophy winners than any other school.

HEISMAN TROPHY WINNERS

Year	Player	Team	Position
1935	Jay Berwanger	Chicago	Halfback
1936	Larry Kelley	Yale	End
1937	Clint Frank	Yale	Halfback
1938	Davey O'Brien	TCU	Quarterback
1939	Nile Kinnick	Iowa	Halfback
1940	Tom Harmon	Michigan	Halfback
1941	Bruce Smith	Minnesota	Halfback

HEISMAN TROPHY WINNERS (Continued)

Year	Player	Team	Position
1942	Frank Sinkwich	Georgia	Tailback
1943	Angelo Bertelli	Notre Dame	Quarterback
1944	Les Horvath	Ohio State	Tailback-Quarterback
1945	Doc Blanchard	Army	Fullback
1946	Glenn Davis	Army	Halfback
1947	Johnny Lubjack	Notre Dame	Quarterback
1948	Doak Walker	SMU	Halfback
1949	Leon Hart	Notre Dame	End
1950	Vic Janowicz	Ohio State	Halfback
1951	Dick Kazmaier	Princeton	Tailback
1952	Billy Vessels	Oklahoma	Halfback
1953	Johnny Lattner	Notre Dame	Halfback
1954	Alan Ameche	Wisconsin	Fullback
1955	Howard Cassady	Ohio State	Halfback
1956	Paul Hornung	Notre Dame	Quarterback
1957	John David Crow	Texas A&M	Halfback
1958	Pete Dawkins	Army	Halfback
1959	Billy Cannon	LSU	Halfback
1960	Joe Bellino	Navy	Halfback
1961	Ernie Davis	Syracuse	Halfback
1962	Terry Baker	Oregon State	Quarterback
1963	Roger Staubach	Navy	Quarterback
1964	John Huarte	Notre Dame	Quarterback
1965	Mike Garrett	Southern Cal	Halfback
1966	Steve Spurrier	Florida	Quarterback
1967	Gary Beban	UCLA	Quarterback
1968	O. J. Simpson	Southern Cal	Halfback
1969	Steve Owens	Oklahoma	Halfback
1970	Jim Plunkett	Stanford	Quarterback
1971	Pat Sullivan	Auburn	Quarterback
1972	Johnny Rodgers	Nebraska	Flanker
1973	John Cappelletti	Penn State	Running Back
1974	Archie Griffin	Ohio State	Running Back
1975	Archie Griffin	Ohio State	Running Back
1976	Tony Dorsett	Pittsburgh	Running Back
1977	Earl Campbell	Texas	Running Back
1978	Billy Sims	Oklahoma	Running Back
1979	Charles White	Southern Cal	Running Back
1980	George Rogers	South Carolina	Running Back
1981	Marcus Allen	Southern Cal	Running Back
1982	Herschel Walker	Georgia	Running Back
1983	Mike Rozier	Nebraska	Running Back
1984	Doug Flutie	Boston College	Quarterback

HEISMAN TROPHY WINNERS (Continued)

Year	Player	Team	Position
1985	Bo Jackson	Auburn	Running Back
1986	Vinny Testarverde	Miami, FL	Quarterback
1987	Tim Brown	Notre Dame	Wide Receiver
1988	Barry Sanders	Oklahoma State	Running Back
1989	Andre Ware	Houston	Quarterback
1990	Ty Detmer	BYU	Quarterback

WINNINGEST COACH ■ COACH EDDIE ROBINSON, GRAMBLING, HAS WON 366 GAMES, THE MOST IN NCAA HISTORY. HIS COMPLETE RECORD IS 366 WINS, 128 LOSSES, 15 TIES THROUGH 1990.

HEISMAN WINNER ■ TY DETMER, BYU, WAS ELECTED THE HEISMAN TROPHY WINNER IN 1990. HE WAS THE FIRST WAC PLAYER TO WIN THE AWARD. DURING THE 1990 SEASON DETMER SET SEVERAL NCAA RECORDS, INCLUDING THE SEASON PASSING YARDAGE RECORD, WITH 5,188 YDS.

COACHES In Division 1-A competition, Paul "Bear" Bryant has won more games than any other coach with 323 victories over 38 years. Bryant coached four teams: Maryland, 1945 (6–2–1); Kentucky, 1956–53 (60–23–5); Texas A&M, 1954–57 (25–14–2); Alabama, 1958–82 (232–46–9). His completed record was 323 wins–85 losses–17 ties, with a .780 winning percentage. In overall NCAA competition, Eddie Robinson, Grambling (Division 1-AA) holds the mark for most victories with 366.

The highest winning percentage in Division 1-A competition is .881 held by Knute Rockne of Notre Dame. Rockne coached the Irish from 1918–30, with a record of 105 wins-12 losses-5 tied. In overall NCAA competition, Bob Reade, Augustana, Ill (Division III) had compiled a .890 winning percentage through 1989.

Attendances It has been estimated that crowds of 120,000 were present for two Notre Dame games played at Soldier Field, Chicago, IL: *v.* Southern Cal (26 November 1927); *v.* Navy (13 October 1928). Official attendance records have been kept by the NCAA since 1948. The highest official crowd for a regular season NCAA game was 106,255 Wolverine fans at Michigan Football Stadium, Ann Arbor MI, on 23 October 1983 for the Michigan *v.* Ohio State game. As Michigan lost 18–15, a record may have been set for the greatest number of depressed people at a football game!

WOLVERINE WORSHIP ▪ THE HIGHEST OFFICIAL CROWD FOR A REGULAR SEASON NCAA GAME WAS 106,255 FANS AT MICHIGAN FOOTBALL STADIUM, ANN ARBOR, ON 23 OCTOBER 1983 FOR THE MICHIGAN V. OHIO STATE GAME. THE BUCKEYES BEAT THE WOLVERINES 18-15, SO MUCH FOR HOME FIELD ADVANTAGE!

The record attendance for a Bowl game is 106,869 people at the 1973 Rose Bowl, where Southern Cal defeated Ohio State 42–17.

The highest average attendance for home games is 105,588 for the six games played by Michigan in 1985.

CANADIAN FOOTBALL LEAGUE (CFL)

ORIGINS The earliest recorded football game in Canada was an intramural contest between students of the University of Toronto on 9 November 1861. As with football in the US, the development of the game in Canada dates from a contest between two universities—McGill and Harvard played in May 1874. In 1909, Lord Earl Grey, the governor general of Canada, donated a trophy that was to be awarded to the Canadian Rugby Football champion. The competition for the Grey Cup evolved during the first half of the 20th century from an open competition for amateurs, college teams and hybrid rugby teams to the championship of the professional Canadian Football League that was formed in 1958.

Canadian football differs in many ways from its counterpart in the US. The major distinctions being: number of players (CFL-12, NFL-11); size of field (CFL-110 yd x 65 yd, NFL-100 yd x 53 yd); downs (CFL-3, NFL-4) and a completely different system for scoring and penalties.

The current CFL is comprised of eight teams in two divisions, the Western and Eastern. The divisional playoff champions meet in the Grey Cup to decide the CFL champion.

CANADIAN FOOTBALL LEAGUE (CFL) RECORDS

POINTS

Game: 36, Bob McNamara, Winnipeg Blue Bombers v. B.C. Lions, 13 October 1956

Season: 233, Paul Osbaldiston, Hamilton Tiger-Cats, 1989

Career: 2,237, Dave Cutler, Edmonton Eskimos, 1969–84

TOUCHDOWNS

Scored

Game: 6, Eddie James, Winnipegs v. Winnipeg St. Johns, 28 September 1932
Bob McNamara, Winnipeg Blue Bombers v. B.C. Lions, 13 October 1956

Season: 20, Pat Abbruzzi, Montreal Alouettes, 1956

Career: 137, George Reed, Saskatchewan Roughriders, 1963–75

Passing

Game: 8, Joe Zugler, Hamilton Tiger-Cats, 15 October 1962

Season: 40, Peter Liske, Calgary Stampeders, 1967

Career: 333, Ron Lancaster, Ottawa Roughriders/Saskatchewan Roughriders, 1960–78

CANADIAN FOOTBALL LEAGUE (CFL) RECORDS (Continued)

TOUCHDOWNS (Continued)

Receptions

Game: 5, Ernie Pitts, Winnipeg Blue Bombers v. Saskatchewan Roughriders, 29 August 1959

Season: 18, Brian Kelly, Edmonton Eskimos, 1984
David Williams, BC Lions, 1988

Career: 97, Brian Kelly, Edmonton Eskimos, 1979–87

Rushing

Game: 5, Earl Lunsford, Calgary Stampeders v. Edmonton Eskimos, 3 September 1962

Season: 18, Gerry James, Winnipeg Blue Bombers, 1957
Jim Germany, Edmonton Eskimos, 1981

Career: 134, George Reed, Saskatchewan Roughriders, 1963–75

PASSING

Yards Gained

Game: 586, Sam Etcheverry, Montreal Alouettes v. Hamilton Tiger-Cats, 16 October 1954

Season: 5,648, Warren Moon, Edmonton Eskimos, 1983

Career: 50,535, Ron Lancaster, Ottawa Roughriders/Saskatchewan Roughriders, 1960–78

Completions

Game: 41, Dieter Brock, Winnipeg Blue Bombers v. Ottawa Roughriders, 3 October 1981

Season: 380, Warren Moon, Edmonton Eskimos, 1983

Career: 3,384, Ron Lancaster, Ottawa Roughriders/Saskatchewan Roughriders, 1960–87

PASS RECEIVING

Receptions

Game: 16, Terry Greer, Toronto Argonauts v. Ottawa Roughriders, 19 August 1983

Season: 116, James Murphy, Winnipeg Blue Bombers, 1986

Career: 655, Rocky DiPietro, Hamilton Tiger-Cats, 1978–89

Yards Gained

Game: 338, Hal Patterson, Montreal Alouettes v. Hamilton Tiger-Cats, 29 September 1956

Season: 2,003, Terry Greer, Toronto Argonauts, 1983

Career: 11,169, Brian Kelly, Edmonton Eskimos, 1979–87

RUSHING

Yards Gained

Game: 287, Ron Stewart, Ottawa Roughriders v. Montreal Alouettes, 10 October 1960

Season: 1,896, Willie Burden, Calgary Stampeders, 1975

Career: 16,116, George Reed, Saskatchewan Roughriders, 1963–75

Source: Canadian Football Hall of Fame & Museum

MOON SHINES ■ WARREN MOON, NOW CHASING NFL RECORDS IN HOUSTON, SET TWO CFL SEASON PASSING RECORDS DURING HIS CAREER WITH THE EDMONTON ESKIMOS: MOST YARDS GAINED (5,648) AND MOST COMPLETIONS (380), BOTH SET IN 1983.

CFL TEAM RECORDS

Longest Winning Streak The Calgary Stampeders won 22 consecutive games between 25 August 1948 to 22 October 1949 to set the CFL mark.

Longest Winless Streak The Hamilton Tiger-Cats hold the dubious distinction of being the CFL's most futile team, amassing a 20-game winless streak (0–19–1), from 28 September 1948 to 2 September 1950.

Highest Scoring Game The Calgary Stampeders defeated Hamilton Tiger-Cats 55–48 on 17 October 1982, to set a CFL combined score record of 103 points.

Highest Score by One Team The Montreal Alouettes rolled over the Hamilton Tiger-Cats 82–14 on 20 October 1956 to set the CFL highest score mark.

GREY CUP GAME RECORDS

POINTS

Game: 23, Don Sweet, Montreal Alouettes *v.* Edmonton Eskimos, 27 November 1977

Career: 72, Dave Cutler, Edmonton Eskimos, 1973–75, 77–80, 82

TOUCHDOWNS

Game: 3, Ross Craig, Hamilton Tigers *v.* Toronto Parkdale, 29 November 1913
Red Storey, Toronto Argonauts *v.* Hamilton Tiger-Cats, 10 December 1938
Jackie Parker, Edmonton Eskimos *v.* Montreal Alouettes, 24 November 1956
Tommy Scott, Edmonton Eskimos *v.* Hamilton Tiger-Cats, 23 November 1980

Career: 5, Hal Patterson, Montreal Alouettes/Hamilton Tiger-Cats, 1955–56, 63
Brian Kelly, Edmonton Eskimos, 1980, 82, 86–87

CONVERTS

Game: 7, Pep Leadlay, Queens *v.* Regina Roughriders, 1 December 1923

Career: 17, Don Sutherin, Hamilton Tiger-Cats/Ottawa Roughriders, 1961–65, 68–69

SINGLES

Game: 8, Hugh Gall, University of Toronto *v.* Toronto Parkdale, 4 December 1909

Career: 12, Hugh Gall, University of Toronto, 1909–10

GREY CUP GAME RECORDS (Continued)

FIELD GOALS

Game: 6, Don Sweet, Montreal Alouettes *v.* Edmonton Eskimos, 27 November 1977
Paul Osbaldiston, Hamilton Tiger-Cats *v.* Edmonton Eskimos, 30 November 1986

Career: 18, Dave Cutler, Edmonton Eskimos, 1973–75, 77–80, 82

Source: Canadian Football Hall of Fame & Museum

GREY CUP RECORD ■ PAUL OSBALDISTON, HAMILTON TIGER-CATS, TIED THE GREY CUP MARK FOR FIELD GOALS, BOOTING SIX IN THE 1986 GAME.

THE GREY CUP

The Toronto Argonauts have won the most Grey Cups with 11 championships: 1914, 1921, 1933, 1937-38, 1945-47, 1950, 1952, 1983.

FRISBEE
(FLYING DISC THROWING)

ORIGINS The design of a carved plastic flying disc was patented in the United States by Fred Morrison in 1948. In 1957 Wham-O Inc. of San Gabriel, CA bought Morrison's patent and trademarked the name *frisbee* in 1958. In 1968 Wham-O helped form the International Frisbee Association (IFA) as a vehicle for organizing the frisbee craze that had swept across the United States. The IFA folded in 1982 and it wasn't until 1986 that the World Flying Disc Federation was formed to organize and standardize rules for the sport.

FRISBEE DISTANCE RECORDS

Men: 623 ft 7 in, Sam Ferrins (US), 2 July 1988

Women: 426 ft 9½ in, Amy Bekkan (US), 25 June 1990

THROW, RUN, CATCH

Men: 303 ft 11 in, Hiroshi Oshima (Japan), 20 July 1988

Women: 196 ft 11 in, Judy Horowitz (US), 29 June 1985

TIME ALOFT

Men: 16.72 sec, Don Cain (US), 26 May 1984

Women: 11.75 sec, Anni Kreml (US), 21 July 1988

GAELIC FOOTBALL

ORIGINS The game developed from interparish "free for all," with no time limit, specific playing areas or rules. The earliest reported match was Meath *v.* Louth, at Slane in 1712. Standardization came with the formation of the Gaelic Athletic Association in Thurles, Ireland on 1 November 1884.

ALL-IRELAND CHAMPIONSHIPS The greatest number of All-Ireland Championships won by one team is 30, by Ciarraidhe (Kerry) between 1903 and 1986.

The greatest number of successive wins is four, by Wexford (1915–18) and Kerry twice (1929–32, 1978–81).

The most finals contested by an individual is 10, including eight wins by the Kerry players Pat Spillane, Paudie O'Shea and Denis Moran, 1975–76, 1978–82, 1984–86.

The highest team score in a final was when Dublin, 27 (5 goals, 12 points), beat Armagh, 15(3 goals, 6 points), on 25 September 1977.

The highest combined score was 45 points when Cork (26) beat Galway (19) in 1973. A goal equals 3 points.

The highest individual score in an All-Ireland final is 2 goals, 6 points, by Jimmy Keaveney (Dublin) *v.* Armagh in 1977, and by Michael Sheehy (Kerry) *v.* Dublin in 1979.

Largest crowd The record crowd is 90,556 for the Down *v.* Offaly final at Croke Park, Dublin in 1961.

GLIDING

ORIGINS Research by Isadore William Deiches has shown evidence of the use of gliders in ancient Egypt *c.* 2500–1500 B.C. Emanuel Swedenborg of Sweden made sketches of gliders *c.* 1714. The earliest man-carrying glider was designed by Sir George Cayley and carried his coachman (possibly John Appleby) about 500 yd across a valley in Brompton Dale, North Yorkshire, England in the summer of 1853.

Most titles The most World Individual Championships (instituted 1937) won is 4, by Ingo Renner (Australia) in 1976 (Standard class), 1983, 1985 and 1987 (Open).

United States The most titles won by a US pilot is two by George Moffat, in the Open category, 1970 and 1974.

Women's altitude records The women's single-seater world record for absolute altitude is 41,449 ft, by Sabrina Jackintell (US) in an Astir GS on 14 February 1979.

The height gain record is 33,506 ft, by Yvonne Loader (New Zealand) at Omarama, New Zealand on 12 January 1988.

HANG GLIDING

ORIGINS In the 11th century the monk Eilmer is reported to have flown from the 60 ft tower of Malmesbury Abbey, Wiltshire, England. The ear-

GLIDING WORLD RECORDS
(Single-seaters)

	DISTANCE	NAME	TYPE OF GLIDER	LOCATION	DATE
Straight Distance:	907.7 mi	Hans-Werner Grosse (West Germany)	ASW-12	Lübeck, W. Germany to Biarritz, France	25 April 1972
Declared Goal Distance:	779.4 mi	Bruce Drake (New Zealand)	Nimbus 2	Te Anau to Te Araroa, New Zealand	14 January 1978
		David Speight (New Zealand)	Nimbus 2	Te Anau to Te Araroa, New Zealand	14 January 1978
		Dick Georgeson (New Zealand)	Nimbus 2	Te Anau to Te Araroa, New Zealand	14 January 1978
Goal and Return:	1,023.2 mi	Tom Knauff (US)	Nimbus 3	Williamsport, PA to Knoxville, TN	25 April 1983
Absolute Altitude:	49,009 ft	Robert R. Harris (US)	Grob G102	California	17 February 1986
Height Gain:	42,303 ft	Paul Bikle (US)	Schweitzer SGSI-23E	Mojave, CA	25 February 1961

GLIDING WORLD RECORDS (Continued)

SPEED OVER TRIANGULAR COURSE

DISTANCE	SPEED	NAME	TYPE OF GLIDER	LOCATION	DATE
100 km:	121.35	Ingo Renner (Australia)	Nimbus 3	Australia	14 December 1982
300 km:	105.32	Jean-Paul Castel (France)	Nimbus 3	South Africa	15 November 1986
500 km:	105.67	Beat Bunzli (Switzerland)	Nimbus 3	South Africa	18 December 1987
750 km:	98.43	Hans-Werner Grosse (West Germany)	ASW-22	Australia	8 January 1985
1,000 km:	90.29	Hans-Werner Grosse (West Germany)	ASW-17	Australia	3 January 1979
1,250 km:	82.79	Hans-Werner Grosse (West Germany)	ASW-17	Australia	9 January 1980

liest modern pioneer was Otto Lilienthal (Germany), with about 2,500 flights in gliders of his own construction between 1891 and 1896. In the 1950s, Professor Francis Rogallo of the National Space Agency developed a flexible "wing" from his space capsule re-entry research.

WORLD CHAMPIONSHIPS The World Team Championships (officially instituted 1976) have been won a record 3 times by Great Britain (1981, 1985 and 1989).

WORLD RECORDS The Fédération Aéronautique Internationale recognizes world records for rigid-wing, flex-wing and multiplace flex-wing. These records are the greatest in each category—all by flex-wing gliders.

Men

Greatest distance in straight line 300.757 miles, Larry Tudor (US), Hobbs, NM, 3 July 1990.

Height gain 14,250 ft, Larry Tudor (US), Owens Valley, CA, 4 August 1985.

Declared goal distance 216.67 miles, Larry Tudor (US), Owens Valley, 30 January 1988.

Out and return distance 192.818 miles, Larry Tudor (US) and Geoffrey Lyons (UK), Owens Valley, CA, 26 June 1988.

Triangular course distance 105 miles, Uli Blumenthal, Markus Hangstangl and Sepp Singhammer (all West Germany), St. André-les-Alps, France, 9 August 1990.

Women

Greatest distance 163.81 miles, Kathrine Yardley (US), Owens Valley, CA, 13 July 1989.

Height gain 11,997 ft, Tover Buas-Hansen (Norway), Owens Valley, CA, 6 July 1989.

Out and return distance 81.99 miles, Tover Buas-Hansen, Owens Valley, CA, 6 July 1989.

Declared goal distance 132.04 miles, Liavan Mallin (Ireland), Owens Valley, CA, 13 July 1989.

Triangular course distance Jenney Ganderton (Australia), 62.76 miles, Forbes, Australia, 22 January 1990.

GOLF

ORIGINS The Chinese Nationalist Golf Association claims that golf (*ch'ui wan*—the ball-hitting game") was played in China in the 3rd or 2nd century B.C. There is evidence that a game resembling golf was played in the Low Countries (present-day Belgium, Holland and northern France) in the Middle Ages. Scotland, however, is generally regarded as the home of the modern game. As early as 1457, the game was banned in Scotland; but the royal patronage of monarchs such as James IV made the game popular throughout Scotland. The oldest club of which there is written evidence is the Honourable Company of Edinburgh Golfers founded in 1744. The Royal & Ancient Club of St. Andrews (R&A), has been in existence since 1754. The R&A is credited with formulating the rules of

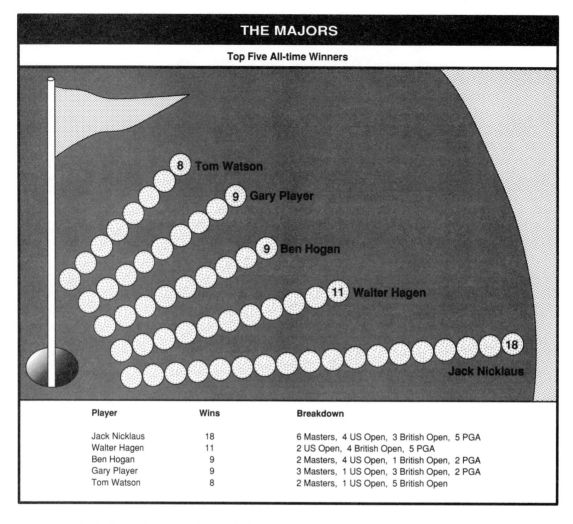

THE MAJORS

Top Five All-time Winners

8 Tom Watson
9 Gary Player
9 Ben Hogan
11 Walter Hagen
18 Jack Nicklaus

Player	Wins	Breakdown
Jack Nicklaus	18	6 Masters, 4 US Open, 3 British Open, 5 PGA
Walter Hagen	11	2 US Open, 4 British Open, 5 PGA
Ben Hogan	9	2 Masters, 4 US Open, 1 British Open, 2 PGA
Gary Player	9	3 Masters, 1 US Open, 3 British Open, 2 PGA
Tom Watson	8	2 Masters, 1 US Open, 5 British Open

golf, upon which the modern game is based. There are claims that golf was played in the United States as early as the 18th century in North Carolina and Virginia. The oldest recognized club in North America is the Royal Montreal Golf Club, Canada formed on November 4, 1873. Two clubs claim to be the first established in the US: the Foxberg Golf Club, Clarion County, PA (1887), and St. Andrews Golf Club of Yonkers, NY (1888). The United States Golf Association (USGA) was founded in 1894 as the governing body of golf in the United States.

GRAND SLAM CHAMPIONSHIPS (MEN)

GRAND SLAM In 1930, Bobby Jones won the US and British Open Championships and the US and British Amateur Championships. This feat was christened the "Grand Slam." In 1960, the profes-sional Grand Slam (the Masters, US Open, British Open and Professional Golfers Association [PGA] Championships), gained recognition when Arnold Palmer won the first two legs, the Masters and the US Open. However, he did not complete the set of titles, and the Grand Slam has still not been attained. Ben Hogan came the closest in 1951, when he won the first three legs, but didn't return to the US from Great Britain in time for the PGA Championship.

The four Grand Slam events are also known as "the majors." Jack Nicklaus has won the most majors, with 18 professional titles (6 Masters, 4 US Opens, 3 British Opens, 5 PGA Championships). Additionally, Nicklaus has won 2 US Amateur titles.

THE MASTERS Inaugurated in 1934, this event is held annually at the 6,980-yd Augusta National Golf Club, Augusta, GA.

MASTERS CHAMPIONS 1934–1990

Year	Champion	Year	Champion
1934	Horton Smith	1963	Jack Nicklaus
1935	Gene Sarazen	1964	Arnold Palmer
1936	Horton Smith	1965	Jack Nicklaus
1937	Byron Nelson	1966	Jack Nicklaus
1938	Henry Picard	1967	Gay Brewer
1939	Ralph Guldahl	1968	Bob Goalby
1940	Jimmy Demaret	1969	George Archer
1941	Craig Wood	1970	Billy Casper
1942	Byron Nelson	1971	Charles Coody
1943	not held	1972	Jack Nicklaus
1944	not held	1973	Tommy Aaron
1945	not held	1974	Gary Player
1946	Herman Keiser	1975	Jack Nicklaus
1947	Jimmy Demaret	1976	Raymond Floyd
1948	Claude Harmon	1977	Tom Watson
1949	Sam Snead	1978	Gary Player
1950	Jimmy Demaret	1979	Fuzzy Zoeller
1951	Ben Hogan	1980	Seve Ballesteros
1952	Sam Snead	1981	Tom Watson
1953	Ben Hogan	1982	Craig Stadler
1954	Sam Snead	1983	Seve Ballesteros
1955	Cary Middlecoff	1984	Ben Crenshaw
1956	Jack Burke Jr.	1985	Bernhard Langer
1957	Doug Ford	1986	Jack Nicklaus
1958	Arnold Palmer	1987	Larry Mize
1959	Art Wall Jr.	1988	Sandy Lyle
1960	Arnold Palmer	1989	Nick Faldo
1961	Gary Player	1990	Nick Faldo
1962	Arnold Palmer		

Most Wins Jack Nicklaus has won the coveted green jacket a record six times (1963, 1965–66, 1972, 1975, 1986).

Consecutive Wins Jack Nicklaus (1965–66) and Nick Faldo (1989–90) are the only two players to have won back-to-back Masters.

Lowest 72-hole total 271, by Jack Nicklaus (67, 71, 64, 69) in 1965; and Raymond Floyd (65, 66, 70, 70) in 1976.

Oldest Champion 46 yr 81 days, Jack Nicklaus (1986).

Youngest Champion 23 yr 2 days, Severiano Ballesteros (1980).

THE UNITED STATES OPEN Inaugurated in 1895, this event is held on a different course each year. The Open was expanded from a three-day, 36-hole Saturday finish to four days of 18 holes of play in 1965.

US OPEN CHAMPIONS 1895–1990

Year	Champion	Year	Champion
1895	Horace Rawlins	1934	Olin Dutra
1896	James Foulis	1935	Sam Parks Jr.
1897	Joe Lloyd	1936	Tony Manero
1898	Fred Herd	1937	Ralph Guldahl
1899	Willie Smith	1938	Ralph Guldahl
1900	Harry Vardon	1939	Byron Nelson
1901	Willie Anderson	1940	Lawson Little
1902	Laurie Auchterlonie	1941	Craig Wood
1903	Willie Anderson	1942	not held
1904	Willie Anderson	1943	not held
1905	Willie Anderson	1944	not held
1906	Alex Smith	1945	not held
1907	Alex Ross	1946	Lloyd Mangrum
1908	Fred McLeod	1947	Lew Worsham
1909	George Sargent	1948	Ben Hogan
1910	Alex Smith	1949	Cary Middlecoff
1911	John McDermott	1950	Ben Hogan
1912	John McDermott	1951	Ben Hogan
1913	Francis Ouimet	1952	Julius Boros
1914	Walter Hagen	1953	Ben Hogan
1915	Jerome Travers	1954	Ed Furgol
1916	Charles Evans Jr.	1955	Jack Fleck
1917	not held	1956	Cary Middlecoff
1918	not held	1957	Dick Mayer
1919	Walter Hagen	1958	Tommy Bolt
1920	Edward Ray	1959	Billy Casper
1921	Jim Barnes	1960	Arnold Palmer
1922	Gene Sarazen	1961	Gene Littler
1923	Bobby Jones	1962	Jack Nicklaus
1924	Cyril Walker	1963	Julius Boros
1925	Willie MacFarlane	1964	Ken Venturi
1926	Bobby Jones	1965	Gary Player
1927	Tommy Armour	1966	Billy Casper
1928	Johnny Farrell	1967	Jack Nicklaus
1929	Bobby Jones	1968	Lee Trevino
1930	Bobby Jones	1969	Orville Moody
1931	Billy Burke	1970	Tony Jacklin
1932	Gene Sarazen	1971	Lee Trevino
1933	Johnny Goodman	1972	Jack Nicklaus

THE MASTER OF THE MAJORS

Who is the best ever? Like almost every sport, golf is dominated by an elite group of players whose fans back their claims to the title "the best ever." If the standard is the player's record in golf's four professional grand slam events (The Masters, US Open, British Open, PGA Championship), also known as "the majors," then one player stands alone: Jack Nicklaus.

As a professional, Nicklaus has competed in 116 grand slam championship events; he has won 18 times, captured second 18 times, came in third 9 times and had 24 other top ten finishes. Additionally, as an amateur, he finished second in the 1960 US Open. His record of 18 victories and 70 top ten finishes overall is unparalleled in the history of golf.

THE MASTERS ■ JACK NICKLAUS HAS WON THE COVETED GREEN JACKET A RECORD SIX TIMES. NICKLAUS CELEBRATES A DRAMATIC PUTT DURING HIS 1975 WIN (LEFT), AND LEAVES THE 18TH GREEN WITH HIS SON, JACK JR. (ABOVE), FOLLOWING HIS FINAL ROUND IN 1986, A VICTORY THAT MADE HIM THE OLDEST MAN TO WIN THE EVENT.

PGA CHAMPIONSHIP ■ NICKLAUS HAS WON THE PGA FIVE TIMES, A RECORD HE SHARES WITH WALTER HAGEN. (ABOVE) NICKLAUS PLAYS A RECOVERY SHOT DURING HIS 1971 WIN, AND CELEBRATES HIS 1975 VICTORY (BELOW RIGHT).

US OPEN ■ NICKLAUS HAS WON THE US OPEN FOUR TIMES, A RECORD HE SHARES WITH THREE OTHER PLAYERS. NICKLAUS CELEBRATES ANOTHER LONG PUTT ON HIS WAY TO VICTORY IN 1967 (UPPER LEFT), AND DISPLAYS THE TROPHY FOLLOWING HIS VICTORIES IN 1972 (ABOVE) AND 1980 (UPPER RIGHT). IN 1980 AT BALTUSROL COUNTRY CLUB, NICKLAUS SHOT 272, THE LOWEST 72-HOLE SCORE IN US OPEN HISTORY.

BRITISH OPEN ■ NICKLAUS HAS WON THE BRITISH OPEN THREE TIMES AND FINISHED SECOND A RECORD SEVEN TIMES. ABOVE, NICKLAUS IS SHOWN CELEBRATING HIS 1980 WIN AT ST. ANDREWS, A VICTORY HE ACKNOWLEDGES AS ONE OF HIS MOST MEMORABLE.

TOP TEN FINISHES (1960–90)

Event	1st	2nd	3rd	4th	5th	6th	7th	8th	9th	10th	Total
Masters	6	4	2	2	1	2	2	1	—	—	20
US Open	4	4	1	1	—	2	1	1	1	2	17
British Open	3	7	3	2	1	1	—	—	—	1	18
PGA	5	4	3	2	—	1	—	—	—	—	15

US OPEN CHAMPIONS 1895–1990
(Continued)

Year	Champion	Year	Champion
1973	Johnny Miller	1982	Tom Watson
1974	Hale Irwin	1983	Larry Nelson
1975	Lou Graham	1984	Fuzzy Zoeller
1976	Jerry Pate	1985	Andy North
1977	Hubert Green	1986	Raymond Floyd
1978	Andy North	1987	Scott Simpson
1979	Hale Irwin	1988	Curtis Strange
1980	Jack Nicklaus	1989	Curtis Strange
1981	David Graham	1990	Hale Irwin

Most Wins Four players have won the title four times: Willie Anderson (1901, 1903–05); Bobby Jones (1923, 1926, 1929–30); Ben Hogan (1948, 1950–51, 1953); Jack Nicklaus (1962, 1967, 1972, 1980).

Consecutive Wins Three, Willie Anderson (1903–05).

Lowest 72-hole total 272 (63, 71, 70, 68), by Jack Nicklaus at Baltusrol Country Club, Springfield, NJ, in 1980.

Oldest Champion 45 yr 15 days, Hale Irwin (1990).

Youngest Champion 19 yr 317 days, John J. McDermott (1911).

THE BRITISH OPEN Inaugurated in 1860, the first dozen tournaments were staged at Prestwick, Scotland. Since 1873, the locations have varied, but all venues are coastal links courses.

BRITISH OPEN CHAMPIONS 1860–1990

Year	Champion	Year	Champion
1860	Willie Park Sr.	1874	Mungo Park
1861	Tom Morris Sr.	1875	Willie Park Sr.
1862	Tom Morris Sr.	1876	Bob Martin
1863	Willie Park Sr.	1877	Jamie Anderson
1864	Tom Morris Sr.	1878	Jamie Anderson
1865	Andrew Strath	1879	Jamie Anderson
1866	Willie Park Sr.	1880	Robert Ferguson
1867	Tom Morris Sr.	1881	Robert Ferguson
1868	Tom Morris Jr.	1882	Robert Ferguson
1869	Tom Morris Jr.	1883	Willie Fernie
1870	Tom Morris Jr.	1884	Jack Simpson
1871	not held	1885	Bob Martin
1872	Tom Morris Jr.	1886	David Brown
1873	Tom Kidd	1887	Willie Park Jr.

BRITISH OPEN CHAMPIONS 1860–1990
(Continued)

Year	Champion	Year	Champion
1888	Jack Burns	1931	Tommy Armour
1889	Willie Park Jr.	1932	Gene Sarazen
1890	John Ball	1933	Densmore Shute
1891	Hugh Kirkaldy	1934	Henry Cotton
1892	Harold H. Hilton	1935	Alfred Perry
1893	William Auchterlonie	1936	Alfred Padgham
1894	John H. Taylor	1937	Henry Cotton
1895	John H. Taylor	1938	Reg Whitcombe
1896	Harry Vardon	1939	Dick Burton
1897	Harold H. Hilton	1940	not held
1898	Harry Vardon	1941	not held
1899	Harry Vardon	1942	not held
1900	John H. Taylor	1943	not held
1901	James Braid	1944	not held
1902	Sandy Herd	1945	not held
1903	Harry Vardon	1946	Sam Snead
1904	Jack White	1947	Fred Daly
1905	James Braid	1948	Henry Cotton
1906	James Braid	1949	Bobby Locke
1907	Arnaud Massy	1950	Bobby Locke
1908	James Braid	1951	Max Faulkner
1909	John H. Taylor	1952	Bobby Locke
1910	James Braid	1953	Ben Hogan
1911	Harry Vardon	1954	Peter Thomson
1912	Edward Ray	1955	Peter Thomson
1913	John H. Taylor	1956	Peter Thomson
1914	Harry Vardon	1957	Bobby Locke
1915	not held	1958	Peter Thomson
1916	not held	1959	Gary Player
1917	not held	1960	Kel Nagle
1918	not held	1961	Arnold Palmer
1919	not held	1962	Arnold Palmer
1920	George Duncan	1963	Bob Charles
1921	Jock Hutchinson	1964	Tony Lema
1922	Walter Hagen	1965	Peter Thomson
1923	Arthur Havers	1966	Jack Nicklaus
1924	Walter Hagen	1967	Roberto de Vicenzo
1925	Jim Barnes	1968	Gary Player
1926	Bobby Jones	1969	Tony Jacklin
1927	Bobby Jones	1970	Jack Nicklaus
1928	Walter Hagen	1971	Lee Trevino
1929	Walter Hagen	1972	Lee Trevino
1930	Bobby Jones	1973	Tom Weiskopf

BRITISH OPEN CHAMPIONS 1860–1990
(Continued)

Year	Champion	Year	Champion
1974	Gary Player	1983	Tom Watson
1975	Tom Watson	1984	Seve Ballesteros
1976	Johnny Miller	1985	Sandy Lyle
1977	Tom Watson	1986	Greg Norman
1978	Jack Nicklaus	1987	Nick Faldo
1979	Steve Ballesteros	1988	Seve Ballesteros
1980	Tom Watson	1989	Mark Calcavecchia
1981	Bill Rogers	1990	Nick Faldo
1982	Tom Watson		

Most Wins Harry Vardon won a record six titles, in 1896, 1898–99, 1903, 1911, 1914.

Consecutive Wins 4, Tom Morris Jr. (1868–70, 1872; the event was not held in 1871).

Lowest 72-hole total 268, (68, 70, 65, 65) by Tom Watson at Turnberry, Scotland in 1977.

Oldest Champion 46 yr 99 days, Tom Morris Sr. (1867).

Youngest Champion 17 yr 249 days, Tom Morris Jr. (1868).

THE PROFESSIONAL GOLFERS ASSOCIATION (PGA) CHAMPIONSHIP Inaugurated in 1916, the tournament was a match-play event, but switched to a 72-hole stroke-play event in 1958.

PGA CHAMPIONSHIP CHAMPIONS 1916–1990

Year	Champion	Year	Champion
1916	Jim Barnes	1932	Olin Dutra
1917	not held	1933	Gene Sarazen
1918	not held	1934	Paul Runyan
1919	Jim Barnes	1935	Johnny Revolta
1920	Jock Hutchinson	1936	Densmore Shute
1921	Walter Hagen	1937	Densmore Shute
1922	Gene Sarazen	1938	Paul Runyan
1923	Gene Sarazen	1939	Henry Picard
1924	Walter Hagen	1940	Byron Nelson
1925	Walter Hagen	1941	Vic Chezzi
1926	Walter Hagen	1942	Sam Snead
1927	Walter Hagen	1943	not held
1928	Leo Diegel	1944	Bob Hamilton
1929	Leo Diegel	1945	Byron Nelson
1930	Tommy Armour	1946	Ben Hogan
1931	Tom Creavy	1947	Jim Ferrier

PGA CHAMPIONSHIP CHAMPIONS 1916–1990 (Continued)

Year	Champion	Year	Champion
1948	Ben Hogan	1970	Dave Stockton
1949	Sam Snead	1971	Jack Nicklaus
1950	Chandler Harper	1972	Gary Player
1951	Sam Snead	1973	Jack Nicklaus
1952	Jim Turnesa	1974	Lee Trevino
1953	Walter Burkemo	1975	Jack Nicklaus
1954	Chick Harbert	1976	Dave Stockton
1955	Doug Ford	1977	Lanny Wadkins
1956	Jack Burke Jr.	1978	John Mahaffey
1957	Lionel Hebert	1979	David Graham
1958	Dow Finsterwald	1980	Jack Nicklaus
1959	Bob Rosburg	1981	Larry Nelson
1960	Jay Herbert	1982	Raymond Floyd
1961	Jerry Barber	1983	Hal Sutton
1962	Gary Player	1984	Lee Trevino
1963	Jack Nicklaus	1985	Hubert Green
1964	Bobby Nichols	1986	Bob Tway
1965	Dave Marr	1987	Larry Nelson
1966	Al Geiberger	1988	Jeff Sluman
1967	Don January	1989	Payne Stewart
1968	Julius Boros	1990	Wayne Grady
1969	Raymond Floyd		

Most Wins Two players have won the title five times: Walter Hagen (1921, 1924–27); and Jack Nicklaus (1963, 1971, 1973, 1975, 1980).

Consecutive Wins 4, Walter Hagen (1924–27).

Lowest 72-hole total 271 (64, 71, 69, 67), by Bobby Nichols at Columbus Country Club, OH in 1964.

Oldest Champion 48 yr 140 days, Julius Boros (1968).

Youngest Champion 20 yr 173 days, Gene Sarazen (1922).

GRAND SLAM CHAMPIONSHIPS (WOMEN)

GRAND SLAM A Grand Slam in ladies' professional golf has been recognized since 1955. From 1955–66, the United States Open, Ladies Professional Golfers Association (LPGA) Championship, Western Open and Titleholders Championship served as the "majors." From 1967–82 the Grand Slam events changed, as first the Western Open (1967) and then the Titleholders Championship (1972)

GRAND SLAM WINNER ■ PATTY BERG HAS WON A RECORD 15 WOMEN'S GRAND SLAM EVENTS.

Year	Champion	Year	Champion
1964	Mickey Wright	1978	Hollis Stacy
1965	Carol Mann	1979	Jerilyn Britz
1966	Sandra Spuzich	1980	Amy Alcott
1967	Catherine Lacoste	1981	Pat Bradley
1968	Susie Berning	1982	Janet Alex
1969	Donna Caponi	1983	Jan Stephenson
1970	Donna Caponi	1984	Hollis Stacy
1971	JoAnne Carner	1985	Kathy Baker
1972	Susie Berning	1986	Jane Geddes
1973	Susie Berning	1987	Laura Davies
1974	Sandra Haynie	1988	Liselotte Neumann
1975	Sandra Palmer	1989	Betsy King
1976	JoAnne Carner	1990	Betsy King
1977	Hollis Stacy		

Most Wins Two players have won the title four times: Betsy Rawls (1951, 1953, 1957, 1960); Mickey Wright (1958–59, 1961, 1964).

Consecutive Wins Two by five players: Mickey Wright (1958–59); Donna Caponi (1969–70); Susie Berning (1972–73); Hollis Stacy (1977–78); Betsy King (1989–90).

Lowest 72-hole total 279 by Pat Bradley at LaGrange Country Club, IL in 1981.

Oldest Champion 40 yr 11 months, Fay Croker (1955).

Youngest Champion 22 yr 5 days, Catherine Lacoste (1967).

LPGA CHAMPIONSHIP Inaugurated in 1955; since 1987 officially called the Mazda LPGA Championship.

were discontinued. Since 1983, the US Open, LPGA Championship, du Maurier Classic and Nabisco Dinah Shore have comprised the Grand Slam events.

Patty Berg has won the most majors with 15 titles (1 US Open, 7 Titleholders, 7 Western Open).

THE UNITED STATES OPEN Inaugurated in 1946. The first event was played as a match-play tournament; however, since 1947, the 72-hole stroke-play format has been used.

	US OPEN CHAMPIONS 1946–1990		
Year	Champion	Year	Champion
1946	Patty Berg	1955	Fay Crocker
1947	Betty Jameson	1956	Kathy Cornelius
1948	Babe Zaharias	1957	Betsy Rawls
1949	Louise Suggs	1958	Mickey Wright
1950	Babe Zaharias	1959	Mickey Wright
1951	Betsy Rawls	1960	Betsy Rawls
1952	Louise Suggs	1961	Mickey Wright
1953	Betsy Rawls	1962	Murle Lindstrom
1954	Babe Zaharias	1963	Mary Mills

	LPGA CHAMPIONSHIP CHAMPIONS 1955–1990		
Year	Champion	Year	Champion
1955	Beverly Hanson	1964	Mary Mills
1956	Marlene Hagge	1965	Sandra Haynie
1957	Louise Suggs	1966	Gloria Ehret
1958	Mickey Wright	1967	Kathy Whitworth
1959	Betsy Rawls	1968	Sandra Post
1960	Mickey Wright	1969	Betsy Rawls
1961	Mickey Wright	1970	Shirley Englehorn
1962	Judy Kimball	1971	Kathy Whitworth
1963	Mickey Wright	1972	Kathy Ahern

LPGA CHAMPIONSHIP CHAMPIONS
1955–1990 (Continued)

Year	Champion	Year	Champion
1973	Mary Mills	1982	Jan Stephenson
1974	Sandra Haynie	1983	Patty Sheehan
1975	Kathy Whitworth	1984	Patty Sheehan
1976	Betty Burfeindt	1985	Nancy Lopez
1977	Chako Higuchi	1986	Pat Bradley
1978	Nancy Lopez	1987	Jane Geddes
1979	Donna Caponi	1988	Sherri Turner
1980	Sally Little	1989	Nancy Lopez
1981	Donna Caponi	1990	Beth Daniel

Most Wins Mickey Wright has won the LPGA a record four times: 1958, 1960–61, 1963.

Consecutive Wins Two by two players: Mickey Wright (1960–61); Patty Sheehan (1983–84).

Lowest 72-hole total 272 by Patty Sheehan at the Jack Nicklaus Sports Center, Kings Island, OH in 1984.

NABISCO DINAH SHORE Inaugurated in 1972. Formerly the Colgate-Dinah Shore (1972–82). The event was designated a "major" in 1983. Mission Hills Country Club, Rancho Mirage, CA is the permanent site.

NABISCO DINAH SHORE CHAMPIONS
1972–1990

Year	Champion	Year	Champion
1972	Jane Blalock	1982	Sally Little
1973	Mickey Wright	1983	Amy Alcott
1974	Jo Ann Prentice	1984	Juli Inkster
1975	Sandra Palmer	1985	Alice Miller
1976	Judy Rankin	1986	Pat Bradley
1977	Kathy Whitworth	1987	Betsy King
1978	Sandra Post	1988	Amy Alcott
1979	Sandra Post	1989	Juli Inkster
1980	Donna Caponi	1990	Betsy King
1981	Nancy Lopez		

Most Wins Three players have won the title two times: Sandra Post (1978–79); Juli Inkster (1984, 1989); Betsy King (1987, 1990).

Consecutive Wins Two, Sandra Post (1978–79).

Lowest 72-hole total 274, Amy Alcott in 1988.

DU MAURIER CLASSIC Inaugurated in 1973; formerly known as La Canadienne (1973) and the Peter Jackson Classic (1974–82). Granted "major" status in 1979, the tournament is held annually at different sites in Canada.

DU MAURIER CLASSIC CHAMPIONS
1973–1990

Year	Champion	Year	Champion
1973	Jocelyne Bourassa	1982	Sandra Haynie
1974	Carole Jo Skala	1983	Hollis Stacy
1975	JoAnne Carner	1984	Juli Inkster
1976	Donna Caponi	1985	Pat Bradley
1977	Judy Rankin	1986	Pat Bradley
1978	JoAnne Carner	1987	Jody Rosenthal
1979	Amy Alcott	1988	Sally Little
1980	Pat Bradley	1989	Tammie Green
1981	Jan Stephenson	1990	Cathy Johnston

Most Wins Pat Bradley has won this event a record three times, 1980, 1985–86.

DU MAURIER CLASSIC ■ CATHY JOHNSTON WON THE 1990 DU MAURIER CLASSIC, THE FINAL LEG OF THE WOMEN'S GRAND SLAM, SHOOTING **276**, AND TIED THE **72-HOLE** LOWEST SCORE HELD BY PAT BRADLEY AND AYAKO OKAMOTO.

Most Consecutive Wins Two, Pat Bradley (1985–86).

Lowest 72-hole total 276 by three players: Pat Bradley and Ayako Okamato tied in regulation play in 1986 at the Board of Trade Country Club, Toronto. Bradley defeated Okamato for the title in a sudden-death playoff. Cathy Johnston matched Bradley and Okamato in 1990 at Westmont Golf and Country Club, Kitchener, Ontario.

PROFESSIONAL GOLFERS ASSOCIATION (PGA) TOUR RECORDS

Most Wins (Season) Byron Nelson won a record 18 tournaments in 1945.

Most Wins (Career) Sam Snead won 84 official PGA tour events from 1936–65.

Consecutive Wins 11, Byron Nelson, 1945.

Most Wins (Tournament) Sam Snead won the Greater Greensboro Open eight times to set the individual tournament win mark. His victories came in 1938, 1946, 1949–50, 1955–56, 1960, 1965.

LOWEST SCORES

18 Holes 59 (30 + 29), by Al Geiberger in the 2nd round of the Danny Thomas Classic, on the 72-par 7,249 yd Colonial Golf Club, Memphis, TN on 10 June 1977.

72 Holes 257, (60, 68, 64, 65), by Mike Souchak in the 1955 Texas Open at San Antonio.

Widest Winning Margin 16 strokes by Bobby Locke in the 1948 Chicago Victory National Championship.

HIGHEST EARNINGS

Season Tom Kite, $1,359,278 in 1989.

Career Tom Kite, $6,258,893.

PGA TOUR LEADING MONEY WINNERS (Career - through 1990)	
Player	Earnings
Tom Kite	$6,258,893
Tom Watson	$5,374,232
Curtis Strange	$5,292,892
Jack Nicklaus	$5,170,465
Lanny Wadkins	$4,614,381

Source: PGA Tour.

Most Times Leading Money Winner Eight, Jack Nicklaus, 1964–65, 1967, 1971–73, 1975–76.

FLYING HIGH! ■ TOM KITE IS THE PGA TOUR ALL-TIME LEADING MONEY WINNER. AT THE END OF THE 1990 SEASON, HIS EARNINGS WERE $6,258,893.

59! ■ AL GEIBERGER SHOT THE LOWEST 18-HOLE SCORE IN PGA TOUR HISTORY IN THE SECOND ROUND OF THE DANNY THOMAS CLASSIC ON 10 JUNE 1977.

Ladies Professional Golf Association (LPGA) Tour Records

Most Wins (Season) Mickey Wright won a record 13 tournaments in 1963.

Most Wins (Career) Kathy Whitworth won 88 official LPGA tour events from 1962–85.

Consecutive Wins Four by two players: Mickey Wright (1962); Kathy Whitworth (1969).

Successive Wins Between May and June 1978, Nancy Lopez won all five tournaments that she entered; however, these events did not follow each other and are therefore not considered consecutive tournament victories.

SUCCESSIVE WINS ■ **BETWEEN MAY AND JUNE 1978, NANCY LOPEZ WON ALL FIVE TOURNAMENTS THAT SHE ENTERED.**

Most Wins (Tournament) Patty Berg won two tournaments; the Titleholders Championship and the Western Open, both now defunct, seven times each. She won the Titleholders: 1937–39, 1948, 1953, 1955, 1957; and the Western: 1941, 1943, 1948, 1951, 1955, 1957–58.

Lowest Scores

18 Holes 62 by two players: Mickey Wright at the 1964 Tall City Open, Hogan Park Country Club, TX; Vicki Fergnon at the 1984 San Jose Classic, San Jose, CA.

72 Holes 268 by Nancy Lopez at the 1985 Henredon Classic in High Point, NC.

Widest Winning Margin 14 strokes by two players: Louise Suggs in the 1949 US Open at Prince Georges Country Club, Landover, MD; Cindy Mackey in the 1986 Mastercard International at Knollwood Country Club, Elmsford, NY.

LPGA MONEY WINNERS ■ **IN 1990, BETH DANIEL (ABOVE, TOP) WON A SEASON RECORD $863,578, WHILE PAT BRADLEY (ABOVE) EXTENDED HER CAREER RECORD EARNINGS TO $3,346,047.**

HIGHEST EARNINGS

Season: Beth Daniel, $863,578 in 1990

Career: Pat Bradley, $3,346,047

Most Times Leading Money Winner 8, Kathy Whitworth, 1965–8, 1970–3.

LPGA TOUR LEADING MONEY WINNERS (Career)

Player	Earnings
Pat Bradley	$3,346,047
Nancy Lopez	$3,026,470
Betsy King	$3,013,537
Beth Daniel	$2,893,482
Patty Sheehan	$2,830,464

Source: LPGA Tour

SENIOR PGA TOUR

The Senior PGA tour was established in 1982. Players 50 years and older are eligible to compete on the tour. Tournaments vary between 54 and 72-hole stroke-play.

Most Wins 24, Miller Barber (1981–90)

Most Wins (Season) Nine, Peter Thomson, 1985

Consecutive Wins Three by two players: Bob Charles and Chi Chi Rodriguez, both in 1987.

Season Earnings Lee Trevino, $1,190,518 in 1990.

SENIOR PGA TOUR LEADING MONEY WINNERS (Career - through 1990)

Player	Earnings
Bob Charles	$2,494,732
Miller Barber	$2,488,787
Chi Chi Rodriguez	$2,235,159
Bruce Crampton	$2,147,530
Orville Moody	$2,136,180

Source: PGA Tour

Lowest Score

18 holes: 61 by Lee Elder in the 1985 Merrill Lynch/Golf Digest Commemorative at Newport, RI.

54 holes (tournament win) 193 by Bob Charles in the 1989 Nynex/Golf Digest Commemorative at Scarborough, NY.

72 holes 263 by Orville Moody at the 1988 Vintage Chrysler International at Indian Wells, CA.

Youngest Winner 50 years 14 days, George Archer (1989 Gatlin Bros SW Classic)

Oldest Winner 63 years 0 days, Mike Fetchik (1985 Hilton Head Sr. International).

US SENIOR OPEN Inaugurated in 1980 for players 55 years and over; in 1981 the minimum age requirement was dropped to 50 years. Arnold

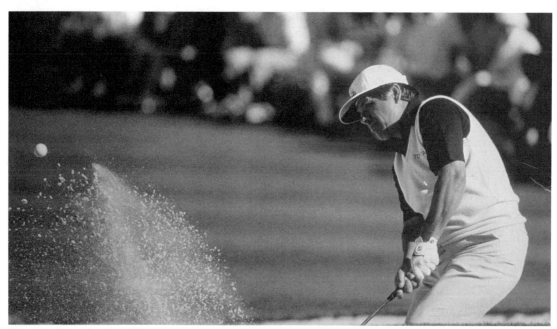

MILLION DOLLAR MEX ■ IN 1990, LEE TREVINO BECAME THE FIRST MILLION DOLLAR WINNER ON THE SENIOR PGA TOUR, EARNING $1,190,518.

Palmer, Billy Casper, Orville Moody and Lee Trevino are the only players to have won both the US Open and US Senior Open.

US SENIOR OPEN CHAMPIONS 1980–1990

Year	Champion	Year	Champion
1980	Roberto de Vicenzo	1986	Dale Douglass
1981	Arnold Palmer	1987	Gary Player
1982	Miller Barber	1988	Gary Player
1983	Billy Casper	1989	Orville Moody
1984	Miller Barber	1990	Lee Trevino
1985	Miller Barber		

Most Wins 3, Miller Barber, 1982, 1984–85.

UNITED STATES AMATEUR CHAMPIONSHIP Inaugurated in 1895, the initial format was match-play competition. In 1965, the format was changed to stroke-play, however, since 1972, the event has been played under the original match-play format.

Most Wins 5, by Bobby Jones, 1924–25, 1927–28, 1930.

Lowest Score (stroke-play) 279, Lanny Wadkins, 1970.

Biggest Winning Margin (match-play: final) 12 & 11, Charles Macdonald, 1895.

NCAA CHAMPIONSHIP The Men's championship was initiated in 1897 as a match-play championship. In 1967 the format was switched to stroke-play. Yale has won the most team championships with 21 victories (1897–98, 1902, 1905–13, 1915, 1924–26, 1931–33, 1936, 1943). The only golfer to win three individual titles is Ben Crenshaw (Texas), 1971–73.

The women's championship was inaugurated in 1982. The team competition has been won a record two times by three teams: Florida (1985–86); Tulsa (1982, 1988); San Jose State (1987, 1989). No golfer has ever won the individual championship more than once.

TEAM COMPETITIONS

RYDER CUP A biennial match-play competition between professional representative teams of the United States and Europe (Great Britain and Ire-

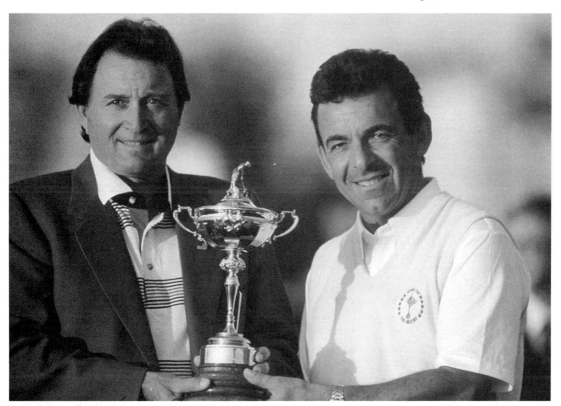

RYDER CUP ■ FIRST PLAYED FOR IN 1927, THE RYDER CUP WAS DOMINATED BY THE US UNTIL 1979, WHEN THE FORMAT EXPANDED TO INCLUDE ALL EUROPEAN PLAYERS. RAY FLOYD (US CAPTAIN) AND TONY JACKLIN (EUROPEAN CAPTAIN) ARE SHOWN HOLDING THE TROPHY AFTER THE 1989 CONTEST, WHICH WAS A TIE.

land prior to 1979). The event was launched in 1927. The US leads the series 21–5, with two ties.

Arnold Palmer (US) has won the most matches in Ryder Cup competition with 22 victories out of 32 played. Christy O'Connor Sr. (Europe) has played in the most contests, with 10 selections 1955–73.

WORLD CUP (FORMERLY CANADA CUP) The World Cup (instituted as the Canada Cup in 1953) has been won a record 17 times by the US: 1955–56, 1960–64, 1966–67, 1969, 1971, 1973, 1975, 1978–79, 1983, 1988.

Arnold Palmer and Jack Nicklaus have been both on winning US teams a record 6 times: Palmer 1960, 1962–64, 1966–67; Nicklaus 1963–64, 1966–67, 1971, 1973. Additionally, Nicklaus has won the individual title a record three times, 1963–64, 1971.

WALKER CUP A biennial match-play competition between amateur representative teams of the US and Great Britain and Ireland. It was instituted in 1921, but has been known as the Walker Cup since 1922. The US leads the series 28–3, with one tie.

Jay Sigel (US) has won a record 14 matches of 27 played. Joseph Carr (Great Britain and Ireland) has played in a record 10 contests, 1947–67.

CURTIS CUP A biennial match-play competition between women's amateur representative teams of the US and Great Britain and Ireland. The US leads the series first held in 1932, 20–4, with two ties.

Longest course The world's longest course is the International Golf Club, Bolton, MA, which is 8,325 yd set at par-77.

Longest hole The longest hole in the world is the 7th hole (par-7), of the Sano Course, Satsuki Golf Club, Japan, which measures 909 yd.

Highest course The Tactu Golf Club, Morococha, Peru is 14,335 ft above sea level.

Lowest course Furnace Creek, Death Valley, CA is 220 ft below sea level.

World one-club record Thad Daber (US), played the 6,037 yd Lochmore Golf Club, Cary, NC in 70 strokes, using only a 6-iron, to win the 1987 World One-club Championship.

Highest score on one hole In the inaugural British Open Championship at Prestwick, Scotland in 1860, a single hole score of 21 is reported; mercifully for the individual concerned, his name is not revealed. Not so fortunate is Ray Ainsley, Ojai, CA, who holds the unenviable record of most shots taken at a single hole in the US Open. Ainsley took

19 at the par-4 16th hole during the 2nd round of the 1938 championship at Cherry Hills Country Club, Denver, CO.

Most holes in 24 hours

On Foot Ian Colston, played 22 rounds and five holes (401 holes) at Bendigo Golf Club, Victoria, Australia, (par-73, 6,061 yd), on 27–28 November 1971.

Via Golf Cart Charles Stock played 783 holes at Boston Hills Golf Club, Hudson, OH (9 holes, 3,110 yd), on 20 July 1987.

HOLES IN ONE

Longest L. Bruce posted a 480-yd "ace" at the 5th hole of the Hope Country Club, AR on November 15, 1962. The women's record is 393 yd by Marie Robie on the 1st hole of the Furnace Brook Golf Club, Wollaston, MA on 4 September 1949.

Consecutive There are at least 18 cases of "aces" being achieved in two consecutive holes, of which the greatest was Norman L. Manley's unique "double albatross" on the par-4 330-yd 7th, and par-4 290-yd 8th holes on the Del Valle Country Club, Saugus, CA on 2 September 1964.

Youngest The youngest golfer to have recorded a hole-in-one is Coby Orr (5 yr) of Littleton, CO on the 103-yd 5th hole at the Riverside Golf Course, San Antonio, TX in 1975.

Oldest The oldest golfer to perform this feat was Otto Bucher, a Swiss native, who sank his "ace" aged 99 yr 244 days on 13 January 1985 at the 130-yd 12th hole at La Manga Golf Club, Spain.

GYMNASTICS

ORIGINS The ancient Greeks and Romans were exponents of gymnastics, as shown by demonstration programs in the Ancient Olympic Games (776 B.C. to A.D. 393). Modern training techniques were developed in Germany toward the end of the 18th century. Johann Friedrich Simon was as the first teacher of the modern methods at Basedow's School, Dessau, Germany in 1776. Friedrich Jahn, who founded the Turnverein in Berlin, Germany in 1811, is regarded as the most influential of the gymnastics pioneers. The International Gymnastics Federation (IGF) was formed in 1891. Gymnastics was included in the first Modern Olympics of 1896, however, women's competition was not included until 1928.

OLYMPIC MEDAL WINNERS

Top Four Men

Gymnast	Country	Total Medals
1. Nikolai Andrianov	USSR	15
2. Boris Shakhlin	USSR	13
Takashi Ono	Japan	13
3. Sawao Kato	Japan	12
4. Viktor Chukarin	USSR	11

OLYMPIC MEDAL WINNERS

Top Four Women

Gymnast	Country	Total Medals
1. Larisa Latynina	USSR	18
2. Vera Caslavska	Czechoslovakia	11
3. Agnes Kaleti	Hungary	10
Polina Astakhova	USSR	10
4. Nadia Comaneci	Romania	9
Lyudmila Tourescheva	USSR	9

OLYMPIC GAMES

Team Records Japan has won the most men's team titles with five (1960, 1964, 1968, 1972, 1976). The USSR has won the most women's titles with nine (1952, 1956, 1960, 1964, 1968, 1972, 1976, 1980, 1988).

Individual Records The most men's individual gold medals is six by two gymnasts: Boris Shakhlin (USSR), one in 1956, four in 1960 and one in 1964; and Nikolai Andrianov (USSR), one in 1972, four in 1976 and one in 1980.

Vera Caslavska-Odlozil (Czechoslovakia) has won the most individual gold medals, with seven, three in 1964 and four (one shared) in 1968. Larisa Latynina (USSR) won six individual gold medals and was on three winning teams from 1956–64, thus earning nine gold medals. She also won five silver and four bronze—18 in all—an Olympic record.

The most medals for a male gymnast (including team medals) is 15, by Nikolai Andrianov (USSR), seven gold, five silver and three bronze from 1972–80.

Aleksandr Dityatin (USSR) is the only man to win a medal in all eight categories in the same Games, with three gold, four silver and one bronze at Moscow in 1980.

MOST MEDALS ■ NIKOLAI ANDRIANOV (USSR) WON 15 OLYMPIC MEDALS, SEVEN GOLD, FIVE SILVER AND THREE BRONZE, FROM 1972–80, THE MOST OF ANY MALE GYMNAST.

UNITED STATES The best US performances were in the 1904 Games. Anton Heida won five gold medals and a silver, and George Eyser, who had a wooden leg, won three gold, two silver and a bronze medal. Mary Lou Retton won a women's record five medals in 1984, gold at all-around, two silver and two bronze.

Highest score Nadia Comaneci (Romania) was the first to achieve a perfect score (10.00) in the Olympics, and achieved seven in all at Montreal, Canada in July 1976.

PERFECTION ■ AT THE 1976 OLYMPIC GAMES, NADIA COMANECI (ROMANIA) BECAME THE FIRST GYMNAST TO BE AWARDED THE PERFECT SCORE, 10.00. IN ALL, SHE WAS AWARDED SEVEN 10'S AT THE MONTREAL OLYMPICS.

US NATIONAL CHAMPIONSHIPS Alfred A. Jochim won a record seven men's all-round US titles, 1925–30 and 1933, and a total of 34 at all exercises between 1923 and 1934. The women's record is six all-round, 1945–46 and 1949–52, and 39 at all exercises, including 11 in succession at balance beam, 1941–51, by Clara Marie Schroth Lomady.

Modern rhythmic gymnastics The most overall individual world titles in modern rhythmic gymnastics is three, by Maria Gigova (Bulgaria) in 1969, 1971 and 1973 (shared). Bulgaria has a record eight team titles in 1969, 1971, 1973, 1981, 1983, 1985, 1987, 1989 (shared). Bianka Panova (Bulgaria) won all four apparatus gold medals, all with maximum scores, and won a team gold in

1987. Marina Lobach (USSR) won the 1988 Olympic title with perfect scores for all events.

Somersaults Ashrita Furman performed 8,341 forward rolls in 10 hr 30 min over 12 miles 390 yd from Lexington to Charleston, MA on 30 April 1986. Shigeru Iwasaki backwards somersaulted 54.68 yd in 10.8 sec at Tokyo, Japan on 30 March 1980.

Static wall "sit" (or Samson's Chair) Paddy Doyle stayed in an unsupported sitting position against a wall for 4 hr 40 min at The Magnet Centre, Erdington, West Midlands, England on 18 April 1990.

HANDBALL

ORIGINS Handball was first played *c.* 1895 in Germany. It was introduced into the Olympic Games at Berlin in 1936 as an 11-man-team outdoor game, with Germany winning, but when re-introduced in 1972 it was an indoor game with a seven-man-team, the standard size of teams since 1952.

The International Handball Federation was founded in 1946. The first international match was held at Halle/Saale on 3 September 1925, when Austria beat Germany 6–3.

MOST CHAMPIONSHIPS

Olympic Games The USSR has won four titles—men 1976 and 1988, women 1976 and 1980. Yugoslavia has also won two men's titles, in 1972 and 1984.

World Championship (instituted 1938) Romania has won four men's and three women's titles (2 outdoor, 1 indoor) from 1956 to 1974. East Germany has also won three women's titles, in 1971, 1975 and 1978.

Highest score The highest score in an international match was recorded when the USSR beat Afghanistan 86–2 in the "Friendly Army Tournament" at Miskolc, Hungary in August 1981.

HARNESS RACING

ORIGINS Trotting races were held in Valkenburg, the Netherlands in 1554. In England the trotting gait (the simultaneous use of the diagonally opposite legs) was known in the 16th century. The sulky first appeared in 1829. Pacers thrust out their fore and hind legs simultaneously on one side.

The sport became very popular in the US in the 19th century, and the National Trotting Association was founded, originally as the National Association for the Promotion of the Interests of the Trotting Turf, in 1870. It brought needed controls to a sport that had been threatened by gambling corruption.

Most successful driver The sulky driver with the most wins in North American harness racing history is Herve Filion of Québec, Canada, who had achieved 12,685 wins and prize earnings of $71,117,462 through 13 January 1991, including a record 814 wins in a year (1989).

John D. Campbell (US) has the highest career earnings of $91,734,541 through 15 January 1991. This includes a season record of $11,620,878 in 1990, when he won 543 races.

Highest price $19.2 million for Nihilator (a pacer), who was syndicated by Wall Street Stable and Almahurst Stud Farm in 1984.

The highest price paid for a trotter is $6 million, for Mack Lobell, by John Erik Magnusson of Vislanda, Sweden in 1988.

Greatest winnings For any harness horse the amount is $3,681,345, by the trotter Ourasi (France) through 1989. The greatest amount won by a pacer horse is $3,225,653, by Nihilator, 1984–85.

The single season records are $1,610,608, by trotter Prakhas in 1985, and $2,091,860, by pacer Beach Towel in 1990.

The largest ever purse was $2,161,000, for the Woodrow Wilson two-year-old race over 1 mile at The Meadowlands, NJ on 16 August 1984. Of this sum, a record $1,080,500 went to the winner, Nihilator, driven by William O'Donnell.

Hambletonian The most famous trotting race in North America, the Hambletonian Stakes, run annually for three-year-olds, was first staged at Syracuse, NY in 1926. The race is named after the great sire Hambletonian, born in 1849, to whom almost all harness horses trace back their pedigree.

The race record time is 1 min 53.3 sec, by Mack Lobell, driven by John Campbell in 1987.

Little Brown Jug Pacing's three-year-old classic has been held annually at Delaware, OH from

---

HARNESS RACING MILE RECORDS

TROTTING

World mile record: 1:52, *Mack Lobell* (driver, John Campbell), Springfield, 21 August 1987

PACING

World: 1:48.4, *Matt's Scooter* (driver, Michel Lachance), Lexington, 23 September 1988

World race record: 1:49.6, Nihilator (driver, William O'Donnell), East Rutherford, 3 August 1985
1:49.6, Call For Rain (driver, Clint Albraith), Lexington, 1 October 1988

1946. The name honors a great 19th-century pacer. The race record time is 1 min 52.1 sec, by Nihilator, driven by Bill O'Donnell in 1985.

HORSE RACING

ORIGINS Horsemanship was an important part of the Hittite culture of Anatolia, Turkey, dating from 1400 B.C. The 33rd ancient Olympic Games of 648 B.C. in Greece featured horse racing. Horse races can be traced in England from the 3rd century. The first sweepstakes race was originated by the 12th Earl of Derby at his estate in Epsom in 1780. The Epsom Derby is still run today and is the classic race of the English flat racing season.

Horses were introduced to the North American continent from Spain by Cortéz in 1519. In colonial America, horse racing was common, Colonel Richard Nicholls, commander of English forces in New York, is believed to have staged the first organized race at Salisbury Plain, Long Island, NY in 1665. Thoroughbred racing was first staged at Saratoga Springs, NY in 1863.

The first Jockey Club to be founded was at Charleston, SC in 1734.

Longest winning sequence Camarero, foaled in 1951, was undefeated in 56 races in Puerto Rico from 19 April 1953 to his first defeat on 17 August 1955 (in his career to 1956, he won 73 of 77 races).

Career Galgo Jr. (foaled 1928) won 137 of 159 starts in Puerto Rico between 1930 and 1936; in 1931 he won a record 30 races in one year.

Career—United States The most wins is 89, by Kingston from 138 starts, 1886–94 including 33 in stakes races. The horse with the most wins in stakes races in the US is Exterminator (foaled 1915), with 34 between 1918 and 1923. John Henry (foaled 1975) won a record 25 graded stakes races, including 16 at Grade 1, 1978–84. On his retirement in 1984, his career prize money was $6,597,947, nearly twice as much as the next best. Of 83 races he won 39, he was second 15 times and third 9 times.

Same race Doctor Syntax (foaled 1811) won the Preston Gold Cup on seven successive occasions, 1815–21.

THE TRIPLE CROWN The races that make up the Triple Crown are the Kentucky Derby, Preakness Stakes and the Belmont Stakes. The Triple Crown is for three-year-olds only and has been achieved by 11 horses.

TRIPLE CROWN WINNERS

Year	Horse	Jockey	Trainer	Owner
1919	Sir Barton	Johnny Loftus	H. Guy Bedwell	J.K.L. Ross
1930	Gallant Fox	Earle Sanders	J.E. Fitzsimmons	Belair Stud
1935	Omaha	Willie Saunders	J.E. Fitzsimmons	Belair Stud
1937	War Admiral	Chas. Kurtsinger	George Conway	Samuel Riddle
1941	Whirlaway	Eddie Arcaro	Ben A. Jones	Calumet Farm
1943	Count Fleet	Johnny Longden	Don Cameron	Mrs. J.D. Hertz
1946	Assault	Warren Mehrtens	Max Hirsch	King Ranch
1948	Citation	Eddie Arcaro	Ben A. Jones	Calumet Farm
1973	Secretariat	Ron Turcotte	Lucien Laurin	Meadow Stable
1977	Seattle Slew	Jean Cruguet	Billy Turner	Karen Taylor
1978	Affirmed	Steve Cauthen	Laz Barrera	Harbor View Farm

Jim Fitzsimmons and Ben Jones are the only trainers to have trained two Triple Crown winners. Eddie Arcaro is the only jockey to have ridden two Triple Crown winners.

HORSES

Most successful The horse with the best won-loss record was Kincsem, a Hungarian mare foaled in 1874, who was unbeaten in 54 races (1876–79) throughout Europe, including the Goodwood Cup of 1878.

KENTUCKY DERBY Held the first Saturday in May at Chuchill Downs, Louisville, KY. The first race was run in 1875 over 1½ miles; the distance was shortened to 1¼ miles in 1896 and is still run at that length.

TRIPLE CROWN WINNERS ■ ELEVEN HORSES HAVE WON THE TRIPLE CROWN. THE FIRST WAS SIR BARTON (LEFT), IN 1919, AND THE LAST TO DATE WAS AFFIRMED (RIGHT FAR SIDE), IN 1978.

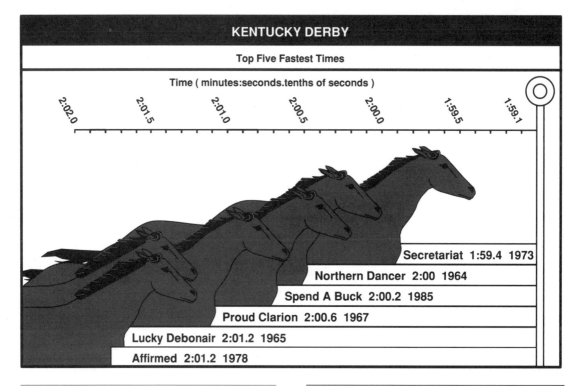

KENTUCKY DERBY

Top Five Fastest Times

Time (minutes:seconds.tenths of seconds)

2:02.0 2:01.5 2:01.0 2:00.5 2:00.0 1:59.5 1:59.1

Secretariat 1:59.4 1973

Northern Dancer 2:00 1964

Spend A Buck 2:00.2 1985

Proud Clarion 2:00.6 1967

Lucky Debonair 2:01.2 1965

Affirmed 2:01.2 1978

KENTUCKY DERBY WINNERS (1875–1990)

Year	Horse	Jockey
1875	Aristides	Oliver Lewis
1876	Vagrant	Bobby Swim
1877	Baden-Baden	Billy Walker
1878	Day Star	Jimmy Carter
1879	Lord Murphy	Charlie Shauer
1880	Fonso	George Lewis
1881	Hindoo	Jim McLaughlin

KENTUCKY DERBY WINNERS (1875–1990) (Continued)

Year	Horse	Jockey
1882	Apollo	Babe Hurd
1883	Leonatus	Billy Donohue
1884	Buchanan	Isaac Murphy
1885	Joe Cotton	Babe Henderson
1886	Ben Ali	Paul Duffy
1887	Montrose	Isaac Lewis

Year	Horse	Jockey	Year	Horse	Jockey
1888	MacBeth II	George Covington	1931	Twenty Grand	Charles Kurtsinger
1889	Spokane	Thomas Kiley	1932	Burgoo King	Eugene James
1890	Riley	Isaac Murphy	1933	Brokers Tip	Don Meade
1891	Kingman	Isaac Murphy	1934	Cavalcade	Mack Garner
1892	Azra	Lonnie Clayton	1935	Omaha	Willie Saunders
1893	Lookout	Eddie Kunze	1936	Bold Venture	Ira Hanford
1894	Chant	Frank Goodale	1937	War Admiral	Charles Kurtsinger
1895	Halma	Soup Perkins	1938	Lawrin	Eddie Arcaro
1896	Ben Brush	Willie Simms	1939	Johnstown	James Stout
1897	Typhoon II	Buttons Garner	1940	Gallahadian	Carroll Bierman
1898	Plaudit	Willie Simms	1941	Whirlaway	Eddie Arcaro
1899	Manuel	Fred Taral	1942	Shut Out	Wayne Wright
1900	Lt. Gibson	Jimmy Boland	1943	Count Fleet	Johnny Longden
1901	His Eminence	Jimmy Winkfield	1944	Pensive	Conn McCreary
1902	Alan-a-Dale	Jimmy Winkfield	1945	Hoop Jr.	Eddie Arcaro
1903	Judge Himes	Hal Booker	1946	Assault	Warren Mehrtens
1904	Elwood	Shorty Prior	1947	Jet Pilot	Eric Guerin
1905	Agile	Jack Martin	1948	Citation	Eddie Arcaro
1906	Sir Huon	Roscoe Troxler	1949	Ponder	Steve Brooks
1907	Pink Star	Andy Minder	1950	Middleground	William Boland
1908	Stone Street	Arthur Pickens	1951	Count Turf	Conn McCreary
1909	Wintergreen	Vincent Power	1952	Hill Gail	Eddie Arcaro
1910	Donau	Fred Herbert	1953	Dark Star	Hank Moreno
1911	Meridian	George Archibald	1954	Determine	Raymond York
1912	Worth	C. H. Shilling	1955	Swaps	Bill Shoemaker
1913	Donerail	Roscoe Goose	1956	Needles	David Erb
1914	Old Rosebud	John McCabe	1957	Iron Liege	Bill Hartack
1915	Regret	Joe Notter	1958	Tim Tam	I. Valenzuela
1916	George Smith	Johnny Loftus	1959	Tomy Lee	Bill Shoemaker
1917	Omar Khayyam	Charles Borel	1960	Venetian Way	Bill Hartack
1918	Exterminator	William Knapp	1961	Carry Back	John Sellers
1919	Sir Barton	Johnny Loftus	1962	Decidedly	Bill Hartack
1920	Paul Jones	Ted Rice	1963	Chateaugay	Braulio Baeza
1921	Behave Yourself	Charles Thompson	1964	Northern Dancer	Bill Hartack
1922	Morvich	Albert Johnson	1965	Lucky Debonair	Bill Shoemaker
1923	Zev	Earl Sande	1966	Kauai King	Don Brumfield
1924	Black Gold	John Mooney	1967	Proud Clarion	Bobby Ussery
1925	Flying Ebony	Earl Sande	1968	Forward Pass	I. Valenzuela
1926	Bubbling Over	Albert Johnson	1969	Majestic Prince	Bill Hartack
1927	Whiskery	Linus McAtee	1970	Dust Commander	Mike Manganello
1928	Reigh Count	Chick Lang	1971	Canonero II	Gustavo Avila
1929	Clyde Van Dusen	Linus McAtee	1972	Riva Ridge	Ron Turcotte
1930	Gallant Fox	Earl Sande	1973	Secretariat	Ron Turcotte

KENTUCKY DERBY WINNERS (1875–1990) (Continued)

Year	Horse	Jockey
1974	Cannonade	Angel Cordero
1975	Foolish Pleasure	Jacinto Vasquez
1976	Bold Forbes	Angel Cordero
1977	Seattle Slew	Jean Cruguet
1978	Affirmed	Steve Cauthen
1979	Spectacular Bid	Ron Franklin
1980	Genuine Risk	Jacinto Vasquez
1981	Pleasant Colony	Jorge Velasquez
1982	Gato Del Sol	E. Delahoussaye
1983	Sunny's Halo	E. Delahoussaye
1984	Swale	Laffit Pincay
1985	Spend A Buck	Angel Cordero
1986	Ferdinand	Bill Shoemaker
1987	Alysheba	Chris McCarron
1988	Winning Colors	Gary Stevens
1989	Sunday Silence	Pat Valenzuela
1990	Unbridled	Craig Perret

Most Wins

Jockey Five, Eddie Arcaro (1938, 1941, 1945, 1948, 1952); Bill Hartack (1957, 1960, 1962, 1964, 1969)

SMELLING THE ROSES ■ EDDIE ARCARO HAS WON THE KENTUCKY DERBY FIVE TIMES, A RECORD HE SHARES WITH BILL HARTACK.

Trainer Six, Ben Jones (1938, 1941, 1944, 1948–49, 1952)

Owner Eight, Calumet Farm (1941, 1944, 1948–49, 1952, 1957–58, 1968)

Fastest Time 1 min 59⅖ sec, Secretariat, 1973.

Largest Field 23 horses in 1974

PREAKNESS STAKES: Inaugurated in 1873 and held annually at Pimlico Race Course, Baltimore, MD. Originally run at 1 ½ miles, the distance was changed several times before being settled at the current length of 1³⁄₁₆ miles in 1925.

PREAKNESS STAKES WINNERS (1873–1990)

Year	Horse	Jockey
1873	Survivor	G. Barbee
1874	Culpepper	W. Donohue
1875	Tom Ochiltree	L. Hughes
1876	Shirley	G. Barbee
1877	Cloverbrook	C. Holloway
1878	Duke of Magenta	C. Holloway
1879	Harold	L. Hughes
1880	Grenada	L. Hughes
1881	Saunterer	T. Costello
1882	Vanguard	T. Costello
1883	Jacobus	G. Barbee
1884	Knight of Ellerslie	S. Fisher
1885	Tecumseh	Jim McLaughlin
1886	The Bard	S. Fisher
1887	Dunboyne	W. Donohue
1888	Refund	F. Littlefield
1889	Buddhist	W. Anderson
1890	Montague	W. Martin
1891	not held	
1892	not held	
1893	not held	
1894	Assignee	F. Taral
1895	Belmar	F. Taral
1896	Margrave	H. Griffin
1897	Paul Kauvar	T. Thorpe
1898	Sly Fox	W. Simms
1899	Half Time	R. Clawson
1900	Hindus	H. Spencer
1901	The Parader	F. Landry
1902	Old England	L. Jackson
1903	Flocarline	W. Gannon
1904	Bryn Mawr	E. Hildebrand

Year	Horse	Jockey	Year	Horse	Jockey
1905	Cairngorm	W. Davis	1948	Citation	Eddie Arcaro
1906	Whimsical	Walter Miller	1949	Capot	Ted Atkinson
1907	Don Enrique	G. Mountain	1950	Hill Prince	Eddie Arcaro
1908	Royal Tourist	Eddie Dugan	1951	Bold	Eddie Arcaro
1909	Effendi	Willie Doyle	1952	Blue Man	Conn McCreary
1910	Layminister	R. Estep	1953	Native Dancer	Eric Guerin
1911	Watervale	Eddie Dugan	1954	Hasty Road	Johnny Adams
1912	Colonel Holloway	C. Turner	1955	Nashua	Eddie Arcaro
1913	Buskin	James Butwell	1956	Fabius	Bill Hartack
1914	Holiday	A. Schuttinger	1957	Bold Ruler	Eddie Arcaro
1915	Rhine Maiden	Douglas Hoffman	1958	Tim Tam	I. Valenzuela
1916	Damrosch	Linus McAtee	1959	Royal Orbit	William Harmatz
1917	Kalitan	E. Haynes	1960	Bally Ache	Bobby Ussery
1918	Jack Hare Jr.	Charles Peak	1961	Carry Back	Johnny Sellers
1919	Sir Barton	Johnny Loftus	1962	Greek Money	John Rotz
1920	Man o'War	Clarence Kummer	1963	Candy Spots	Bill Shoemaker
1921	Broomspun	F. Coltiletti	1964	Northern Dancer	Bill Hartack
1922	Pillory	L. Morris	1965	Tom Rolfe	Ron Turcotte
1923	Vigil	B. Marinelli	1966	Kauai King	Don Brumfield
1924	Nellie Morse	John Merimee	1967	Damascus	Bill Shoemaker
1925	Coventry	Clarence Kummer	1968	Forward Pass	I. Valenzuela
1926	Display	John Maiben	1969	Majestic Prince	Bill Hartack
1927	Bostonian	Whitey Abel	1970	Personality	Eddie Belmonte
1928	Victorian	Sonny Workman	1971	Canonero II	Gustavo Avila
1929	Dr. Freeland	Louis Schaefer	1972	Bee Bee Bee	Eldon Nelson
1930	Gallant Fox	Earl Sande	1973	Secretariat	Ron Turcotte
1931	Mate	George Ellis	1974	Little Current	Miguel Rivera
1932	Burgoo King	John Maiben	1975	Master Derby	Derrel Mchargue
1933	Head Play	Chas. Kurtsinger	1976	Elocutionist	John Lively
1934	High Quest	Robert Jones	1977	Seattle Slew	Jean Cruguet
1935	Omaha	Willie Saunders	1978	Affirmed	Steve Cauthen
1936	Bold Venture	George Woolf	1979	Spectacular Bid	Ron Franklin
1937	War Admiral	Chas. Kurtsinger	1980	Codex	Angel Cordero
1938	Dauber	Maurice Peters	1981	Pleasant Colony	Jorge Valasquez
1939	Challedon	George Seabo	1982	Aloma's Ruler	Jack Kaenel
1940	Bimelech	F. A. Smith	1983	Deputed Testamony	Donald Miller
1941	Whirlaway	Eddie Arcaro	1984	Gate Dancer	Angel Cordero
1942	Alsab	Basil James	1985	Tank's Prospect	Pat Day
1943	Count Fleet	Johnny Longden	1986	Snow Chief	Alex Solis
1944	Pensive	Conn McCreary	1987	Alysheba	Chris McCarron
1945	Polynesian	W. D. Wright	1988	Risen Star	E. Delahoussaye
1946	Assault	Warren Mehrtens	1989	Sunday Silence	Pat Valenzuela
1947	Faultless	Doug Dobson	1990	Summer Squall	Pat Day

Most Wins

Jockey Six, Eddie Arcaro (1941, 1948, 1950–51, 1955, 1957)

Trainer Seven, Robert Wyndham Walden (1875, 78–82, 88)

Owner Five, George Lorillard (1878–82)

Fastest Time 1 min 53⅕ sec, Tank's Prospect, 1985

Largest Field 18 horses in 1928

BELMONT STAKES The third leg of the Triple Crown, first run in 1867 at Jerome Park, NY. Since 1905 the race has been staged at Belmont Park, NY. Originally run over 1 mile and 5 furlongs, the current distance of 1½ miles has been set since 1926.

BELMONT STAKES (1867–1990)

Year	Horse	Jockey
1867	Ruthless	J. Gilpatrick
1868	General Duke	Bobby Swim
1869	Fenian	C. Miller

BELMONT STAKES (1867–1990) (Continued)

Year	Horse	Jockey
1870	Kingfisher	W. Dick
1871	Harry Bassett	W. Miller
1872	Joe Daniels	James Rowe
1873	Springbok	James Rowe
1874	Saxon	G. Barbee
1875	Calvin	Bobby Swim
1876	Algerine	Billy Donohue
1877	Cloverbrook	C. Holloway
1878	Duke of Magenta	L. Hughes
1879	Spendthrift	George Evans
1880	Grenada	L. Hughes
1881	Saunterer	T. Costello
1882	Forester	Jim McLaughlin
1883	George Kinney	Jim McLaughlin
1884	Panique	Jim McLaughlin
1885	Tyrant	Paul Duffy
1886	Inspector B	Jim McLaughlin
1887	Hanover	Jim McLaughlin

PREAKNESS PACESETTER ■ TANK'S PROSPECT WON THE 1985 PREAKNESS STAKES IN A RECORD TIME OF 1 MIN 53⅕ SEC.

Year	Horse	Jockey
1888	Sir Dixon	Jim McLaughlin
1889	Eric	W. Hayward
1890	Burlington	Pike Barnes
1891	Foxford	Ed Garrison
1892	Patron	W. Hayward
1893	Comanche	Willie Simms
1894	Henry of Navarre	Willie Simms
1895	Belmar	Fred Taral
1896	Hastings	H. Griffin
1897	Scottish Chieftain	J. Scherrer
1898	Bowling Brook	F. Littlefield
1899	Jean Bereaud	R. Clawson
1900	Ildrim	Nash Turner
1901	Commando	H. Spencer
1902	Masterman	John Bullman
1903	Africander	John Bullman
1904	Delhi	George Odom
1905	Tanya	E. Hildebrand
1906	Burgomaster	Lucien Lyne
1907	Peter Pan	G. Mountain
1908	Colin	Joe Notter
1909	Joe Madden	E. Dugan
1910	Sweep	James Butwell
1911	not held	
1912	not held	
1913	Prince Eugene	Roscoe Troxler
1914	Luke McLuke	Merritt Buxton
1915	The Finn	George Byrne
1916	Friar Rock	E. Haynes
1917	Hourless	James Butwell
1918	Johren	Frank Robinson
1919	Sir Barton	John Loftus
1920	Man o'War	Clarence Kummer
1921	Grey Lag	Earl Sande
1922	Pillory	C. H. Miller
1923	Zev	Earl Sande
1924	Mad Play	Earl Sande
1925	American Flag	Albert Johnson
1926	Crusader	Albert Johnson
1927	Chance Shot	Earl Sande
1928	Vito	Clarence Kummer
1929	Blue Larkspur	Mack Garner
1930	Gallant Fox	Earl Sande

Year	Horse	Jockey
1931	Twenty Grand	Chas. Kurtsinger
1932	Faireno	Tom Malley
1933	Hurryoff	Mack Garner
1934	Peace Chance	W. D. Wright
1935	Omaha	Willie Saunders
1936	Granville	James Stout
1937	War Admiral	Chas. Kurtsinger
1938	Pasteurized	James Stout
1939	Johnstown	James Stout
1940	Bimelech	Fred Smith
1941	Whirlaway	Eddie Arcaro
1942	Shut Out	Eddie Arcaro
1943	Count Fleet	Johnny Longden
1944	Bounding Home	G. L. Smith
1945	Pavot	Eddie Arcaro
1946	Assault	Warren Mehrtens
1947	Phalanx	R. Donoso
1948	Citation	Eddie Arcaro
1949	Capot	Ted Atkinson
1950	Middleground	William Boland
1951	Counterpoint	David Gorman
1952	One Count	Eddie Arcaro
1953	Native Dancer	Eric Guerin
1954	High Gun	Eric Guerin
1955	Nashua	Eddie Arcaro
1956	Needles	David Erb
1957	Gallant Man	Bill Shoemaker
1958	Cavan	Pete Anderson
1959	Sword Dancer	Bill Shoemaker
1960	Celtic Ash	Bill Hartack
1961	Sherluck	Braulio Baeza
1962	Jaipur	Bill Shoemaker
1963	Chateaugay	Braulio Baeza
1964	Quadrangle	Manuel Ycaza
1965	Hail to All	John Sellers
1966	Amberoid	William Boland
1967	Damascus	Bill Shoemaker
1968	Stage Door Johnny	Gus Gustines
1969	Arts and Letters	Braulio Baeza
1970	High Echelon	John Rotz
1971	Pass Catcher	Walter Blum
1972	Riva Ridge	Ron Turcotte
1973	Secretariat	Ron Turcotte

BELMONT STAKES (1867–1990) (Continued)

Year	Horse	Jockey
1974	Little Current	Miguel Rivera
1975	Avatar	Bill Shoemaker
1976	Bold Forbes	Angel Cordero
1977	Seattle Slew	Jean Cruguet
1978	Affirmed	Steve Cauthen
1979	Coastal	Ruben Hernandez
1980	Temperence Hill	Eddie Maple
1981	Summing	George Martens
1982	Conquistador Cielo	Laffit Pincay
1983	Caveat	Laffit Pincay
1984	Swale	Laffit Pincay
1985	Creme Fraiche	Eddie Maple
1986	Danzig Connection	Chris McCarron
1987	Bet Twice	Craig Perret
1988	Risen Star	E. Delahoussaye
1989	Easy Goer	Pat Day
1990	Go and Go	Michael Kinane

Most Wins

Jockey Six, Jim McLaughlin (1882–84, 1886–88) Eddie Arcaro (1941–42, 1945, 1948, 1952, 1955)

Trainer Eight, James Rowe Sr. (1883–84, 1901, 1904, 1907–08, 1910, 1913)

Owner Five, Dwyer Brothers (1883–84, 1886–88); James R. Keene (1901, 1904, 1907–08, 1910); William Woodward Sr. (Belair Stud) (1930, 1932, 1935–36, 1939)

Fastest Time 2 min 24 sec, Secretariat, 1973

Largest Field 15 horses in 1983

BREEDERS' CUP

The highest prize money for a day's racing is $10 million, for the Breeders' Cup series of seven races staged annually since 1984. Included each year is a record $3 million for the Breeders' Cup Classic.

The jockey who has won the most Breeders' Cup races is Laffit Pincay Jr., with six from 1985 to 1990; the trainer with the most wins is D. Wayne Lukas, with 10.

BELMONT'S BEST ■ TRIPLE CROWN WINNER SECRETARIAT STRIDES TO AN EMPHATIC VICTORY IN THE 1973 BELMONT STAKES. SECRETARIAT'S WIN WAS BOTH THE FASTEST AND THE WIDEST MARGIN OF VICTORY IN THE HISTORY OF THE RACE.

JOCKEYS

Most successful Bill Shoemaker (US) rode a record 8,833 winners from 40,350 mounts from his first ride on 19 March 1949 and first winner on 20 April 1949 to his retirement on 3 February 1990. Laffit Pincay Jr. (Panama) has earned a career record $154,659,844 from 1964 to the end of 1990.

The most races won by a jockey in a year is 598 from 2,312 rides, by Kent Desormeaux in 1989. The highest earnings won in a year is $14,877,298, by José Adeon Santos (US) in 1988.

Wins The most winners ridden in one day is nine, by Chris Antley (US) on 31 October 1987. They consisted of four in the afternoon at Aqueduct, NY and five in the evening at The Meadowlands, NJ.

One card The most winners ridden on one card is eight, by Hubert S. Jones, 17, from 13 rides at Caliente, CA on 11 June 1944; Oscar Barattuci, at Rosario City, Argentina on 15 December 1957; Dave Gall, from 10 rides at Cahokia Downs, East St. Louis, IL on 18 October 1978; Chris Loseth, from 10 rides at Exhibition Park, Vancouver, BC, Canada on 9 April 1984; Robert Williams, from 10 rides at Lincoln, NE on 29 September 1984; and Pat Day, from only nine rides at Arlington, IL, on 13 September 1989.

Consecutive The longest winning streak is 12, by Sir Gordon Richards (one race at Nottingham, England on 3 October, six out of 6 at Chepstow on 4 October and the first 5 races next day at Chepstow) in 1933; and by Pieter Stroebel at Bulawayo, Southern Rhodesia (now Zimbabwe), 7 June–7 July 1958.

TRAINERS

Jack Charles Van Berg (US) has the greatest number of wins in a year, 496 in 1976. The career record is 5,540 by Dale Baird (US) through 1990. The greatest amount won in a year is $17,842,358, by D. Wayne Lukas (US) in 1988. The only trainer to saddle the first five finishers in a championship race is Michael William Dickinson), in the Cheltenham Gold Cup (UK) on 17 March 1983; he won a record 12 races in one day, 27 December 1982.

OWNERS

The most lifetime wins by an owner is 4,775, by Marion H. Van Berg in North America in 35 years. The most wins in a year is 494, by Dan R. Lasater (US) in 1974. The greatest amount won in a year is $5,858,168, by Ogden Phipps (US) in 1988.

HURLING

ORIGINS A game of very ancient origin, hurling was included in the Tailteann Games (instituted 1829 B.C.) It only became standardized with the formation of the Gaelic Athletic Association in Thurles, Ireland on 1 November 1884. The Irish Hurling Union was formed on 24 January 1879.

Most titles

ALL-IRELAND The greatest number of All-Ireland Championships won by one team is 27, by Cork between 1890 and 1990. The greatest number of successive wins is four, by Cork (1941–44).

Most appearances The most appearances in All-Ireland finals is 10, shared by Christy Ring (Cork and Munster) and John Doyle (Tipperary). They also share the record of All-Ireland medals won, with eight each. Ring's appearances on the winning side were in 1941–44, 1946 and 1952–54, while Doyle's were in 1949–51, 1958, 1961–62 and 1964–65. Ring also played in a record 22 interprovincial finals (1942–63), and was on the winning side 18 times.

Highest and lowest scores The highest score in an All-Ireland final (60 min) was in 1989, when

Tipperary, 41 (4 goals, 29 points), beat Antrim 18 (3 goals, 9 points). The record aggregate score was when Cork, 39 (6 goals, 21 points), defeated Wexford, 25 (5 goals, 10 points), in the 80-minute final of 1970. A goal equals three points. The highest recorded individual score was by Nick Rackard (Wexford), who scored seven goals and seven points against Antrim in the 1954 All-Ireland semifinal. The lowest score in an All-Ireland final was when Tipperary (1 goal, 1 point) beat Galway (zero) in the first championship at Birr in 1887.

Longest hit The greatest distance for a "lift and stroke" is one of 129 yd credited to Tom Murphy of Three Castles, Kilkenny, in a "long puck" contest in 1906.

Largest crowd The largest crowd was 84,865 for the All-Ireland final between Cork and Wexford at Croke Park, Dublin in 1954.

ICE HOCKEY

ORIGINS There is pictorial evidence that a hockey-like game (*kalv*) was played on ice in the early 16th century in The Netherlands. The game was probably first played in North America on 25 December 1855 at Kingston, Ontario, Canada, but Halifax also lays claim to priority. The International Ice Hockey Federation was founded in 1908.

NATIONAL HOCKEY LEAGUE (NHL)

ORIGINS The National Hockey League (NHL) was founded on 22 November 1917 in Montreal, Canada. The formation of the NHL was precipitated by the collapse of the National Hockey Association of Canada (NHA). Four teams formed the original league: the Montreal Canadiens, Montreal Wanderers, Ottawa Senators, Quebec Bulldogs. The Toronto Arenas were admitted as a 5th team, but the Bulldogs were unable to operate, and the league began as a four-team competition. The first NHL game was played on 19 December 1917. The NHL is now comprised of 21 teams, seven from Canada and 14 from the United States, divided into two divisions within two conferences: Adams and Patrick Divisions in the Wales Conference; Norris and Smythe Division in the Campbell Conference. At the end of the regular season, 16 teams compete in the Stanley Cup playoffs to decide the NHL Champion. (For further details of the Stanley Cup see below.)

Most Wins in One Season The Montreal Canadiens won 60 games during the 1976–77 season.

In 80 games, "the Habs" won 60, lost 8, tied 12, which set the all-time points mark of 132.

Most Losses in One Season The Washington Capitals hold the unenviable record of having lost the most games in one season. During the 1974–75 season, the first for the franchise, the Capitals lost 67 of 80 games played. They managed to win only eight games, the fewest in the modern era. The fewest wins in any season was four by the Quebec Bulldogs, in 24 games, in 1919–20.

Longest Winning Streak The New York Islanders won 15 consecutive games from 21 January–20 February 1982. The longest undefeated streak in one season is 35 games by the Philadelphia Flyers. The Flyers won 25 games and tied 10 from 14 October 1979–6 January 1980.

Longest Losing Streak The Washington Capitals lost 17 consecutive games from 18 February–26 March 1975. The Winnipeg Jets set the mark for the longest winless streak at 30 games. From 19 October to 20 December 1980, the Jets lost 23 games and tied seven.

Most Games Played Gordie Howe played 1,767 games over a record 26 seasons for the Detroit Red Wings (1946–71) and Hartford Whalers (1979–80). The most games played by a goaltender is 971 by Terry Sawchuk, who played 21 seasons for five teams: Detroit Red Wings, Boston Bruins, Toronto Maple Leafs, Los Angeles Kings and New York Rangers (1949–70).

Most Consecutive Games Doug Jarvis played 962 consecutive games over 12 seasons from 8 October 1975 to 5 April 1987. During the streak Jarvis played for three teams: the Montreal Canadiens, Washington Capitals and Hartford Whalers.

Fastest Goal The fastest goal from the start of a game is 5 sec by Doug Smail (Winnipeg Jets) *v.* St. Louis Blues at Winnipeg on 20 December 1981, and by Bryan Trottier (New York Islanders) *v.* Boston Bruins at Boston on 22 March 1984. The fastest goal from the start of any period was after 4 sec by Claude Provost (Montreal Canadiens) *v.* Boston Bruins in the 2nd period at Montreal on 9 November 1957, and by Denis Savard (Chicago Blackhawks) *v.* Hartford Whalers in the 3rd period at Chicago on 12 January 1986.

Most Goals in One Game The NHL record for goals in one game is 21, which has occurred on two occasions. The mark was set on 10 January 1920, when the Montreal Canadiens defeated the Toronto St. Patricks, 14–7, at Montreal. This record was matched on 11 December 1985, when the

NATIONAL HOCKEY LEAGUE RECORDS (1917 through 1989–90)

GOALS

Period: 4, Busher Jackson, Toronto Maple Leafs v. St. Louis Eagles, 20 November 1934
Max Bentley, Chicago Blackhawks v. New York Rangers, 28 January 1943
Clint Smith, Chicago Blackhawks v. Montreal Canadiens, 4 March 1945
Red Berenson, St. Louis Blues v. Philadelphia Flyers, 7 November 1968
Wayne Gretzky, Edmonton Oilers v. St. Louis Blues, 18 February 1981
Grant Mulvey, Chicago Blackhawks v. St. Louis Blues, 3 February 1982
Bryan Trottier, New York Islanders v. Philadelphia Flyers, 13 February 1982
Al Secord, Chicago Blackhawks v. Toronto Maple Leafs, 7 January 1987
Joe Nieuwendyk, Calgary Flames v. Winnipeg Jets, 11 January 1989

Game: 7, Joe Malone, Quebec Bulldogs v. Toronto St. Patricks, 31 January 1920

Season: 87, Wayne Gretzky, Edmonton Oilers (80 games), 1981–82

Career: 801, Gordie Howe, Detroit Red Wings; Hartford Whalers, 1946–71; 1979–80

ASSISTS

Period: 5, Dale Hawerchuk, Winnipeg Jets v. Los Angeles Kings, 6 March 1984

Game: 7, Billy Taylor, Detroit Red Wings v. Chicago Blackhawks, 16 March 1947
Wayne Gretzky, Edmonton Oilers v. Washington Capitals, 15 February 1980
Wayne Gretzky, Edmonton Oilers v. Chicago Blackhawks, 11 December 1985
Wayne Gretzky, Edmonton Oilers v. Quebec Nordiques, 14 February 1986

Season: 163, Wayne Gretzky, Edmonton Oilers (80 games), 1985–86

Career: 1,302, Wayne Gretzky, Edmonton Oilers; Los Angeles Kings, 1979–90

THE GREAT ONE ■ WAYNE GRETZKY, LOS ANGE-LES KINGS, HAS COMPLETELY REWRITTEN THE NHL RECORD BOOK SINCE HIS ARRIVAL IN EDMONTON IN 1979. HE HOLDS CAREER AND SEASON RECORDS IN MOST OFFENSIVE CATEGORIES, AND IN 1990 BE-CAME THE FIRST PLAYER TO ACHIEVE 2,000 POINTS.

Edmonton Oilers beat the Chicago Blackhawks, 12–9, at Chicago.

Most Goals by One Team in a Game The Montreal Canadiens pounded the Quebec Bulldogs 16–3, on 3 March 1920 to set the single game scoring record. To make matters worse for Quebec, it was on home ice!

Most Hat Tricks The most hat tricks (3 or more goals in a game) in a career is 46 by Wayne Gretzky for the Edmonton Oilers and Los Angeles Kings in 11 seasons (1979–90). "The Great One" has recorded 33 three-goal games, 9 four-goal games and 4 five-goal games. Gretzky also holds the record for most hat tricks in a season, 10, in both the 1981–82 and 1983–84 seasons for the Edmonton Oilers.

Most Consecutive 50-or-More Goal Seasons Mike Bossy (New York Islanders) scored at least 50 goals in nine consecutive seasons from 1977–78 through 1985–86. Wayne Gretzky (Edmonton Oilers, Los Angeles Kings) has also scored at least 50 goals in one season nine times, but his longest streak is eight seasons.

Longest Shutout Sequence by a Goaltender Alex Connell (Ottawa Senators) played 461 min,

NATIONAL HOCKEY LEAGUE RECORDS (1917 through 1989–90)
(Continued)

POINTS

Period: 6, Bryan Trottier, New York Islanders v. New York Rangers, 23 December 1978

Game: 10, Darryl Sittler, Toronto Maple Leafs v. Boston Bruins, 7 February 1976

Season: 215, Wayne Gretzky, Edmonton Oilers (80 games), 1985–86

Career: 1,979, Wayne Gretzky, Edmonton Oilers; Los Angeles Kings, 1979–90

GOALTENDERS
Shutouts

Season: 22, George Hainsworth, Montreal Canadiens (44 games), 1928–29

Career: 103, Terry Sawchuk, Detroit Red Wings; Boston Bruins; Toronto Maple Leafs; Los Angeles Kings; New York Rangers, 1949–70

Wins

Season: 47, Bernie Parent, Philadelphia Flyers, 1973–74

Career: 435, Terry Sawchuk, Detroit Red Wings; Boston Bruins; Toronto Maple Leafs; Los Angeles Kings; New York Rangers , 1949–70

PERIOD PIECE ■ BRYAN TROTTIER SET RECORDS FOR MOST GOALS (4) AND MOST POINTS (6) IN ONE PERIOD WHILE PLAYING FOR THE NEW YORK ISLANDERS.

Source: NHL

29 sec without conceding a goal in the 1927–28 season.

Longest Undefeated Streak by a Goaltender Gerry Cheevers (Boston Bruins) went 32 games (24 wins, 8 ties), undefeated during the 1971–72 season.

Longest Consecutive Point Scoring Streak The most consecutive games scoring at least one point is 51, by Wayne Gretzky (Edmonton Oilers) between 5 October 1983 and 27 January 1984. During the streak, Gretzky scored 61 goals, 92 assists for 153 points.

Defensemen Denis Potvin (New York Islanders 1973–88) set career records for most goals (310),

OFFENSIVE DEFENSEMAN ■ IN 1970–72, BOBBY ORR, BOSTON BRUINS, ESTABLISHED SEASON RECORDS FOR ASSISTS (102) AND POINTS (139) BY A DEFENSEMAN. ORR MAY ALSO HAVE THE RECORD FOR MOST APPEARANCES BY A HOCKEY PLAYER IN THE "NEW YORK TIMES" CROSSWORD PUZZLE.

assists (742) and points (1,052) by a defenseman. Paul Coffey (Edmonton Oilers) scored a record 48 goals in 1985–86. Bobby Orr (Boston Bruins) holds the single season marks for assists (102) and points (139), both of which were set in 1970–71.

Hart Trophy Awarded annually since the 1923–24 season by the Professional Hockey Writers Association to the Most Valuable Player of the NHL. Wayne Gretzky has won the award a record nine times, 1980–87, 1989.

Coaches Scotty Bowman holds the records for most victories and highest winning percentage by an NHL coach. He won 739 games (110, St. Louis Blues 1967–71; 419, Montreal Canadiens 1971–79; 210, Buffalo Sabres 1979–87). His career record is 739 wins, 327 losses, 210 ties for a record .661 winning percentage. Dick Irvin has coached a record 1,437 games with three teams: Chicago Blackhawks (1930–31; 55–56); Toronto Maple Leafs (1931–40); Montreal Canadiens (1940–55). Irvin's career record was 690 wins, 521 losses, 226 ties.

Longest Game The longest game was played between the Detroit Red Wings and the Montreal Maroons and lasted 2 hr 56 min 30 sec. Played at the Forum, Montreal, the Red Wings won when Mud Bruneteau scored the only goal of the game in the 6th period of overtime at 2:25 A.M. on 25 March 1936.

STANLEY CUP

The Stanley Cup is currently the oldest competition in North American professional sports. The cup was donated to the Canadian Amateur Hockey Association (AHA) by Sir Frederick Arthur Stanley, Lord Stanley of Preston in 1893. The inaugural championship was presented to the AHA champion, but since 1894 there has always been a play-off. The playoff format underwent several changes until 1926 when the National Hockey League (NHL) playoffs became the permanent forum to decide the Stanley Cup champion.

Year	Champion	Loser	Series
1893	Montreal A.A.A.	(no challenger)	——
1894	Montreal A.A.A.	Ottawa Generals	3–1*

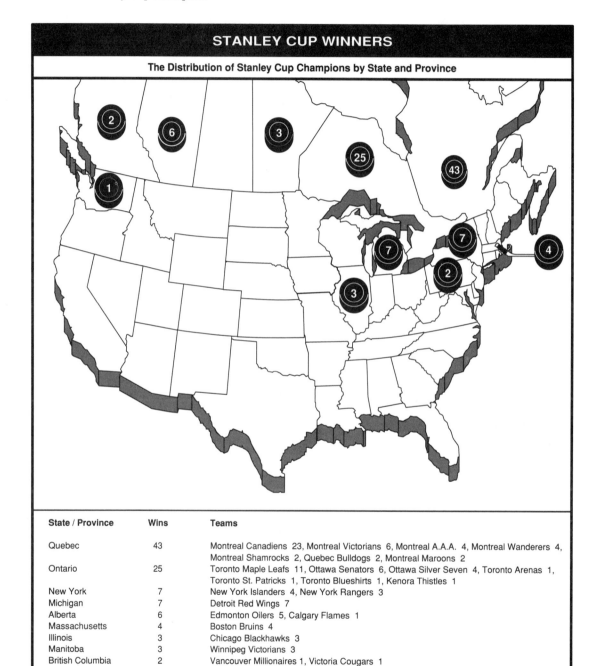

STANLEY CUP WINNERS

The Distribution of Stanley Cup Champions by State and Province

State / Province	Wins	Teams
Quebec	43	Montreal Canadiens 23, Montreal Victorians 6, Montreal A.A.A. 4, Montreal Wanderers 4, Montreal Shamrocks 2, Quebec Bulldogs 2, Montreal Maroons 2
Ontario	25	Toronto Maple Leafs 11, Ottawa Senators 6, Ottawa Silver Seven 4, Toronto Arenas 1, Toronto St. Patricks 1, Toronto Blueshirts 1, Kenora Thistles 1
New York	7	New York Islanders 4, New York Rangers 3
Michigan	7	Detroit Red Wings 7
Alberta	6	Edmonton Oilers 5, Calgary Flames 1
Massachusetts	4	Boston Bruins 4
Illinois	3	Chicago Blackhawks 3
Manitoba	3	Winnipeg Victorians 3
British Columbia	2	Vancouver Millionaires 1, Victoria Cougars 1
Pennsylvania	2	Philadelphia Flyers 2
Washington	1	Seattle Metropolitans 1

Year	Champion	Loser	Series
1895	Montreal Victorias	(no challenger)	——
1896	Winnipeg Victorias (February)	Montreal Victorias	2–0*
	Montreal Victorias (December)	Winnipeg Victorias	6–5*
1897	Montreal Victorias	Ottawa Capitals	15–2*
1898	Montreal Victorias	(no challenger)	——
1899	Montreal Victorias (February)	Winnipeg Victorias	2–0
	Montreal Shamrocks (March)	Queen's University	6–2*
1900	Montreal Shamrocks	Halifax Crescents Winnipeg Victorias	**
1901	Winnipeg Victorias	Montreal Shamrocks	2–0
1902	Winnipeg Victorias (January)	Toronto Wellingtons	2–0
	Montreal A.A.A. (March)	Winnipeg Victorias	2–1
1903	Montreal A.A.A. (February)	Winnipeg Victorias	2–2–1+
	Ottawa Silver Seven (March)	Rat Portage Thistles Montreal Victorias	**
1904	Ottawa Silver Seven	Brandon Wheat Kings Montreal Wanderers Toronto Marlboros Winnipeg Rowing Club	**
1905	Ottawa Silver Seven	Rat Portage Thistles Dawson City Nuggets	**
1906	Ottawa Silver Seven (February)	Montreal Wanderers Smith's Falls Queen's University	**
	Montreal Wanderers (March)	New Glasgow Clubs Ottawa Silver Seven	**
1907	Kenora Thistles (January)	Montreal Wanderers	2–0
	Montreal Wanderers (March)	Kenora Thistles	1–1+
1908	Montreal Wanderers	Edmonton Eskimos Toronto Trolley Leaguers Winnipeg Maple Leafs Ottawa Victorias	**
1909	Ottawa Senators	(no challenger)	
1910	Montreal Wanderers	Berlin Union Jacks Edmonton Eskimos Galt	**
1911	Ottawa Senators	Port Arthur Bearcats Galt	**
1912	Quebec Bulldogs	Moncton Victorias	2–0
1913	Quebec Bulldogs	Sydney Miners	2–0
1914	Toronto Blueshirts	Victoria Cougars Montreal Canadiens	**
1915	Vancouver Millionaires	Ottawa Senators	2–0

Year	Champion	Loser	Series
1916	Montreal Canadiens	Portland Rosebuds	3–2
1917	Seattle Metropolitans	Montreal Canadiens	3–1
1918	Toronto Arenas	Vancouver Millionaires	3–2
1919	no decision		
1920	Ottawa Senators	Seattle Metropolitans	3–2
1921	Ottawa Senators	Vancouver Millionaires	3–2
1922	Toronto St. Patricks	Vancouver Millionaires	3–2
1923	Ottawa Senators	Vancouver Maroons Edmonton Eskimos	**
1924	Montreal Canadiens	Vancouver Maroons Calgary Tigers	**
1925	Victoria Cougars	Montreal Canadiens	3–1
1926	Montreal Maroons	Victoria Cougars	3–1
1927	Ottawa Senators	Boston Bruins	2–0
1928	New York Rangers	Montreal Maroons	3–2
1929	Boston Bruins	New York Rangers	2–0
1930	Montreal Canadiens	Boston Bruins	2–0
1931	Montreal Canadiens	Chicago Blackhawks	3–2
1932	Toronto Maple Leafs	New York Rangers	3–0
1933	New York Rangers	Toronto Maple Leafs	3–1
1934	Chicago Blackhawks	Detroit Red Wings	3–1
1935	Montreal Maroons	Toronto Maple Leafs	3–0
1936	Detroit Red Wings	Toronto Maple Leafs	3–1
1937	Detroit Red Wings	New York Rangers	3–2
1938	Chicago Blackhawks	Toronto Maple Leafs	3–1
1939	Boston Bruins	Toronto Maple Leafs	4–1
1940	New York Rangers	Toronto Maple Leafs	4–2
1941	Boston Bruins	Detroit Red Wings	4–0
1942	Toronto Maple Leafs	Detroit Red Wings	4–3
1943	Detroit Red Wings	Boston Bruins	4–0
1944	Montreal Canadiens	Chicago Blackhawks	4–0
1945	Toronto Maple Leafs	Detroit Red Wings	4–3
1946	Montreal Canadiens	Boston Bruins	4–1
1947	Toronto Maple Leafs	Montreal Canadiens	4–2
1948	Toronto Maple Leafs	Detroit Red Wings	4–0
1949	Toronto Maple Leafs	Detroit Red Wings	4–0
1950	Detroit Red Wings	New York Rangers	4–3
1951	Toronto Maple Leafs	Montreal Canadiens	4–1
1952	Detroit Red Wings	Montreal Canadiens	4–0
1953	Montreal Canadiens	Boston Bruins	4–1
1954	Detroit Red Wings	Montreal Canadiens	4–3
1955	Detroit Red Wings	Montreal Canadiens	4–3
1956	Montreal Canadiens	Detroit Red Wings	4–1
1957	Montreal Canadiens	Boston Bruins	4–1
1958	Montreal Canadiens	Boston Bruins	4–2

Year	Champion	Loser	Series
1959	Montreal Canadiens	Toronto Maple Leafs	4–1
1960	Montreal Canadiens	Toronto Maple Leafs	4–0
1961	Chicago Blackhawks	Detroit Red Wings	4–2
1962	Toronto Maple Leafs	Chicago Blackhawks	4–2
1963	Toronto Maple Leafs	Detroit Red Wings	4–1
1964	Toronto Maple Leafs	Detroit Red Wings	4–3
1965	Montreal Canadiens	Chicago Blackhawks	4–3
1966	Montreal Canadiens	Detroit Red Wings	4–2
1967	Toronto Maple Leafs	Montreal Canadiens	4–2
1968	Montreal Canadiens	St. Louis Blues	4–0
1969	Montreal Canadiens	St. Louis Blues	4–0
1970	Boston Bruins	St. Louis Blues	4–0
1971	Montreal Canadiens	Chicago Blackhawks	4–3
1972	Boston Bruins	New York Rangers	4–2
1973	Montreal Canadiens	Chicago Blackhawks	4–2
1974	Philadelphia Flyers	Boston Bruins	4–2
1975	Philadelphia Flyers	Buffalo Sabres	4–2
1976	Montreal Canadiens	Philadelphia Flyers	4–0

Year	Champion	Loser	Series
1977	Montreal Canadiens	Boston Bruins	4–0
1978	Montreal Canadiens	Boston Bruins	4–2
1979	Montreal Canadiens	New York Rangers	4–1
1980	New York Islanders	Philadelphia Flyers	4–2
1981	New York Islanders	Minnesota North Stars	4–1
1982	New York Islanders	Vancouver Canucks	4–0
1983	New York Islanders	Edmonton Oilers	4–0
1984	Edmonton Oilers	New York Islanders	4–1
1985	Edmonton Oilers	Philadelphia Flyers	4–1
1986	Montreal Canadiens	Calgary Flames	4–1
1987	Edmonton Oilers	Philadelphia Flyers	4–3
1988	Edmonton Oilers	Boston Bruins	4–0
1989	Calgary Flames	Montreal Canadiens	4–2
1990	Edmonton Oilers	Boston Bruins	4–1

* Final score of single challenge game.
** Multiple challenger series.
+ Series decided on total goals scored. The 1919 final between the Montreal Canadiens and the Seattle Metropolitans was cancelled because of an influenza epidemic.

STANLEY CUP TEAM RECORDS (1918–1990)

Most Championships: 22, Montreal Canadiens, 1924, 1930–31, 1944, 1946, 1953, 1956–60, 1965–66, 1968–69, 1971, 1973, 1976–79, 1986

Most Consecutive Wins: 5, Montreal Canadiens, (1956–60)

GOALS

Game (one team): 13, Edmonton Oilers v. Los Angeles Kings (3), 9 April 1987

Game (combined score): 18, Los Angeles Kings (10) Edmonton Oilers (8), 7 April 1982

Period (one team): 7, Montreal Canadiens (3rd period) v. Toronto Maple Leafs (final 11–0), 30 March 1944

Period (combined): 9, New York Rangers (6) Philadelphia Flyers (3) (3rd period), (final 8–3) 24 April 1979
Los Angeles Kings (5) Calgary Flames (4) (2nd period), (final 12–4) 10 April 1990

POWER-PLAY GOALS

Period (one team): 4, Toronto Maple Leafs (2nd period) v. Boston Bruins (final 8–3), 26 March 1936
Minnesota North Stars (2nd period) v. Edmonton Oilers (final 5–8), 28 April 1984

Game (one team): 6, Boston Bruins v. Toronto Maple Leafs, 2 April 1969

Series (one team): 15, New York Islanders v. Philadelphia Flyers, 1980

Season (one team): 32, Edmonton Oilers (18 games), 1988

STANLEY CUP INDIVIDUAL RECORDS (1918–90) (Continued)

SHORTHANDED GOALS

Game (one team): 3, Boston Bruins v. Minnesota North Stars, 11 April 1981
New York Islanders v. New York Rangers, 17 April 1983

Series (one team): 5, Edmonton Oilers v. Calgary Flames, 1983
New York Rangers v. Philadelphia Flyers, 1979

Season (one team): 10, Edmonton Oilers (16 games), 1983

GOALS

Period: 4, Tim Kerr, Philadelphia Flyers v. New York Rangers, 13 April 1985
Mario Lemieux, Pittsburgh Penguins v. New York Rangers, 25 April 1989

Game: 5, Newsy Lalonde, Montreal Canadiens v. Ottawa Senators, 1 March 1919
Maurice Richard, Montreal Canadiens v. Toronto Maple Leafs, 23 March 1944
Darryl Sittler, Toronto Maple Leafs v. Philadelphia Flyers, 22 April 1976
Reggie Leach, Philadelphia Flyers v. Boston Bruins, 6 May 1976
Mario Lemieux, Pittsburgh Penguins v. Philadelphia Flyers, 25 April 1989

Series (any round): 12, Jari Kurri, Edmonton Oilers v. Chicago Blackhawks, 1985

Series (Final): 9, Babe Dye, Toronto St. Patricks v. Vancouver Millionaires, 1922

Season: 19, Newsy Lalonde, Montreal Canadiens (10 games), 1919
Reggie Leach, Philadelphia Flyers (16 games), 1976
Jari Kurri, Edmonton Oilers (18 games), 1985

Career: 92, Jari Kurri, Edmonton Oilers, 1980–90

POWER-PLAY GOALS

Period: 3, Tim Kerr, Philadelphia Flyers v. New York Rangers, 13 April 1985

Series: 6, Chris Kontos, Los Angeles Kings v. Edmonton Oilers, 1989

Season: 9, Mike Bossy, New York Islanders, 1981

Career: 35, Mike Bossy, New York Islanders, 1977–87

POINTS

Period: 4, Maurice Richard, Montreal Canadiens v. Toronto Maple Leafs, 29 March 1945
Dickie Moore, Montreal Canadiens v. Boston Bruins, 25 March 1954
Barry Pederson, Boston Bruins v. Buffalo Sabres, 8 April 1982
Peter McNab, Boston Bruins v. Buffalo Sabres, 11 April 1982
Tim Kerr, Philadelphia Flyers v. New York Rangers, 13 April 1985
Ken Linseman, Boston Bruins v. Montreal Canadiens, 14 April 1985
Wayne Gretzky, Edmonton Oilers v. Los Angeles Kings, 12 April 1987
Glenn Anderson, Edmonton Oilers v. Winnipeg Jets, 6 April 1988
Mario Lemieux, Pittsburgh Penguins v. Philadelphia Flyers, 25 April 1989

Game: 8, Patrik Sundstrom, New Jersey Devils v. Washington Capitals, 22 April 1988
Mario Lemieux, Pittsburgh Penguins v. Philadelphia Flyers, 25 April 1989

Series (any round): 19, Rick Middleton, Boston Bruins v. Buffalo Sabres, 1983

Series (Final): 13, Wayne Gretzky, Edmonton Oilers v. Boston Bruins, 1988

Season: 47, Wayne Gretzky, Edmonton Oilers (18 games), 1985

Career: 284, Wayne Gretzky, Edmonton Oilers; Los Angeles Kings, 1979–90

STANLEY CUP INDIVIDUAL RECORDS (1918–90) (Continued)

ASSISTS

Period: 3, This feat has been recorded 48 times.

Games: 6, Mikko Leinonen, New York Rangers v. Philadelphia Flyers, 8 April 1982
Wayne Gretzky, Edmonton Oilers v. Los Angeles Kings, 9 April 1987

Series (any round):   14, Rick Middleton, Boston Bruins v. Buffalo Sabres, 1983
Wayne Gretzky, Edmonton Oilers v. Chicago Blackhawks, 1985

Series (Final):   10, Wayne Gretzky, Edmonton Oilers v. Boston Bruins, 1988

Season: 31, Wayne Gretzky, Edmonton Oilers (19 games), 1988

Career: 195, Wayne Gretzky, Edmonton Oilers; Los Angeles Kings, 1979–90

GOALTENDERS
Shutouts

Consecutive Games: 3, Clint Benedict, Montreal Maroons, 1926

Season: 4, Clint Benedict, Montreal Maroons (8 games), 1926
Clint Benedict, Montreal Maroons (9 games), 1928
Dave Kerr, New York Rangers (9 games), 1937
Frank McCool, Toronto Maple Leafs (13 games), 1945
Terry Sawchuk, Detroit Tigers (8 games), 1952
Bernie Parent, Philadelphia Flyers (17 games), 1975
Ken Dryden, Montreal Canadiens (14 games), 1977

Career: 15, Clint Benedict, Ottawa Senators; Montreal Marrons, 1917–30

Minutes Played

Season: 1,540, Ron Hextall, Philadelphia Flyers (26 games), 1987

Career: 7,645, Billy Smith, New York Islanders, 1971–89

Wins

Season: 16, Grant Fuhr, Edmonton Oilers (19 games), 1988
Mike Vernon, Calgary Flames (22 games), 1989
Bill Ranford, Edmonton Oilers (22 games), 1990

Career: 88, Billy Smith, New York Islanders, 1975–88

PENALTY MINUTES

Game: 42, Dave Schultz, Philadelphia Flyers v. Toronto Maple Leafs, 22 April 1976

Career: 505, Dale Hunter, Quebec Nordiques; Washington Capitals, 1980–90

Source: NHL

Most Games Played   Larry Robinson has played in 213 Stanley Cup playoff games for the Montreal Canadiens (1973–89, 203 games) and the Los Angeles Kings (1990, 10 games).

Fastest Goal   The fastest goal from the start of any playoff game was scored by Don Kozak (Los Angeles Kings) past Gerry Cheevers (Boston Bruins) with 6 sec elapsed. The Kings went on to win 4–2, the game was played on 17 April 1977. Kozak's goal shares the mark for fastest goal from the start of any period with one scored by Pelle Eklund (Philadelphia Flyers). Eklund scored in the 2nd period of a game against the Pittsburgh Penguins in Pittsburgh on 25 April 1989; his effort was in vain, however, as the Penguins won 10–7.

MOST GOALS ■ JARI KURRI SCORED A RECORD 92 STANLEY CUP PLAYOFF GOALS FOR THE EDMONTON OILERS, 1980–90.

MOST POINTS ■ PATRIK SUNDSTROM, NEW JERSEY DEVILS, SET THE RECORD FOR MOST POINTS IN A PLAYOFF GAME, 8, ON 22 APRIL 1988.

Shorthanded Goals The most shorthanded goals scored by one player in a single period is two shared by three players: Bryan Trottier was the first player to perform this feat on 8 April 1990 for the New York Islanders *v.* the Los Angeles Kings. His goals came in the 2*nd* period of an 8–1 Islanders victory. Bobby Lalonde (Boston Bruins) matched Trottier on 11 April 1981. His double came in the 3*rd* period of a Bruins 6–3 loss to the Minnesota North Stars. Jari Kurri (Edmonton Oilers) joined this club on 24 April 1983. His goals came in the 3rd period of an Oilers 8–4 win over the Chicago Blackhawks.

Bill Barber (Philadelphia Flyers) holds the record for most shorthanded goals in a playoff series with three. Barber's goals came in a Flyers 4–1 series victory over the Minnesota North Stars in 1980.

Mark Messier (Edmonton Oilers) holds the mark for career playoff goals at 11 in 148 games (1979–90).

SHUTOUTS ■ BERNIE PARENT, PHILADELPHIA FLYERS, SHARES THE RECORD OF FOUR SHUTOUTS IN A PLAYOFF SEASON WITH FIVE OTHER GOALIES. PARENT PERFORMED THIS FEAT IN 1975.

GOON RECORD ▪ DALE HUNTER (32) HOLDS THE PLAYOFF CAREER RECORD FOR MOST PENALTY MINUTES, 505, ACQUIRED FROM 1980 TO 1990.

Defensemen During his career with the Edmonton Oilers, 1980–87, Paul Coffey set marks for the most points in a playoff game (6) and in a season (37)—both set in 1985. Also in 1985, Coffey set the record for most goals by a defenseman in a playoff season with 12 in 18 games. The record for most goals in a game by a defenseman is three shared by five players: Bobby Orr (Boston Bruins *v.* Montreal Canadiens, 11 April 1971); Dick Redmond (Chicago Blackhawks *v.* St. Louis Blues, 4 April 1973); Denis Potvin (New York York Islanders *v.* Edmonton Oilers, 17 April 1981); Paul Reinhart, twice, (Calgary Flames *v.* Edmonton Oilers, 14 April 1983; *v.* Vancouver Canucks, 8 April 1984); Doug Halward (Vancouver Canucks *v.* Calgary Flames, 7 April 1984).

Point-Scoring Streak Bryan Trottier (New York Islanders) scored a point in 27 playoff games over three seasons (1980–82), scoring 16 goals and 26 assists for 42 points.

Goal-Scoring Streak Reggie Leach (Philadelphia Flyers) scored at least one goal in nine consecutive playoff games in 1976. The streak started on 17 April *v.* the Toronto Maple Leafs, and ended on 9 May when he was shut out by the Montreal Canadiens. Overall, Leach scored 14 goals during his record-setting run.

Consecutive Wins by a Goaltender Gerry Cheevers (Boston Bruins) set a playoff record 10 straight victories, anchoring the Bruins to a Stanley Cup title in 1970.

Longest Shutout Sequence In the 1936 semifinal contest between the Detroit Red Wings and the Montreal Maroons, Norm Smith, the Red Wings goaltender, shut out the Maroons for 248 min, 32 sec. The Maroons failed to score in the first two games (the second game lasted 116 min, 30 sec, the longest overtime game in playoff history), and finally breached Smith's defenses at 12:02 of the 1st period in game three. After such a stellar performance, it is no surprise that the Red Wings swept the series 3–0.

Coaches "Toe" Blake coached the Montreal Canadiens to eight championships (1956–60, 1965–66, 1968), the most of any coach. Al Arbour and Scotty Bowman share the record for most playoff wins at 114: Arbour (4, St. Louis Blues, 1970–73; 110, New York Islanders, 1973–86, 1988–90); Bowman (26, St. Louis Blues, 1967–71; 70, Montreal Canadiens, 1971–79; 18, Buffalo Sabres, 1979–87). Dick Irvin holds the mark for most games coached at 190 with three clubs: Chicago Blackhawks (1930–31, 1955–56); Toronto Maple Leafs (1931–40); Montreal Canadiens (1940–55).

MOST WINS ▪ COACHES AL ARBOUR (ABOVE) AND SCOTTY BOWMAN SHARE THE RECORD FOR MOST PLAYOFF VICTORIES, 114.

WORLD CHAMPIONSHIPS AND OLYMPIC GAMES

World Championships were first held for amateurs in 1920 in conjunction with the Olympic

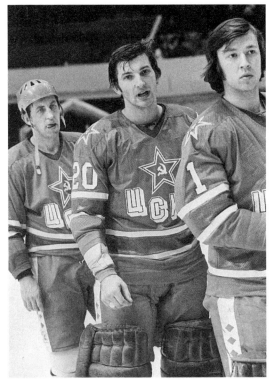

MOST GOLDS ▪ SOVIET GOALIE VLADISLAV TRETYAK (20) IS ONE OF FIVE SOVIET PLAYERS TO HAVE WON A RECORD THREE OLYMPIC GOLD MEDALS.

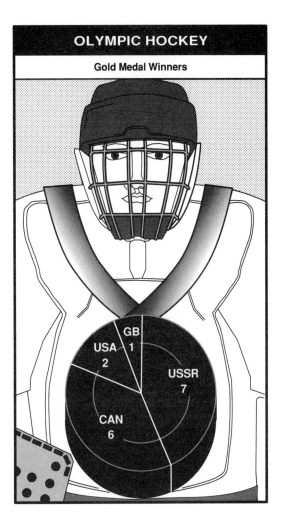

Games, which were also considered as world championships up to 1968. From 1977, World Championships have been open to professionals. The USSR won 22 world titles between 1954 and 1990, including the Olympic titles of 1956, 1964 and 1968. They have a record seven Olympic titles with a further four, 1972, 1976, 1984 and 1988. The longest Olympic career is that of Richard Torriani (Switzerland) from 1928 to 1948. The most gold medals won by any player is three, achieved by USSR players Vitaliy Semyenovich Davidov, Anatoliy Vasilyevich Firssov, Viktor Grigoryevich Kuzkin and Aleksandr Pavlovich Ragulin in 1964, 1968 and 1972, and by Vladislav Aleksandrovich Tretyak in 1972, 1976 and 1984.

Women The first world championships were won by Canada, who beat the US 5–2, at Ottawa, Canada on 24 March 1990.

Most goals The greatest number of goals recorded in a world championship match was when Australia beat New Zealand 58–0 at Perth on 15 March 1987.

ICE SKATING

ORIGINS The earliest reference to ice skating is in Scandanavian literature dating to the 2nd century A.D. Some historians argue that the origins date to at least 10 centuries earlier. It is believed that the modern form of speed skating originated in the Netherlands in the 18th century, where skating on frozen canals became popular. Figure skating originated in Scotland, where the first known skating club, the Edinburgh Skating Club, was formed in c. 1742.

The first recorded race was from Wisbech to Whittlesey, England in 1763. The first artificial ice rink was opened in London, England on 7 January 1876. Ice skating may be divided into two sports: figure skating and speed skating. The world governing body for both is the International Skating Union (ISU), founded in 1892.

FIGURE SKATING

OLYMPIC GAMES The most Olympic gold medals won by a figure skater is three, by: Gillis Grafström (Sweden) in 1920, 1924 and 1928; by Sonja Henie (Norway) in 1928, 1932 and 1936; and by Irina Rodnina (USSR), with two different partners, in the Pairs in 1972, 1976 and 1980.

WORLD CHAMPIONSHIPS The greatest number of men's individual world figure skating titles (instituted 1896) is 10, by Ulrich Salchow (Sweden), in 1901–05 and 1907–11. The women's record (instituted 1906) is also 10 individual titles, by Sonja Henie between 1927 and 1936. Irina Rodnina has won 10 pairs titles (instituted 1908), four with Aleksey Ulanov, 1969–72, and six with her hus-

ICE QUEENS ■ SONJA HENIE OF NORWAY (LEFT) WON THREE OLYMPIC TITLES, 1928, 1932 AND 1936, AND TEN WORLD TITLES, 1927–36. THIS FEAT WAS MATCHED BY IRINA RODNINA OF THE USSR (BELOW), WHO WON THREE OLYMPIC PAIRS TITLES, 1972, 1976 AND 1980, AND TEN WORLD TITLES, 1969–78. RODNINA HAD TWO PARTNERS DURING HER CAREER. SHE IS SHOWN SKATING WITH HER SECOND PARTNER, ALEKSANDR ZAITSEV.

band, Aleksandr Zaitsev, 1973–78. The most ice dance titles (instituted 1952) won is six, by Lyudmila Pakhomova and her husband, Aleksandr Gorshkov (USSR), 1970–74 and 1976. They also won the first ever Olympic ice dance title in 1976.

Dick Button set US records with two Olympic gold medals, 1948 and 1952, and five world titles, 1948–52. Five women's world titles were won by Carol Elizabeth Heise, 1956–60, as well as the 1960 Olympic gold.

US CHAMPIONSHIPS The US Championships were first held in 1914. The most titles won by an individual is nine, by Maribel Y. Vinson 1928–33 and 1935–37. She also won six pairs titles, and her aggregate of 15 titles is equaled by Therese Blanchard (née Weld) who won six individual and nine pairs titles between 1914 and 1927. The men's individual record is seven, by Roger Turner 1928–34 and by Dick Button, 1946–52. At age 16 in 1946, Button was the youngest ever winner.

Highest marks The highest tally of maximum six marks awarded in an international championship was 29, to Jayne Torvill and Christopher Dean (UK) in the World Ice Dance Championships at Ottawa, Canada on 22–24 March 1984. This comprised seven in the compulsory dances, a perfect set of nine for presentation in the set pattern dance and 13 in the free dance, including another perfect set from all nine judges for artistic presentation. They previously gained a perfect set of nine sixes for artistic presentation in the free dance at the 1983 World Championships in Helsinki, Finland and at the 1984 Winter Olympic Games in Sarajevo, Yugoslavia. In their career, Torvill and Dean received a record total of 136 sixes.

The most by a soloist is seven, governed by Donald Jackson (Canada) in the World Men's Championship at Prague, Czechoslovakia in 1962; and by Midori Ito (Japan) in the World Ladies' Championships at Paris, France in 1989.

Most midair rotations Kurt Browning (Canada) was the first to achieve a quadruple jump in competition—a toe loop—in the World Championships at Budapest, Hungary on 25 March 1988. Midori Ito (Japan) was the first woman to complete a jump exceeding three rotations—a triple axel—in the World Championships at Paris, France on 18 March 1989.

Distance Robin Cousins (UK) achieved 19 ft 1 in in an axel jump and 18 ft with a back flip at Richmond Ice Rink, Surrey, England on 16 November 1983.

Largest rink The world's largest indoor ice rink is the Moscow Olympic arena, which has an ice area of 86,800 ft². The five rinks at Fujikyu Highland Skating Center, Japan total 285,243 ft².

SPEED SKATING

OLYMPIC GAMES The most gold medals won by one skater is six by Lidiya Skoblikova (USSR); two in 1960 and four in 1964. Clas Thunberg (Finland) and Eric Heiden (US) share the men's record at five medals each. Thunberg won his medals in 1924 and 1928, Heiden won his at the 1980 Lake Placid Games, the most ever by one athlete for individual events at any Olympiad.

WORLD CHAMPIONSHIPS Oscar Mathisen (Norway) and Clas Thunberg (Finland) have won a record five overall world titles (instituted 1893). Mathisen won titles in 1908–09 and 1912–14; Thunberg in 1923, 1925, 1928–29 and 1931. Karein Kania (née Enke, East Germany), holds the women's mark, also at five. She won in 1982, 1984, 1986–88.

SPEED SKATING WORLD RECORDS
MEN

Distance	Min. Sec.	Name (Country)	Place	Date
500 Meters:	36.45	Uwe-Jens Mey (East Germany)	Calgary, Canada	14 February 1988
	36.23ᵁ	Nick Thometz (US)	Medeo, USSR	26 March 1987
1,000 Meters:	1:12.58	Igor Zhelozovsky (USSR)	Heerenveen, Netherlands	25 Febuary 1989
	1:12.58ᴬ	Pavel Pegov (USSR)	Medeo, USSR	25 November 1983
	1:12.05ᵁ	Nick Thometz (US)	Medeo, USSR	27 March 1987

SPEED SKATING WORLD RECORDS (Continued)

MEN (Continued)

Distance	Min. Sec.	Name (Country)	Place	Date
1,500 Meters:	1:52.06	André Hoffmann (East Germany)	Calgary, Canada	20 February 1988
3,000 Meters:	3:57.52	Johann Olav Koss (Norway)	Heerenveen, Netherlands	13 March 1990
	3:56.65	Sergey Martyuk (USSR)	Medeo, USSR	11 March 1977
5,000 Meters:	6:43.59	Geir Karlstad (Norway)	Calgary, Canada	6 December 1987
10,000 Meters:	13:48.20	Tomas Gustafsson (Sweden)	Calgary, Canada	21 February 1988

WOMEN

Distance	Min. Sec.	Name (Country)	Place	Date
500 Meters:	39.10	Bonnie Blair (US)	Calgary, Canada	22 February 1988
1,000 Meters:	1:17.65	Christa Rothenberg (now Luding; East Germany)	Calgary, Canada	26 February 1988
1,500 Meters:	1:59.30	Karin Kania (East Germany)	Medeo, USSR	22 March 1986
3,000 Meters:	4:11.94	Yvonne van Gennip (Netherlands)	Calgary, Canada	23 February 1988
5,000 Meters:	7:14.13	Yvonne van Gennip (Netherlands)	Calgary, Canada	28 February 1988
10,000 Meters +:	15:25.25	Yvonne van Gennip (Netherlands)	Heerenveen, Netherlands	19 March 1988

u unofficial.
A set at high altitude.
+ Record not officially recognized for this distance.

SPEED RECORDS ■ NICK THOMETZ (RIGHT) HOLDS US SPEED SKATING RECORDS AT 500 M AND 1,000 M. ERIC FLAIM (LEFT) HOLDS THE US RECORDS FOR 1,500 M, 5,000 M AND 10,000 M.

U.S. SPEED SKATING RECORDS

MEN

Meters	Time	Name	Place	Date
500	36.23*	Nick Thometz	Medeo, USSR	27 March 1987
1,000	1:12.05*	Nick Thometz	Medeo, USSR	27 March 1987
1,500	1:52.12	Eric Flaim	Calgary, Canada	20 February 1988
5,000	6:47.09	Eric Flaim	Calgary, Canada	17 February 1988
10,000	14:05.57	Eric Flaim	Calgary, Canada	21 February 1988

WOMEN

Meters	Time	Name	Place	Date
500	39.10	Bonnie Blair	Calgary, Canada	22 February 1988
1,000	1:18.31	Bonnie Blair	Calgary, Canada	26 February 1988
1,500	2:03.89	Bonnie Blair	Calgary, Canada	5 December 1987
3,000	4:25.26	Jan Goldman	Calgary, Canada	23 February 1988
5,000	7:36.98	Jan Goldman	Calgary, Canada	28 February 1988

* Not recognized as an official world record by the International Skating Union.

UNITED STATES Eric Heiden won three overall world titles 1977–79, the most by any US skater. His sister Beth became the only American woman to win an overall championship in 1979.

Longest race The "Elfstedentocht" ("Tour of the Eleven Towns"), which originated in the 17th century, was held in the Netherlands from 1909–63, and again in 1985 and 1986, covering 124 miles 483 yd. As the weather does not permit an annual race in the Netherlands; alternative "Elfstedentocht" take place at suitable venues. These venues have included Lake Vesijärvi, near Lahti, Finland; Ottawa River, Canada; and Lake Weissenssee, Austria. The record time for 200 km is: (men) 5 hr 40 min 37 sec, by Dries van Wijhe (Netherlands); and (women) 5 hr 48 min 8 sec, by Alida Pasveer (Netherlands), both at Lake Weissensee (altitude 3,609 ft), Austria on 11 February 1989. Jan-Roelof Kruithof (Netherlands) won the race eight times—1974, 1976–77, 1979–83. An estimated 16,000 skaters took part in 1986.

24 hours Martinus Kuiper (Netherlands) skated 339.681 miles in 24 hr in Alkmaar, Netherlands on 12–13 December 1988.

JAI ALAI (PELOTA VASCA)

ORIGINS The game, which originated in Italy as *longue paume* and was introduced into France in the 13th century, is said to be the fastest of all ball games. The glove or *gant* was introduced *c.* 1840 and the *chistera* was invented by Jean "Gantchiki" Dithurbide of Ste. Pée, France. The *grand chistera* was invented by Melchior Curuchague of Buenos Aires, Argentina in 1888. The world's largest *frontón* (enclosed stadium) is the World Jai Alai at Miami, FL, which had a record attendance of 15,052 on 27 December 1975.

WORLD CHAMPIONSHIPS The Federacion Internacional de Pelota Vasca stage, World Championships every four years (first in 1952). The most successful pair have been Roberto Elias and Juan Labat (Argentina), who won the *Trinquete Share* four times, in 1952, 1958, 1962 and 1966. Labat won a record seven world titles in all. The most wins in the long-court game *Cesta Punta* is three, by Hamuy of Mexico, with two different partners, in 1958, 1962 and 1966.

Highest speed An electronically measured ball velocity of 188 mph was recorded by José Ramon Areitio at the Newport Jai Alai, RI on 3 August 1979.

JUDO

ORIGINS Judo is a modern combat sport that developed from an amalgam of several old Japanese martial arts, the most popular of which was jujitsu (jiu-jitsu), which is thought to be of Chinese origin. Judo has greatly developed since 1882, when it was first devised by Dr. Jigoro Kano. The International Judo Federation was founded in 1951.

WORLD CHAMPIONSHIPS AND OLYMPIC GAMES World Championships were inaugurated in Tokyo, Japan in 1956. Women's championships were first held in 1980 in New York. Yashiro Yamashita won four world titles; Over 95 kg in 1979, 1981 and 1983; Open in 1981. He retired undefeated after 203 successive wins between 1977 and 1985. Two other men have won four world titles: Wilhelm Ruska (Netherlands): Over 93 kg in 1967, 1971 and 1972; Olympic and Open titles, and Shozo Fujii (Japan): Under 80 kg in 1971, 1973 and 1975; Under 75 kg in 1979. The only men to have won two Olympic gold medals are Wilhelm Ruska (Netherlands), Over 93 kg and Open in 1972; Peter Seisenbacher (Austria), 86 kg in 1984 and 1988; and Hitoshi Saito (Japan), Over 95 kg in 1984 and 1988. Ingrid Berghmans (Belgium) has won a record six women's world titles (first held 1980): Open 1980, 1982, 1984 and 1986 and Under 72 kg in 1984 and 1989.

The only US judo practitioners to win world titles have been Michael Swain, in men's 71 kg class in 1987, and Ann-Maria Bernadette Burns, in women's 56 kg in 1984.

Highest grades The efficiency grades in judo are divided into pupil (*kyu*) and master (*dan*) grades. The highest awarded is the extremely rare red belt *judan* (10th dan), given to only 13 men so far. The Judo protocol provides for an 11th dan (*juichidan*) who also would wear a red belt, a 12th dan (*junidan*) who would wear a white belt twice as wide as an ordinary belt, and the highest of all, *shihan* (ductor), but these have never been bestowed, save for the 12th dan, to the founder of the sport Dr. Jigoro

JUMP ROPE

10 mile skip-run Vadivelu Karunakaren (India) jump roped 10 miles in 58 min at Madras, India, 1 February 1990.

Most turns

10 sec 128 by Albert Rayner (Great Britain), Stanford Sports Birmingham, England 19 November 1982.

1 min 425 by Robert Commers (US) at The Holiday Inn, Jamestown, NY, 23 February 1990.

One hour 13,783 by Robert Commers (US), at Woodbridge, NJ, 13 May 1989.

On a single rope, team of 90 160, by students from the Nishigoshi Higashi Elementary School, Kumamoto, Japan, 27 February 1987.

On a tightrope 58 (consecutive), by Bryan Andro (ne Dewhurst), TROS TV, the Netherlands, 6 August 1981.

Most consecutive multiple turns

Double 10,709, by Frank Oliveri (US), at Rochester, NY, 7 May 1988.

Double (with cross) 2,411, by Ken Solis (US), at North Shore-Elite Fitness and Racquets Club, Glendale, WI, 29 March 1988.

Treble 423, by Shozo Hamada (Japan), at Saitama, Japan, 1 June 1987.

Quadruple 51, by Katsumi Suzuki (Japan), at Saitama, Japan, 29 May 1975.

Quintuple 6, by Hideyuki Tateda (Japan), at Aomori, Japan, 19 June 1982.

Most on a rope (minimum 12 turns obligatory) 200, by a team at the International Rope Skipping Competition, Greeley, CO, 30 June 1989.

KARATE

ORIGINS Based on techniques devised from the 6th century Chinese art of Shaolin boxing (*kempo*), karate was developed by an unarmed populace in Okinawa as a weapon against armed Japanese oppressors *c.* 1500. Transmitted to Japan in the 1920s by Funakoshi Gichin, this method of combat was refined into karate and organized into a sport with competitive rules. The five major styles of karate in Japan are: *shotokan, wado-ryu, goju-ryu, shito-ryu* and *kyo-kushinkai*, each of which places different emphasis on speed and power, etc. Other styles include *sankukai, shotokai* and *shukokai*. *Wu shu* is a comprehensive term embracing all Chinese martial arts.

WORLD CHAMPIONSHIPS Great Britain has won a record six world titles (instituted 1970) at the kumite team event, in 1975, 1982, 1984, 1986, 1988 and 1990. Two men's individual kumite titles have been won by: Pat McKay (UK) in Under 80 kg, in 1982 and 1984; Emmanuel Pinda (France) in Open, in 1984; and Over 80 kg, in 1988; and Theirry Masci (France) in Under 70 kg, in 1986 and 1988. Four women's kumite titles have been won by Guus van Mourik (Netherlands), in Over 60 kg, in 1982, 1984, 1986 and 1988. Three individual kata titles have been won by men: Tsuguo Sakumoto (Japan), in 1984, 1986 and 1988; women: Mie Nakayama (Japan), in 1982, 1984 and 1986.

LACROSSE

ORIGINS The game is of American Indian origin, derived from the intertribal game *baggataway* and was played before 1492 by Iroquois Indians in lower Ontario, Canada and upper New York State. The French named it after their game of *chouler á la crosse*, known in 1381. Lacrosse was included in the Olympic Games of 1904 and 1908, and featured as an exhibition sport in the 1928, 1932 and 1948 Games. The US Amateur Lacrosse Association was founded in 1879.

WORLD CHAMPIONSHIPS The US has won five of the six World Championships, in 1967, 1974, 1982, 1986 and 1990. Canada won the other world title in 1978, beating the US 17–16.

NCAA CHAMPIONSHIPS National champions were determined by committee from 1936, and they received the Wilson Wingate Trophy; from 1971 they have been decided by NCAA playoffs. John Hopkins University has the most wins overall: seven NCAA titles between 1974 and 1987, and six wins and five ties between 1941 and 1970.

Highest scores The highest score in an international match is the US 32–8 win over England at Toronto, Canada in 1986.

MODERN PENTATHLON

ORIGINS Comprised of five activities; fencing, horseback-riding, pistol shooting, swimming and cross-country running, the Modern Pentathlon derived from military training in the 19th century, which was based on a messenger being able to travel across country on horseback, fighting his way through with sword and pistol, and being prepared to swim across rivers and complete his journey on foot. Each event is scored on points, determined either against the other competitors or against scoring tables. There is no standard course, therefore points totals are not comparable. The sport has been included at every Olympic Games since 1912. L'Union Internationale de Pentathlon Moderne (UIPM) was formed in 1948 and expanded to include the administration of the Biathlon in 1957. The first US national championship was held in 1955. The United States Modern Pentathlon and Biathlon Association was established in 1971, but this body was split to create the US Modern Pentathlon Association in 1978.

OLYMPIC GAMES The greatest number of Olympic gold medals won is three, by András Balczó (Hung-

WORLD CHAMPIONS ■ IN 1979, ROBERT NIEMAN (ABOVE) BECAME THE FIRST AMERICAN TO WIN THE MODERN PENTATHLON WORLD TITLE. IN 1989, LORI NORWOOD (TOP) BECAME THE FIRST US WOMAN TO WIN A WORLD CHAMPIONSHIP.

ary), a member of the winning team in 1960 and 1968 and the 1972 individual champion. Lars Hall (Sweden) is unique in having won two individual championships (1952, 1956). Pavel Lednyev (USSR) won a record seven medals (two team gold, one team silver, one individual silver, three individual bronze), in 1968, 1972, 1976 and 1980. The only US individual Olympic medalist has been Robert Lee Beck, who won the bronze in 1960.

WORLD CHAMPIONSHIPS András Balczó (Hungary) won a record number of world titles (instituted 1949), six individual and seven team. He won the world individual title in 1963, 1965–67 and 1969 and the Olympic title in 1972. His seven team titles (1960–70) comprised five world and two Olympic. The USSR has won a record 14 world and four Olympic team titles. Hungary has also won a record four Olympic team titles and 10 world titles.

Women's World Championships were first held in 1981. Great Britain won three team titles 1981–83, with Sarah Parker a member of each of those teams. The only double individual champion has been Irina Kiselyeva (USSR), 1986–87. Wendy Norman (UK) won the individual title in 1982 and team goals in 1981–82. She also won the individual World Cup title in 1980 and Great Britain won three World Cup team titles, 1978–80.

The only US modern pentathletes to win world titles have been Robert Nieman, in 1979, when the men's team also won, and Lori Norwood (women's) in 1989.

US NATIONAL CHAMPIONSHIPS The men's championship was inaugurated in 1955. Mike Burley has won a record four titles (1977, 1979, 1981, 1985). The women's championship was first held in 1977; Kim Dunlop (née Arata) has won a record eight titles (1979–80, 1984–89).

MOTO-CROSS

ORIGINS Moto-cross, also known as scrambling, developed in Great Britain in the 1920's. The typical Moto-cross course is a dirt circuit with continuous undulations, climbs, drops and curves. A 500cc class World Championship was established in 1957, with a 250cc class added in 1962 and a 125cc event in 1975.

WORLD CHAMPIONSHIPS Joël Robert (Belgium) won six 250cc Moto-cross World Championship (1964, 1968–72). Between 25 April 1964 and 18 June 1972, he won a record fifty 250cc Grands

Prix. The youngest moto-cross world champion was Dave Strijbos (Netherlands), who won the 125cc title at age 18yr 296 days, on 31 August 1986. Eric Geboers (Belgium) is the only person to have won all three categories of the Moto-cross World Championships, at 125cc in 1983, 250cc in 1987 and 500cc in 1988.

MOTORCYCLE RACING

ORIGINS The first recorded motorcycle race took place on 20 September 1896 when eight riders took part in a 139-mi race from Paris, France to Nantes, France and back. The winner was M. Chevalier on a Michelin-Dion tricycle, he covered the course in 4 hr 10 min 37 sec. The first race for two-wheeled motorcycles was held on a one-mile oval track at Sheen House, Richmond, England on 29 November 1897. The Federation Internationale Motorcycliste (FIM) was founded in 1904 and is the world governing body.

WORLD CHAMPIONSHIPS The FIM instituted World Championships in 1949 for 125, 250, 350 and 500cc classes. In 1962, a 50cc class was introduced, which was upgraded to 80cc in 1983. In 1982, the 350cc class was discontinued.

Most Championships

Overall 15, Giacomo Agostini (Italy): 7–350cc (1968–74); 8–500cc (1966–72, 1975).

50cc 6, Angel Nieto (Spain), 1969–70, 1972, 1975–77.

80cc 3, Jorge Martinez (Spain), 1986–88.

125cc 7, Angel Nieto (Spain), 1971–72, 1979, 1981–84.

250cc 4, Phil Read (UK), 1964–65, 1968, 1971.

350cc 7, Giacomo Agostini (Italy), 1968–74.

500cc 8, Giacomo Agostini (Italy), 1966–72, 1975.

United States The most world titles won by an American rider is four by Eddie Lawson at 500cc in 1984, 1986, 1988–89.

In 1985 Freddie Spencer (US) became the first man ever to win the 250cc and 500cc titles in the same year.

Most Grand Prix Wins

Overall 122, Giacomo Agostini (Italy): 54–350cc; 68–500cc.

50cc 27, Angel Nieto (Spain)

80cc 21, Jorge Martinez (Spain)

125cc 62, Angel Nieto (Spain)

137.150 mph) by Barry Sheene (UK) on a 495cc 4-cylinder Suzuki during the Belgian Grand Prix on 3 July 1977. On that occasion he set a record time for this 10-lap (87.74-mile) race of 38 min 58.5 sec (average speed 135.068 mph).

Longest race The longest race was the Liége 24 hr run on the old Francorchamps circuit. The greatest distance ever covered is 2,761.9 mi (average speed 115.08 mph) by Jean-Claude Chemarin and Christian Leon, both of France, on a 941cc 4-cylinder Honda on the Francorchamps circuit on 14–15 August 1976.

Longest circuit The 37.73-mile "Mountain" circuit on the Isle of Man, over which the principal TT races have been run since 1911 (with minor amendments in 1920), has 264 curves and corners and is the longest used for any motorcycle race.

MOUNTAINEERING

Although Bronze Age artifacts have been found on the summit of the Riffelhorn, Switzerland (9,605 ft), mountaineering as a sport has a continuous history dating back only to 1854. Isolated instances of climbing for its own sake exist back to the 13th century. The Atacamenans built sacrificial platforms near the summit of Llullaillaco (22,057 ft) in late pre-Columbian times *c.* 1490.

Mt. Everest Everest (29,078 ft) was first climbed at 11:30 A.M. on 29 May 1953, when the summit was reached by Edmund Hillary (New Zealand) and Sherpa Tenzing Norgay (Nepal). The successful expedition was led by Colonel Henry Cecil John Hunt.

Most conquests Sherpa Ang Rita (Nepal), with ascents in 1983, 1984, 1985, 1987, 1988 and 1990, has scaled Everest six times—all without the use of bottled oxygen.

Solo Reinhold Messner (Italy) was the first to make the entire climb solo on 20 August 1980. Also, Messner, with Peter Habeler, (Austria), made the first entirely oxygen-less ascent on 8 May 1978.

First woman Junko Tabei (Japan) reached the summit on 16 May 1975.

Oldest Richard Daniel Bass (US) was 55 yr 130 days when he reached the summit on 30 April 1985.

Most successful expedition The Mount Everest International Peace Climb, a team of American, Soviet and Chinese climbers, led by James W. Whittaker (US), in 1990 succeeded in putting the

GRAND PRIX LEADER ■ GIACOMO AGOSTINI, ITALY, HAS WON A RECORD 122 MOTORCYCLE GRAND PRIX RACES.

250cc 33, Anton Mang (West Germany)

350cc 54, Giacomo Agostini (Italy)

500cc 68, Giacomo Agostini (Italy)

Most successful machines Japanese Yamaha machines won 39 World Championships between 1964 and 1989.

Youngest and oldest world champions Johnny Cecotto (Venezuela) is the youngest to win a World Championship. He was 19 yr 211 days when he won the 350cc title on 24 August 1975. The oldest was Hermann-Peter Müller (West Germany), who won the 250cc title in 1955 at age 46.

Fastest circuits The highest average lap speed attained on any closed circuit is 160.288 mph, by Yvon du Hamel (Canada) on a modified 903cc 4-cylinder Kawasaki Z1 at the 31-degree banked 2.5 mile Daytona International Speedway, FL in March 1973. His lap time was 56.149 sec.

The fastest road circuit was the Francorchamps circuit near Spa, Belgium, then 8.74 miles long. It was lapped in 3 min 50.3 sec (average speed

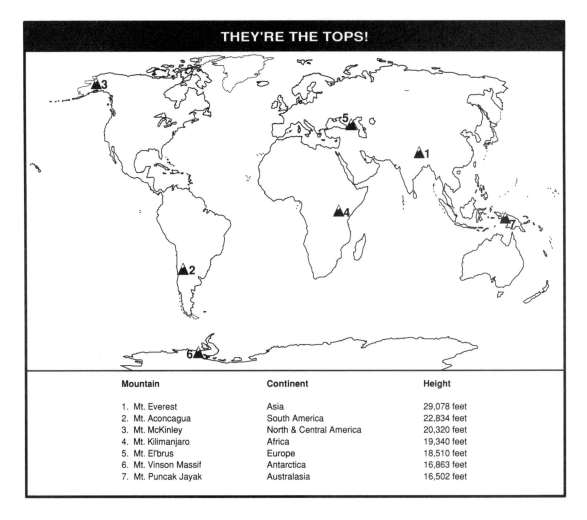

THEY'RE THE TOPS!

Mountain	Continent	Height
1. Mt. Everest	Asia	29,078 feet
2. Mt. Aconcagua	South America	22,834 feet
3. Mt. McKinley	North & Central America	20,320 feet
4. Mt. Kilimanjaro	Africa	19,340 feet
5. Mt. El'brus	Europe	18,510 feet
6. Mt. Vinson Massif	Antarctica	16,863 feet
7. Mt. Puncak Jayak	Australasia	16,502 feet

greatest number of people on the summit, 20, from 7–10 May 1990.

Sea level to summit Timothy Macartney-Snape (Australia) traversed Mount Everest's entire altitude from sea level to summit. He set off on foot from the Bay of Bengal near Calcutta, India on 5 February 1990 and reached the summit on 11 May, having walked approximately 745 miles.

All continents The first person to climb the highest mountain in each of the seven continents (Africa: Kilimanjaro, 19,340 ft; Antarctica: Vinson Massif, 16,863 ft; Asia: Everest, 29,078 ft; Europe: El'brus, 18,510 ft; North and Central America: McKinley, 20,320 ft; South America: Aconcagua, 22,834 ft; and Australasia: Puncak Jayak, 16,502 ft) was Patrick Morrow (Canada). He climbed the last of the seven mountains, Puncak Jayak, on 7 May 1986.

Mountaineer Reinhold Messner was the first person to successfully scale all 14 of the world's mountains of over 26,250 ft, all without oxygen. With his ascent of Kanchenjunga in 1982, he became the first person to climb the world's three highest mountains, having earlier reached the summits of Everest and K2.

Greatest walls The highest final stage in any wall climb is that on the south face of Annapurna I (26,545 ft). It was climbed by the British expedition led by Chris Bonington (UK), when from 2 April to 27 May 1970, using 18,000 ft of rope, Donald Whillans (UK) and Dougal Haston (UK) both scaled to the summit. The longest wall climb is on the Rupal-Flank from the base camp at 11,680 ft to the South Point at 26,384 ft of Nanga Parbat—vertical ascent of 14,704 ft. This was scaled by the Austro-German-Italian expedition led by Dr. Karl Maria Herrligkoffer in April 1970.

The most demanding free climbs in the world are those rated at 5.13, the premier location for these being in the Yosemite Valley, CA.

Highest bivouac Four Nepalese summiters bivouacked at more than 28,870 ft in their descent from the summit of Everest on the night of 23 April 1990. They were Ang Rita Sherpa on his record-breaking 6th ascent of Everest, Ang Kami Sherpa, Pasang Norbu Sherpa and Top Bahadur Khatri.

Oldest Teiichi Igarashi (Japan) climbed Mount Fuji (Fuji-yama) (12,388 ft) at the age of 99 yr 302 days on 20 July 1986.

OLYMPIC GAMES

ORIGINS The exact date of the first Olympic Games is uncertain. The earliest date for which there is documented evidence is July 776 B.C. By order of Theodosius I, emperor of Rome, the Games were prohibited in A.D. 394. The revival of the Olympic Games is credited to Pierre de Fredi, Baron de Coubertin, a French aristocrat, who was commissioned by his government to form a universal sports association in 1889. Coubertin presented his proposals for a modern Games on November 25, 1892 in Paris, which led to the formation of the International Olympic Committee (IOC) in 1894 and thence to the staging of the Olympic Games, which were opened in Athens,

OLYMPIC MEDAL ■ AT THE FIRST MODERN OLYMPIC GAMES HELD IN 1896, WINNERS RECEIVED A SILVER MEDAL (ABOVE) AND A CROWN OF OLIVE LEAVES.

Greece on 6 April 1896. In 1906, the IOC organized the Intercalated Games in Athens, to celebrate the 10th anniversary of the revival of the Games. Records from this event are included in this section. In 1924, the first Winter Olympics were held in Chamonix, France.

OLYMPIC CHAMPION ■ BOB GARRETT OF THE US WON SIX MEDALS AT THE FIRST MODERN OLYMPICS, INCLUDING THE DISCUS, AN EVENT HE WAS COMPETING IN FOR THE FIRST TIME.

VENUES OF SUMMER GAMES		
Year	City	Country
1896	Athens	Greece
1900	Paris	France
1904	St. Louis	USA
1906*	Athens	Greece
1908	London	England
1912	Stockholm	Sweden
1920	Antwerp	Belgium
1924	Paris	France
1928	Amsterdam	Netherlands

VENUES OF SUMMER GAMES (Continued)

Year	City	Country
1932	Los Angeles	USA
1936	Berlin	Germany
1948	London	England
1952	Helsinki	Finland
1956	Melbourne	Australia
1960	Rome	Italy
1964	Tokyo	Japan
1968	Mexico City	Mexico
1972	Munich	West Germany
1976	Montreal	Canada
1980	Moscow	USSR
1984	Los Angeles	USA
1988	Seoul	South Korea
1992	Barcelona	Spain
1996	Atlanta	USA

*Intercalated Games

SUMMER OLYMPIC GAMES (1896–1988)
Table of Medal Winners

Country	Gold	Silver	Bronze	Total
USA	746	560	475	1,781
USSR	395	323	299	1,017
Great Britain	174	223	207	604
Germany*	157	207	207	571
France	153	167	177	497
Sweden	131	139	169	439
East Germany**	153	129	127	409
Italy	147	121	124	392
Hungary	124	112	136	372
Finland	97	75	110	282
Japan	87	75	82	244
Australia	71	67	87	225
Romania	55	64	82	201
Poland	40	56	95	191
Canada	39	62	73	174
Switzerland	40	66	57	163
Netherlands	43	47	63	153
Bulgaria	37	62	52	151
Denmark	33	58	53	144
Czechoslovakia	45	48	49	142
Belgium	35	48	42	125
Norway	42	33	33	108
Greece	22	39	39	100

SUMMER OLYMPIC GAMES (1896–1988) (Continued)
Table of Medal Winners

Country	Gold	Silver	Bronze	Total
Yugoslavia	26	29	28	83
Austria	19	26	34	79
South Korea	19	22	29	70
China	20	19	21	60
Cuba	23	21	15	59
New Zealand	26	6	23	55
South Africa	16	15	21	52
Turkey	24	13	10	47
Argentina	13	18	13	44
Mexico	9	12	18	39
Brazil	7	9	20	36
Kenya	11	9	11	31
Iran	4	11	15	30
Spain	4	12	8	24
Jamaica	4	10	8	22
Estonia+	6	6	9	21
Egypt	6	6	6	18
India	8	3	3	14
Ireland	4	4	5	13
Portugal	2	4	7	13
North Korea++	2	5	5	12
Mongolia	0	5	6	11
Ethiopia	5	1	4	10
Pakistan	3	3	3	9
Uruguay	2	1	6	9
Venezuela	1	2	5	8
Chile	0	6	2	8
Trinidad	1	2	4	7
Philippines	0	1	6	7
Morocco	3	1	2	6
Uganda	1	3	1	5
Tunisia	1	2	2	5
Colombia	0	2	3	5
Lebanon	0	2	2	4
Nigeria	0	1	3	4
Puerto Rico	0	1	3	4
Peru	1	2	0	3
Latvia+	0	2	1	3
Taipei (Taiwan)	0	1	2	3
Ghana	0	1	2	3
Thailand	0	1	2	3
Luxembourg	1	1	0	2

Table of Medal Winners

Country	Gold	Silver	Bronze	Total
Bahamas	1	0	1	2
Tanzania	0	2	0	2
Cameroon	0	1	1	2
Haiti	0	1	1	2
Iceland	0	1	1	2
Algeria	0	0	2	2
Panama	0	0	2	2
Surinam	1	0	0	1
Zimbabwe	1	0	0	1
Costa Rica	0	1	0	1
Indonesia	0	1	0	1
Ivory Coast	0	1	0	1
Netherlands Antilles	0	1	0	1
Senegal	0	1	0	1
Singapore	0	1	0	1
Sri Lanka	0	1	0	1
Syria	0	1	0	1
Virgin Islands	0	1	0	1
Bermuda	0	0	1	1
Djibouti	0	0	1	1
Dominican Republic	0	0	1	1
Guyana	0	0	1	1
Iraq	0	0	1	1
Niger	0	0	1	1
Zambia	0	0	1	1

* Germany 1896–1964 West Germany from 1968
** East Germany from 1968
+ Estonia and Latvia up to 1936
++ North Korea from 1964

Most Competitors The greatest number of participants at a Summer Games is 8,465 (6,279 men, 2,186 women), who represented a record 159 countries, at Seoul, South Korea in 1988.

VENUES OF WINTER GAMES

Year	City	Country
1924	Chamonix	France
1928	St. Moritz	Switzerland
1932	Lake Placid	USA
1936	Garmisch-Partenkirchen	Germany
1948	St. Moritz	Switzerland
1952	Oslo	Norway
1956	Cortina d'Ampezzo	Italy
1960	Squaw Valley	USA

VENUES OF WINTER GAMES (Continued)

Year	City	Country
1964	Innsbruck	Austria
1968	Grenoble	France
1972	Sapporo	Japan
1976	Innsbruck	Austria
1980	Lake Placid	USA
1984	Sarajevo	Yugoslavia
1988	Calgary	Canada
1992	Albertville	France
1994	Lilliehammer	Norway

WINTER OLYMPIC GAMES (1924–88)

Table of Medal Winners

Country	Gold	Silver	Bronze	Total
USSR	79	57	59	195
Norway	54	60	54	168
USA	42	47	34	123
East Germany*	39	36	35	110
Finland	33	43	34	110
Austria	28	38	32	98
Sweden	36	25	31	92
Germany**	26	26	23	75
Switzerland	23	25	25	73
Canada	14	13	17	44
Netherlands	13	17	12	42
France	13	10	16	39
Italy	14	10	9	33
Czechoslovakia	2	8	13	23
Great Britain	7	4	10	21
Lichtenstein	2	2	5	9
Japan	1	4	2	7
Hungary	0	2	4	6
Belgium	1	1	2	4
Poland	1	1	2	4
Yugoslavia	0	3	1	4
Spain	1	0	0	1
North Korea+	0	1	0	1
Bulgaria	0	0	1	1
Romania	0	0	1	1

* East Germany from 1968
** Germany 1924–64 West Germany from 1968
+ North Korea from 1964

Most Competitors The most participants at the Winter Games is 1,428 (1,113 men, 315 women), representing 57 countries, at Calgary, Canada in 1988.

The first modern Games were opened in Athens, Greece on 6 April 1896. Forty-four events were staged, but none for women. Women were allowed to compete at the second Olympiad at Paris, France in 1900, but the only events were golf and tennis. Charlotte Cooper, Great Britain, became the first female Olympic champion when she won the singles title on 9 July. The track and field program did not add women's events until 1928, and these did not include races beyond 800 m. In 1972, a 1,500-m women's race was held, but it wasn't until 1984 that female athletes finally received recognition when events such as the 3,000 m and the marathon were added to the schedule.

The United States has won more gold medals (788) and more total medals (1,904) than any other nation in the history of the Summer and Winter Olympics. Recognized here are some of the female Olympic record holders who have contributed to that total and proved that female athletes belong in the Olympic Games.

TRACK AND FIELD ■ THE MOST MEDALS WON BY AN AMERICAN TRACK ATHLETE IS FIVE, BY FLORENCE GRIFFITH-JOYNER: SILVER AT 200 M IN 1984; GOLD AT 100 M, 200 M AND 4 X 100 M RELAY, AND SILVER AT 4 X 400 M RELAY IN 1988.

DIVING ■ THE MOST GOLD MEDALS WON BY AN AMERICAN ATHLETE IS FOUR, BY PATRICIA MC-CORMICK. SHE WON BOTH THE HIGHBOARD AND SPRINGBOARD EVENTS IN 1952 AND 1956.

SWIMMING ■ SHIRLEY BABASHOFF HOLDS THE RECORD FOR WINNING THE MOST SILVER MEDALS IN OLYMPIC COMPETITION, SIX (1972–76).

SPEED SKATING ■ BONNIE BLAIR WON THE GOLD MEDAL FOR 500 M AT CALGARY, CANADA IN 1988.

GYMNASTICS ■ AT THE LOS ANGELES OLYMPICS IN 1984, MARY LOU RETTON BECAME THE FIRST AMERICAN WOMAN TO WIN THE OVERALL CHAMPIONSHIP.

FIGURE SKATING ■ DOROTHY HAMILL WON THE 1976 LADIES' CHAMPIONSHIP AT INNSBRUCK, AUSTRIA.

INDIVIDUAL RECORDS

Most Medals (Gold, Silver, Bronze) Larisa Latynina (USSR) won 18 medals, (9 gold, 5 silver, 4 bronze), in gymnastics from 1956–64. The most medals won by a man is 15 (7 gold, 5 silver, 3 bronze), by Nikolai Andrianov (USSR) in gymnastics 1972–80.

Most Gold Medals Ray Ewry (US) won 10 gold medals (1900–08) in standing high, long and triple jumps. Larissa Latynina (USSR) has won the most gold medals by a women with nine in gymnastics (1956–64).

Most Silver Medals Shirley Babashoff (US) won six silver medals in swimming (1972–76). The men's record is also six, held by Aleksandr Dityatin (USSR) in gymnastics (1976–80) and Mikhail Voronin (USSR) in gymnastics (1968–72).

Most Bronze Medals Heikki Savolainen (Finland) won six bronze medals in gymnastics (1928–52).

Most Gold Medals at One Olympiad Swimmer Mark Spitz (US) won a record seven gold medals at Munich in 1972. His victories came in the 100-meter freestyle, 200-meter freestyle, 100-meter butterfly, 200-meter butterfly, and three relay events. Speed skater Eric Heiden (US) won a record five individual events at Lake Placid, NY in 1980.

Most Medals at One Olympiad Gymnast Aleksandr Dityatin (USSR) won eight medals (3 gold, 4 silver, 1 bronze) at Moscow, USSR in 1980.

Consecutive Gold Medals in Same Event Al Oerter (US) is the only athlete to win the same event, the discus, at four consecutive Olympiads, 1956–68. Paul B. Elvstrom (Denmark) won four successive gold medals at monotype yachting events, 1948–60, but there was a class change (1948 Firefly class, 1952–60 Finn class).

Oldest Gold Medalist Oscar Swahn (Sweden) was aged 64 years 258 days, when he won an Olympic gold medal in 1912 as a member of the winning Running Deer shooting team.

Youngest Gold Medalist The youngest ever winner was an unnamed French boy who coxed the Netherlands pair to victory in the 1900 rowing event. He was believed to be 7–10 years old. The youngest ever woman champion was Marjorie Gestring (née Bowman) (US), who at age 13 years 268 days, won the 1936 women's springboard diving event.

GOLD MEDAL STREAK ■ AL OERTER OF THE US IS THE ONLY ATHLETE TO WIN THE SAME EVENT, THE DISCUS, AT FOUR CONSECUTIVE OLYMPIADS, 1956–68.

Most Games Three Olympians have competed in eight Games: show jumper Raimondo d'Inzeo (Italy, 1948–76); yachtsman Paul B. Elvstrom (Denmark, 1948–60, 1968–72, 1984–88); yachtsman, Durwood Knowles (Great Britain/Bahamas, 1948–72, 1988). The most appearances by a woman is seven by fencer Kerstin Palm (Sweden, 1964–88).

Summer/Winter Games Gold Medalist The only person to have won gold medals in both Summer and Winter Olympiads is Edward Eagan (US), who won the 1920 light-heavyweight boxing title and was a member of the 1932 four-man bobsled winning team.

UNITED STATES RECORDS

Most Gold Medals The records for most gold medals overall and at one Games are both held by American athletes (see above). The most gold medals won by an American woman is four by Patricia McCormick (née Keller), both in highboard and springboard diving, 1952 and 1956.

Most Medals (Gold, Silver, Bronze) The most medals won by an American Olympian is 11 by two athletes: Carl Osburn, shooting, five gold, four silver, two bronze (1912–24); Mark Spitz, swimming, nine gold, one silver, one bronze (1968–72). The most medals won by an American woman is eight by Shirley Babashoff, swimming, two gold, six silver (1972–76).

Oldest Gold Medalist The oldest US Olympic champion was Galen Spencer, who won a gold medal in archery in 1904, at age 64 years 2 days.

Youngest Gold Medalist The youngest gold medalist was Jackie Fields (né Finkelstein), who won the 1924 featherweight boxing title at age 16 years 162 days.

Youngest Medalist The youngest American medal winner, and youngest ever participant, was Dorothy Poynton who won a bronze medal at the 1928 Games at age 13 years 23 days. The youngest men's medalist was Donald Douglas Jr., who won a silver medal at 6-meter yachting in 1932, at age 15 years 40 days.

Olympic Torch Relay The longest journey of the torch within one country was for the XV Olympic Winter Games in Canada in 1988. The torch arrived from Greece at St. John's, Newfoundland on 17 November 1987 and was then transported 11,222 miles (5,088 miles by foot, 4,419 miles by aircraft/ferry, 1,712 miles by snowmobile and 3 miles by dogsled), until its arrival at Calgary on 13 February 1988.

ORIENTEERING

ORIGINS Orienteering, the sport that combines cross-country running and compass and map navigation, can be traced to Scandinavia at the turn of the 20th century. Major Ernst Killander (Sweden) is regarded as the father of orienteering, having founded the first large race in Saltsjobaden, Sweden in 1919. The Swedish federation, Svenska Orienteringsforbundet, was founded in 1936. The International Orienteering Federation was established in 1961. Orienteering

INTO THE WOODS ■ SHARON CRAWFORD (RIGHT) HAS WON A RECORD 11 US NATIONAL ORIENTEERING CHAMPIONSHIPS, 1977–82, 1984–87, 1989. PETER GAGARIN (LEFT) HOLDS THE MEN'S MARK WITH FIVE WINS, 1976–79, 1983.

was introduced to the US in the 1940s. The first US Orienteering Championships were held on 17 October 1970. The US Orienteering Federation (USOF) was founded on 1 August 1971.

WORLD CHAMPIONSHIPS The men's relay has been won a record seven times by Norway—1970, 1978, 1981, 1983, 1985, 1987 and 1989. Sweden has won the women's relay eight times—1966, 1970, 1974, 1976, 1981, 1983, 1985 and 1989. Three women's individual titles have been won by Annichen Kringstad-Svensson (Sweden) in 1981, 1983 and 1985. The men's title has been won twice by: Age Hadler (Norway), in 1966 and 1972; Egil Johansen (Norway), in 1976 and 1978; and Oyvind Thon (Norway), in 1979 and 1981.

US NATIONAL CHAMPIONSHIPS First held on 17 October 1970, Sharon Crawford, New England Orienteering Club, has won a record 11 overall women's titles: 1977–82, 1984–87, 1989. Peter Gagarin, New England Orienteering Club, has won a record five overall men's titles: 1976–79, 1983.

Most Competitors: The most participants in a one-day event is 38,000 in the Ruf des Herbstes held in Sibiu, Romania in 1982. The largest event is the five-day Swedish O-Ringen at Smaland, which attracted 120,000 competitors in 1983.

POLO

ORIGINS Polo originated in Central Asia, possibly as early as 3,100 B.C. in the Manipur state. The name is derived from the Tibetan word "pulu." The modern era began in India in the 1850s when British army officers were introduced to the game. The Cachar Club, Assam, India was founded in 1859, and is believed to be the first Polo Club of the modern era. The game was introduced in England in 1869. The world governing body, the Hurlingham Polo Association, was founded in London, England in 1874 and drew up the laws of the game in 1875.

Polo was introduced to the US by James Gordon Bennett in 1876, when he arranged for the first indoor game at Dickel's Riding Academy, NY. The United States Polo Association was formed in 1890. The United States Open Championship was inaugurated in 1904 and has been played continuously, with the exception of 1942–45, since 1919.

WORLD CHAMPIONSHIPS The first World Championships were held in West Berlin, West Germany in 1989. The US won the title defeating Great Britain 7–6 in the final.

Highest handicap The highest handicap based on eight 7 ½-min "chukkas" is 10 goals introduced in the US in 1891 and in the UK and in Argentina in 1910. A total of 55 players have received 10-goal handicaps. A match of two 40-goal teams was staged, for the only time, at Palermo, Buenos Aires, Argentina in 1975.

Highest score The highest aggregate number of goals scored in an international match is 30, when Argentina beat the US 21–9 at Meadowbrook, Long Island, NY in September 1936.

Sports World Records The playing field for polo is the largest of any sport, with maximum length of 300 yd x 200 yd, without boards, or 160 yd with boards. Also, as the chart below indicates, polo may be able to claim the world's wealthiest amateur sportsmen.

POLO INCOME FACTS	
Household Income	
Average	$174,000.00
$500,000 +	8.5%
$200,000 +	27.0%
$100,000 +	51.8%
Net Worth	
Average	$966,000.00
$1 million +	31.9%
$500,000 +	53.9%
Primary Residence Valuation	
Average	$515,000.00
$1 million +	10.0%
$500,000 +	31.4%
Occupation	
Prof/Managerial	93.6%
Chairman/President	40.5%

Source: Polo Magazine

POOL

Pool or championship pocket billiards with numbered balls began to become standardized c. 1890. The greatest exponents were Ralph Greenleaf (US), who won the "world" professional title 19 times (1919–37), and Willie Mosconi (US), who dominated the game from 1941 to 1957.

The longest consecutive run in an American straight pool match is 625 balls, by Michael Eufemia at Logan's Billiard Academy, Brooklyn, NY on

2 February 1960. The greatest number of balls pocketed in 24 hr is 16,009, by Paul Sullivan at Selby, England on 8–9 April 1989.

The record times for potting all 15 balls in a speed competition are: (men) 37.9 sec, by Rob McKenna at Blackpool, England on 7 November 1987, and (women) 44.5 sec, by Susan Thompson at Shrublands Community Centre, Gorleston, England, on 20 April 1990.

A record break of 132 for 14–1 pool was set by Ross McInnes at Pontin's, Heysham, England on 3 October 1984.

POWERBOAT RACING

ORIGINS A gasoline engine was first installed in a boat by Jean Lenoir on the River Seine, Paris, France in 1865. Powerboat racing started at the turn of the century. The first major international competition was the Harnsworth Trophy launched in 1903. Powerboat racing is broken down into two main types: circuit racing in sheltered waterways and offshore racing. Offshore events were initially for displacement (nonplaning) cruisers, but in 1958 the 170-miles Miami, FL to Nassau, Bahamas race was staged for planing cruisers.

APBA GOLD CUP The American Power Boat Association (APBA) was formed in 1903; it held its first Gold Cup race at the Columbia Yacht Club on the Hudson River, NY in 1904, when the winner was *Standard*, piloted by C. C. Riotto at an average speed of 23.6 mph. The most wins by a pilot is eight by Bill Muncey, 1956–57, 1961–62, 1972, 1977–79. The most successful boat has been *Atlas Van Lines*, piloted by Muncey to victory in 1972, 1977–79, and by Chip Hanauer in 1982–84. Hanauer went on to complete a record seven successive victories to 1988.

Fastest speeds The fastest speed recorded by a propeller-driven boat is 229 mph, by *The Texan*, a Kurtis Top Fuel Hydro Drag boat, driven by Eddie Hill (US) on 5 September 1982 at Chowchilla, CA. He also set a 440 yd elapsed time record of 5.16 sec in this boat at Firebird Lake, AZ on 13 November 1983. The official American Drag Boat Association record is 223.88 mph by *Final Effort*, a Blown Fuel Hydro boat driven by Robert T. Burns at Creve Coeur Lake, St. Louis, MO on 15 July 1985 over a ¼-mile course.

The fastest speed recognized by the Union Internationale Motonautique for an outboard-powered boat is in Class (e): 177.61 mph by P. R. Knight in a Chevrolet-engined Lautobach hull on Lake Ruataniwha, New Zealand in 1986. Robert F. Hering (US) set the world Formula One record at 165.338 mph at Parker, AZ on 21 April 1986.

The fastest speed recognized for an offshore boat is 154.438 mph for one way and 148.238 mph for two runs by Tom Gentry (US), in his 49-ft catamaran, powered by four Gentry Turbo Eagle V8 Chevrolets.

The fastest speed recorded for a diesel (compression ignition) boat is 135.532 mph by the hydroplane *Iveco World Leader*, powered by an Aifo-Fiat engine, driven by Carlo Bonomi at Venice, Italy on 4 April 1985.

Fastest race speeds The fastest speed recorded in an offshore race is 103.29 mph, by Tony Garcia (US) in a Class I powerboat at Key West, FL in November 1983.

Longest races The longest offshore race has been the Port Richborough London to Monte Carlo Marathon Offshore international event. The race extended over 2,947 mi in 14 stages from 10–25 June 1972. It was won by *H.T.S.* (UK), piloted by Mike Bellamy, Eddie Chater and Jim Brooker in 71 hr 35 min 56 sec, for an average speed of 41.15 mph. The longest circuit race is the 24-hr race held annually since 1962 on the River Seine at Rouen, France.

POWERLIFTING

ORIGINS Powerlifting developed from the many different lifts practiced by weightlifters during their training for that sport. There are 11 weight categories for men and 10 for women in three classifications: the squat, bench press and dead lift (all performed two-handed). The first United States Championships were first held in 1964. The International Powerlifting Federation was founded in 1972, a year after the first, unofficial world championships were held. Official championships have been held annually for men from 1973 and for women from 1980.

WORLD CHAMPIONSHIPS The winner of the most world titles is Hideaki Inaba (Japan), with 15, at 52 kg, 1974–83, 1985–89. The most by a women is six, by Beverley Francis (Australia) at 75 kg, 1980, 1982; 82.5 kg 1981, 1983–85.

Powerlifting feats Lamar Gant (US) was the first man to deadlift five times his own body weight, lifting 661 lb when 132 lb in 1985.

WORLD POWERLIFTING RECORDS (All weights in kilograms)

Class	Squat	Bench Press	Deadlift	Total
MEN				
52 kg	243 Hideaki Inaba (Japan) 1986	146.6 Joe Cunha (US) 1982	237.5 Hideaki Inaba (Japan) 1987	587.5 Hideaki Inaba (Japan) 1987
56 kg	242.5 Hideaki Inaba (Japan) 1988	160.5 Hiroyuki Isagawa (Japan) 1989	289.5 Lamar Gant (US) 1982	625 Lamar Gant (US) 1982
60 kg	295 Joe Bradley (US) 1980	180 Joe Bradley (US) 1980	310 Lamar Gant (US) 1988	707.5 Joe Bradley (US) 1982
67.5 kg	300 Jessie Jackson (US) 1987	200 Kristoffer Hulecki (Sweden) 1985	315 Daniel Austin (US) 1989	762.5 Daniel Austin (US) 1989
75 kg	328 Ausby Alexander (US) 1989	217.5 James Rouse (US) 1980	333 Jarmo Virtanen (Finland) 1988	850 Rick Gaugler (US) 1982
82.5 kg	379.5 Mike Bridges (US) 1982	240 Mike Bridges (US) 1981	357.5 Veli Kumpuniemi (Finland) 1980	952.5 Mike Bridges (US) 1982
90 kg	375 Fred Hatfield (US) 1980	255 Mike MacDonald (US) 1980	372.5 Walter Thomas (US) 1982	937.5 Mike Bridges (US) 1980
100 kg	422.5 Ed Coan (US) 1989	261.5 Mike MacDonald (US) 1977	378 Ed Coan (US) 1989	1,032.5 Ed Coan (US) 1989
110 kg	393.5 Dan Wohleber (US) 1981	270 Jeffrey Magruder (US) 1982	395 John Kuc (US) 1980	1,000 John Kuc (US) 1980
125 kg	412.5 David Waddington (US) 1982	278.5 Tom Hardman (US) 1982	387.5 Lars Norén (Sweden) 1987	1,005 Ernie Hackett (US) 1982
125 + kg	445 Dwayne Fely (US) 1982	300 Bill Kazmaier (US) 1981	406 Lars Norén (Sweden) 1988	1,100 Bill Kazmaier (US) 1981
WOMEN				
44 kg	142.5 Delcy Palk (US) 1988	75 Teri Hoyt (US) 1982	165 Nancy Belliveau (US) 1985	352.5 Marie-France Vassart (Bel) 1985
48 kg	147.5 Keiko Nishio (Japan) 1987	82.5 Michelle Evris (US) 1981	182.5 Majik Jones (US) 1984	390 Majik Jones (US) 1984
52 kg	173.5 Sisi Dolman (Neth) 1989	95 Mary Ryan (US) 1984	197.5 Diana Rowell (US) 1984	427.5 Diana Rowell (US) 1984
56 kg	191 Mary Jeffrey (née Ryan; US) 1989	115 Mary Jeffrey (US) 1988	200.5 Joy Burt (Canada) 1989	485 Mary Jeffrey (US) 1988
60 kg	200.5 Ruthi Shafer (US) 1983	105.5 Judith Auerbach (US) 1989	213 Ruthi Shafer (US) 1983	502.5 Vicki Steenrod (US) 1985
67.5 kg	230 Ruthi Shafer (US) 1984	117.5 Vicki Steenrod (US) 1989	244 Ruthi Shafer (US) 1984	565 Ruthi Shafer (US) 1984
75 kg	225 Sumita Laha (Ind) 1989	142.5 Liz Odendaal (Neth) 1989	230 Liz Odendaal (Neth) 1989	577.5 Liz Odendaal (Neth) 1989
82.5 kg	230 Juanita Trujillo (US) 1986	150 Beverley Francis (Aus) 1981	227.5 Vicky Gagne (US) 1981	577.5 Beverley Francis (Aus) 1983
90 kg	252.5 Lorraine Constanzo (US) 1988	130 Lorraine Constanzo (US) 1988	227.5 Lorraine Constanzo (US) 1988	607.5 Lorraine Constanzo (US) 1988
90 + kg	262.5 Lorraine Constanzo (US) 1987	137.5 Myrtle Augee (GB) 1989	237.5 Lorraine Constanzo (US) 1987	622.5 Lorraine Constanzo (US) 1987

The greatest powerlift by a woman is a squat of 628 lb by Lorraine Constanzo (US) at Dayton, OH on 21 November 1987. Cammie Lynn Lusko (US) became the first woman to lift more than her body weight with one arm, with 131 lb at a body weight of 128.5 lb, at Milwaukee, WI on 21 May 1983.

24-hr and 1-hr lifts A deadlifting record of 5,519,634 lb in 24 hr was set by a team of 10 from HM Prison Wandsworth, London, England on 26–27 May 1990. The 24-hr deadlift record by an individual is 818,108 lb, by Anthony Wright at HM Prison Featherstone, Wolverhampton, England on 31 August–1 September 1990.

A bench press record of 8,529,565 lb was set by a nine-man team from the Hogarth Barbell Club, Chiswick, England on 18–19 July 1987. A squat record of 4,780,919 lb was set by a 10-man team from St. Albans Weightlifting Club and Ware Boys Club, Hertfordshire, England on 20–21 July 1986. A record 133,380 arm-curling repetitions using three 48¼-lb weightlifting bars and dumbbells was achieved by a team of nine from Intrim Health and Fitness Club at Gosport, England on 4–5 August 1989.

Michael Williams achieved 1,438 repetitions of his body weight (147.7 lb) in one hour of bench presses at Don Styler's Gymnasium, Gosport, England on 17 April 1989.

RACQUETBALL

ORIGINS Racquetball, using a 40 ft x 20 ft court, was invented in 1950 by Joe Sobek at the Green-wich YMCA, CT, originally as Paddle Rackets. The International Racquetball Association was founded in 1968 by Bob Kendler (US). It changed its name in 1980 to the American Amateur Racquetball Association.

WORLD CHAMPIONSHIPS First held in 1982 and staged biennially, the men's competition has been won by different players on each occasion. Three Americans have been world champions. Ed Andrews (1982), Egan Inoue (1986) and Andy Roberts (1988). Cindy Baxter (US) has won a record two world titles in 1982 and 1986.

US NATIONAL CHAMPIONSHIPS The governing body for the sport in the US is the American Amateur Racquetball Association (AARA), whose championships were initiated in 1968. A record four men's open titles have been won by Ed Andrews of California, 1980–81 and 1985–86, and a record four women's open titles by Cindy Baxter of Pennsylvania, 1981, 1983, 1985–86.

RODEO

ORIGINS Rodeo originated in Mexico, developing from 18th century fiestas, and moved north to the US and Canada with the expansion of the North American cattle industry in the 18th and 19th centuries. There are several claims as to the earliest organized rodeo, the Professional Rodeo Cowboys Association (PRCA) sanctions the West of the Pecos Rodeo, Pecos, TX, as the oldest; it was first held in 1883.

WORLD CHAMPIONSHIPS The Rodeo Association of America organized the first World Champion-

STAYING POWER ■ LARRY MAHAN HAS WON A RECORD SIX ALL-AROUND WORLD TITLES, A RECORD HE SHARES WITH TOM FERGUSON.

ships in 1929. The championship has been organized under several different formats and sponsored by different groups throughout its existence. The current championship is a season-long competition based on PRCA earnings. The PRCA has organized the championship since 1945 (as the Rodeo Cowboy Association through 1976).

RODEO WORLD CHAMPIONSHIPS			
Event	Wins	Rider	Year
All-Around	6	Larry Mahan Tom Ferguson	1966–70, 1973 1974–79
Saddle Bronc Riding	6	Casey Tibbs	1949, 1951-54, 1959
Bareback Riding	5	Joe Alexander Bruce Ford	1971–75 1979–80, 1982–83, 1987
Bull Riding	8	Don Gay	1975–81, 1984
Calf Roping	8	Dean Oliver	1955, 1958, 1960–64, 1969
Steer Roping	6	Everett Shaw	1945–46, 1948, 1951, 1959, 1962
Steer Wrestling	6	Homer Pettigrew	1940, 1942–45, 1948
Team Roping	5	Jake Barnes & Clay O'Brien Cooper	1985–89
Women's Barrel Racing	7	Charmayne Rodman	1984–90

Source: PRCA

Earnings Records Roy Cooper holds the career rodeo earnings mark at $1,239,256 (1976–90). The single season record is $213,772 by Ty Murray in 1990.

PRCA EARNINGS RECORDS BY EVENT

Event	Rider	Earnings	Year
Saddle Bronc Riding	Robert Etbauer	$113,411	1990
Bareback Riding	Lewis Feild	$114,675	1986
Bull Riding	Tuff Hederman	$137,061	1986
Calf Roping	Roy Cooper	$122,455	1983
Steer Wrestling	Steve Duhon	$114,535	1986
Steer Roping	Guy Allen	$44,386	1989
Team Roping	Jake Barnes & Clay O'Brien Cooper	$99,048 each	1985
Women's Barrel Racing	Charmayne Rodman	$151,969	1986

Source: PRCA

Big Bucks ■ Charmayne Rodman (above) set a barrel racing earnings mark of $151,969 in 1986. Ty Murray (top right) set a PRCA single-season earnings record of $213,772 in 1990.

Time records Records for PRCA timed events, such as calf roping and steer wrestling, are not always comparable, because of the widely varying conditions attributable to the sizes of arenas and amount of start given the stock. The fastest time recorded for calf roping under the current PRCA rules is 6.7 sec, by Joe Beaver at West Jordan, UT in 1986, and the fastest time for steer wrestling is 2.4 sec, by: James Bynum, at Marietta, OK in 1955; Carl Deaton at Tulsa, OK in 1976; and Gene Melton at Pecatonica, IL in 1976. The fastest team roping time is 3.7 sec, by Bob Harris and Tee Woolman at Spanish Fork, UT in 1986.

Bull riding Jim Sharp of Kermit, TX became the first rider to ride all 10 bulls at a National Finals Rodeo at Las Vegas in December 1988.

The highest score in bull riding was 98 points out of a possible 100, by Denny Flynn on Red Lightning at Palestine, IL in 1979.

The top bucking bull Red Rock dislodged 312 riders, 1980–88, and was finally ridden to the 8-sec bell by Lane Frost on 20 May 1988. Red Rock was retired at the end of the 1987 season but still continued to make guest appearances.

Saddle bronc riding The highest scored saddle bronc ride is 95 out of a possible 100, by Doug Vold at Meadow Lake, Saskatchewan, Canada in 1979. Descent, a saddle bronc owned by Beutler Brothers and Cervi Rodeo Company, received a record six PRCA saddle bronc of the year awards, 1966–69, 1971–72.

Bareback riding Joe Alexander of Cora, WY scored 93 out of a possible 100 at Cheyenne, WY in 1974.

ROLLER SKATING

ORIGINS Roller skates were invented by Joseph Merlin of Belgium. He demonstrated his new mode of transport at a masquerade party in London in 1760 with disastrous consequences—he was unable to stop and crashed into a large mirror, receiving near-fatal wounds. In 1863, James L. Plimpton of Medfield, MA, patented the modern four-wheeled roller skate. In 1866, he opened the first public roller skating rink in the US in Newport, RI. The International Roller Skating Federation was founded in 1924 and is now headquartered in Lincoln, NE. In 1937, the first World Championships were held for speed skating in Monza, Italy.

WORLD CHAMPIONSHIPS (SPEED) The most world speed titles won is 18, by two women: Alberta Vianello

(Italy), eight track and 10 road 1953–65; and Annie Lambrechts (Belgium), one track and 17 road, 1964–81, at distances from 500 m to 10,000 m.

WORLD CHAMPIONSHIPS (FIGURE) The records for figure titles are: five, by Karl Heinz Losch in 1958–59, 1961–62 and 1966; and four by Astrid Bader in 1965–68, both of West Germany. The most world pair titles is four, by Dieter Fingerle (West Germany) in 1959, 1965–67 with two different partners, and by John Arishita and Tammy Jeru (US) 1983–86.

Speed skating The fastest speed achieved in an official world record is 26.85 mph, when Luca Antoniel (Italy) recorded 24.99 sec for 300 m on a road at Gujan Mestras, France on 31 July 1987. The women's record is 25.04 mph by Marisa Canafoglia (Italy) for 300 m on the road at Grenoble, France on 27 August 1987. The world records for 10,000 m on a road or track are: (men) 14 min 55.64 sec, Giuseppe de Persio (Italy) at Gejun Mestras, France on 1 August 1988; (women) 15 min 58.022 sec, Marisa Canofogilia (Italy) at Grenoble, France on 30 August 1987.

Largest rink The greatest indoor rink ever to operate was located in the Grand Hall, Olympia, London, England. Opened in 1890 and closed in 1912, it had an actual skating area of 68,000 ft². The current largest is the main arena of 34,981 ft² at Guptill Roll-Arena, Boght Corner, NY. The total rink area is 41,380 ft².

Endurance Theodore James Coombs of Hermosa Beach, CA skated 5,193 miles from Los Angeles, CA to New York and back to Yates Center, KS from 30 May to 14 September 1979.

ROWING

ORIGINS Forms of rowing can be traced back to ancient Egypt; however, the modern sport of rowing dates to 1715, when the Doggett's Coat and Badge scull race was established in London, England. Types of regattas are believed to have taken place in Venice, Italy in 1300, but the modern regatta can also be traced to England, where races were staged in 1775 on the River Thames at Ranleigh Gardens, Putney. The earliest mention of a rowing competition in the US appears in a New York newspaper in 1811. The first regatta is thought to be that held on the Hudson River, off Peekskill, NY, in 1848. The world governing body is the Federation Internationale des Societes d'Aviron (FISA), founded in 1892. Rowing has been part of the Olympic Games since 1900.

OLYMPIC GAMES Six oarsmen have won three gold medals: John Kelly (US), Single Sculls (1920) and Double Sculls (1920 and 1924); his cousin Paul Costello (US), Double Sculls (1920, 1924 and 1928); Jack Beresford Jr. (UK), Single Sculls (1924), Coxless Fours (1932) and Double Sculls (1936); Vyacheslav Ivanov (USSR), Single Sculls (1956, 1960 and 1964); Siegfried Brietzke (East Germany), Coxless Pairs (1972) and Coxless Fours (1976, 1980); and Pertti Karppinen (Finland), Single Sculls 1976, 1980 and 1984.

WORLD CHAMPIONSHIPS World rowing championships distinct from the Olympic Games were first held in 1962, at first every four years, but from 1974 annually, except in Olympic years.

The most gold medals won at World Championships and Olympic Games is seven at coxed pairs by the Italian brothers, Giuseppe and Carmine Abbagnale. In women's events, Jutta Behrendt (née Hampe [East Germany]) has won six gold medals.

The most wins at Single Sculls is five, by Peter-Michael Kolbe (West Germany), in 1975, 1978, 1981, 1983 and 1986, and by Pertti Karppinen, 1979 and 1985, with his three Olympic wins (above); in the women's events by Christine Hahn (née Scheiblich, [East Germany], 1974–75, 1977–78 (and the 1976 Olympic title).

Fastest speed The fastest recorded speed on nontidal water for 2,000 m is by an American eight in 5 min 27.14 sec (13.68 mph) at Lucerne, Switzerland on 17 June 1984. A crew from Penn AC, was timed in 5 min 18.8 sec (14.03 mph) in the FISA Championships on the River Meuse, Liège, Belgium on 17 August 1930.

24 hours The greatest distance rowed in 24 hr (upstream and downstream) by an eight is 130 miles, by members of the Renmark Rowing Club, South Australia on 20–21 April 1984.

Longest race The longest annual rowing race is the annual Tour du Lac Leman, Geneva, Switzerland for coxed fours (the five-man crew taking turns as cox) over 99 miles. The record winning time is 12 hr 52 min, by LAGA Delft, Netherlands on 3 October 1982.

RUGBY

ORIGINS As with baseball in the US, the origins of rugby are obscure, but a traditional "history" has become so imbedded in the national psyche, in this case Great Britain, that any historical revision is either ignored or not tolerated. The tradition is that the game began when William Webb Ellis picked up the ball during a soccer game at Rugby School in November 1823 and ran with it. The "new" handling code of soccer developed and was played at Cambridge University in 1839. The first rugby club was formed at Guy's Hospital, London, England in 1843 and the Rugby Football Union (RFU) was founded in January 1871. The International Rugby Football Board (IRFB) was founded in 1886.

OLYMPIC GAMES Held at four Games from 1900 to 1924, the only double gold medalist was the US, which won in 1920 and 1924, defeating France in the final on both occasions.

WORLD CUP The inaugural World Cup was contested in Australia and New Zealand by 16 national teams in 1987. The final in Auckland on 20 June 1987 was won by New Zealand, which beat France 29–9. The highest team score was New Zealand's 74–13 victory over Fiji at Christchurch, New Zealand on 27 May 1987. The individual match record was 30 points (3 tries, 9 conversions), by Didier Camberabero (France) v. Zimbabwe at Auckland, New Zealand on 2 June 1987.

INTERNATIONAL RUGBY RECORDS

Highest Score The highest score by a team in a full international game is 106 points, which has occurred twice: New Zealand 106 Japan 4, at Tokyo, Japan on 1 November 1987; France 106 Paraguay 12, at Asuncion, Paraguay on 28 June 1988.

Most Points by an Individual Player The record for a game is 34 points (2 tries, 10 conversions, 2 penalty goals) by Phil Bennett for Wales v. Japan at Tokyo on 24 September 1975, as Wales won 82–6. The most points in an international career is 538 in 41 games scored by Michael Lynagh (Australia, 1984–90).

Most Tries Scored The most tries scored in a game is five by two players: George Lindsay, Scotland v. Wales at Edinburgh, Scotland on 26 February 1887; Douglas Lambert, England v. France at Richmond, England on 5 January 1907. The record for tries scored in a career is 36 by David Campese (Australia, 1982–90).

Most International Appearances Mike Gibson has played in a record 81 international games, Ireland (69 games); British Lions (12 games).

Consecutive Games The record for consecutive international games is 53 shared by two players: Gareth Edwards (Wales, 1967–78); Willie John McBride (Ireland, 1962–75).

WELSH WIZARD ■ PHIL BENNETT, WALES, HOLDS THE RECORD FOR MOST POINTS SCORED IN AN INTERNATIONAL RUGBY GAME, WITH **34** IN WALES V. JAPAN ON **24** SEPTEMBER 1975.

SHOOTING

ORIGINS The earliest recorded shooting club is the Lucerne Shooting Guild (Switzerland), formed *c.* 1466. The first known shooting competition was held at Zurich, Switzerland in 1472. The American Rifle Association was formed in 1871. The international governing body, the Union International de Tir (UIT), was formed in Zurich in 1907.

OLYMPIC GAMES

Shooting has been part of the Olympic program since the first modern Games in 1896. Separate events for women were first staged in 1984, although they had been competing against men since the 1968 Games.

Most Medals The record number of medals won is 11 (5 gold, 4 silver, 2 bronze), by Carl Osburn (US) in 1912, 1920 and 1924.

SHOOTING-INDIVIDUAL WORLD RECORDS

In 1986 the International Shooting Union introduced new regulations for determining major championships and world records. Now the leading competitors undertake an additional round with a target subdivided to tenths of a point for rifle and pistol shooting and an extra 25 shots for trap and skeet. The table below shows the world records for the 13 Olympic shooting disciplines giving in parentheses the score for the number of shots specified plus the score in the additional round.

MEN			
Event	Points	Marksman	Date
Free Rifle 50 m 3 x 40 shots	1,283.4 (1,183 + 100.4)	Petr Kurka (Czechoslovakia)	1 October 1987
Free Rifle 50 m 60 Shots Prone	704.9 (599 + 105.9) 704.9 (598 + 106.9)	Petr Kurka (Czechoslovakia) Goran Maksimovic (Yugoslavia)	2 June 1987 21 October 1988
Air Rifle 10 m 60 shots	699.4 (596 + 103.4)	Rajmond Debevec (Yugoslavia)	8 June 1990
Free Pistol 50 m 60 shots	671 (579 + 92)	Sergey Pyzhyanov (USSR)	31 May 1990
Rapid-fire Pistol 25 m 60 shots	698 (598 + 100)	Afanasiy Kuzmin (USSR)	23 September 1988
Air Pistol 10 m 60 shots	695.1 (593 + 102.1)	Sergey Pyzhyanov (USSR)	October 1989
Running Game Target 50 m 30 + 30 shots	691 (594 + 97) 691 (596 + 95)	Sergey Luzov (USSR) Nikolay Lapin (USSR)	7 September 1986 25 July 1987

WOMEN

Event	Points	Markswoman	Date
Standard Rifle 50 m 3 x 20 shots	691.6 (587 + 104.6)	Vessela Letcheva (Bulgaria)	22 May 1987
Air Rifle 10 m 40 shots	496.9 (397 + 99.9)	Valentina Cherkasova (USSR)	3 March 1989
Sport Pistol 25 m 60 shots	696 (597 + 99)	Lulita Svetkova (USSR)	10 April 1989
Air Pistol 10 m 40 shots	488.8 (388 + 100.8)	Svetlana Smirnova (USSR)	2 March 1989

OPEN

Event	Points	Marksman	Date
Trap 200 targets	224 (199 + 25)	Miloslav Bednarik (Czechoslovakia)	14 September 1986
Skeet 200 targets	224 (199 + 25)	Matthew Dryke (US)	8 September 1986
	224 (199 + 25)	Luca Scribani Rossi (Italy)	11 June 1988
	224 (200 + 24)	Ole Riber Rasmussen (Denmark)	11 June 1988

Six other marksmen have won five gold medals, including three Americans: Alfred P. Lane 1912–20; Willis Augustus Lee Jr. all in 1920; and Morris Fisher 1920 and 1924.

The first US woman to win an Olympic medal was Margaret L. Murdock (née Thompson), who took the silver at small-bore rifle three positions in mixed competition in 1976. The first to win an Olympic gold medal was Patricia Spurgin, at women's air rifle in 1984.

WORLD RECORD The first world record by a woman at any sport for a category in direct and measurable competition with men was by Margaret Murdock, who set a world record for small-bore rifle (kneeling position) of 391 in 1967.

SKIING

ORIGINS Skiing traces its history to Scandinavia; *ski* is the Norwegian word for snowshoe. A ski discovered in a peat bog in Hoting, Sweden dates to *c.* 2500 B.C., and records note the use of skis at the Battle of Isen, Norway in A.D. 1200. The first ski races were held in Norway and Australia in the 1850s and 1860s. Two men stand out as pioneers of the development of skiing in the 19th century: Sondre Nordheim, a Norwegian, who designed equipment and developed skiing techniques, and Mathias Zdarsky, an Austrian, who pioneered Alpine skiing. The first national governing body was that of Norway, formed in 1833. The International Ski Commission was founded in 1910 and was succeeded as the world governing body in 1924 by the International Ski Federation (FIS). The first ski club in the US was formed at Berlin, NH in January 1872. The United States Ski Association was originally founded as the National Ski Association in 1905; in 1962, it was renamed the United States Ski Association, and in 1990 was renamed US Skiing. In the modern era, skiing has evolved into two main categories, Nordic and Alpine. Nordic skiing covers ski jumping events and cross-country racing. Alpine skiing encompasses downhill and slalom racing.

OLYMPIC GAMES

ALPINE SKIING

Downhill and slalom events were first included at the 1936 Olympic Games.

Most Gold Medals In men's competition, the most gold medals won is three by two skiers: Toni Sailer (Austria), who won all three events, downhill, slalom and giant slalom, in 1956; and Jean Claude Killy (France), who matched Sailer's feat in 1968. For women the record is two golds achieved by six skiers: Andrea Mead-Lawrence (US; slalom, giant slalom 1952); Marielle Goitschel (France; giant slalom 1964, slalom 1968); Marie-Therese Nadig (Switzerland; downhill, giant slalom 1972); Rosi Mittermaier (West Germany; downhill, slalom 1976); Hanni Wenzel (Liechtenstein; giant slalom, slalom 1980); Vreni Schneider (Switzerland; giant slalom, slalom 1988).

Most Medals Hanni Wenzel (Liechtenstein) holds the record for most medals with four. Wenzel won a bronze in the 1976 slalom, two gold medals in the 1980 giant slalom and slalom, and a silver in the 1980 downhill.

NORDIC SKIING

Ski jumping and cross-country racing have been included in every Winter Olympic Games.

Most Gold Medals

Cross Country In men's competition, three skiers have each won four gold medals: Sixten Jernberg (Sweden; 50 km 1956, 30 km 1960, 50 km and 4 x 10 km relay 1964); Gunde Svan (Sweden; 15 km and 4 x 10 km relay 1984; 50 km and 4 x 10 km relay 1988); Thomas Wassberg (Sweden; 15 km 1980, 50 km and 4 x 10 km relay 1984; 4 x 10 km relay 1988). The women's record is also four golds, won by Galina Kulakova (USSR; 5 km, 10 km and 3 x 5 km relay 1972; 4 x 5 km relay 1976).

Ski Jumping Matti Nykanen (Finland) has won a record four gold medals, 90 m hill in 1984 and 70 m, 90 m and team event in 1988.

Most Medals The most medals won in Nordic events is nine for both men and women. Sixten Jernberg (Sweden) holds the men's record (4 gold, 3 silver, 2 bronze 1956–64) and Raise Smetanina (USSR) holds the women's (3 gold, 5 silver, 1 bronze 1976-88).

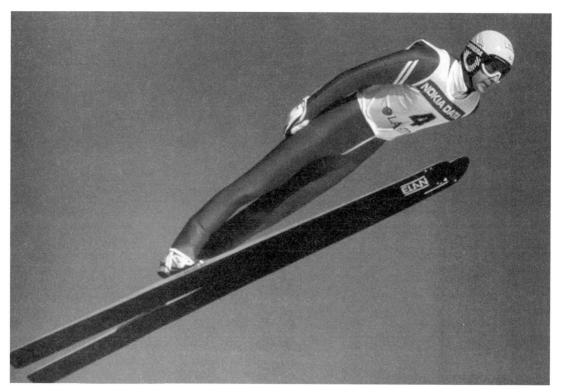

Is It a Bird? ■ Ski jumper Matti Nykanen, Finland, has won a record four Olympic gold medals, 1984 and 1988.

WORLD CHAMPIONSHIPS

Alpine Skiing Inaugurated in 1931 at Murren, Switzerland. From 1931–39 the championships were held annually and biennially from 1950. Up to 1980, the Olympic Games were considered the World Championships, except in 1936. In 1985, the championship schedule was changed so as not to coincide with an Olympic year.

Most Gold Medals Christel Cranz (Germany) won a record 12 titles: Four slalom (1934, 1937–39); three downhill (1935, 1937, 1939); five combined (1934–35, 1937–39). Toni Sailer (Austria) holds the men's record with seven titles: one slalom (1956); two giant slalom (1956, 1958); two downhill (1956, 1958); two combined (1956, 1958).

WORLD CUP

Alpine Skiing Contested annually since 1967, the World Cup is a circuit of races where points are earned during the season, with the champion being the skier with the most points at the end of the season.

MOST WORLD CUP TITLES

Event	Wins	Skier, Country	Year
MEN			
Overall	4	Gustavo Thoeni, Italy	1971–73, 1975
		Pirmin Zurbriggen, Switzerland	1984, 1987–88, 1990
Downhill	5	Franz Klammer, Austria	1975–78, 1983
Slalom	8	Ingemar Stenmark, Sweden	1975–81, 1983
Giant Slalom	7	Ingemar Stenmark, Sweden	1975–76, 1978–81, 1984
Super Giant Slalom	4	Pirmin Zurbriggen, Switzerland	1987–90
WOMEN			
Overall	6	Annemarie Moser, Austria	1971–75, 1979
Downhill	7	Annemarie Moser, Austria	1971–75, 1978–79
Slalom	4	Erika Hess, Switzerland	1981–83, 1985

SLALOM SPECIALIST ■ INGEMAR STENMARK, SWEDEN, WON A RECORD 86 WORLD CUP RACES (46 GIANT SLALOM, 40 SLALOM), OUT OF 287 CONTESTED, 1974–89.

MOST WORLD CUP TITLES (Continued)

WOMEN (Continued)

Event	Wins	Skier, Country	Year
Giant Slalom	3	Annemarie Moser, Austria	1971–72, 1975
		Lise-Marie Morerod, Switzerland	1976–78
		Vreni Schneider, Switzerland	1986–87, 1989
Super Giant Slalom	2	Carole Merle, France	1989–90

Individual Racing Records

Most Wins (Men) Ingemar Stenmark (Sweden) won a record 86 races (46 giant slalom, 40 slalom) from 287 contested, 1974–89.

Most Wins (Women) Annemarie Moser (née Proll, Austria) won a record 62 races, 1970–79.

Most Wins (Season) Ingemar Stenmark (Sweden) won 13 races in 1978–79 to set the men's mark. Vreni Schneider (Switzerland) won 13 races in 1988–89 to set the women's mark.

Consecutive Wins Ingemar Stenmark (Sweden) won 14 successive giant slalom races from 18 March 1978 to 21 January 1980. The women's record is 11 wins by Annemarie Moser (née Proll) in the downhill from December 1972 to January 1974.

NORDIC SKIING

Contested annually since 1981.

WORLD CUP TITLES

MEN

Event	Wins	Skier, Country	Year
Ski Jumping	4	Matti Nykanen, Finland	1983, 1985–86, 1988
Cross-Country	5	Gunde Svan, Sweden	1984–86, 1988–89

WOMEN

Event	Wins	Skier, Country	Year
Cross-Country	3	Marjo Matikainen, Finland	1986–88

UNITED STATES NATIONAL CHAMPIONSHIPS

ALPINE SKIING

Most Titles (Men)

Event	Titles	Skier	Year
Downhill	3	Dick Durrance	1937, 1939–40
Giant Slalom	5	Phil Mahre	1975, 1977–79, 1981

UNITED STATES NATIONAL CHAMPIONSHIPS (Continued)

ALPINE SKIING (Continued)

Most Titles (Men) (Continued)

Event	Titles	Skier	Year
Slalom	4	Cary Adgate	1974, 1976–77, 1979
		Steve Mahre	1975, 1980–81, 1984
		Felix McGrath	1985, 1988–90

NORDIC SKIING (OVERALL)

Most Titles (Men)

Event	Titles	Skier	Year
Cross-Country	12	Audun Endestad	1984–90
Ski Jumping	7	Lars Haugen	1912–28

ALPINE SKIING

Most Titles (Women)

Event	Titles	Skier	Year
Downhill	3	Nancy Greene	1960, 1965, 1967
		Cindy Nelson	1973, 1978, 1980
		Pam Fletcher	1983, 1987–88
Giant Slalom	3	Becky Dorsey	1975, 1977–78
Slalom	7	Tamara McKinney	1982–84, 1986–89

NORDIC SKIING (OVERALL)

Cross-Country	14	Martha Rockwell	1969–75

Fastest speed The official world record, as recognized by the International Ski Federation, for a skier is 139.030 mph, by Michael Prufer (Monaco), and the fastest by a woman is 133.234 mph, by Tarja Mulari (Finland), both at Les Arcs, France on 16 April 1988.

The fastest average speed in the Olympic downhill race was 64.95 mph, by Bill Johnson (US) at Sarajevo, Yugoslavia on 16 February 1984. The fastest in a World Cup downhill is 67.00 mph, by Harti Weirather (Austria) at Kitzbühel, Austria on 15 January 1982.

Fastest speed—cross-country Bill Koch (US) on 26 March 1981 skied 10 times round a 3.11 mile loop on Marlborough Pond, near Putney, VT. He completed the course in 1 hr 59 min 47 sec—an average speed of 15.57 mph. A race includes uphill and downhill sections; Gunde Svan (Sweden) posted the record time for a race in World Championships or Olympic Games of 2 hr 4 min 30.9 sec, in 1988, an average speed of 14.97 mph.

Longest ski jump The longest ski jump ever recorded is one of 636 ft, by Piotr Fijas (Poland) at

Planica, Yugoslavia on 14 March 1987. The women's record is 361 ft, by Tiina Lehtola (Finland) at Ruka, Finland on 29 March 1981.

Highest altitude Jean Afanassieff and Nicolas Jaeger skied from 26,900 ft to 20,340 ft on the 1978 French expedition on Mt. Everest.

Steepest descent The steepest descents in alpine skiing history have been made by Sylvain Saudan. At the start of his descent from Mont Blanc on the northeast side down the Couloir Gervasutti from 13,937 ft on 17 October 1967, he skied to gradients of *c.* 60°.

Longest races The world's longest Nordic ski race is the Vasaloppet, which commemorates an event of 1521 when Gustav Vasa, later King Gustavus Eriksson, fled 53.3 miles from Mora to Sälen, Sweden. He was overtaken by loyal, speedy scouts on skis, who persuaded him to return eastwards to Mora to lead a rebellion and become the king of Sweden. The reenactment of this return journey is now an annual event at 55.3 miles. There were a record 10,934 starters on 6 March 1977 and a record 10,633 finishers on 4 March 1979. The fastest time is 3 hr 48 min 55 sec, by Bengt Hassis (Sweden) on 2 March 1986.

The longest downhill race is the Inferno in Switzerland, 9.8 miles from the top of the Schilthorn to Lauterbrunnen. The record number of entries was 1,401 in 1981 and the record time 15 min 26.44 sec, by Ueli Grossniklaus (Switzerland) in 1987.

Long-distance (cross-country) In 24 hours, Seppo-Juhani Savolainen covered 258.2 miles at Saariselkä, Finland on 8–9 April 1988. The women's record is 205.05 miles, by Sisko Kainulaisen at Jyväskylä, Finland on 23–24 March 1985.

Longest lift The longest gondola ski lift is 3.88 miles at Grindelwald- Männlichen, Switzerland (in two sections, but one gondola). The longest chair lift in the world was the Alpine Way to Kosciusko Chalet lift above Thredbo, near the Snowy Mountains, New South Wales, Australia. It took from 45 to 75 min to ascend the 3.5 miles, according to the weather. It has now collapsed. The highest is at Chacaltaya, Bolivia, rising to 16,500 ft.

SLED DOG RACING

ORIGINS Racing between harnessed dog teams (usually huskies) is believed to have been prac-

ticed by Inuits in North America, and also by the peoples of Scandinavia long before the first recorded formal race, the All- America Sweepstakes, which took place in 1908. Sled dog racing was a demonstration sport at the 1932 Olympic Games and a World Championship was inaugurated in 1936. The best known race is the Iditarod Trail Sled Dog Race, first run in 1973.

IDITAROD TRAIL SLED DOG RACE

The annual 1,049-mile race from Anchorage to Nome, Alaska commemorates the 1925 midwinter emergency mission to get medical supplies to Nome during a diptheria epidemic. Raced over alternate courses, the northern and southern trail, the Iditarod was first run in 1973.

IDITAROD WINNERS		
Year	Musher	Elapsed Time
1973	Dick Wilmarth	20 days, 00:49:41
1974	Carl Huntington	20 days, 15:02:07
1975	Emmitt Peters	14 days, 14:43:45
1976	Gerald Riley	18 days, 22:58:17
1977	Rick Swenson	16 days, 16:27:13
1978	Rick Mackey	14 days, 18:52:24
1979	Rick Swenson	15 days, 10:37:47
1980	Joe May	14 days, 07:11:51
1981	Rick Swenson	12 days, 08:45:02
1982	Rick Swenson	16 days, 04:40:10
1983	Rick Mackey	12 days, 14:10:44
1984	Dean Osmar	12 days, 15:07:33
1985	Libby Riddles	18 days, 00:20:17
1986	Susan Butcher	11 days, 15:06:00
1987	Susan Butcher	11 days, 02:05:13
1988	Susan Butcher	11 days, 11:41:40
1989	Joe Runyan	11 days, 05:24:34
1990	Susan Butcher	11 days, 01:53:23

Most Wins 4, Rick Swenson (1977, 1979, 1981–82), Susan Butcher (1986–88, 1990)

Record Time 11 days, 1 hr 53 min 23 sec by Susan Butcher in 1990.

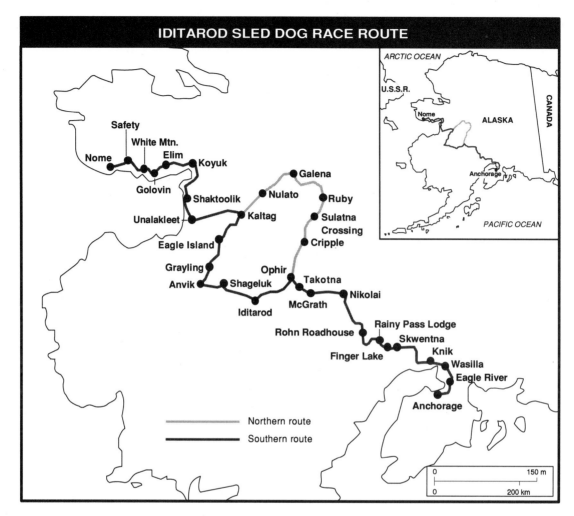

IDITAROD SLED DOG RACE ROUTE

Northern route
Southern route

SNOOKER

ORIGINS Neville Chamberlain, a British army officer, is credited with inventing the game in Jubbulpore, India in 1875. Snooker is a hybrid of pool and pyramids. Chamberlain added a set of colored balls to the 15 red ones used in pyramids and devised a scoring system based on "potting" the balls in sequence: red, color, red, color until all the reds have been cleared, leaving the colored balls to be potted in numerical order. The modern scoring system: a red ball is worth one point, yellow—2, green—3, brown—4, blue—5, pink—6 and black—7, was adopted in England in 1891. The sequence of potting the balls is called a break, the maximum possible being 147. The name snooker comes from the term coined for new recruits at the Woolwich Military Academy and which Chamberlain labeled anyone who lost at his game.

WORLD PROFESSIONAL CHAMPIONSHIPS

First organized in 1927, Joe Davis (England) won the title on the first 15 occasions it was contested, and this still stands as the all-time record for victories. The youngest player to win the event was Stephen Hendry (Scotland), who became champion at 21 yrs 106 days on 29 April 1990. The only 147 "maximum break" in world championship competition was compiled by Cliff Thorburn (Canada) on 23 April 1988.

SOCCER

ORIGINS A game called *Tsu chu* ("to kick a ball of stuffed leather") was played in China more than 2,500 years ago. However, the ancestry of the modern game is traced to England. In 1314, King

Edward II prohibited the game because of excessive noise. Three subsequent monarchs also banned the game. Nevertheless, "football," the name by which soccer is known throughout the rest of the world, continued its development in England. In 1848, the first rules were drawn up at Cambridge University; in 1863, the Football Association (FA) was founded in England. The sport grew in popularity worldwide, and the Federation Internationale de Football Association (FIFA), the world governing body, was formed in Paris, France in 1904. FIFA currently has more than 160 members.

WORLD CUP

The first World Cup for the Jules Rimet Trophy was held in Uruguay in 1930 and has been staged quadrennially since, with a break from 1939–49 because of World War II. In 1970, Brazil won its third World Cup and was awarded permanent possession of the Jules Rimet Trophy. Countries now compete for the FIFA World Cup.

WORLD CUP FINALS

Year	Winner	Loser	Score
1930	Uruguay	Argentina	4–2
1934	Italy	Czechoslovakia	2–1
1938	Italy	Hungary	4–2
1950	Uruguay	Brazil	2–1
1954	West Germany	Hungary	3–2
1958	Brazil	Sweden	5–2
1962	Brazil	Czechoslovakia	3–1
1966	England	West Germany	4–2
1970	Brazil	Italy	4–1
1974	West Germany	Netherlands	2–1
1978	Argentina	Netherlands	3–1
1982	Italy	West Germany	3–1
1986	Argentina	West Germany	3–2
1990	West Germany	Argentina	1–0

TEAM RECORDS

Most Wins Three countries have won the World Cup on three occasions: Brazil (1958, 1962, 1970); Italy (1934, 1938, 1982); West Germany (1954, 1974, 1990).

WORLD CUP WINNERS ■ WEST GERMAN PLAYERS CELEBRATE THEIR 1990 WORLD CUP VICTORY IN ITALY. THIS WAS WEST GERMANY'S THIRD TITLE, WHICH TIED THE MARK OF BRAZIL AND ITALY.

Most Appearances Brazil is the only country to qualify for all 14 World Cup tournaments.

Most Goals The highest score by one team in a game is 10 by Hungary in a 10–1 defeat of El Salvador at Elche, Spain on 15 June 1982. The most goals in tournament history is 148 (from 66 games) by Brazil.

Highest Scoring Game The highest scoring game took place on 26 June 1954 when Austria defeated Switzerland 7–5.

INDIVIDUAL RECORDS

CHAMPIONSHIP GAME

Most Wins Pele (Brazil) is the only player to have played on three winning teams. Mario Zagalo (Brazil) was the first man to play in (1958, 1962) and be manager of (1970) a World Cup winning team. Franz Beckenbauer emulated Zagalo, when he managed the West German team to victory in 1990. He had previously captained the 1974 winning team. Beckenbauer is the only man to have both captained and managed a winning side.

Most Goals The most goals scored in a final is three by Geoff Hurst for England *v.* West Germany on 30 July 1966.

FINALS TOURNAMENT

Most Games Played Two players have appeared in 21 games in the finals tournament: Uwe Seeler (West Germany, 1958–70); Wladyslaw Zmuda (Poland, 1974–86).

Most Goals Scored The most goals scored by a player in a game is four, which has occurred nine times (see below). The most goals scored in one tournament is 13 by Just Fontaine (France) in 1958, from six games. The most goals scored in a career is 14 by Gerd Muller (West Germany), 10 goals in 1970 and 4 in 1974.

OLYMPIC GAMES

Soccer has been an official sport at the Olympics since 1908, except for 1932, when it was not staged in Los Angeles. The leading gold medal winner is Hungary with three wins (1952, 1964, 1968).

NORTH AMERICAN SOCCER LEAGUE (NASL)

The North American Soccer League was formed in 1968 and folded in 1985. During its heyday in the mid-1970s the NASL attracted large crowds and sparked US interest in the "world game." The fall of the NASL was even more spectacular than

---

GOAL-SCORING RECORDS

CLUB COMPETITION

Game: 16, Stephan Stanis (Racing Club Lens *v.* Aubry-Asturies), 13 December 1942

Career: 1,329, Artur Friedenreich (Germania, CA Ipiranga, Americano, CA Paulistano, Sao Paulo, Flamengo), 1909–35

INTERNATIONAL COMPETITION

Game: 10, Sofus Nielsen (Denmark *v.* France), 1908

Career: 97, Pele (Brazil), 1957–70

WORLD CUP FINALS

Game: 4, Leonidas (Brazil *v.* Poland), 1938
Ernst Willimowski (Poland *v.* Brazil), 1938
Gustav Wetterstrom (Sweden *v.* Cuba), 1938
Juan Schiaffino (Uruguay *v.* Bolivia), 1950
Ademir (Brazil *v.* Sweden), 1950
Sandor Kocsis (Hungary *v.* West Germany), 1954
Just Fontaine (France *v.* West Germany), 1958
Eusebio (Portugal *v.* North Korea), 1966
Emilio Butragueno (Spain *v.* Denmark), 1986

Career: 14, Gerd Muller (West Germany), 1970, 1974

HAT-TRICK HERO ■ GEOFF HURST PIVOTS TO DRIVE HOME HIS SECOND OF THREE GOALS IN ENGLAND'S 4–2 WORLD CUP TRIUMPH OVER WEST GERMANY IN 1966. HURST IS THE ONLY PLAYER TO HAVE SCORED A HAT-TRICK IN THE WORLD CUP FINAL.

its rise. In 1979 the NASL consisted of 24 teams; by 1985 the league had collapsed.

NASL Champions

Year	Champion	Year	Champion
1968	Atlanta Chiefs	1977	New York Cosmos
1969	Kansas City Spurs	1978	New York Cosmos
1970	Rochester Lancers	1979	Vancouver Whitecaps
1971	Dallas Tornados	1980	New York Cosmos
1972	New York Cosmos	1981	Chicago Sting
1973	Philadelphia Atoms	1982	New York Cosmos
1974	Los Angeles Aztecs	1983	Tulsa Roughnecks
1975	Tampa Bay Rowdies	1984	Chicago Sting
1976	Toronto Metro-Croatia		

Most Wins 5, New York Cosmos (1972, 1977–78, 1980, 1982)

MAJOR INDOOR SOCCER LEAGUE (MISL)

Founded in 1978, the most championships is six by the San Diego Sockers, 1983, 1985–86, 1988–90.

MISL Champions

Year	Champion	Year	Champion
1979	New York Arrows	1985	San Diego Sockers
1980	New York Arrows	1986	San Diego Sockers
1981	New York Arrows	1987	Dallas Sidekicks
1982	New York Arrows	1988	San Diego Sockers
1983	San Diego Sockers	1989	San Diego Sockers
1984	Baltimore Blast	1990	San Diego Sockers

NCAA DIVISION I CHAMPIONSHIPS

Men The University of St. Louis has won the most Division I titles (first held in 1959) with 10 victories, which includes one tie: 1959–60, 1962–63, 1965, 1967, 1969–70, 1972–73.

Women The University of North Carolina has won a record eight Division I titles, (first held in 1982). Its victories came in 1982–84, 1986–90.

SOFTBALL

ORIGINS Softball, a derivative of baseball, was invented by George Hancock at the Farragut Boat Club of Chicago, IL in 1887. Rules were first codified in Minneapolis, MN in 1895 as kitten ball. The name softball was introduced by Walter Hakanson at a meeting of the National Recreation Congress in 1926. The name was adopted throughout the US in 1930. Rules were formalized in 1933 by the International Joint Rules Committee for Softball and adopted by the Amateur Softball Association of America. The International Softball Federation was formed in 1950 as governing body for both fast pitch and slow pitch. It was reorganized in 1965.

WORLD CHAMPIONSHIPS The US has won the men's World Championship (instituted 1966) five times, 1966, 1968, 1976 (shared), 1980 and 1988, and the women's title (instituted 1965) three times, in 1974, 1978 and 1986.

US NATIONAL CHAMPIONSHIPS The most wins in the fast pitch championships (first held in 1933) for men is 10, by the Clearwater (Florida) Bombers between 1950 and 1973, and for women is 20, by the Hi Ho (formerly Raybestos) Brakettes of Stratford, CT, between 1958 and 1988.

Slow pitch championships have been staged annually since 1953 for men and since 1962 for women. Three wins for men have been achieved by Skip Hogan A. C. of Pittsburgh, 1962, 1964–65 and by Joe Gatliff Auto Sales of Newport, KY, 1956–57, 1963. At super slow pitch three wins have been achieved by Howard's Western Steer, Denver, CO, 1981, 1983–84, and by Steele's Silver Bullets, Grafton, OH, 1985–87. The Dots of Miami, FL have a record five women's titles, playing as the Converse Dots, 1969, Marks Brothers, N. Miami Dots, 1974–75 and Bob Hoffman Dots, 1978–79.

SPEEDWAY

ORIGINS Motorcycle racing on large dirt track surfaces has been traced back to 1902 in the US. The first fully documented motorcycle track races were at the Portman Road Ground, Ipswich, Suffolk, England on 2 July 1904. Two heats and a final were contested, F. E. Barker winning in 5 min 54.2 sec for three miles. Modern speedway has developed from the "short track" races held at the West Maitland Agricultural Show (New South Wales, Australia) on 22 December 1923, by Johnnie Hoskins (New Zealand).

WORLD CHAMPIONSHIPS The World Speedway Championship was inaugurated at London, England on 10 September 1936. The most wins have been six, by Ivan Mauger (New Zealand) in 1968–70, 1972, 1977 and 1979. Barry Briggs (New Zealand) made a record 17 consecutive appearances in the finals (1954–70) and won the world title in 1957–58, 1964 and 1966. He scored a record 201 points in world championship competition from 87 races.

The only American rider to win a world title is Bruce Penhall, who won in 1981 and 1982.

The World Pairs Championship instituted in 1968 has been won a record seven times, by Great Britain (1972, 1976–78, 1980 and 1983–84) and Denmark (1979, 1985–90). The most successful individuals in the World Pairs have been Erik Gundersen and Hans Neilsen with five wins for Denmark. They won as a pair, 1986–89, and Gundersen won with Tommy Krudeen in 1985, Nielsen with Jan Pedersen in 1990.

The US has won the Pairs title two times: 1981 (Bruce Penhall and Bobby Schwartz), 1982 (Dennis Sigalos and Bobby Schwartz).

SQUASH

ORIGINS Squash is an offshoot of rackets and is believed to have been first played at Harrow School, London, England in 1817. The first recognized national champion was John A. Miskey of Philadelphia, PA, who won the US Amateur Championship in 1907, the year the U.S. Squash Racquets Association was formed. The International Squash Rackets Federation (ISRF) was founded in 1967. The Women's International Squash Rackets Federation was formed in 1976.

WORLD OPEN CHAMPIONSHIPS

Both the men's and women's events were first held in 1976. The men's competition is an annual event, but the women's tournament was biennial until 1989 when it switched to the same system as the men's event. There was no championship in 1978.

Jahangir Khan (Pakistan) has won the most titles with six victories, 1981–85 and 1988. Susan Devoy (New Zealand) holds the mark in the women's event with three victories, 1985, 1987, 1990.

Fastest speed In tests at Wimbledon Squash and Badminton Club, England in January 1988, Roy Buckland hit a squash ball by an overhead service at a measured speed of 144.6 mph over the distance to the front wall. This is equivalent to an initial speed at the racket of 150.8 mph.

SURFING

ORIGINS The Polynesian sport of surfing in a canoe (*ehorooe*) was first recorded by the British explorer Captain James Cook in December 1771 during his exploration of Tahiti. The modern sport developed in Hawaii, California and Australia in the mid-1950s. Although Hawaii is one of the 50 states that comprise the USA, Hawaii is allowed to compete separately from the US in international surfing competition.

WORLD AMATEUR CHAMPIONSHIP

First held in May 1964 in Sydney, Australia. The open championship is the most prestigious event in both men's and women's competition. In the women's division the title has been won a record 2 times by two surfers: Joyce Hoffman (US), 1965–66; and Sharon Weber (Hawaii), 1970 and 1972. The men's title has been won by different surfer's on each occasion.

WORLD PROFESSIONAL CHAMPIONSHIPS

First held in 1970, the World Championship has been organized by the Association of Surfing Professionals (ASP) since 1976. The World Championship is a circuit of events held throughout the year, with the winner gaining the most points over the course of the year.

The most titles won by a professional surfer is five by Mark Richards (Australia), 1975, 1979–82. The women's record is four by Frieda Zamba (US), 1984–86, 1988.

SWIMMING & DIVING

SWIMMING

ORIGINS The earliest references to swimming races were in Japan in 36 B.C. The first national swimming association, the Metropolitan Swimming Clubs Association, was founded in England in 1791. Swimming was included in the first modern Olympic Games in 1896 and has been in every one since. The first United States Swimming Championships were staged by the Amateur Athletic Union on 25 August 1888 in New York City. The International governing body for swimming, diving and water polo—the Federation Internationale de Natation Amateur (FINA)—was founded in 1908.

Fastest swimmer In a 25-yd pool, Tom Jager (US) achieved an average speed of 5.37 mph for 50 yards in 19.05 sec at Nashville, TN on 23 March 1990. The women's fastest is 4.48 mph, by Yang Wenyi (China) in her 50 m world record (see World Record table).

Most world records Men: 32, Arne Borg (Sweden), 1921–29. Women: 42, Ragnhild Hveger (Denmark), 1936–42. For currently recognized events (only metric distances in 50 m pools) the most is 26, by Mark Spitz (US), 1967–72, and 23, by Kornelia Ender (East Germany), 1973–76. The most by a US woman is 15, by Debbie Meyer, 1967–70.

OLYMPIC GAMES
Most medals

Men The greatest number of Olympic gold medals won is nine, by Mark Spitz (US): 100 m and 200 m freestyle, 1972; 100 m and 200 m butterfly, 1972; 4 x 100 m freestyle, 1968 and 1972; 4 x 200 m freestyle, 1968 and 1972; 4 x 100 m medley, 1972. *All but one of these performances (the 4 x 200 m freestyle of 1968) were also new world records.* He also won a silver (100 m butterfly) and a bronze (100 m freestyle) in 1968 for a record 11 medals. His record seven medals at one Games in 1972 was equaled by Matt Biondi (US), who took five gold, one silver and one bronze in 1988.

Women The record number of gold medals won by a woman is six by Kristin Otto (East Germany) at Seoul, S. Korea in 1988: 100 m freestyle, backstroke and butterfly, 50 m freestyle, 4 x 100 m freestyle and 4 x 100 m medley. Dawn Fraser (Australia) is the only swimmer to win the same event, the 100 m freestyle, on three successive occasions (1956, 1960 and 1964).

The most medals won by a woman is eight, by: Dawn Fraser, four golds: 100 m freestyle, 1956, 1960 and 1964, 4 x 100 m freestyle, 1956 and four silvers: 400 m freestyle, 1956, 4 x 100 m freestyle, 1960 and 1964, 4 x 100 m medley, 1960; Kornelia Ender, four golds: 100 m and 200 m freestyle, 100 m butterfly and 4 x 100 m medley in 1976 and four silvers: 200 m individual medley, 1972, 4 x 100 m medley, 1972, 4 x 100 m freestyle, 1972 and 1976; and Shirley Babashoff (US), who won two golds (4 x 100 m freestyle, 1972 and 1976) and six silvers (100 m freestyle, 1972; 200 m freestyle, 1972 and 1976; 400 m and 800 m freestyle, 1976; 4 x 100 m medley, 1976).

Most individual gold medals The record number of individual gold medals won is four, by:

Charles Meldrum Daniels (US) (100 m freestyle, 1906 and 1908, 220 yd freestyle 1904, 440 yd freestyle, 1904); Roland Matthes (East Germany) with 100 m and 200 m backstroke in 1968 and 1972; Mark Spitz and Kristin Otto (see above); and the divers Pat McCormick and Greg Louganis (see below).

Closest verdict The closest verdict in the Olympic Games was in Los Angeles, CA on 29 July 1984, when Nancy Lynn Hogshead and Carrie Lynne Steinseifer, both of the US, dead-heated for the women's 100 m freestyle gold medal in 55.92 sec. In the 1972 men's 400 m individual medley, Gunnar Larsson (Sweden) beat Aleksander Timothy McKee (US) by just 2/1,000 th second, just 3 mm. Now timings are determined only to hundredths.

WORLD CHAMPIONSHIPS

In the World Championships (instituted 1973), the most medals won is 10, by Kornelia Ender (East Germany), with eight gold and two silver in 1973 and 1975. The most by a man is eight, by Rowdy Gaines (US), five gold and three silver, in 1978 and 1982. The most gold medals won is six (two individual and four relay), by James Montgomery (US) in 1973 and 1975. The most medals won at a single championship is seven, by Matt Biondi (US), three gold, one silver, three bronze, in 1986.

The most gold medals won by an American woman is five, by Tracy Caulkins, all in 1978. The most medals is nine, by Mary T. Meagher, two gold, five silver, two bronze, 1978–82.

SWIMMING—WORLD RECORDS (set in 50 m pools)

MEN
FREESTYLE

Event	Time	Name, country	Date
50 meters:	21.81	Tom Jager (US)	24 March 1990
100 meters:	48.42	Matt Biondi (US)	10 August 1988
200 meters:	1:46.69	Giorgio Lamberti (Italy)	15 August 1989
400 meters:	3:46.95	Uwe Dassler (East Germany)	23 September 1988
800 meters:	7:50.64	Vladimir Salinkov (USSR)	4 July 1986
1,500 meters:	14:54.76	Vladimir Salnikov (USSR)	22 February 1983
4 x 100 meters relay:	3:16.53	United States (Christopher Jacobs, Troy Dalbey, Tom Jager, Matt Biondi)	23 September 1988
4 x 200 meters relay:	7:12.51	United States (Troy Dalbey, Matthew Cetlinski, Douglas Gjertsen, Matt Biondi)	21 September 1988

BREASTSTROKE

100 meters:	1:01.49	Adrian Moorhouse (Great Britain)	15 August 1989
	1:01.49	Adrian Moorhouse (Great Britian)	25 January 1990
	1:01.49	Adrian Moorhouse (Great Britain)	26 July 1990
200 meters:	2:11.53	Michael Barrowman (US)	20 July 1990

BUTTERFLY

100 meters:	52.84	Pablo Morales (US)	23 June 1986
200 meters:	1:56.24	Michael Gross (West Germany)	28 June 1986

BACKSTROKE

100 meters:	54.51	David Berkoff (US)	24 September 1988
200 meters:	1:58.14	Igor Polyanskiy (USSR)	3 March 1985

FLOATS LIKE A BUTTERFLY ■ PABLO MORALES, US, SET THE WORLD RECORD FOR 100 M BUTTERFLY AT 52.84 SEC ON 23 JUNE 1986.

SWIMMING—WORLD RECORDS (set in 50 m pools)(Continued)

MEN (Continued)
MEDLEY

Event	Time	Name, country	Date
200 meters:	2:00.11	David Wharton (US)	20 August 1989
400 meters:	4:14.75	Tamás Darnyi (Hungary)	21 September 1988
4 x 100 meters relay:	3:36.93	United States (David Berkoff, Richard Schroeder, Matt Biondi, Christopher Jacobs)	25 September 1988

WOMEN
FREESTYLE

Event	Time	Name, country	Date
50 meters:	24.98	Yang Wenyi (China)	11 April 1988
100 meters:	54.73	Kristin Otto (East Germany, relay first leg)	19 August 1986
200 meters:	1:57.55	Heike Friedrich (East Germany)	18 June 1986
400 meters:	4:03.85	Janet Evans (US)	22 September 1988
800 meters:	8:16.22	Janet Evans (US)	20 August 1989
1,500 meters:	15:52.10	Janet Evans (US)	26 March 1988
4 x 100 meters relay:	3:40.57	East Germany (Kristin Otto, Manuela Stellmach, Sabina Schulze, Heike Friedrich)	19 August 1986

SWIMMING—WORLD RECORDS (set in 50 m pools)(Continued)

WOMEN

FREESTYLE (Continued)

Event	Time	Name, country	Date
4 x 200 meters relay:	7:55.47	East Germany (Manuela Stellmach, Astrid Strauss, Anke Möhring, Heike Friedrich)	18 August 1987

BREASTSTROKE

100 meters:	1:07.91	Silke Hörner (East Germany)	21 August 1987
200 meters:	2:26.71	Silke Hörner (East Germany)	21 September 1988

BUTTERFLY

100 meters:	57.93	Mary T. Meagher (US)	16 August 1981
200 meters:	2:05.96	Mary T. Meagher (US)	13 August 1981

BACKSTROKE

100 meters:	1:00.59	Ina Kleber (East Germany relay first leg)	24 August 1984
200 meters:	2:08.60	Betsy Mitchell (US)	27 June 1986

MEDLEY

200 meters:	2:11.73	Ute Geweniger (East Germany)	4 July 1981
400 meters:	4:36.10	Petra Schneider (East Germany)	1 August 1982
4 x 100 meters relay:	4:03.69	East Germany (Ina Kleber, Sylvia Gerasch, Ines Geissler, Birgit Meineke)	24 August 1984

US NATIONAL CHAMPIONSHIPS

Tracy Caulkins won a record 48 US swimming titles and set 60 US records in her career, 1977–84.

The men's record is 36 titles, by Johnny Weissmuller, between 1921 and 1928.

U.S. NATIONAL RECORDS (SET IN 50 M POOLS)

MEN

FREESTYLE

Event	Time	Name	Date
50 meters:	21.81	Tom Jager	24 March 1990
100 meters:	48.42	Matt Biondi	10 August 1988
200 meters:	1:47.72	Matt Biondi	8 August 1988
400 meters:	3:48.06	Matthew Cetlinski	11 August 1988
800 meters:	7:52.45	Sean Killion	27 July 1987

U.S. NATIONAL RECORDS (SET IN 50 M POOLS) (Continued)

MEN

FREESTYLE (Continued)

Event	Time	Name	Date
1,500 meters:	15:01.51	George DiCarlo	30 June 1984
4 x 100 meter relay:	3:16.53	United States (Christopher Jacobs, Troy Dalbey, Tom Jager, Matt Biondi)	23 September 1988
4 x 200 meter relay:	7:12.51	United States (Troy Dalbey, Matthew Cetlinski, Douglas Gjertsen, Matt Biondi)	21 September 1988

BREASTSTROKE

100 meters:	1:01.65	Steve Lundquist	29 July 1984
200 meters:	2:11.53	Michael Barrowman	20 July 1990

BUTTERFLY

100 meters:	52.84	Pablo Morales	23 June 1986
200 meters:	1:57.75	Pablo Morales	3 August 1984

BACKSTROKE

100 meters:	54.51	David Berkoff	24 September 1988
200 meters:	1:58.86	Rick Carey	27 June 1984

MEDLEY

200 meters:	2:00.11	David Wharton	20 August 1989
400 meters:	4:15.57	Eric Namesnick	30 July 1990
4 x 100 meter relay:	3:36.93	United States (David Berkoff, Richard Schroeder, Matt Biondi, Christopher Jacobs)	25 September 1988

WOMEN

FREESTYLE

50 meters:	25.50	Leigh Ann Fetter	13 August 1988
100 meters:	55.30	Dara Torres (relay first leg)	25 March 1988
200 meters:	1:58.23	Cynthia Woodhead	3 September 1979
400 meters:	4:03.85	Janet Evans	22 September 1988
800 meters:	8:16.22	Janet Evans	20 August 1989
1,500 meters:	15:52.10	Janet Evans	26 March 1988
4 x 100 meter relay:	3:43.43	United States (Jenna Leigh Johnson, Carrie Steinseifer, Dara Torres, Nancy Lyn Hogshead)	31 July 1984

MULTI-RECORD HOLDER ■ JANET EVANS HOLDS FOUR US NATIONAL RECORDS: 400 M, 800 M, 1,500 M FREESTYLE AND 400 M MEDLEY.

U.S. NATIONAL RECORDS (SET IN 50 M POOLS) (Continued)

WOMEN (Continued)
FREESTYLE

Event	Time	Name	Date
4 x 200 meter relay:	8:02.12	United States (Betsy Mitchell, Mary T. Meagher, Kim Brown, Mary Alice Wayte)	17 August 1986

BREASTSTROKE

100 meters:	1:08.91	Tracey McFarlane	11 August 1988
200 meters:	2:29.58	Amy Shaw	16 August 1987

BUTTERFLY

100 meters:	57.93	Mary T. Meagher	16 August 1981
200 meters:	2:05.96	Mary T. Meagher	13 August 1981

BACKSTROKE

100 meters:	1:01.20	Betsy Mitchell	24 June 1986
200 meters:	2:08.60	Betsy Mitchell	27 June 1986

MEDLEY

200 meters:	2:12.64	Tracy Caulkins	3 August 1984
400 meters:	4:37.76	Janet Evans	19 September 1988
4 x 100 meter relay:	4:06.94	United States (Betsy Mitchell, Tracey McFarlane, Janel Jorgensen, Nicole Haislett)	23 July 1990

LONG-DISTANCE SWIMMING

Longest swims The greatest recorded distance ever swum is 1,826 miles down the Mississippi River between Ford Dam near Minneapolis, MN and Carrollton Ave, New Orleans, LA, by Fred P. Newton, of Clinton, OK from 6 July to 29 December 1930. He was in the water for 742 hrs. The greatest distance covered in a continuous swim is 299 miles, by Ricardo Hoffmann, from Corrientes to Santa Elena, Argentina in the River Paraná, in 84 hr 37 min on 3–6 March 1981.

The longest ocean swim is one of 128.8 miles by Walter Poenisch Sr. (US), who started from Havana, Cuba, on 11 July 1978 and arrived at Little Duck Key, FL (in a shark cage and wearing flippers) 34 hr 15 min later on 13 July 1978.

In 1966 Mihir Sen of Calcutta, India swam the Palk Strait from Sri Lanka to India (in 25 hr 36 min on 5–6 April); the Straits of Gibraltar (in 8 hr 1 min on 24 August), the length of the Dardanelles (in 13 hr 55 min on 12 September), the Bosphorus (in 4 hr on 21 September), and the length of the Panama Canal (in 34 hr 15 min on 29–31 October). He is the only person to have accomplished this feat.

English Channel swimming The first to swim the English Channel from shore to shore (without a life jacket) was the Merchant Navy Captain Matthew Webb, who swam from Dover, England to Calais Sands, France, in 21 hr 45 min from 12:56 P.M. to 10:41 A.M., 24–25 August 1875. He swam an estimated 38 miles to make the 21-mile crossing. The first woman to succeed was Gertrude Caroline Ederle (US), who swam from Cap Gris-Nez, France to Deal, England on 6 August 1926, in the then overall record-time of 14 hr 39 min.

24 hours Anders Forvass (Sweden) swam 63.3 miles at the 25-meter Linköping public swimming pool, Sweden on 28–29 October 1989. In a 50-meter pool, Evan Barry (Australia) swam 60.08 miles, at the Valley Pool, Brisbane, Australia on 19–20 December 1987.

The women's record is 51.01 miles, by Irene van der Laan (Netherlands) at Amersfoort, Netherlands on 20–21 September 1985.

Long-distance relay The New Zealand national relay team of 20 swimmers swam a record 113.59 miles in Lower Hutt, New Zealand in 24 hours, passing 100 miles in 20 hr 47 min 13 sec on 9–10 December 1983.

DIVING

OLYMPIC GAMES The most medals won by a driver is five, by Klaus Dibiasi (Austria, [Italy] (3 gold, 2 silver), 1964–76; and Greg Louganis (US) (4 gold, 1 silver), 1976, 1984–1988. Dibiasi is the only diver to win the same event (highboard) at three successive Games (1968, 1972 and 1976). Two divers have won the highboard and springboard doubles at two Games: Pat McCormick (née Keller, [US]), 1952 and 1956, and Greg Louganis, 1984 and 1988.

Highest Score Greg Louganis achieved record scores at the 1984 Olympics, with 754.41 points for the 11-dive springboard event and 710.91 for the highboard.

WORLD CHAMPIONSHIPS Greg Louganis (US) has won a record five world titles, highboard in 1978 and the highboard/springboard double in 1982 and 1986. Philip Boggs (US) is the only diver to win three gold medals at one event, springboard, 1973, 1975 and 1978.

PERFECT "10.0" The first diver to be awarded a perfect score of 10.0 by all seven judges was Michael Finneran in the 1972 US Olympic Trials, in Chicago, IL, for a backward 1½ somersault, 2½ twist, from the 10 m board. Greg Louganis is the only diver to have been awarded 10.0 in world championship competition. He achieved perfection at the 1984 event in Guayaquil, Ecuador, for his highboard inward 1½ somersault in the pike position.

Deep diving records The record depth for the extremely dangerous activity of breath-held diving is 344 ft, by Jacques Mayol (France) off Elba, Italy, in December 1983. He descended on a sled in 104 sec and ascended in 90 sec.

The record for women is 246 ft ¾ in, by Rossana Majorca (Italy) off Syracuse, Sicily on 31 July 1987.

The record dive with scuba (self-contained underwater breathing apparatus) is 437 ft by John J. Gruener and R. Neal Watson (US) off Freeport, Grand Bahama on 14 October 1968.

For women, the record is 345 ft by Marty Dunwoody (US) off Bimini, Bahama Islands on 20 December 1987.

The record dive utilizing gas mixtures (nitrogen, oxygen and helium) is a simulated dive of 2,250 ft in a dry chamber by Stephen Porter, Len Whitlock and Erik Kramer at Duke University Medical Center in Durham, NC on 3 February 1981 in a 43-day trial.

A team of six divers (four Comex and two French Navy) descended to and worked efficiently at a depth of 1,706 ft off Marseilles, France as part of the Hydro VIII operation during six days in the spring of 1988. They used "hydreliox"—a synthetic breathing mixture containing a high percentage of hydrogen.

TABLE TENNIS

ORIGINS The earliest evidence relating to a game resembling table tennis has been found in the catalogs of London sporting goods manufacturers in the 1880s. The International Table Tennis Federation (ITTF) was founded in 1926 and the United States Table Tennis Association was established in 1933. In 1971, a US table tennis team was invited to play in the People's Republic of China, thereby initiating the first officially sanctioned Chinese-American cultural exchange in almost 20 years.

WORLD CHAMPIONSHIPS

The ITTF instituted European Championships in 1926 and later designated this event as the World Championship. The tournament was staged annually until 1957, when the event became biennial.

SWAYTHLING CUP The men's team championship is named after Lady Swaythling who donated the trophy in 1926. The most wins is 12 by Hungary (1926, 1928–31, 1933 [two events were held this year, with Hungary winning both times], 1935, 1938, 1949, 1952, 1979).

The United States has won the team title once, 1937.

CORBILLON CUP The women's team championship is named after M. Marcel Corbillon, president of the French Table Tennis Association, who donated the trophy in 1934. China has won the most titles with nine wins, (1965, 1975, 1977, 1979, 1981, 1983, 1985, 1987, 1989).

The United States has won the trophy twice, 1937 and 1949.

Men's Singles The most victories in singles is five, by Viktor Barna (Hungary; 1931, 1932–35).

Women's Singles The most victories is six, by Angelica Rozeanu (Romania; 1950–55).

Men's Doubles The most victories is eight, by Viktor Barna (Hungary; 1929–35 [twice in 1933], 1939). The partnership that has won the most titles is Viktor Barna and Miklos Szabados (Hungary; 1929–33, 1935).

Women's Doubles The most victories is seven, by Maria Mednyanszky (Hungary; 1928, 1930–35).

The team that has won the most titles is Maria Mednyanszky and Anna Sipos (Hungary; 1930–35).

Mixed Doubles Maria Mednyanszky (Hungary) has won a record six mixed doubles titles: 1927–28, 1930–31, 1933 (twice). The pairing of Miklos Szabados and Maria Mednyansky (Hungary) won the title a record three times: 1930–31, 1933.

US NATIONAL CHAMPIONSHIPS US national championships were first held in 1931. Leah Neuberger (née Thall) won a record 29 titles between 1941 and 1961: nine women's singles, 12 women's doubles. Richard Mills won a record 10 men's singles titles between 1945 and 1962.

Counter hitting The record number of hits in 60 sec is 172, by Thomas Busin and Stefan Renold, both of Switzerland, on 4 November 1989. The women's record is 168, by the sisters Lisa and Jackie Bellinger, at Crest Hotel, Luton, England on 14 July 1987. With a bat in each hand, Gary D. Fisher of Olympia, WA completed 5,000 consecutive volleys over the net in 44 min 28 sec on 25 June 1979.

TAEKWONDO

Taekwondo is a martial art, with all activities based on defensive spirit, developed over 20 centuries in Korea. It was officially recognized as part of Korean tradition and culture on 11 April 1955. The first World Taekwondo Championships were organized by the Korean Taekwondo Association and were held at Seoul, South Korea in 1973. The World Taekwondo Federation was then formed and has organized biennial championships.

WORLD CHAMPIONSHIPS

These biennial championships were first held in Seoul, South Korea in 1973, when they were staged by the Korean Taekwondo Association. Women's events were first staged unofficially in 1983 and have been officially recognized since 1987.

Most Titltes Chung Kook-hyun (South Korea) has won a record four world titles: light middleweight, 1982–83, welterweight 1985, 1987. The only American to win a world title is Lynette Love at heavyweight in 1987.

OLYMPIC GAMES

Taekwondo was included as a demonstration sport at the 1988 Games. Three American women won gold medals: Dana Hee (60kg), Arlene Limas (65kg), Lynette Love (over 70kg).

TENNIS

ORIGINS The modern game evolved from the indoor sport of real tennis. There is an account of a game called "Field Tennis" in an English sports periodical dated 29 September 1793, however the "father" of lawn tennis is regarded as being Major Walter Wingfield who patented a type of tennis called "sphairistike" in 1874. The Marylebone Cricket Club, England revised Wingfield's initial rules in 1877, and the famed All-England Croquet Club (home of the Wimbledon Championships) added the name Lawn Tennis to its title in 1877. The "open" era of tennis was introduced in 1968, when amateurs were permitted to play with and against professionals.

GRAND SLAM

The modern grand slam is achieved by winning all four grand slam events—the Australian Open, French Open, Wimbledon and US Open—in succession. The traditional slam is winning the four events in one calendar year.

GRAND SLAM ■ DON BUDGE OF THE US (TOP LEFT) WAS THE FIRST PLAYER TO WIN ALL FOUR LEGS OF THE GRAND SLAM, 1937–38. ROD LAVER OF AUSTRALIA (ABOVE) IS THE ONLY PLAYER TO HAVE COMPLETED THE SLAM TWICE, 1962 AND 1969.

GRAND SLAM WINNERS

Singles Don Budge (US) was the first player to hold all four championships simultaneously, when he won the last two events of 1937 and the first two of 1938. He was also the first to win all four in the same year, 1938. The only player to have won the grand slam twice is Rod Laver (Australia), who accomplished this in 1962 and 1969. Four woman have completed the grand slam: Maureen Connolly (US), in 1953; Margaret Court (née Smith [Australia]), in 1970; Martina Navrátilová (US), in 1983–84, (last three slams of 1983 and first three of 1984); Steffi Graf (West Germany), in 1988.

Most Singles Championships Won The most singles championships won in grand slam tournaments is 24, by Margaret Court (née Smith [Australia]): 11 Australian, five French, three Wimbledon, five US Open between 1960 and 1973. The men's record is 12, by Roy Emerson (Australia): six Australian, two French, two Wimbledon, two US Open, between 1961 and 1967.

Doubles The only men to win the grand slam for doubles were Frank Sedgman and Ken McGregor (Australia) in 1951. Four women have won the grand slam: Louise Brough (US) in 1949–50 (last three of 1949 and first of 1950); Maria Bueno (Brazil) in 1960; Martina Navrátilová and Pam Shriver (US) in 1984. Navrátilová and Shriver won eight consecutive doubles titles from 1983–85.

MOST GRAND SLAM TITLES ■ MARGARET COURT (NÉE SMITH) OF AUSTRALIA HAS WON MORE GRAND SLAM SINGLES TITLES THAN ANY OTHER PLAYER: 24.

DOUBLES ■ LOUISE BROUGH, US, WON 20 GRAND SLAM DOUBLES CHAMPIONSHIPS WITH HER PARTNER MARGARET DU PONT, US. THIS RECORD WAS MATCHED IN 1989 BY MARTINA NAVRÁTILOVÁ AND PAM SHRIVER, BOTH OF THE US.

Most Doubles Championships won The most wins by a doubles partnership is 20, by: Louise Brough (US) and Margaret Du Pont (US), who won three French, five Wimbledon and 12 US Opens, 1942–57; and by Martina Navrátilová (US) and Pam Shriver (US). They won seven Australian, four French, five Wimbledon, four US Opens, 1981–89.

Mixed Doubles Ken Fletcher and Margaret Court (Australia) won all four legs of the grand slam in 1963.

WIMBLEDON CHAMPIONSHIPS

"The Lawn Tennis Championships" at the All-England Club, Wimbledon are generally regarded as the most prestigious in tennis and currently form the third leg of the grand slam events. They were first held in 1877 and, until 1922, were organized on a challenge round system (the defending champion automatically qualifies for the following year's final and plays the winner of the challenger event). Wimbledon became an Open Championship (professionals could compete) in 1968.

WIMBLEDON CHAMPIONS (1877–1990)

MEN'S SINGLES

Year	Player	Country
1877	Spencer Gore	Great Britain
1878	Frank Hadlow	Great Britain
1879	Rev. John Hartley	Great Britain
1880	Rev. John Hartley	Great Britain
1881	William Renshaw	Great Britain
1882	William Renshaw	Great Britain
1883	William Renshaw	Great Britain
1884	William Renshaw	Great Britain
1885	William Renshaw	Great Britain
1886	William Renshaw	Great Britain
1887	Herbert Lawford	Great Britain
1888	Ernest Renshaw	Great Britain
1889	William Renshaw	Great Britain
1890	Willoughby Hamilton	Great Britain
1891	Wilfred Baddeley	Great Britain
1892	Wilfred Baddeley	Great Britain
1893	Joshua Pim	Great Britain
1894	Joshua Pim	Great Britain
1895	Wilfred Baddeley	Great Britain
1896	Harold Mahoney	Great Britain
1897	Reginald Doherty	Great Britain
1898	Reginald Doherty	Great Britain
1899	Reginald Doherty	Great Britain
1900	Reginald Doherty	Great Britain
1901	Arthur Gore	Great Britain
1902	Lawrence Doherty	Great Britain
1903	Lawrence Doherty	Great Britain
1904	Lawrence Doherty	Great Britain
1905	Lawrence Doherty	Great Britain
1906	Lawrence Doherty	Great Britain
1907	Norman Brookes	Australia
1908	Arthur Gore	Great Britain
1909	Arthur Gore	Great Britain
1910	Tony Wilding	New Zealand
1911	Tony Wilding	New Zealand
1912	Tony Wilding	New Zealand
1913	Tony Wilding	New Zealand
1914	Norman Brookes	Australia
1915	not held	
1916	not held	
1917	not held	
1918	not held	

WIMBLEDON CHAMPIONS (1877–1990)
(Continued)

MEN'S SINGLES (Continued)

Year	Player	Country
1919	Gerald Patterson	Australia
1920	Bill Tilden	United States
1921	Bill Tilden	United States
1922	Gerald Patterson	Australia
1923	William Johnston	United States
1924	Jean Borotra	France
1925	Rene Lacoste	France
1926	Jean Borotra	France
1927	Henri Cochet	France
1928	Rene Lacoste	France
1929	Henri Cochet	France
1930	Bill Tilden	United States
1931	Sidney Wood	United States
1932	Ellsworth Vines	United States
1933	Jack Crawford	Australia
1934	Fred Perry	Great Britain
1935	Fred Perry	Great Britain
1936	Fred Perry	Great Britain
1937	Don Budge	United States
1938	Don Budge	United States
1939	Bobby Riggs	United States
1940	not held	
1941	not held	
1942	not held	
1943	not held	
1944	not held	
1945	not held	
1946	Yvon Petra	France
1947	Jack Kramer	United States
1948	Bob Falkenburg	United States
1949	Ted Schroeder	United States
1950	Budge Patty	United States
1951	Dick Savitt	United States
1952	Frank Sedgman	Australia
1953	Vic Seixas	United States
1954	Jaroslav Drobny	Egypt
1955	Tony Trabert	United States
1956	Lew Hoad	Australia
1957	Lew Hoad	Australia
1958	Ashley Cooper	Australia
1959	Alex Olmedo	United States
1960	Neale Fraser	Australia

MEN'S SINGLES (Continued)

Year	Player	Country
1961	Rod Laver	Australia
1962	Rod Laver	Australia
1963	Chuck McKinley	United States
1964	Roy Emerson	Australia
1965	Roy Emerson	Australia
1966	Manuel Santana	Spain
1967	John Newcombe	Australia
1968	Rod Laver	Australia
1969	Rod Laver	Australia
1970	John Newcombe	Australia
1971	John Newcombe	Australia
1972	Stan Smith	United States
1973	Jan Kodes	Czechoslovakia
1974	Jimmy Connors	United States
1975	Arthur Ashe	United States
1976	Bjorn Borg	Sweden
1977	Bjorn Borg	Sweden
1978	Bjorn Borg	Sweden
1979	Bjorn Borg	Sweden
1980	Bjorn Borg	Sweden
1981	John McEnroe	United States
1982	Jimmy Connors	United States
1983	John McEnroe	United States
1984	John McEnroe	United States
1985	Boris Becker	West Germany
1986	Boris Becker	West Germany
1987	Pat Cash	Australia
1988	Stefan Edberg	Sweden
1989	Boris Becker	West Germany
1990	Stefan Edberg	Sweden

WOMEN'S SINGLES

Year	Player	Country
1884	Maud Watson	Great Britain
1885	Maud Watson	Great Britain
1886	Blanche Bingley	Great Britain
1887	Lottie Dod	Great Britain
1888	Lottie Dod	Great Britain
1889	Blanche Hillyard (née Bingley)	Great Britain
1890	Helene Rice	Great Britain
1891	Lottie Dod	Great Britain
1892	Lottie Dod	Great Britain
1893	Lottie Dod	Great Britain

WOMEN'S SINGLES (Continued)

Year	Player	Country
1894	Blanche Hillyard (née Bingley)	Great Britain
1895	Charlotte Cooper	Great Britain
1896	Charlotte Cooper	Great Britain
1897	Blanche Hillyard (née Bingley)	Great Britain
1898	Charlotte Copper	Great Britain
1899	Blanche Hillyard (née Bingley)	Great Britain
1900	Blanche Hillyard (née Bingley)	Great Britain
1901	Charlotte Sterry (née Cooper)	Great Britain
1902	Muriel Robb	Great Britain
1903	Dorothea Douglass	Great Britain
1904	Dorothea Douglass	Great Britain
1905	May Sutton	United States
1906	Dorothea Douglass	Great Britain
1907	May Sutton	United States
1908	Charlotte Sterry (née Cooper)	Great Britain
1909	Dora Boothby	Great Britain
1910	Dorothea Lambert-Chambers (née Douglass)	Great Britain
1911	Dorothea Lambert-Chambers (née Douglass)	Great Britain
1912	Ethel Larcombe	Great Britain
1913	Dorothea Lambert-Chambers (née Douglass)	Great Britain
1914	Dorothea Lambert-Chambers (née Douglass)	Great Britain
1915	not held	
1916	not held	
1917	not held	
1918	not held	
1919	Suzanne Lenglen	France
1920	Suzanne Lenglen	France
1921	Suzanne Lenglen	France
1922	Suzanne Lenglen	France
1923	Suzanne Lenglen	France
1924	Kathleen McKane	Great Britain
1925	Suzanne Lenglen	France
1926	Kathleen Godfree (née McKane)	Great Britain
1927	Helen Wills	United States
1928	Helen Wills	United States
1929	Helen Wills	United States
1930	Helen Moody (née Wills)	United States
1931	Cilly Aussem	Germany

Year	Player	Country
1932	Helen Moody (née Wills)	United States
1933	Helen Moody (née Wills)	United States
1934	Dorothy Round	Great Britain
1935	Helen Moody (née Wills)	United States
1936	Helen Jacobs	United States
1937	Dorothy Round	Great Britain
1938	Helen Moody (née Wills)	United States
1939	Alice Marble	United States
1940	not held	
1941	not held	
1942	not held	
1943	not held	
1944	not held	
1945	not held	
1946	Pauline Betz	United States
1947	Margaret Osborne	United States
1948	Louise Brough	United States
1949	Louise Brough	United States
1950	Louise Brough	United States
1951	Doris Hart	United States
1952	Maureen Connolly	United States
1953	Maureen Connolly	United States
1954	Maureen Connolly	United States
1955	Louise Brough	United States
1956	Shirley Fry	United States
1957	Althea Gibson	United States
1958	Althea Gibson	United States
1959	Maria Bueno	Brazil
1960	Maria Bueno	Brazil
1961	Angela Mortimer	Great Britain
1962	Karen Susman	United States
1963	Margaret Smith	Australia
1964	Maria Bueno	Brazil
1965	Margaret Smith	Australia
1966	Billie Jean King	United States
1967	Billie Jean King	United States
1968	Billie Jean King	United States
1969	Ann Jones	Great Britain
1970	Margaret Court (née Smith)	Australia
1971	Evonne Goolagong	Australia
1972	Billie Jean King	United States
1973	Billie Jean King	United States

Year	Player	Country
1974	Chris Evert	United States
1975	Billie Jean King	United States
1976	Chris Evert	United States
1977	Virginia Wade	Great Britain
1978	Martina Navrátilová	Czechoslovakia
1979	Martina Navrátilová	Czechoslovakia
1980	Evonne Cawley (née Goolagong)	Australia
1981	Chris Evert	United States
1982	Martina Navrátilová	United States
1983	Martina Navrátilová	United States
1984	Martina Navrátilová	United States
1985	Martina Navrátilová	United States
1986	Martina Navrátilová	United States
1987	Martina Navrátilová	United States
1988	Steffi Graf	West Germany
1989	Steffi Graf	West Germany
1990	Martina Navrátilová	United States

Most Wins Men Overall the most titles is seven by William Renshaw (Great Britain), 1881–86, 1889. Since the abolition of the Challenge Round in 1922, the most wins is five by Bjorn Borg (Sweden), 1976–80.

Most Wins Women Martina Navrátilová has won a record nine titles; 1978–79, 1982–87, 1990.

Men's Doubles

Most Wins Lawrence and Reginald Doherty (Great Britain) won the doubles title a record eight times: 1897–1901, 1903–05.

Women's Doubles

Most Wins Suzanne Lenglen (France) and Elizabeth Ryan (United States) won the doubles a record six times: 1919–23, 1925. Elizabeth Ryan was a winning partner on a record 12 occasions, 1914, 1919–23, 1925–27, 1930, 1933–34.

Mixed Doubles The team of Ken Fletcher and Margaret Court (née Smith), both of Australia, won the mixed doubles a record four times: 1963, 1965–66, 1968. Fletcher's four victories tie him for the men's record for wins, which is shared by two other players: Vic Seixas (US), 1953–56; Owen Davidson (Australia), 1967, 1971, 1973–74. Elizabeth Ryan (US) holds the women's record with seven wins: 1919, 1921, 1923, 1927–28, 1930, 1932.

Most Titles Overall Billie Jean King (US) has won a record 20 Wimbledon titles from 1961–79; six singles, 10 doubles, four mixed doubles.

Youngest Champions The youngest champion was Lottie Dod (Great Britain), who was 15 yr 285 days when she won in 1887. The youngest men's champion was Boris Becker (West Germany), who was 17 yr 227 days when he won in 1985.

UNITED STATES OPEN CHAMPIONSHIPS

The first official US Championships were staged in 1881. From 1884–1911, the contest was based on a challenger format. In 1968 and 1969, separate amateur and professional events were held. Since 1970, there has only been an Open competition. On the current schedule the US Open is the fourth and final leg of the grand slam and is played at the US National Tennis Center, Flushing Meadow, NY.

WIMBLEDON MARK ECLIPSED ■ HELEN MOODY (NÉE WILLS) OF THE US (ABOVE) WON HER LAST AND EIGHTH WIMBLEDON SINGLES TITLE IN 1938. IN 1990 MARTINA NAVRATILOVA OF THE US (BELLOW) PASSED MOODY'S MARK BY WINNING HER NINTH WIMBLEDON CROWN.

US OPEN CHAMPIONS 1881–1990

MEN'S SINGLES

Year	Player	Country
1881	Richard Sears	United States
1882	Richard Sears	United States
1883	Richard Sears	United States
1884	Richard Sears	United States
1885	Richard Sears	United States
1886	Richard Sears	United States
1887	Richard Sears	United States
1888	Henry Slocum Jr.	United States
1889	Henry Slocum Jr.	United States
1890	Oliver Campbell	United States
1891	Oliver Campbell	United States
1892	Oliver Campbell	United States
1893	Robert Wrenn	United States
1894	Robert Wrenn	United States
1895	Fred Hovey	United States
1896	Robert Wrenn	United States
1897	Robert Wrenn	United States
1898	Malcolm Whitman	United States
1899	Malcolm Whitman	United States
1900	Malcolm Whitman	United States
1901	William Larned	United States
1902	William Larned	United States
1903	Lawrence Doherty	Great Britain
1904	Holcombe Ward	United States

MEN'S SINGLES (Continued)

Year	Player	Country
1905	Beals Wright	United States
1906	William Clothier	United States
1907	William Larned	United States
1908	William Larned	United States
1909	William Larned	United States
1910	William Larned	United States
1911	William Larned	United States
1912	Maurice McLoughlin	United States
1913	Maurice McLoughlin	United States
1914	Norris Williams	United States
1915	William Johnston	United States
1916	Norris Williams	United States
1917	Lindley Murray	United States
1918	Lindley Murray	United States
1919	William Johnston	United States
1920	Bill Tilden	United States
1921	Bill Tilden	United States
1922	Bill Tilden	United States
1923	Bill Tilden	United States
1924	Bill Tilden	United States
1925	Bill Tilden	United States
1926	Rene Lacoste	France
1927	Rene Lacoste	France
1928	Henri Cochet	France
1929	Bill Tilden	United States
1930	John Doeg	United States
1931	Ellsworth Vines	United States
1932	Ellsworth Vines	United States
1933	Fred Perry	Great Britain
1934	Fred Perry	Great Britain
1935	Wilmer Allison	United States
1936	Fred Perry	Great Britain
1937	Don Budge	United States
1938	Don Budge	United States
1939	Bobby Riggs	United States
1940	Donald McNeil	United States
1941	Bobby Riggs	United States
1942	Ted Schroeder	United States
1943	Joseph Hunt	United States
1944	Frank Parker	United States
1945	Frank Parker	United States
1946	Jack Kramer	United States

MEN'S SINGLES (Continued)

Year	Player	Country
1947	Jack Kramer	United States
1948	Pancho Gonzalez	United States
1949	Pancho Gonzalez	United States
1950	Arthur Larsen	United States
1951	Frank Sedgman	Australia
1952	Frank Sedgman	Australia
1953	Tony Trabert	United States
1954	Vic Seixas	United States
1955	Tony Trabert	United States
1956	Ken Rosewall	Australia
1957	Malcolm Anderson	Australia
1958	Ashley Cooper	Australia
1959	Neale Fraser	Australia
1960	Neale Fraser	Australia
1961	Roy Emerson	Australia
1962	Rod Laver	Australia
1963	Raphael Osuna	Mexico
1964	Roy Emerson	Australia
1965	Manuel Santana	Spain
1966	Fred Stolle	Australia
1967	John Newcombe	Australia
1968	Arthur Ashe	United States
1968	Arthur Ashe	United States*
1969	Stan Smith	United States
1969	Rod Laver	Australia*
1970	Ken Rosewall	Australia
1971	Stan Smith	United States
1972	Ilie Nastase	Romania
1973	John Newcombe	Australia
1974	Jimmy Connors	United States
1975	Manuel Orantes	Spain
1976	Jimmy Connors	United States
1977	Guillermo Vilas	Argentina
1978	Jimmy Connors	United States
1979	John McEnroe	United States
1980	John McEnroe	United States
1981	John McEnroe	United States
1982	Jimmy Connors	United States
1983	Jimmy Connors	United States
1984	John McEnroe	United States
1985	Ivan Lendl	Czechoslovakia

* Open event

MEN'S SINGLES (Continued)

Year	Player	Country
1986	Ivan Lendl	Czechoslovakia
1987	Ivan Lendl	Czechoslovakia
1988	Mats Wilander	Sweden
1989	Boris Becker	West Germany
1990	Pete Sampras	United States

WOMEN'S SINGLES

Year	Player	Country
1887	Ellen Hansell	United States
1888	Bertha Townsend	United States
1889	Bertha Townsend	United States
1890	Ellen Roosevelt	United States
1891	Mabel Cahill	United States
1892	Mabel Cahill	United States
1893	Aline Terry	United States
1894	Helen Helwig	United States
1895	Juliette Atkinson	United States
1896	Elisabeth Moore	United States
1897	Juliette Atkinson	United States
1898	Juliette Atkinson	United States
1899	Marion Jones	United States
1900	Myrtle McAteer	United States
1901	Elisabeth Moore	United States
1902	Marion Jones	United States
1903	Elisabeth Moore	United States
1904	May Sutton	United States
1905	Elisabeth Moore	United States
1906	Helen Homans	United States
1907	Evelyn Sears	United States
1908	Maud Bargar-Wallach	United States
1909	Hazel Hotchkiss	United States
1910	Hazel Hotchkiss	United States
1911	Hazel Hotchkiss	United States
1912	Mary Browne	United States
1913	Mary Browne	United States
1914	Mary Browne	United States
1915	Molla Bjurstedt	United States
1916	Molla Bjurstedt	United States
1917	Molla Bjurstedt	United States
1918	Molla Bjurstedt	United States
1919	Hazel Wightman (née Hotchkiss)	United States
1920	Molla Mallory (née Bjurstedt)	United States
1921	Molla Mallory (née Bjurstedt)	United States
1922	Molla Mallory (née Bjurstedt)	United States

WOMEN'S SINGLES (Continued)

Year	Player	Country
1923	Helen Wills	United States
1924	Helen Wills	United States
1925	Helen Wills	United States
1926	Molla Mallory (née Bjurstedt)	United States
1927	Helen Wills	United States
1928	Helen Wills	United States
1929	Helen Wills	United States
1930	Betty Nuthall	Great Britain
1931	Helen Moody (née Wills)	United States
1932	Helen Jacobs	United States
1933	Helen Jacobs	United States
1934	Helen Jacobs	United States
1935	Helen Jacobs	United States
1936	Alice Marble	United States
1937	Anita Lizana	Chile
1938	Alice Marble	United States
1939	Alice Marble	United States
1940	Alice Marble	United States
1941	Sarah Cooke	United States
1942	Pauline Betz	United States
1943	Pauline Betz	United States
1944	Pauline Betz	United States
1945	Sarah Cooke	United States
1946	Pauline Betz	United States
1947	Louise Brough	United States
1948	Margaret Du Pont	United States
1949	Margaret Du Pont	United States
1950	Margaret Du Pont	United States
1951	Maureen Connolly	United States
1952	Maureen Connolly	United States
1953	Maureen Connolly	United States
1954	Doris Hart	United States
1955	Doris Hart	United States
1956	Shirley Fry	United States
1957	Althea Gibson	United States
1958	Althea Gibson	United States
1959	Maria Bueno	Brazil
1960	Darlene Hard	United States
1961	Darlene Hard	United States
1962	Margaret Smith	Australia
1963	Maria Bueno	Brazil
1964	Maria Bueno	Brazil

WOMEN'S SINGLES (Continued)

Year	Player	Country
1965	Margaret Smith	Australia
1966	Maria Bueno	Brazil
1967	Billie Jean King	United States
1968	Margaret Court (née Smith)	Australia
1968	Virginia Wade	Great Britain*
1969	Margaret Court (née Smith)	Australia
1969	Margaret Court (née Smith)	Australia*
1970	Margaret Court (née Smith)	Australia
1971	Billie Jean King	United States
1972	Billie Jean King	United States
1973	Margaret Court (née Smith)	Australia
1974	Billie Jean King	United States
1975	Chris Evert	United States
1976	Chris Evert	United States
1977	Chris Evert	United States
1978	Chris Evert	United States
1979	Tracy Austin	United States
1980	Chris Evert	United States
1981	Tracy Austin	United States
1982	Chris Evert	United States
1983	Martina Navrátilová	United States
1984	Martina Navrátilová	United States
1985	Hanna Mandlikova	Czechoslovakia
1986	Martina Navrátilová	United States
1987	Martina Navrátilová	United States
1988	Steffi Graf	West Germany
1989	Steffi Graf	West Germany
1990	Gabriela Sabatini	Argentina

*Open event

US OPEN CHAMPION ■ BILL TILDEN, US, HAS WON THE US OPEN SEVEN TIMES, 1920–25, 1929, A RECORD HE SHARES WITH RICHARD SEARS, US, AND WILLIAM LARNED, US.

Most Wins Men Seven by three players: Richard Sears (US), 1881–87; William Larned (US), 1901–02, 1907–11; Bill Tilden (US), 1920–25, 1929.

Most Wins Women Molla Mallory (née Bjurstedt [US]), has won a record eight titles; 1915–18, 1920–22, 1926.

Men's Doubles The most wins by one pair is five by Richard Sears and James Dwight (US), 1882–84, 1886–87. The most wins by an individual player is six by two players: Richard Sears, 1882–84, 1886–87, with Dwight and 1885 with Joseph Clark; Holcombe Ward 1899–1901 (with Dwight Davis), 1904–06 (with Beals Wright).

Women's Doubles The most wins by a pair is 12 by Louise Brough and Margaret Du Pont (née Osborne), both of the US. They won 1942–50, 1955–57. Margaret Du Pont holds the record for an individual player with 13 wins, adding to her victories with Brough was the 1941 title with Sarah Cooke.

Mixed Doubles The most wins by one pair is four by William Talbert and Margaret Osborne (US), who won 1943–46. The most titles won by any individual is nine by Margaret Du Pont (née Osborne). She won 1943–46, 1950, 1956, 1958–60. The most titles won by a man is four accomplished by six players: Edwin Fischer (US), 1894–96, 1898; Wallace Johnson (US), 1907, 1909, 1911, 1920; Bill Tilden (US), 1913–14, 1922–23; William Talbert (US) 1943–46; Owen Davidson (Australia), 1966–67, 1971, 1973; Marty Riessen (US), 1969–70, 1972, 1980.

Most Titles Overall Margaret Du Pont (née Osborne) has won a record 25 US Open titles from 1941–60, three singles, 13 doubles, nine mixed doubles.

Youngest Champions The youngest singles champion was Tracy Austin (US), who was 16 yr 271 days when she won the women's singles in 1979. The youngest men's champion was Pete Sampras (US), who was 19 yr 28 days when he won the 1990 title.

YOUNGEST MEN'S CHAMPION ■ AT 19 YEARS 28 DAYS, PETE SAMPRAS BECAME THE YOUNGEST MEN'S US OPEN CHAMPION WHEN HE WON IN 1990.

FRENCH OPEN CHAMPIONSHIPS

The first French Championships were held in 1891, however entry was restricted to members of French clubs until 1925. Grand Slam records only include the French Open from 1925. This event has been staged at the Stade Roland Garros since 1928 and currently is the second leg of the grand slam.

FRENCH OPEN CHAMPIONS (1925–1990)

MEN'S SINGLES		
Year	Player	Country
1925	Rene Lacoste	France
1926	Henri Cochet	France
1927	Rene Lacoste	France
1928	Henri Cochet	France
1929	Rene Lacoste	France
1930	Henri Cochet	France
1931	Jean Borotra	France
1932	Henri Cochet	France
1933	Jack Crawford	Australia

FRENCH OPEN CHAMPIONS (1925–1990) (Continued)

MEN'S SINGLES (Continued)		
Year	Player	Country
1934	Gottfried Von Cramm	Germany
1935	Fred Perry	Great Britain
1936	Gottfried Von Cramm	Germany
1937	Henner Henkel	Germany
1938	Don Budge	United States
1939	Donald McNeil	United States
1940	not held	
1941	not held	
1942	not held	
1943	not held	
1944	not held	
1945	not held	
1946	Marcel Bernard	France
1947	Jozsef Asboth	Hungary
1948	Frank Parker	United States
1949	Frank Parker	United States
1950	Budge Patty	United States
1951	Jaroslav Drobny	Egypt
1952	Jaroslav Drobny	Egypt
1953	Ken Rosewall	Australia
1954	Tony Trabert	United States
1955	Tony Trabert	United States
1956	Lew Hoad	Australia
1957	Sven Davidson	Sweden
1958	Mervyn Rose	Australia
1959	Nicola Pietrangeli	Italy
1960	Nicola Pietrangeli	Italy
1961	Manuel Santana	Spain
1962	Rod Laver	Australia
1963	Roy Emerson	Australia
1964	Manuel Santana	Spain
1965	Fred Stolle	Australia
1966	Tony Roche	Australia
1967	Roy Emerson	Australia
1968	Ken Rosewall	Australia
1969	Rod Laver	Australia
1970	Jan Kodes	Czechoslovakia
1971	Jan Kodes	Czechoslovakia
1972	Andres Gimeno	Spain
1973	Ilie Nastase	Romania
1974	Bjorn Borg	Sweden
1975	Bjorn Borg	Sweden

MEN'S SINGLES (Continued)

Year	Player	Country
1976	Adriano Panatta	Italy
1977	Guillermo Vilas	Argentina
1978	Bjorn Borg	Sweden
1979	Bjorn Borg	Sweden
1980	Bjorn Borg	Sweden
1981	Bjorn Borg	Sweden
1982	Mats Wilander	Sweden
1983	Yannick Noah	France
1984	Ivan Lendl	Czechoslovakia
1985	Mats Wilander	Sweden
1986	Ivan Lendl	Czechoslovakia
1987	Ivan Lendl	Czechoslovakia
1988	Mats Wilander	Sweden
1989	Michael Chang	United States
1990	Andres Gomez	Ecuador

WOMEN'S SINGLES

Year	Player	Country
1925	Suzanne Lenglen	France
1926	Suzanne Lenglen	France
1927	Kea Bouman	Netherlands
1928	Helen Moody (née Wills)	United States
1929	Helen Moody (née Wills)	United States
1930	Helen Moody (née Wills)	United States
1931	Cilly Aussem	Germany
1932	Helen Moody (née Wills)	United States
1933	Margaret Scriven	Great Britain
1934	Margaret Scriven	Great Britain
1935	Hilde Sperling	Germany
1936	Hilde Sperling	Germany
1937	Hilde Sperling	Germany
1938	Simone Mathieu	France
1939	Simone Mathieu	France
1940	not held	
1941	not held	
1942	not held	
1943	not held	
1944	not held	
1945	not held	
1946	Margaret Osborne	United States
1947	Pat Todd	United States
1948	Nelly Landry	France
1949	Margaret Du Pont (née Osborne)	United States

WOMEN'S SINGLES (Continued)

Year	Player	Country
1950	Doris Hart	United States
1951	Shirley Fry	United States
1952	Doris Hart	United States
1953	Maureen Connolly	United States
1954	Maureen Connolly	United States
1955	Angela Mortimer	Great Britain
1956	Althea Gibson	United States
1957	Shirley Bloomer	Great Britain
1958	Zsuzsi Kormoczy	Hungary
1959	Christine Truman	Great Britain
1960	Darlene Hard	United States
1961	Ann Haydon	Great Britain
1962	Margaret Smith	Australia
1963	Lesley Turner	Australia
1964	Margaret Smith	Australia
1965	Lesley Turner	Australia
1966	Ann Jones (née Haydon)	Great Britain
1967	Francoise Durr	France
1968	Nancy Richey	United States
1969	Margaret Court (née Smith)	Australia
1970	Margaret Court (née Smith)	Australia
1971	Evonne Goolagong	Australia
1972	Billie Jean King	United States
1973	Margaret Court (née Smith)	Australia
1974	Chris Evert	United States
1975	Chris Evert	United States
1976	Sue Barker	Great Britain
1977	Mimi Jausovec	Yugoslavia
1978	Virginia Ruzici	Romania
1979	Chris Evert	United States
1980	Chris Evert	United States
1981	Hana Mandlikova	Czechoslovakia
1982	Martina Navrátilová	United States
1983	Chris Evert	United States
1984	Martina Navrátilová	United States
1985	Chris Evert	United States
1986	Chris Evert	United States
1987	Steffi Graf	West Germany
1988	Steffi Graf	West Germany
1989	Aranxta Sanchez Vicario	Spain
1990	Monica Seles	Yugoslavia

Most Wins Men Bjorn Borg (Sweden) has won the French title a record six times, 1974–75, 1978–81.

Most Wins Women Chris Evert has won a record seven French titles, 1974–75, 1979–80, 1983, 1985–86.

Men's Doubles Roy Emerson (Australia) has won the men's doubles a record six times, 1960–65, with five different partners.

Women's Doubles The pair of Martina Navrátilová and Pam Shriver (both US), have won the doubles title a record four times, 1984–85, 1987–88. The most wins by an individual player is seven, by Martina Navrátilová, four times with Pam Shriver, 1984–85, 1987–88, and with three other players in 1975, 1982, 1986.

Mixed Doubles Two teams have won the mixed title three times: Ken Fletcher and Margaret Smith (Australia), 1963–65; Jean-Claude Barclay and Francoise Durr (France), 1968, 1971, 1973. Margaret Court (née Smith) has won the title the most times with four wins, winning with Marty Riessen (US), 1969, in addition to her three wins with Fletcher. Fletcher and Barclay share the men's record of three wins.

Most Titles Overall Margaret Court (née Smith) has won a record 13 French Open titles: 1962–73; five singles, four doubles, four mixed doubles.

Youngest Champions The youngest singles champion at the French Open was Monica Seles (Yugoslavia) in 1990, at 16 yr 169 days. The youngest men's winner is Michael Chang (US), who was 17 yr 109 days when he won the 1989 title.

AUSTRALIAN OPEN CHAMPIONSHIPS

The first Australasian championships were held in 1905, with New Zealand hosting the event in 1906 and 1912. The tournament changed to the Australian Open in 1925 and is counted as a grand slam event from that year. There were two championships in 1977 because the event was moved from early season (January) to December. It reverted to a January date in 1987, which meant there was no championship in 1986. Currently the tournament is held at the Australian Tennis Center in Melbourne and is the first leg of the grand slam.

AUSTRALIAN OPEN CHAMPIONS (1925–1990)

MEN'S SINGLES

Year	Player	Country
1925	James Anderson	Australia
1926	John Hawkes	Australia
1927	Gerald Patterson	Australia
1928	Jean Borotra	France
1929	John Gregory	Australia
1930	Gar Moon	Australia
1931	Jack Crawford	Australia
1932	Jack Crawford	Australia
1933	Jack Crawford	Australia
1934	Fred Perry	Great Britain
1935	Jack Crawford	Great Britain
1936	Adrian Quist	Australia
1937	V. B. McGrath	Australia
1938	Don Budge	United States
1939	John Bromwich	Australia
1940	Adrian Quist	Australia
1941	not held	
1942	not held	
1943	not held	
1944	not held	
1945	not held	
1946	John Bromwich	Australia
1947	Dinny Pails	Australia
1948	Adrian Quist	Australia
1949	Frank Sedgman	Australia
1950	Frank Sedgman	Australia
1951	Dick Savitt	United States
1952	Ken McGregor	Australia
1953	Ken Rosewall	Australia
1954	Mervyn Rose	Australia
1955	Ken Rosewall	Australia
1956	Lew Hoad	Australia
1957	Ashley Cooper	Australia
1958	Ashley Cooper	Australia
1959	Alex Olmedo	United States
1960	Rod Laver	Australia
1961	Roy Emerson	Australia
1962	Rod Laver	Australia
1963	Roy Emerson	Australia
1964	Roy Emerson	Australia
1965	Roy Emerson	Australia
1966	Roy Emerson	Australia

MEN'S SINGLES (Continued)

Year	Player	Country
1967	Roy Emerson	Australia
1968	Bill Bowrey	Australia
1969	Rod Laver	Australia
1970	Arthur Ashe	United States
1971	Ken Rosewall	Australia
1972	Ken Rosewall	Australia
1973	John Newcombe	Australia
1974	Jimmy Connors	United States
1975	John Newcombe	Australia
1976	Mark Edmondson	Australia
1977	Roscoe Tanner	United States
1977	Vitas Gerulaitis	United States
1978	Guillermo Vilas	Argentina
1979	Guillermo Vilas	Argentina
1980	Brian Teacher	United States
1981	Johan Kriek	South Africa
1982	Johan Kriek	South Africa
1983	Mats Wilander	Sweden
1984	Mats Wilander	Sweden
1985	Stefan Edberg	Sweden
1986	not held	
1987	Stefan Edberg	Sweden
1988	Mats Wilander	Sweden
1989	Ivan Lendl	Czechoslovakia
1990	Ivan Lendl	Czechoslovakia

WOMEN'S SINGLES

Year	Player	Country
1925	Daphne Akhurst	Australia
1926	Daphne Akhurst	Australia
1927	Esna Boyd	Australia
1928	Daphne Akhurst	Australia
1929	Daphne Akhurst	Australia
1930	Daphne Akhurst	Australia
1931	Coral Buttsworth	Australia
1932	Coral Buttsworth	Australia
1933	Joan Hartigan	Australia
1934	Joan Hartigan	Australia
1935	Dorothy Round	Great Britain
1936	Joan Hartigan	Australia
1937	Nancye Wynne	Australia
1938	Dorothy M. Bundy	Australia
1939	Emily Westacott	Australia

WOMEN'S SINGLES (Continued)

Year	Player	Country
1940	Nancye Wynne	Australia
1941	not held	
1942	not held	
1943	not held	
1944	not held	
1945	not held	
1946	Nancye Bolton (née Wynne)	Australia
1947	Nancye Bolton (née Wynne)	Australia
1948	Nancye Bolton (née Wynne)	Australia
1949	Doris Hart	United States
1950	Louise Brough	United States
1951	Nancye Bolton (née Wynne)	Australia
1952	Thelma Long	Australia
1953	Maureen Connolly	United States
1954	Thelma Long	Australia
1955	Beryl Penrose	Australia
1956	Mary Carter	Australia
1957	Shirley Fry	United States
1958	Angela Mortimer	Great Britain
1959	Mary Reitano (née Carter)	Australia
1960	Margaret Smith	Australia
1961	Margaret Smith	Australia
1962	Margaret Smith	Australia
1963	Margaret Smith	Australia
1964	Margaret Smith	Australia
1965	Margaret Smith	Australia
1966	Margaret Smith	Australia
1967	Nancy Richey	United States
1968	Billie Jean King	United States
1969	Margaret Court (née Smith)	Australia
1970	Margaret Court (née Smith)	Australia
1971	Margaret Court (née Smith)	Australia
1972	Virginia Wade	Great Britain
1973	Margaret Court (née Smith)	Australia
1974	Evonne Goolagong	Australia
1975	Evonne Goolagong	Australia
1976	Evonne Cawley (née Goolagong)	Australia
1977	Kerry Reid	Australia
1977	Evonne Cawley (née Goolagong)	Australia
1978	Christine O'Neill	Australia
1979	Barbara Jordan	United States
1980	Hana Mandlikova	Czechoslovakia

AUSTRALIAN OPEN CHAMPIONS
(1925–1990) (Continued)
WOMEN'S SINGLES (Continued)

Year	Player	Country
1981	Martina Navrátilová	United States
1982	Chris Evert	United States
1983	Martina Navrátilová	United States
1984	Chris Evert	United States
1985	Martina Navrátilová	United States
1986	not held	
1987	Hana Mandlikova	Czechoslovakia
1988	Steffi Graf	West Germany
1989	Steffi Graf	West Germany
1990	Steffi Graf	West Germany

Most Wins Men Six by Roy Emerson (Australia), 1961, 1963–67.

Most Wins Women 11 by Margaret Court (née Smith) of Australia, 1960–66, 1969–71, 1973.

ON TOP DOWN UNDER ■ ROY EMERSON, AUS-TRALIA, HAS WON A MEN'S RECORD 12 GRAND SLAM SINGLES TITLES, INCLUDING A RECORD SIX AUSTRA-LIAN TITLES.

Men's Doubles The most wins by one pair is eight by John Bromwich and Adrian Quist (Australia), 1938–40, 1946–50. In addition, Quist holds the record for most wins by one player with 10, winning in 1936–37 with Don Turnbull, to add to his triumphs with Bromwich.

Women's Doubles The most wins by one pair is 10 by Nancye Bolton (née Wynne) and Thelma Long (née Coyne), both Australian. Their victories came in 1936–40, 1947–49, 1951–52. Long also holds the record for most wins with 12, winning in 1956, 1958 with Mary Hawton.

Mixed Doubles The most wins by one pair is four by two teams: Harry Hopman and Nell Hopman (née Hall) (Australia), 1930, 1936–37, 1939; Colin Long and Nancye Bolton (née Wynne), (Australia), 1940, 1946–48.

Most Overall Titles Margaret Court (née Smith) has won a record 21 Australian Open titles between 1960 and 1973—11 singles, eight doubles, two mixed doubles.

Youngest Champions The youngest women's singles champion was Margaret Smith, who won the event, when aged 17 years 5 months.

OLYMPIC GAMES Tennis was reintroduced to the Olympic Games in 1988, having originally been included at the Games from 1896 to 1924. It was also a demonstration sport in 1968 and 1984.

A record four gold medals as well as a silver and a bronze, were won by Max Decugis (France), 1900–20. A women's record five medals (1 gold, 2 silver, 2 bronze) were won by Kitty McKane (later Kitty Godfree, [Great Britain]) in 1920 and 1924.

DAVIS CUP (INSTITUTED 1900) The most wins in the Davis Cup, the men's international team championship, has been 29, by the US. The most appearances for Cup winners is eight, by Roy Emerson (Australia), 1959–62, 1964–67. Bill Tilden (US) played in a record 28 matches in the final, winning a record 21, 17 out of 22 singles and four out of six doubles. He was in seven winning sides, 1920–26, and then four losing sides, 1927–30.

Nicola Pietrangeli (Italy) played a record 163 matches (66 ties), 1954 to 1972, winning 120. He played 109 singles (winning 78) and 54 doubles (winning 42).

Ilie Nastase (Romania) set a singles season mark of 18 wins (with 2 losses) in 1971.

DAVIS CUP WINNERS

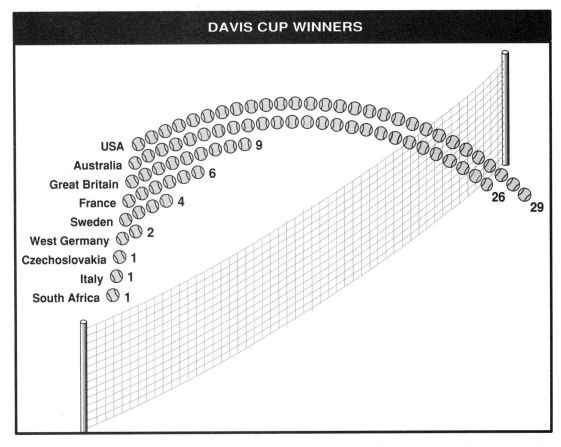

USA 9
Australia 6
Great Britain 4
France 2
Sweden 1
West Germany 1
Czechoslovakia 1
Italy 1
South Africa 1

26
29

DAVIS CUP ■ MEMBERS OF THE US TEAM CELEBRATE THEIR VICTORY OVER AUSTRALIA IN THE 1990 DAVIS CUP FINAL. FOR THE US THIS WAS A RECORD 29TH WIN IN THE COMPETITION.

US TEAM RECORDS

Most Years on Team	11, Bill Tilden, Stan Smith
Most Matches	25, John McEnroe
Most Wins, Singles	39, John McEnroe
Most Wins, Doubles	22, John Van Ryn
Most Wins, Total	54, John McEnroe

FEDERATION CUP (INSTITUTED 1963) The most wins in the Federation Cup, the women's international team championship, is 14, by the US. Virginia Wade (Great Britain) played each year from 1967 to 1983, in a record 57 ties, playing 100 matches, including 56 singles (winning 36) and 44 doubles (winning 30). Chris Evert (US) won her first 29 singles matches, 1977–86. Her overall record (1977–89) is 40 wins in 42 singles and 16 wins in 18 doubles matches.

Highest Earnings Ivan Lendl (Czechoslovakia) won a men's season's record $2,344,367 in 1989 and holds the career mark at $16,722,078 at the end of 1990. The season's record for women is $2,173,556 in 1984 (including a $1 million Grand Slam bonus) by Martina Navrátilová (US). Navrátilová also holds the career mark at $16,674,607 through 1990.

MEN'S CAREER EARNINGS
Top Five

Player	Prize Money
Ivan Lendl	$16,772,078
John McEnroe	$11,265,336
Stefan Edberg	$8,633,696
Boris Becker	$8,160,207
Jimmy Connors	$8,107,685

Source: ATP

WOMEN'S CAREER EARNINGS
Top Five

Player	Prize Money
Martina Navrátilová	$16,674,607
Chris Evert	$8,896,195
Steffi Graf	$7,173,198
Pam Shriver	$4,323,497
Gabriela Sabatini	$3,656,136

Source: WTC

Fastest service The fastest service timed with modern equipment is 138 mph, by Steve Denton (US) at Beaver Creek, CO on 29 July 1984. The fastest *ever* measured was one of 163.6 mph, by Bill Tilden (US) in 1931.

"Golden set" The only known example of a "Golden set" (to win a set 6–0 without dropping a single point) in professional tennis was achieved by Bill Scanlon (US) against Marcos Hocevar (Brazil) in the first round of the WCT Gold Coast Classic at Del Ray, FL on 22 February 1983. Scanlon won the match, 6–2, 6–0.

Longest game The longest known singles game was one of 37 deuces (80 points) between Anthony Fawcett (Rhodesia) and Keith Glass (Great Britain) in the first round of the Surrey Championships at Surbiton, England on 26 May 1975. It lasted 31 min. Noëlle van Lottum and Sandra Begijn played a game lasting 52 min in the semifinals of the Dutch Indoor Championships at Ede, Gelderland on 12 February 1984.

The longest tiebreak was 26–24 for the 4th and decisive set of a first round men's doubles at the Wimbledon Championships on 1 July 1985. Jan Gunnarsson (Sweden) and Michael Mortensen (Denmark) defeated John Frawley (Australia) and Victor Pecci (Paraguay) 6–3, 6–4, 3–6, 7–6.

The longest rally in tournament play was one of 643 times over the net between Vicky Nelson and Jean Hepner at Richmond, VA in October 1984. The 6 hr 22 min match was won by Nelson 6–4, 7–6. It concluded with a 1 hr 47 min tiebreak, 13–11, for which one point took 29 minutes.

TRACK AND FIELD

ORIGINS Competition in running, jumping or throwing must have occurred from the earliest days of mankind. The earliest evidence of organized running is from 3800 B.C. in Egypt. The ancient Olympic Games were cultural festivals that highlighted the ancient Greek ideal of perfection of mind and body. The modern Olympic Games staged in 1896 focused on athletic achievement and the spirit of competition and have provided the focus for track and field as a sport ever since. In 1983, a separate World Championship was introduced.

Fastest speed An analysis of split times at each 10 meters in the 1988 Olympic Games 100 m final in Seoul, South Korea on 24 September 1988, which was won by Ben Johnson (Canada) in 9.79 (average speed 22.85 mph but later disallowed as a world record because of testing positive for steroids) from Carl Lewis (US) 9.92, showed that both Johnson and Lewis reached a peak speed (40 m–50 m and 80 m–90 m respectively) of 0.83 sec for 10 m, i.e., 26.95 mph.

Highest jump above own head The greatest height cleared above an athlete's own head is 23¼ in, by Franklin Jacobs (US), who jumped 7 ft 7¼ in in New York City on 27 January 1978. He is 5 ft 8 in tall. The greatest height cleared by a woman above her own head is 12 in, by Cindy John Holmes (US), 5 ft tall, who jumped 6 ft at Provo, UT on 1 June 1982.

Most records in a day Jesse Owens (US) set six world records in 45 min at Ann Arbor, MI on 25 May 1935, with a 9.4 sec 100 yd at 3:15 P.M., a 26 ft 8¼ in long jump at 3:25 P.M., a 20.3 sec 220 yd (and 200 m) at 3:45 P.M. and a 22.6 sec 220-yd (and 200-m) low hurdles at 4:00 P.M.

MOST RECORDS IN A DAY ■ JESSE OWENS, US, SET SIX WORLD RECORDS IN 45 MIN AT ANN ARBOR, MI ON 25 MAY 1935. HE SET RECORDS AT 100 YD, LONG JUMP, 220 YD, 200 M, 220-YD HURDLES AND 200-M HURDLES.

OLYMPIC GAMES

The first modern Olympic Games were staged in Athens, Greece, 6–15 April 1896. 59 athletes from 10 nations competed; women's events were not added until 1928.

Gold Medals Ray Ewry (US) holds the all-time record for most appearances atop the winners podium with 10 gold medals: standing high jump (1900, 1904, 1906, 1908); standing long jump (1900, 1904, 1906, 1908); standing triple jump (1900, 1904). The women's record is four shared by three athletes: Fanny Blankers-Koen (Netherlands): 100 m, 200 m, 80 m hurdles and 4 x 100 m relay in 1948; Betty Cuthbert (Australia): 100 m, 200 m, 4 x 100 m relay in 1956, and 400 m in 1964; Barbel Wockel (née Eckert [East Germany]): 200 m and 4 x 100 m relay in both 1976 and 1980.

Most Wins at One Games Paavo Nurmi (Finland) won five gold medals at the 1924 Games. His victories came in the 1,500 m, 5,000 m, 10,000 m cross-country, 3,000 m team and cross-country team. The most wins at individual events (not including relay or other team races) is four by Alvin Kraenzlein (US) in 1900 at 60 m, 110 m hurdles, 200 m hurdles and the long jump. The women's record is four set by Fanny Blankers-Koen (Netherlands [see above]).

FINNISH FIRST ■ PAAVO NURMI, FINLAND, WON A RECORD 12 TRACK AND FIELD OLYMPIC MEDALS (9 GOLD, 3 SILVER), IN THE 1920, 1924 AND 1928 GAMES.

WORLD RECORDS

MEN

World records for the men's events scheduled by the International Amateur Athletic Federation. Fully automatic electric timing is mandatory for events up to 400 meters.

RUNNING

100 meters: 9.92,* Carl Lewis (US), Seoul, South Korea, 24 September 1988

200 meters: 19.72,[A] Pietro Mennea (Italy), Mexico City, Mexico, 12 September 1979

400 meters: 43.29, Butch Reynolds Jr. (US), Zürich, Switzerland, 17 August 1988

800 meters: 1:41.73, Sebastian Coe (Great Britain), Florence, Italy, 10 June 1981

1,500 meters: 3:29.46, Saïd Aouita (Morocco), Berlin, West Germany, 23 August 1985

1 mile: 3:46.32, Steve Cram (Great Britain), Oslo, Norway, 27 July 1985

5,000 meters: 12:58.39, Saïd Aouita (Morocco), Rome, Italy, 22 July 1987

10,000 meters: 27:08.23, Arturo Barrios (Mexico), Berlin, West Germany, 18 August 1989

* Ben Johnson (Canada) ran 100 m in 9.79 sec at Seoul, South Korea on 24 September 1988, but was subsequently disqualified on testing positive for steroids. He later admitted to having taken drugs over many years, which invalidated his 9.83 sec at Rome, Italy on 30 August 1987.

[A] This record was set at high altitude—Mexico City 7,349 ft. Best mark at low altitude: 200 m: 19.75 sec, Carl Lewis, Indianapolis, IN, 19 June 1983 and Joe DeLoach (US) at Seoul, South Korea on 28 September 1988.

HURDLING

110 meters: 12.92, Roger Kingdom (US), Zürich, Switzerland, 16 August 1989

400 meters: 47.02, Edwin Moses (US), Koblenz, West Germany, 31 August 1983

3,000 meters steeplechase: 8:05.35, Peter Koech (Kenya), Stockholm, Sweden, 4 July 1989

RELAYS

4 x 100 meters: 37.83, United States (Sam Graddy, Ron Brown, Calvin Smith, Carl Lewis), Los Angeles, CA, 11 August 1984

4 x 400 meters: 2:56.16[A], United States (Vince Matthews, Ron Freeman, Larry James, Lee Evans), Mexico City, Mexico, 20 October 1968
2:56.16, United States (Danny Everett, Steve Lewis, Kevin Robinzine, Butch Reynolds), Seoul, South Korea, 1 October 1988

[A] Set at high altitude

FIELD EVENTS

High Jump: 8' 0" Javier Sotomayor (Cuba), San Juan, Puerto Rico, 29 July 1989

Pole Vault: 19' 10½" Sergey Bubka (USSR), Nice, France, 10 July 1988

Long Jump: 29' 2½"[A] Bob Beamon (US), Mexico City, Mexico, 18 October 1968

Triple Jump: 58' 11" Willie Banks (US), Indianapolis, IN, 16 June 1985

Shot 16 lb: 75' 10¼" Randy Barnes (US), Los Angeles, CA, 20 May 1990

Discus 4 lb 8 oz: 243' 0" Jürgen Schult (East Germany), Neubrandenburg, East Germany, 6 June 1986

Hammer 16 lb: 284' 7" Yuriy Sedykh (USSR), Stuttgart, West Germany, 30 August 1986

Javelin: 298' 6"[†] Stephen Backley (Great Britain), London, UK, 20 July 1990

[A] Set at high altitude; the low altitude best: 28 ft 10 ¼ in, Carl Lewis at Indianapolis, IN on 19 July 1983.

[†] With the new javelin, which has the center of gravity moved back, introduced in 1986. The best performance with the old javelin was 343 ft 10 in by Uwe Hohn (East Germany) at East Berlin, East Germany on 20 July 1984.

MEN (Continued)
DECATHLON

8,847 points: Daley Thompson (Great Britain) (1st day: 100 m 10.44 sec, Long Jump 26' 3½", Shot Put 51' 7", High Jump 6' 8", 400 m 46.97 sec), (2nd day: 110 m Hurdles 14.33 sec, Discuss 152' 9", Pole Vault 16' 4¾", Javelin 214' 0", 1,500 m 4:35.00 sec), Los Angeles, CA, 8–9 August 1984

WOMEN

World records for the women's events scheduled by the International Amateur Athletic Federation. The same stipulation about automatically timed events applies in the six events up to 400 meters as in the men's list.

RUNNING

100 meters: 10.49, Florence Griffith Joyner (US), Indianapolis, IN, 16 July 1988

200 meters: 21.34, Florence Griffith Joyner (US), Seoul, South Korea, 29 September 1988

400 meters: 47.60, Marita Koch (East Germany), Canberra, Australia, 6 October 1985

800 meters: 1:53.28, Jarmila Kratochvilová (Czechoslovakia), Münich, West Germany, 26 July 1983

1,000 meters: 2:30.6, Tatyana Providokhina (USSR), Podolsk, USSR, 20 August 1978

1,500 meters: 3:52.47, Tatyana Kazankina (USSR), Zürich, Switzerland, 13 August 1980

1 mile: 4:15.61, Paula Ivan (Romania), Nice, France, 10 July 1989

2,000 meters: 5:28.69, Maricica Puica (Romania), London, England, 11 July 1986

3,000 meters: 8:22.62, Tatyana Kazankina (USSR), Leningrad, USSR, 26 August 1984

5,000 meters: 14:37.33, Ingrid Kristiansen (née Christensen [Norway]), Stockholm, Sweden, 5 August 1986

10,000 meters: 30:13.74, Ingrid Kristiansen (Norway), Oslo, Norway, 5 July 1986

HURDLING

100 meters: 12.21, Yordanka Donkova (Bulgaria), Stara Zagora, Bulgaria, 20 August 1988

400 meters: 52.94, Marina Styepanova (née Makeyeva [USSR]), Tashkent, USSR, 17 September 1986

RELAYS

4 x 100 meters: 41.37, East Germany (Silke Gladisch [now Möller], Sabine Rieger [now Günther], Ingrid Auerswald [née Brestrich], Marlies Göhr [née Oelsner]), Canberra, Australia, 6 October 1985

4 x 400 meters: 3:15.17, USSR (Tatyana Ledovskaya, Olga Nazarova, Maria Pinigina [née Kulchunova], Olga Bryzgina [née Vladykina]), Seoul, South Korea 1 October 1988

FIELD EVENTS

High Jump: 6' 10¼", Stefka Kostadinova (Bulgaria), Rome, Italy, 30 August 1987

Long Jump: 24' 8¼", Galina Chistyakova (USSR), Leningrad, USSR, 11 June 1988

Triple Jump: 47' 8½", Li Huirong (China), Sapporo, Japan, 25 August 1990

Shot 8 lb 13 oz: 74' 3" Natalya Lisovskaya (USSR), Moscow, USSR, 7 June 1987

Discus 2 lb 3 oz: 252' 0" Gabriele Reinsch (East Germany), Neubrandenburg, East Germany, 9 July 1988

Javelin 247 oz: 262' 5" Petra Felke (East Germany), Potsdam, East Germany, 9 September 1988

HEPTATHLON

7,291 points: Jacqueline Joyner-Kersee (US) (100 m hurdles 12.69 sec; High Jump 6 ft 1¼ in; Shot 51 ft 10 in; 200 m 22.56 sec; Long Jump 23 ft 10 in; Javelin 149 ft 9 in; 800 m 2 min 08.51 sec), Seoul, South Korea, 23–24 September 1988

Most Medals Won Paavo Nurmi (Finland) won a record 12 medals (9 gold, 3 silver) in the Games of 1920, 1924 and 1928. The women's record is seven shared by two athletes: Shirley de la Hunty (Australia), three gold, one silver, three bronze in the 1948, 1952 and 1956 Games; Irena Szewinska (Poland), three gold, two silver, two bronze in the 1964, 1968, 1972 and 1976 Games.

United States Athletes Ray Ewry holds the Olympic mark for most golds (see above). His 10 gold medals are also the most overall medals won by any US athlete in Olympic history. The women's record for gold medals is three set by four athletes: Wilma Rudolph, 100 m, 200 m and 4 x 100 m relay in 1960; Wyomia Tyus, 100 m in 1964, 100 m and 4 x 100 m relay in 1968; Valerie Brisco, 200 m, 400 m and 4 x 400 m relay in 1984; Florence Griffith Joyner, 100 m, 200 m and 4 x 100 m relay in 1988.

The most gold medals won at one Games by a US athlete is four shared by three men: Alvin Kraenzlein (see above), Jesse Owens, 100 m, 200 m, long jump and 4 x 100 m relay in 1936; Carl Lewis, 100 m, 200 m, long jump, 4 x 100 m relay in 1984. The women's record is three golds held by Wilma Rudolph, Valerie Brisco and Florence Griffith Joyner (see above).

The most medals won overall by a female athlete is five by Florence Griffith Joyner, three golds, two silver in the 1984 and 1988 Games.

WORLD CHAMPIONSHIPS

Quadriennial World Championships distinct from the Olympic Games were first held in 1983 at Helsinki, Finland.

The most medals won is six (5 gold 1 silver) by Carl Lewis (US). In 1983, he won the long jump, 100 m and 4 x 100 m relay; in 1987, he repeated his long jump and relay feats, but could only gain the silver in the 100 m. The most medals won by a women is four shared by two athletes: Marita Koch (East Germany), three gold (200 m, 4 x 100

POLE VAULT ■ SERGEY BUBKA, USSR, IS THE WORLD RECORD HOLDER IN THE POLE VAULT. HIS MARK OF 19 FT 10½ IN WAS SET AT NICE, FRANCE ON 10 JULY 1988.

US NATIONAL RECORDS

MEN

RUNNING

100 meters: 9.92, Carl Lewis, Seoul, South Korea, 24 September 1988

200 meters: 19.75, Carl Lewis, Indianapolis, IN, 19 June 1983
19.75, Joe DeLoach, Seoul, South Korea, 28 September 1988

400 meters: 43.29, Butch Reynolds, Jr, Zürich, Switzerland, 17 August 1988

800 meters: 1:42.60, Johnny Gray, Koblenz, West Germany, 28 August 1985

1,500 meters: 3:29.77, Sydney Maree, Cologne, West Germany, 25 August 1985

1 mile: 3:47.69, Steve Scott, Oslo, Norway, 7 July 1982

3,000 meters: 7:33.37,[#] Sydney Maree, London, England 17 July 1982
7:35.84, Doug Padilla, Oslo, Norway, 9 July 1983

5,000 meters: 13:01.5, Sydney Maree, Oslo, Norway, 27 July 1985

10,000 meters: 27:20.56, Marcus Nenow, Brussels, Belgium, 5 September 1986

[#] Prior to obtaining US citizenship

HURDLING

110 meters: 12.92, Roger Kingdom, Zürich, Switzerland, 16 August 1989

400 meters: 47.02, Edwin Moses, Koblenz, West Germany, 31 August 1983

3,000 meter steeplechase: 8:09.17, Henry Marsh, Koblenz, West Germany, 28 August 1985

RELAYS

4 x 100 meters: 37.83, National Team (Sam Graddy, Ron Brown, Calvin Smith, Carl Lewis), Los Angeles, CA, 11 August 1984

4 x 400 meters: 2:56.16,[A] National Team (Vince Matthews, Ron Freeman, Larry James, Lee Evans) Mexico City, Mexico, 20 October 1968
2:56.16, National Team (Danny Everett, Steve Lewis, Kevin Robinzine, Butch Reynolds), Seoul, South Korea, 1 October 1988

[A] Set at high altitude

FIELD EVENTS

High jump: 7' 10", Hollis Conway, Norman, OK, 30 July 1989

Pole vault: 19' 6½", Joe Dial, Norman, OK, 18 June 1987

Long jump: 29' 2½",[A] Bob Beamon, Mexico City, Mexico, 18 October 1968

Triple Jump: 58' 11½", Willie Banks, Indianapolis, IN, 16 June 1985

Shot: 75' 10¼", Randy Barnes, Westwood, LA, 20 May 1990

Discus: 237' 4",* Ben Plunknett, Stockholm, Sweden, 7 July 1981

Hammer: 268' 8", Judson Logan, University Park, PA, 22 April 1988

Javelin: 280' 1",[†] Thomas Petranoff, Helsinki, Finland, 7 July 1986

[A] Set at high altitude; the low altitude best: 28 ft 10 1/4 in, Carl Lewis at Indianapolis, IN on 19 June 1983.
* Ratified despite the fact that it was achieved after testing positive for drugs
[†] Petranoff has also thrown 283 ft 8 in at Port Elizabeth, South Africa on 5 March 1990.

US NATIONAL RECORDS (Continued)

MEN (Continued)
DECATHLON

8,634 points: Bruce Jenner (1st day: 100 m 10.94 sec, Long jump 23 ft 8¼ in, Shot put 50 ft 4 ½ in, High jump 6 ft 8 in, 400 m 47.51 sec), (2nd day: 110m hurdles 14.84 sec, Discus 164 ft 2 in, Pole vault 15 ft 9 in, Javelin 224 ft 10 in, 1,500 m 4:12.61 sec), Montreal, Canada, 29–30 July 1976

WOMEN
RUNNING

100 meters: 10.49, Florence Griffith Joyner, Indianapolis, IN, 16 July 1988

200 meters: 21.34, Florence Griffith Joyner, Seoul, South Korea, 29 September 1988

400 meters: 48.83, Valerie Brisco, Los Angeles, CA, 6 August 1984

800 meters: 1:56.90, Mary Slaney (née Decker), Berne, Switzerland, 16 August 1985

1,500 meters: 3:57.12, Mary Slaney, Stockholm, Sweden, 26 July 1983

1 mile: 4:16.71, Mary Slaney, Zürich, Switzerland, 21 August 1985

3,000 meters: 8:25.83, Mary Slaney, Rome, Italy, 7 September 1985

5,000 meters: 15:00.00, Patti-Sue Plumer, Stockholm, Sweden, 3 July 1989

10,000 meters: 31:35.3, Mary Slaney, Eugene, OR, 16 July 1982

HURDLING

100 meters: 12.61, Yolanda Devers (now Roberts), Los Angeles, CA, 21 May 1988
12.61, Jacqueline Joyner Kersee, San Jose, CA, 28 May 1988

400 meters: 53.37, Sandra Marie Farmer-Patrick, New York, NY, 22 July 1989

RELAYS

4 x 100 meters: 41.55, National Team (Alice Regina Brown, Diane Williams, Florence Griffith, Pam Marshall), Berlin, West Germany, 21 August 1987

4 x 400 meters: 3:15.51, National Team (Denean Howard, Diane Lynn Dixon, Valerie Brisco, Florence Griffith Joyner), Seoul, South Korea, 1 October 1988

FIELD EVENTS

High jump: 6′ 8", Louise Ritter, Austin, TX, 8 July 1988
6′ 8", Louise Ritter, Seoul, South Korea, 30 September 1988

Long jump: 24′ 5½", Jacqueline Joyner-Kersee, Indianapolis, IN, 13 August 1987

Triple jump: 46′ 0¾", Sheila Hudson, Durham, NC, 2 June 1990

Shot: 66′ 2½", Ramona Lu Pagel (née Ebert), San Diego, CA, 25 June 1988

Discus: 216′ 10", Carol Therese Cady, San Jose, CA, 31 May 1986

Javelin: 227′ 5", Kate Schmidt, Fürth, West Germany, 11 September 1977

HEPTATHLON

7,291 points: Jacqueline Joyner-Kersee (100 m hurdles 12.69 sec, High jump 6 ft 1¼ in; Shot 51 ft 10 in; 200 m 22.56 sec; Long jump 23 ft 10 in; Javelin 149 ft 9 in; 800 m 2 min 08.51 sec), Seoul, South Korea, 23–24 September 1988

TOP FLOP ■ 1988 OLYMPIC HIGH JUMP CHAMPION LOUISE RITTER ALSO HOLDS THE US RECORD FOR THE EVENT. TWICE SHE HAS JUMPED 6 FT 8 IN, 8 JULY 1988 AND 30 SEPTEMBER 1988.

relay 4 x 400 m relay), one silver (100 m) in 1983; Silke Gladisch (East Germany), three gold (4 x 100 m relay in 1983; 100 m, 200 m in 1987); one silver (4 x 100 m relay in 1987).

Most US national titles The most American national titles won at all events, indoors and out, is 65, by Ronald Owen Laird at various walks events between 1958 and 1976. Excluding the walks, the record is 41, by Stella Walsh (née Walasiewicz), who won women's events between 1930 and 1954: 33 outdoors and eight indoors.

Longest winning sequence Iolanda Balas (Romania) won a record 140 consecutive competitions at high jump from 1956 to 1967. The record at a track event was 122, at 400 meters hurdles, by Edwin Moses (US) between his loss to Harald Schmid (West Germany) at Berlin, West Germany on 26 August 1977 and that to Danny Harris (US) at Madrid, Spain on 4 June 1987.

MARATHON

The marathon is run over a distance of 26 miles 385 yd. This distance was that used for the race at the 1908 Olympic Games, run from Windsor to the White City stadium, London, England and that became standard from 1924. The marathon was introduced to the 1896 Olympic Games to commemorate the legendary run of Pheidippides (or Philippides) from the battlefield of Marathon to Athens in 490 B.C. The 1896 Olympic marathon was preceded by trial races that year. The first Boston Marathon, the world's longest-lasting major marathon, was held on 19 April 1897 at 24 miles 1,232 yd, and the first national marathon championship was that of Norway in 1897.

The first championship marathon for women was organized by the Road Runners Club of America on 27 September 1970.

Fastest There are as yet no official records for the marathon, and it should be noted that courses may vary in severity. The following are the best times recorded, all on courses with verified distances: (men) 2 hr 6 min 50 sec, by Belayneh Dinsamo (Ethiopia) at Rotterdam, Netherlands on 17 April 1988, and (women) 2 hr 21 min 6 sec by Ingrid Kristiansen (née Christensen, [Norway]) at London, England on 21 April 1985.

OLYMPIC GAMES The marathon has been run at every Olympic Games of the modern era, however a women's race wasn't included in the Games until 1984. The record for most wins in the men's race is two by two marathoners: Abebe Bikila (Ethiopia, 1960 and 1964); Waldemar Cierpinski (East Germany, 1976 and 1980). The women's event has been run twice, with different winners. The Olympic record for the marathon is 2 hr 9 min 21 sec by Carlos Lopes (Portugal) in 1984. The women's record is 2 hr 24 min 52 sec by Joan Benoit (US) in 1984.

BOSTON MARATHON First run by 15 men on 19 April 1897 over a distance of 24 miles 1,232 yd, the Boston Marathon is the world's oldest annual race. The full marathon distance was first run in 1927. It is run every year from Hopkinton, MA to Boston, MA on or about the 19th April, Patriot's Day, which honors the famed ride of Paul Revere.

The most wins is seven, by Clarence DeMar in 1911, 1922–24, 1927–28 and 1930.

Kathy Switzer (US) contested the race in 1967, although the race director tried to prevent her, but pioneering efforts helped force the acceptance of women runners, and they were admitted officially for the first time in 1972. Rosa Mota (Portugal) has a record three wins, 1987–88 and 1990, in the women's race.

The course record for men is 2 hr 8 min 19 sec, by Gelindo Bordin (Italy), and for women is 2 hr 22 min 43 sec, by Joan Benoit (now Samuelson) in 1983.

NEW YORK CITY MARATHON The race was run in Central Park each year from 1970 to 1976, when, to celebrate the US Bicentennial, the course was changed to a route through all five boroughs of the city. From that year, when there were 2,090 runners, the race has become one of the world's great sporting occasions; in 1989 there were a record 24,588 finishers.

Bill Rodgers had a record four wins—1976–79, and Grete Waitz (née Anderson [Norway]) was the women's winner nine times—1978–80, 1982–86 and 1988.

The course record for men is 2 hr 8 min 1 sec, by Juma Ikangaa (Tanzania), and for women is 2 hr 25 min 30 sec, by Ingrid Kristiansen (Norway) in 1989. On a course subsequently remeasured as about 170 yd short, Grete Waitz was the 1981 women's winner in 2 hr 25 min 29 sec.

Most run by an individual Sy Mah (US) ran 524 marathons of 26 miles385 yd or longer from 1966 to his death in 1988.

Highest altitude The highest start to a marathon is the biennially held Everest Marathon, first run on 27 November 1987. It begins at Gorak Shep, 17,100 ft and descends to Namche Bazar at 11,300 ft. The fastest time to complete this race is 3 hr 59 min 4 sec, by Jack Maitland in 1989.

Oldest finishers The oldest man to complete a marathon was Dimitrion Yordanidis (Greece), aged 98, in Athens, Greece on 10 October 1976. He finished in 7 hr 33 min. Thelma Pitt-Turner (New Zealand) set the women's record in August 1985, completing the Hastings, New Zealand Marathon in 7 hr 58 min at the age of 82.

Longest running race The longest races ever staged were the 1928 (3,422 miles) and 1929 (3,665 miles) transcontinental races from New York City to Los Angeles, CA. Johnny Salo (US) was the winner in 1929 in 79 days, from 31 March to 18 June. His elapsed time of 525 hr 57 min 20 sec (averaging 6.97 mph) left him only 2 min 47 sec ahead of Englishman Peter Gavuzzi.

The longest race staged annually is Australia's Westfield Run from Paramatta, New South Wales to Doncaster, Victoria (Sydney to Melbourne). The distance run has varied slightly, but the record is by Yiannis Kouros (Greece) in 5 days 2 hr 27 min 27 sec in 1989, when the distance was 658 miles.

Longest runs The longest run by an individual is one of 11,134 miles around the US, by Sarah Covington-Fulcher (US), starting and finishing in Los Angeles, CA, between 21 July 1987 and 2 October 1988. Robert J. Sweetgall (US) ran 10,608 miles around the perimeter of the US, starting and finishing in Washington D.C., between October 1982 and 15 July 1983. Ron Grant (Australia) ran around Australia, 8,316 miles in 217 days 3 hr 45 min, 28 March–31 October 1983. Max Telford (New Zealand) ran 5,110 miles from Anchorage, AK to Halifax, Nova Scotia, in 106 days 18 hr 45 min from 25 July to 9 November 1977.

The fastest time for the cross-America run is 46 days 8 hr 36 min, by Frank Giannino Jr. (US) for the 3,100 miles from San Francisco to New York from 1 September–17 October 1980. The women's trans-America record is 69 days 2 hr 40 min, by Mavis Hutchinson (South Africa) from 12 March–21 May 1978.

Backwards running Scott Weiland (US) ran the Detroit marathon backwards in 4 hr 7 min 54 sec on 13 October 1982. Donald Davis (US) ran 1 mile backwards in 6 min 7.1 sec at the University of Hawaii on 21 February 1983. Ferdie Ato Adoboe (Ghana) ran 100 yd backwards in 12.8 sec

(100 m in 14.0 sec) at Amherst, MA on 28 July 1983.

Arvind Pandya (India) ran backwards across America, Los Angeles to New York, in 107 days, 18 August–3 December 1984.

WALKING

OLYMPIC GAMES Walking races have been included in the Olympic events since 1906. The only walker to win three gold medals has been Ugo Frigerio (Italy), with the 3,000 m in 1920, and 10,000 m in 1920 and 1924. He also holds the record of most medals, with four (he won the bronze medal at 50,000 m in 1932), a total shared with Vladimir Golubnichiy (USSR), who won gold medals for the 20,000 m in 1960 and 1968, the silver in 1972 and the bronze in 1964.

24 hours The greatest distance walked in 24 hr is 140 miles 1,229 yd, by Paul Forthomme (Belgium) on a road course at Woluwé, Belgium on 13–14 October 1984. The best by a woman is 125.7 miles by Annie van der Meer at Rouen, France on 30 April–1 May 1984 over a 1.185–km lap road course.

Backwards walking The greatest ever exponent of reverse pedestrianism has been Plennie L. Wingo of Abilene, TX, who completed his 8,000 miles trans-continental walk from Santa Monica, CA to Istanbul, Turkey from 15 April 1931 to 24 October 1932. The longest distance recorded for walking backwards in 24 hr is 84.0 miles by Anthony Thornton (US) in Minneapolis, MN on 31 December 1985–1 January 1986.

TRAMPOLINING

ORIGINS Trampolining has been part of circus acts for many years. The sport of trampolining dates from 1936, when the prototype "T" model trampoline was designed by George Nissen of the US. The first official tournament took place in 1947.

WORLD CHAMPIONSHIPS

Instituted in 1964, they have been staged biennially since 1968. The World Championships recognize champions, both men and women, in four events: Individual, Synchronized Pairs, Tumbling, Double Mini Trampoline.

MOST TITLES			
MEN			
Event	Titles	Champion	Year
Individual	2	Wayne Miller (US)	1966, 1970
		Dave Jacobs (US)	1967–68
		Richard Tisson (France)	1974, 1976
		Yevgeniy Yanes (USSR)	1976, 1978
		Lionel Pioline (France)	1984, 1986

TRACK WALKING

WORLD RECORDS

The International Amateur Athletic Federation recognizes men's records at 20 km, 30 km, 50 km and 2 hours, and women's at 5 km and 10 km.

MEN

20 km: 1:18:40.0, Ernesto Canto (Mexico), Fana, Norway, 5 May 1984

30 km: 2:07:59.8, Jose Marin (Spain), Barcelona, Spain, 8 April 1979

50 km: 3:41:38.4, Raul Gonzalez (Mexico), Fana, Norway, 25 May 1979

2 hours: 28,165 m, Jose Marin (Spain), Barcelona, Spain, 8 April 1979

WOMEN

5 km: 20:17.19, Kerry Ann Saxby (Australia), Sydney, Australia, 14 January 1990

10 km: 41:56.21, Nadezhda Ryashkina (USSR), Seattle, WA, 24 July 1990

Event	Titles	Champion	Year
MEN(Continued)			
Synchronized Pairs	3	Igor Bogachev & Vadim Krasnochapka (USSR)	1984, 1986, 1988
Tumbling	2	Jim Bertz (US)	1976, 1978
		Steve Elliott (US)	1982, 1984
Double Mini Trampoline	3	Brett Austine (Australia)	1982, 1984, 1986
WOMEN			
Individual	5	Judy Wills (US)	1964–68
Synchronized Pairs	2	Judy Wills & Nancy Smith (US)	1966–67
Tumbling	3	Jill Hollembeak (US)	1982, 1984, 1986
Double Mini Trampoline	2	Leigh Hennessy (US)	1976, 1978

TRIATHLON

ORIGINS The triathlon combines long distance swimming, cycling and running. The sport was developed by a group of dedicated athletes who founded the Hawaii "Ironman" in 1974. After a series of unsuccessful attempts to create a world governing body, L'Union Internationale de Triathlon (UIT) was founded in Avignon, France in 1989. The UIT staged the first official World Championships in Avignon on 6 August 1989.

WORLD CHAMPIONSHIPS

An unofficial World Championship has been held in Nice, France from 1982. The three legs comprised a 3,200 m swim (4,000 m from 1988), 120 km bike ride and 32 km run. Mark Allen (US) has won a record seven times, 1982–86, 1989–90. Allen also won the first official championship in Avignon, France in 1989. The women's champion was Erin Baker (New Zealand).

HAWAII IRONMAN

The first, and best known, of the triathlons. Instituted on 18 February 1978, the first race was contested by 15 athletes. The Ironman grew rapidly in popularity and 1,000 athletes entered the 1984 race. Contestants must first swim 2.4 miles, then cycle 112 miles and finally run a full marathon of 26 miles 385 yd. Dave Scott (US) has won the Ironman a record six times, 1980, 1982–84, 1986–

87. Mark Allen (US) holds the record for fastest time at 8 hr 9 min 16 sec in 1989. The women's event has been won a record three times by Paula Newby-Fraser (Zimbabwe) in 1986, 1988–89. Newby-Fraser holds the course record at 9 hr 56 sec.

Fastest Time The fastest time ever recorded over the Ironman distances is 8 hr 1 min 32 sec by Dave Scott (US) at Lake Biwas, Japan on 30 July 1989.

Largest Field The most competitors to finish a triathlon race has been the 3,888 who completed the 1987 Bud Lite US Triathlon in Chicago, IL.

VOLLEYBALL

ORIGINS The game was invented as *mintonette* in 1895 by William G. Morgan at the YMCA gymnasium at Holyoke, MA. The International Volleyball Association (IVA) was formed in Paris, France in April 1947.

WORLD CHAMPIONSHIPS World Championships were instituted in 1949 for men and 1952 for women. The USSR has won six men's titles (1949, 1952, 1960, 1962, 1978 and 1982) and four women's (1952, 1956, 1960 and 1970).

OLYMPIC GAMES The sport was introduced to the Olympic Games for both men and women in 1964. The USSR has won a record three men's (1964, 1968 and 1980) and four women's (1968, 1972, 1980 and 1988) titles. The only player to win four medals is Inna Ryskal (USSR), who won women's silver medals in 1964 and 1976 and golds in 1968 and 1972. The record for men is held by Yuriy Poyarkov (USSR) who won gold medals in 1964 and 1968 and a bronze in 1972, and by Katsutoshi Nekoda (Japan) who won gold in 1972, silver in 1968 and bronze in 1964.

The US won the men's title in 1984 and 1988. Three men played on each of those teams and on the only US teams to win the World Championships (1986): Craig Buck, Karch Kiraly and Stephen Timmons. Kiraly is the only player to win an Olympic gold medal and the World Championship of Beach Volleyball (1989).

WATER POLO

ORIGINS Originally played in England as "water soccer" in 1869. The first rules were drafted in 1876. Water polo has been an Olympic event since 1900. In 1908, FINA (see swimming) became the governing body for water polo. The first World Championships were held in 1973.

OLYMPIC GAMES Hungary has won the Olympic tournament most often, with six wins, in 1932, 1936, 1952, 1956, 1964 and 1976. Five players share the record of three gold medals: Britons George Wilkinson, in 1900, 1908, 1912; Paul Radmilovic, and Charles Smith, in 1908, 1912, 1920; and Hungarians Deszö Gyarmati and György Kárpáti, in 1952, 1956, 1964.

US teams took all the medals in 1904, but there were no foreign contestants. Since then their best result has been silver in 1984.

WORLD CHAMPIONSHIPS First held at the World Swimming Championships in 1973. The USSR is the only double winner, 1975 and 1982. A women's competition was introduced in 1986, when it was won by Australia.

Most goals The greatest number of goals scored by an individual in an international is 13, by Debbie Handley for Australia (16) *v.* Canada (10) at the World Championship in Guayaquil, Ecuador in 1982.

WATER SKIING

ORIGINS Modern water skiing was pioneered in the 1920s. Ralph Samuelson, who skied on Lake Pepin, MN in 1922 using two curved pine boards, is generally credited as being the "father" of the sport. Forms of skiing on water can be traced back centuries to people attempting to walk on water with planks and aquaplaning. The development of the motor boat to tow skiers was the largest factor in the sports growth. The world governing body is the World Water Ski Union (WWSU), which succeeded the Union Internationale de Ski Nautique that had been formed in Geneva, Switzerland in 1946. The first World Championships were held in 1949. The American Water Ski Association was founded in 1939 and held the first national championships that year.

WORLD CHAMPIONSHIPS World Overall Championships (instituted 1949) have been won four times by Sammy Duvall (US), in 1981, 1983, 1985 and 1987, and three times by two women, Willa McGuire (née Worthington) of the US, in 1949–50 and 1955 and Liz Allan-Shetter (US), in 1965, 1969 and 1975. Allan-Shetter has won a record eight individual championship events and is the only person to win all four titles—slalom, jumping, tricks and overall in one year, at Copenhagen, Denmark in 1969. The US has won the team championship on 17 successive occasions, 1957–89.

US NATIONAL CHAMPIONSHIPS US national championships were first held at Marine Stadium, Jones Beach State Park, Long Island, NY on 22 July

LET US SPRAY ■ SAMMY DUVALL, US, HAS WON THE WORLD OVERALL WATER SKIING TITLE A RECORD FOUR TIMES, 1981, 1983, 1985 AND 1987.

1939. The most overall titles is eight, by Willa Worthington McGuire, 1946–51 and 1954–55 and by Liz Allan-Shetter 1968–75. The men's record is six titles, by Chuck Stearns 1957–58, 1960, 1962, 1965 and 1967.

Fastest speed The fastest water skiing speed recorded is 143.08 mph by Christopher Massey (Australia) on the Hawkesbury River, Windsor, Australia on 6 March 1983. His drag boat driver was Stanley Sainty. Donna Patterson Brice set a women's record of 111.11 mph at Long Beach, CA on 21 August 1977.

Longest run The greatest distance traveled is 1,321.16 miles, by Steve Fontaine (US) on 24–26 October 1988 at Jupiter Hills, FL.

Most skiers towed by one boat A record 100 water skiers were towed on double skis over a nautical mile by the cruiser *Reef Cat* at Cairns, Queensland, Australia on 18 October 1986. This feat, organized by the Cairns and District Powerboat and Ski Club, was then replicated by 100 skiers on single skis.

Barefoot The first person to water ski barefoot is reported to be Dick Pope Jr. at Lake Eloise, FL on 6 March 1947. The barefoot duration record is 2 hr 42 min 39 sec, by Billy Nichols (US) on Lake Weir, FL on 19 November 1978. The backward barefoot record is 39 min, by Paul McManus (Australia).

The official barefoot speed record is 119.36 mph, by Scott Pellaton (US) over a quarter-mile course at Chowchilla, CA on 4 September 1983. The fastest by a woman is 73.67 mph, by Karen Toms (Australia) on the Hawkesbury River, Windsor, Australia on 31 March 1984.

The fastest official speed backwards barefoot is 62 mph, by Robert Wing (Australia) on 3 April 1982.

The barefoot jump record is: (men) 72 ft 6 in, by Brett Sands (Australia) at Cohuna, Australia on 29 February 1989 and (women) 47 ft 6¾ in, by Debbie Pugh (Australia) at Hellas Park, Australia on 5 February 1989.

WEIGHTLIFTING

ORIGINS Competitions for lifting weights of stone were held in the ancient Olympic Games. The first championships entitled "world" were staged in London, England on 28 March 1891 and then in Vienna, Austria on 19–20 July 1898, subsequently recognized by the International Weightlifting Federation (IWF). Prior to that time, weightlifting consisted of professional exhibitions in which some of the advertised poundages were open to doubt.

The Fédération Internationalé Haltérophile et Culturiste, now the International Weightlifting Federation (IWF), was established in 1905, and its first official championships were held in Tallinn, Estonia on 29–30 April 1922.

There are two standard lifts: the "snatch" and the "clean and jerk". Totals of the two lifts determine competition results. The "press," which had been a standard lift, was abolished in 1972.

OLYMPIC GAMES Norbert Schemansky (US) won a record four Olympic medals: gold, middle heavyweight 1952; silver, heavyweight 1948; bronze, heavyweight 1960 and 1964.

Three US lifters won two gold medals: John Davis Jr., heavyweight 1948 and 1952; Tommy Kono, lightweight 1952, light heavyweight 1956; Chuck Vinci Jr., bantamweight 1956 and 1960.

WORLD CHAMPIONSHIPS The IWF held its first World Championships at Tallinn, Estonia in 1922, but has subsequently recognized 18 championships held in Vienna, Austria between 1898 and 1920. The championships have been held annually since 1946, with the Olympic Games recognized as World Championships in the year of the Games until 1988, when a championship separate from the Olympics was staged. From 1928 to 1972, the results were decided on the aggregate of press, snatch and jerk; from 1973, just on snatch and jerk.

MOST TITLES The record for most titles is eight held by three lifters: John Davis (US), 1938, 1946–52; Tommy Kono (US), 1952–59; Vasiliy Alekseyev (USSR), 1970–77.

US NATIONAL CHAMPIONSHIPS The most titles won is 13 by Anthony Terlazzo at 137 lb, 1932 and 1936 and at 148 lb, 1933, 1935, 1937–45.

Heaviest lift to body weight The first man to clean and jerk more than three times his body weight was Stefan Topurov (Bulgaria), who lifted 396¾ lb at Moscow, USSR on 24 October 1983. The first man to snatch two-and-a-half times his own body weight was Naim Suleymanoglü (Turkey), who lifted 330½ lb at Cardiff, Wales on 27 April 1988. The first woman to clean and jerk more than two times her own body weight was Cheng Jinling (China), who lifted 198 lb in the class of the World Championships at Jakarta, Indonesia in December 1988.

WORLD WEIGHTLIFTING RECORDS

FLYWEIGHT
52 kg 114½lb

Snatch: 264½ Sevdalin Marinov (Bulgaria), 18 September 1988

Jerk: 341¾ Ivan Ivanov (Bulgaria), 16 September 1989

Total: 600¾ Ivan Ivanov (Bulgaria), 16 September 1989

BANTAMWEIGHT
56 kg 123¼lb

Snatch: 296½ Liu Shoubin (China), 1 March 1989

Jerk: 377 Neno Terziiski (Bulgaria), 6 September 1987

Total: 661¼ Naim Suleimanov (Bulgaria),* 11 May 1984

FEATHERWEIGHT
60 kg 132¼lb

Snatch: 336 Naim Suleymanoglü (Turkey),* 20 September 1988

Jerk: 418¾ Naim Suleymanoglü (Turkey),* 20 September 1988

Total: 755 Naim Suleymanoglü (Turkey),* 20 September 1988

* Formerly Naim Suleimanov or Neum Shalamanov of Bulgaria

AARGH!!! ■ NAIM SULEYMANOGLÜ, TURKEY, HOLDS WEIGHTLIFTING WORLD RECORDS IN THE BANTAMWEIGHT AND FEATHERWEIGHT CLASSES.

WORLD WEIGHTLIFTING RECORDS (Continued)

LIGHTWEIGHT
67.5 kg 148¾lb

Snatch: 352¾ Israil Militosyan (USSR), 18 September 1989

Jerk: 442 Mikhail Petrov (Bulgaria), 8 September 1987

Total: 782½ Mikhail Petrov (Bulgaria), 5 December 1987

MIDDLEWEIGHT
75 kg 165¼ lb

Snatch: 374¾ Angel Guenchev (Bulgaria), 11 December 1987

Jerk: 475 Aleksandr Varbanov (Bulgaria), 5 December 1987

Total: 843¼ Aleksandr Varbanov (Bulgaria), 20 February 1988

LIGHT-HEAVYWEIGHT
82.5 kg 181¾lb

Snatch: 403¼ Asen Zlatev (Bulgaria), 7 December 1986

Jerk: 496 Asen Zlatev (Bulgaria), 12 November 1986

Total: 892¾ Yurik Vardanyan (USSR), 14 September 1984

MIDDLE-HEAVYWEIGHT
90 kg 198¼lb

Snatch: 431 Blagoi Blagoyev (Bulgaria), 1 May 1983

Jerk: 518 Anatoliy Khrapatliy (USSR), 29 April 1988

Total: 931¼ Viktor Solodov (USSR), 15 September 1984

100 kg 220¼lb

Snatch: 442 Nicu Vlad (Romania), 14 November 1986

Jerk: 534½ Aleksandr Popov (USSR), 5 March 1988

Total: 970 Yuriy Zakharevich (USSR), 4 March 1983

HEAVYWEIGHT
110 kg 242½lb

Snatch: 462¾ Yuiry Zakharevich (USSR), 27 September 1988

Jerk: 552¼ Yuriy Zakharevich (USSR), 30 April 1988

Total: 1,003 Yuriy Zakharevich (USSR), 27 September 1988

SUPER-HEAVYWEIGHT
Over 110 kg 242½ lb

Snatch: 476 Antonio Krastev (Bulgaria), 13 September 1987

Jerk: 586¼ Leonid Taranenko (USSR), 26 November 1988

Total: 1,047 Leonid Taranenko (USSR), 26 November 1988

Women's World Championships These are held annually—the first at Daytona Beach, FL in October 1987. Women's world records have been ratified for the best marks at these championships. The heaviest lift for any of the nine weight categories has been the 303 lb jerk by Han Changmei (China) for over 82.5 kg at Manchester, England in November of 1989.

WRESTLING

ORIGINS Wrestling was the most popular sport in the ancient Olympic Games; wall drawings dating to *circa*. 2600 B.C. show that the sport was active long before the Greeks. Wrestling was included in the first modern Games. The International Amateur Wrestling Association (FILA) was founded in 1912. There are two forms of wrestling at international level, Freestyle and Greco-Roman—the use of the legs and holds below the waist are prohibited in Greco-Roman.

OLYMPIC GAMES Three Olympic titles have been won by: Carl Westergren (Sweden) in 1920, 1924 and 1932; Ivar Johansson (Sweden) in 1932 (two) and 1936; and Aleksandr Medved (USSR) in 1964, 1968 and 1972.

The one US wrestler to win two Olympic freestyle titles was George Mehnert, flyweight in 1904 and bantamweight in 1908. The first, and only, US men to win Greco-Roman titles were Steven Fraser at light heavyweight and Jeffrey Blatnick at super-heavyweight in 1984.

WORLD CHAMPIONSHIPS The freestyler Aleksandr Medved (USSR) won a record 10 World Championships, 1962–64, 1966–72 at three weight categories. The only wrestler to win the same title in seven successive years has been Valeriy Rezantsev (USSR) in the Greco-Roman 90 kg class in 1970–76, including the Olympic Games of 1972 and 1976.

The most world titles won by a US wrestler is three, by Leroy Kemp, welterweight, 1978–79, 1982.

NCAA DIVISION I CHAMPIONSHIP Oklahoma State University was the first unofficial national champion in 1928. Including five unofficial titles, Oklahoma State has won a record 29 NCAA titles, in 1928–31, 1933–35, 1937–42, 1946, 1948–49, 1954–56, 1958–59, 1961–62, 1964, 1966, 1968, 1971, 1989–90. The University of Iowa has won the most consecutive titles with nine championships from 1978–86.

Longest bout The longest recorded bout was one of 11 hr 40 min, when Martin Klein (Estonia representing Russia) beat Alfred Asikáinen (Finland) for the Greco-Roman 75 kg "A" event silver medal in the 1912 Olympic Games in Stockholm, Sweden.

Heaviest heavyweight The heaviest wrestler in Olympic history is Chris Taylor, bronze medalist in the super-heavyweight class in 1972, who stood 6 ft 5 in tall and weighed over 420 lb. FILA introduced an upper weight limit of 286 lb for international competition in 1985.

SUMO WRESTLING

The sport's origins in Japan dates from *circa*. 23 B.C. The heaviest ever *rikishi* is Samoan-American Salevaa Fuali Atisnoe of Hawaii, known as Konishiki, who in 1988 had a peak weight of 556 lb. He is also the first foreign *rikishi* to attain the second highest rank of *ozeki*, or champion.

The most successful wrestlers have been *yokozuna* Sadaji Akiyoshi known as Futabayama, winner of 69 consecutive bouts in the 1930s; *yokozuna* Koki Naya, known as Taiho ("Great Bird"), who won the Emperor's Cup 32 times up to his retirement in 1971; and the *ozeki* Tameemon Torokichi, known as Raiden, who in 21 years (1789–1810) won 254 bouts and lost only 10 for the highest ever winning percentage of 96.2. Taiho and Futabayama share the record of eight perfect tournaments without a single loss. The youngest of the 62 men to attain the rank of *yokozuna* (grand champion) was Toshimitsu Ogata, known as Kitanoumi, in July 1974 at age 21 yr and 2 months. He set a record in 1978, winning 82 of the 90 bouts that top *rikishi* fight annually, and had a record 804 wins in the top *Makunouchi* division.

Yokozuna Mitsugu Akimoto, known as Chiyonofuji, set a record for domination of one of the six annual tournaments by winning the Kyushu Basho for eight successive years, 1981–88. Hawaiian-born Jesse Kuhaulua, now a Japanese citizen named Daigoro Watanabe, known as Takamiyama, was the first non-Japanese to win an official top-division tournament, in July 1972.

Yukio Shoji, known as Aobajo, did not miss a single bout in his 22-year career, 1964–86, and contested a record 1,631 consecutive bouts. Kenji Hatano, known as Oshio, contested a record 1,891 nonconsecutive bouts in his 26-year career, 1962–88, the longest in modern sumo history. He holds the record for the most career wins with 1,017.

YACHTING

ORIGINS Sailing as a sport dates from the 17th century. Originating in the Netherlands, it was introduced to England by Charles II, who participated in a 23 mile race along the River Thames in 1661. The oldest yacht club in the world is the Royal Cork Yacht Club, which claims descent from the Cork Harbor Water Club, founded in Ireland in 1720. The oldest continuously existing yacht club in the US is the New York Yacht Club, founded in 1844.

AMERICA'S CUP The America's Cup was originally won as an outright prize by the schooner *America* on 22 August 1851 at Cowes, England and was later offered by the New York Yacht Club as a challenge trophy. On 8 August 1870 J. Ashbury's *Cambria* (UK) failed to capture the trophy from *Magic*, owned by F. Osgood (US). The Cup has been challenged 27 times, the US was undefeated, winning 77 races and only losing eight until 1983, when *Australia II*, skippered by John Bertrand and owned by a Perth syndicate headed by Alan Bond, beat *Liberty* 4–3, the narrowest series victory, at Newport, RI.

The most times a single helmsman has steered a cup defender is in three separate series. This was achieved by Charlie Barr (US), who defended in 1899, 1901 and 1903, and by Harold S. Vanderbilt (US) in 1930, 1934 and 1937. Dennis Conner (US) has been helmsman of American boats four times in succession: in 1980, when he successfully defended; in 1983, when he steered the defender, but lost; in 1987, when the American challenger regained the trophy, and in 1988, when he again successfully defended.

The largest yacht to have competed in the America's Cup was the 1903 defender, the gaff rigged cutter *Reliance*, with an overall length of 144 ft, a record sail area of 16,160 ft² and a rig of 175 ft high.

AMERICA'S CUP WINNERS

Year	Cup Winner	Skipper	Challenger	Series
1851	America	Richard Brown	—	—
1870	Magic	Andrew Comstock	Cambria (England)	—
1871	Columbia	Nelson Comstock	Livonia (England)	4–1
1876	Madeleine	Josephus Williams	Countess of Dufferin (Canada)	2–0

AMERICA'S CUP WINNERS (Continued)

Year	Cup Winner	Skipper	Challenger	Series
1881	Mischief	Nathaniel Cook	Atalanta (Canada)	2–0
1885	Puritan	Aubrey Crocker	Genesta (England)	2–0
1886	Mayflower	Martin Stone	Galatea (England)	2–0
1887	Volunteer	Henry Haff	Thistle (Scotland)	2–0
1893	Vigilant	William Hansen	Valkyrie II (England)	3–0
1895	Defender	Henry Haff	Valkyrie III (England)	3–0
1899	Columbia	Charlie Barr	Shamrock (England)	3–0
1901	Columbia	Charlie Barr	Shamrock II (England)	3–0
1903	Reliance	Charlie Barr	Shamrock III (England)	3–0

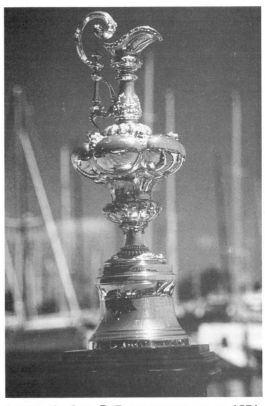

AMERICA'S CUP ■ FIRST PRESENTED IN 1851, THE AMERICA'S CUP TROPHY (ABOVE) IS THE OLDEST IN INTERNATIONAL SPORTS.

CUP'S AWAY! ■ IN SEPTEMBER 1983, AUSTRALIA II BEAT LIBERTY (PORT), SNAPPING THE LONGEST WINNING STREAK IN SPORTS HISTORY, 132 YEARS. IN 1987 STARS & STRIPES (STARBOARD), CAPTAINED BY DENNIS CONNER, REGAINED THE CUP FOR THE US.

AMERICA'S CUP WINNERS (Continued)

Year	Cup Winner	Skipper	Challenger	Series
1920	Resolute	Charles Adams	Shamrock IV (England)	3–2
1930	Enterprise	Harold Vanderbilt	Shamrock V (England)	4–0
1934	Rainbow	Harold Vanderbilt	Endeavour (England)	4–2
1937	Ranger	Harold Vanderbilt	Endeavour II (England)	4–0
1958	Columbia	Briggs Cunningham	Sceptre (England)	4–0
1962	Weatherly	Emil Mosbacher Jr.	Gretel (Australia)	4–1
1964	Constellation	Bob Bavier Jr.	Sovereign (England)	4–0
1967	Intrepid	Emil Mosbacher Jr.	Dame Pattie (Australia)	4–0
1970	Intrepid	Bill Fricker	Gretel II (Australia)	4–1

AMERICA'S CUP WINNERS (Continued)

Year	Cup Winner	Skipper	Challenger	Series
1974	Courageous	Ted Hood	Southern Cross (Australia)	4–0
1977	Courageous	Ted Turner	Australia (Australia)	4–0
1980	Freedom	Dennis Conner	Australia (Australia)	4–1
1983	Australia II	John Bertrand	Liberty (US)	4–3
1987	Stars & Stripes	Dennis Conner	Kookaburra III (Australia)	4–0
1988	Stars & Stripes	Dennis Conner	New Zealand (New Zealand)	2–0

OLYMPIC GAMES Bad weather caused the abandonment of yachting events at the first modern Games in 1896. However, the weather has stayed "fair" ever since, and yachting has been part of every Games program.

Most Gold Medals Paul B. Elvstrom (Denmark) has won a record four gold medals in yachting, and in the process became the first competitor in Olympics history to win individual gold medals in four successive Games. Elvstrom's titles came in the Firefly class in 1948, and the Finn class in 1952, 1956 and 1960.

Father and Son Hilary and Paul Smart (US) became the first, and so far only, father and son to combine to win a team event at the Olympic Games when they won the Star class at the 1948 Games.

United States The only US yachtsman to have won two gold medals is Herman Whiton, at 6 meter class, in 1948 and 1952.

Longest race The world's longest non-stop sailing race is the Vendée Globe Challenge, the first of which started from Les Sables d'Olonne, France on 26 November 1989. The distance circumnavigated without stopping was 22,500 nautical miles. The race is for boats between 50–60 ft, sailed single-handed. The record time on the course is 109 days 8 hr 48 min 50 sec, by Titouan Lamazou (France) in the sloop *Ecureuil d'Aquitaine*, which finished at Les Sables on 19 March 1990.

The oldest regular sailing race around the world is the quadrennial Whitbread Round the World race (instituted August 1973), organized by the Royal Naval Sailing Association (Great Britain). It starts in England, and the course around the world and the number of legs with stops at specified ports are varied race to race. The distance for 1989–90 was 32,000 nautical miles from Southampton, England and return, with stops and restarts at Punta Del Este, Uruguay; Fremantle,

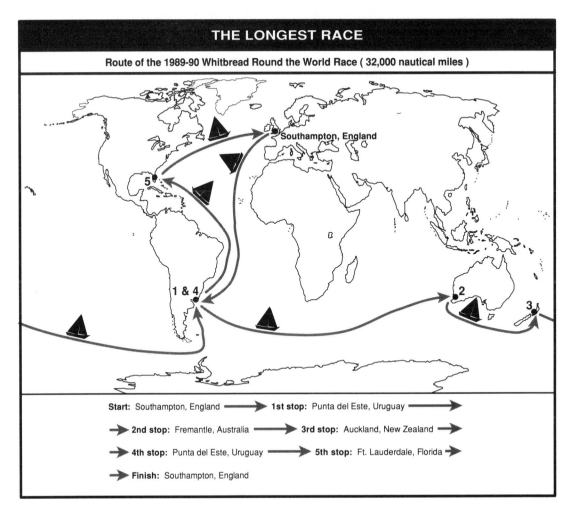

THE LONGEST RACE

Route of the 1989-90 Whitbread Round the World Race (32,000 nautical miles)

Southampton, England
5
1 & 4
2
3

Start: Southampton, England ⟶ **1st stop:** Punta del Este, Uruguay ⟶

⟶ **2nd stop:** Fremantle, Australia ⟶ **3rd stop:** Auckland, New Zealand ⟶

⟶ **4th stop:** Punta del Este, Uruguay ⟶ **5th stop:** Ft. Lauderdale, Florida ⟶

⟶ **Finish:** Southampton, England

Australia; Auckland, New Zealand; Punta del Este, Uruguay, and Fort Lauderdale, FL.

Fastest speed The fastest speed reached under sail on water by any craft over a 500 m timed run is by a boardsailer Pascal Maka (France) at 42.91 knots at Saintes Maries de-la-Mer canal, Camargue, France on 27 February 1990. The women's record was set at the same venue by Brigitte Gimenez (France) who achieved 39.13 knots on 28 October 1989.

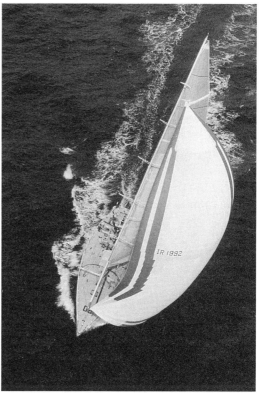

CIRCUMNAVIGATION ■ THE QUADRENNIAL WHITBREAD ROUND THE WORLD RACE IS THE OLDEST AROUND-THE-WORLD SAILING EVENT. LIVERPOOL ENTERPRISE (PORT) AND NBC IRELAND (STARBORAD) WERE TWO OF THE COMPETITORS IN THE 1989–90 RACE, WHICH COVERED A DISTANCE OF 32,000 NAUTICAL MILES.

OVERTIME

The following records were set too late to be included in the main section of the book.

BASKETBALL

NATIONAL BASKETBALL ASSOCIATION (NBA)

Highest Scoring Game On 11 November 1990, the Phoenix Suns defeated the Denver Nuggets, 173-143, in Phoenix, AZ. During the game several NBA records were either set or matched. The Suns' 107 points during the first half broke the NBA record, which ironically had been posted by the Nuggets the previous week, 8 November 1990, in a game v. San Antonio Spurs. The Suns also set marks for most field goals—43—and most assists—33—in a half. In the second quarter, Phoenix scored 57 points, surpassing the Baltimore Bullets' record of 52. Phoenix's total 173 points tied the mark for a nonovertime game set by the Boston Celtics in 1959.

Most Assists Scott Skiles, Orlando Magic, set an NBA single-game record of 30 assists on 30 December 1990. Skiles broke Kevin Porter's 12-year record when Jerry Reynolds converted a 20-foot shot with 19.6 sec left on the clock.

NCAA

Most Points On 6 January 1991 Loyola Marymount defeated United States International University 186-140, breaking its own NCAA record for most points in a game. Also, Kevin Bradshaw (US International), with 72 points, set the NCAA mark for most points scored versus a Division I opponent.

Most Blocked Shots Shawn Bradley, BYU, tied the mark for most blocked shots with 14 v. Eastern Kentucky on 7 December 1990.

Most 3-Pointers UNLV tied the NCAA mark for most 3-point field goals in a game, when the team hit 21 v. Nevada on 7 December 1990.

FOOTBALL

NATIONAL FOOTBALL LEAGUE (NFL)

Longest Field Goal (playoffs) Pete Stoyanovich, Miami Dolphins, booted a record-breaking 58-yd field goal during the Dolphins' 17-16 wild-card victory over the Kansas City Chiefs on 5 January 1991.

SUPER BOWL

Super Bowl XXV was played on 27 January 1991 at Tampa Stadium, Tampa, FL. The New York Giants defeated the Buffalo Bills, 20-19. The game, which was generally regarded as one of the few "great" Super Bowls, set only three records:

Narrowest Margin of Victory The Giants' one-point win was the narrowest victory margin in the history of the game, breaking the previous record of three points, set in Super Bowl V, when the Baltimore Colts edged the Dallas Cowboys 16-13.

Longest Touchdown Drive The Giants completed the longest elapsed time touchdown drive, but not the longest in yardage, in Super Bowl history, with a 75-yard 14-play drive that lasted 9 min 29 sec. The drive opened the third quarter and O.J. Anderson's one-yard touchdown plunge gave New York a 17-12 lead.

Longest Time of Possession The New York Giants had possession of the ball for 40 min 33 sec to set a Super Bowl record.

GOLF

Skins Game Jack Nicklaus won a record $285,000 skin in the Senior Skins Game at Mauna Lani Resort, Hawaii on 27 January 1991. Nicklaus's record skin was earned with a 40-foot eagle putt in a playoff with Gary Player. The skin was in fact the accumulated prize money of nine skins in the winner take-all format of this popular, non-PGA tour event. Nicklaus held the previous mark at $240,000, set in 1984.

HORSE RACING

Most Stakes Wins (Season) Craig Perret's 57 stakes victories in 1990 tied Jorge Velasquez's mark set in 1985.

ICE HOCKEY

NATIONAL HOCKEY LEAGUE (NHL)

Most Points On 27 October 1990, Wayne Gretzky, Los Angeles Kings, became the first NHL player to achieve 2,000 points. The historic point came on an assist to Tomas Sandstrom v. Winnipeg Jets in Winnipeg. At the NHL All-Star break, 18 January 1991, Gretzky had extended his career leading points total to 2,070 (705 goals, 1,365 assists). On 3 January 1991, Gretzky became the fourth player to score 700 goals. In that game v. New York Islanders, Gretzky scored three goals and thus extended his career hat-tricks record to 47. On 26 January 1991, his 30th birthday, Gretzky scored his 48th career hat-trick in a 5-4 Kings' victory over the Vancouver Canucks.

SWIMMING & DIVING

Youngest Champion Fu Mingxa (China) became the youngest world champion in the history of aquatic sports when she won the women's 10-m platform diving title in Perth, Australia on 5 January 1991. Fu was only 12 years old.

**SWIMMING
WORLD RECORDS**

The following world records were set at the World Swimming Championships in Perth, Australia.

1,500 m freestyle	14:50.36, Joerg Hoffman, Germany, 13 January 1991
100 m breaststroke	1:01.45, Norbert Rozsa, Hungary, 7 January 1991
200 m breaststroke	2:11.23, Mike Barrowman, USA, 11 January 1991
100 m butterfly	1:55.69, Melvin Stewart, USA, 12 January 1991
200 m individual medley	1:59.36, Tamas Darnyi, Hungary, 13 January 1991
400 m individual medley	4:12.36, Tamas Darnyi, Hungary, 8 January 1991

US RECORDS

MEN

200 m breaststroke	2:11.23, Mike Barrowman, 11 January 1991
100 m butterfly	1:55.69, Melvin Stewart, 12 January 1991
400 m individual medley	4:15.21, Eric Namesnick, 8 January 1991

WOMEN

50 m freestyle	25.50,* Leigh Ann Fetter, 8 January 1991
100 m freestyle	55.17, Nicole Haislett, 7 January 1991
4 x 100 m relay	3:46.26, United States (Nicole Haislett, Julie Cooper, Whitney Hedgepeth, Jenny Thompson), 11 January 1991

* Tied previous record

Most Medals At the conclusion of the 1991 World Championships, Michael Gross (Germany) had set a record for the most overall medals won in a career, with 13 medals (five gold, five silver, three bronze: 1982-91). Matt Biondi set an American career record with 11 medals (six gold, two silver, three bronze: 1986, 1991).

TENNIS

Largest Purse On 16 December 1990, Pete Sampras (US) won the inaugural Grand Slam Cup in Munich, Germany. Sampras's first-place prize money was $2 million, the largest in tennis history. The Grand Slam Cup matches the 16 players with the best records in the four grand slam events. In the final Sampras defeated Brad Gilbert (US) 6-3, 6-4, 6-2.

1991 AUSTRALIAN OPEN CHAMPIONSHIPS

Winners
Men, Boris Becker, Germany
Women, Monica Seles, Yugoslavia

Youngest Women's Champion At age 17 years 55 days, Monica Seles, Yugoslavia, became the youngest women's singles champion in Australian Open history.

THE 1990 SPORTS YEAR IN REVIEW

A selective listing of results and winners from the 1990 sports calendar.

ARCHERY

IFAA WORLD CHAMPIONSHIPS (AT VALLA PARK, AUSTRALIA)
Freestyle (Men) Terry Ragsdale (US)
Freestyle (Women) Michelle Ragsdale (US)
Freestyle Limited (Men) Tim Strickland (US)
Freestyle Limited (Women) Patti Curtiss (US)

AUTO RACING

CART PPG-INDY CAR SERIES

Series Champion Al Unser Jr.

RACE WINNERS
AUTOWORKS 200 Rick Mears
TOYOTA GRAND PRIX OF LONG BEACH Al Unser Jr.
INDIANAPOLIS 500 Arie Luyendyk (Netherlands)
MILLER GENUINE DRAFT 200 Al Unser Jr.
DETROIT GRAND PRIX Michael Andretti
BUDWEISER/G.I. JOE'S 200 Michael Andretti
CLEVELAND GRAND PRIX Danny Sullivan
MARLBORO GRAND PRIX Michael Andretti
MOLSON INDY TORONTO Al Unser Jr.
MARLBORO 500 Al Unser Jr.
GRAND PRIX OF DENVER Al Unser Jr.
MOLSON INDY VANCOUVER Al Unser Jr.
RED ROOF INNS 200 Michael Andretti

TEXACO/HAVOLINE 200 Michael Andretti
BOSCH SPARK PLUG GRAND PRIX Emerson Fittipaldi (Brazil)
CHAMPION SPARK PLUG 300 km Danny Sullivan

NASCAR, WINSTON CUP SERIES

WINSTON CUP CHAMPION Dale Earnhardt

RACE WINNERS
DAYTONA 500 Derrike Cope
PONTIAC EXCITEMENT 400 Mark Martin
GOODWRENCH 500 Kyle Petty
MOTOCRAFT QUALITY PARTS 500 Dale Earnhardt
TRANSOUTH 500 Dale Earnhardt
VALLEYDALE MEATS 500 Davey Allison
FIRST UNION 400 Brett Bodine
HANES ACTIVEWEAR 500 Geoff Bodine
WINSTON 500 Dale Earnhardt
COCA-COLA 600 Rusty Wallace
MILLER GENUINE DRAFT 500 Harry Grant
MILLER GENUINE DRAFT 400 Dale Earnhardt
PEPSI 400 Dale Earnhardt
AC SPARK PLUG 500 Geoff Bodine
DIEHARD 500 Dale Earnhardt
BUDWEISER AT THE GLEN Ricky Rudd
CHAMPION SARK PLUG 400 Mark Martin
BUSCH 500 Ernie Irvan
HEINZ SOUTHERN 500 Dale Earnhardt
MILLER GENUINE DRAFT 400 Dale Earnhardt

PEAK ANTI-FREEZE 500 Bill Elliot

GOODY'S 500 Geoff Bodine

TYSON HOLLY FARMS 400 Mark Martin

MELLO YELLO 500 Davey Allison

AC DELCO 500 Alan Kulwicki

CHECKER 500 Dale Earnhardt

ATLANTA JOURNAL 500 Morgan Shepherd

FORMULA ONE GRAND PRIX CHAMPIONSHIP

Formula One World Champion Ayrton Senna (Brazil)

RACE WINNERS

PHOENIX GRAND PRIX Ayrton Senna (Brazil)

BRAZILIAN GRAND PRIX Alain Prost (France)

SAN MARINO GRAND PRIX Riccardo Patrese (Italy)

MONACO GRAND PRIX Ayrton Senna (Brazil)

CANADIAN GRAND PRIX Ayrton Senna (Brazil)

MEXICAN GRAND PRIX Alain Prost (France)

FRENCH GRAND PRIX Alain Prost (France)

BRITISH GRAND PRIX Alain Prost (France)

WEST GERMAN GRAND PRIX Ayrton Senna (Brazil)

HUNGARIAN GRAND PRIX Thierry Boutsen (Belgium)

BELGIAN GRAND PRIX Ayrton Senna (Brazil)

ITALIAN GRAND PRIX Ayrton Senna (Brazil)

PORTUGUESE GRAND PRIX Nigel Mansell (UK)

SPANISH GRAND PRIX Alain Prost (France)

JAPANESE GRAND PRIX Nelson Piquet (Brazil)

AUSTRIALIAN GRAND PRIX Nelson Piquet (Brazil)

MISCELLANEOUS RACES

DAYTONA 500 Derrike Cope

INDIANAPOLIS 500 Arie Luyendyk (Netherlands)

24 HOURS OF LE MANS John Nielsen (Denmark)/Price Cobb (US)/Martin Brundle (UK)

24 HOURS OF DAYTONA Davy Jones (US)/Jan Lammers (Netherlands)/Andy Wallace (UK)

WORLD SOLAR CHALLENGE "The Spirit of Biel" (Switzerland)

BASEBALL

MAJOR LEAGUE BASEBALL

1990 REGULAR SEASON FINAL STANDINGS

AMERICAN LEAGUE EAST				
Team	W	L	Pct	GB
Boston	88	74	.543	—
Toronto	86	76	.531	2
Detroit	79	83	.488	9
Cleveland	77	85	.475	11
Baltimore	76	85	.472	11½
Milwaukee	74	88	.457	14
New York	67	95	.414	21
AMERICAN LEAGUE WEST				
Oakland	103	59	.636	—
Chicago	94	68	.580	9
Texas	83	79	.512	20
California	80	82	.494	23
Seattle	77	85	.475	26
Kansas City	75	86	.466	27½
Minnesota	74	88	.457	29
NATIONAL LEAGUE EAST				
Pittsburgh	95	67	.586	—
New York	91	71	.562	4
Montreal	85	77	.525	10
Philadelphia	77	85	.475	18
Chicago	77	85	.475	18
St. Louis	70	92	.432	25
NATIONAL LEAGUE WEST				
Cincinnati	91	71	.562	—
Los Angeles	86	76	.531	5
San Francisco	85	77	.525	6
San Diego	75	87	.463	16
Houston	75	87	.463	16
Atlanta	65	97	.401	26

BASEBALL AWARDS

MOST VALUABLE PLAYER (MVP)

American League Rickey Henderson (Oakland A's)

National League Barry Bonds (Pittsburgh Pirates)

CY YOUNG AWARD

American League Bob Welch (Oakland A's)

National League Doug Drabek (Pittsburgh Pirates)

MANAGER OF THE YEAR

American League Jeff Torborg (Chicago White Sox)

National League Jim Leyland (Pittsburgh Pirates)

ROOKIE OF THE YEAR AWARD

American League Sandy Alomar Jr. (Cleveland Indians)

National League Dave Justice (Atlanta Braves)

1990 STATISTICAL LEADERS

BATTING AVERAGE

American League .329 George Brett (Kansas City Royals)

National League .335 Willie McGee (St. Louis Cardinals)

HOME RUNS

American League 51 Cecil Fielder (Detroit Tigers)

National League 40 Ryne Sandberg (Chicago Cubs)

RBIs

American League 132 Cecil Fielder (Detroit Tigers)

National League 122 Matt Williams (San Francisco Giants)

WINS

American League 27-6 Bob Welch (Oakland A's)

National League 22-6 Doug Drabek (Pittsburgh Pirates)

EARNED RUN AVERAGE (ERA)

American League 1.93 Roger Clemens (Boston Red Sox)

National League 2.21 Danny Darwin (Houston Astros)

SAVES

American League 57 Bobby Thigpen (Chicago White Sox)

National League 33 John Franco (New York Mets)

LEAGUE CHAMPIONSHIP SERIES (LCS)

AMERICAN LEAGUE CHAMPIONSHIP SERIES (ALCS)

Oakland A's 4 Boston Red Sox 0

Game 1 (at Boston) Oakland 9 Boston 1

Game 2 (at Boston) Oakland 4 Boston 1

Game 3 (at Oakland) Oakland 4 Boston 1

Game 4 (at Oakland) Oakland 3 Boston 1

MVP Dave Stewart (Oakland)

NATIONAL LEAGUE CHAMPIONSHIP SERIES (NLCS)

Cincinnati Reds 4 Pittsburgh Pirates 2

Game 1 (at Cincinnati) Pittsburgh 4 Cincinnati 3

Game 2 (at Cincinnati) Cincinnati 2 Pittsburgh 1

Game 3 (at Pittsburgh) Cincinnati 6 Pittsburgh 3

Game 4 (at Pittsburgh) Cincinnati 5 Pittsburgh 3

Game 5 (at Pittsburgh) Pittsburgh 3 Cincinnati 2

Game 6 (at Cincinnati) Cincinnati 2 Pittsburgh 1

MVP Randy Meyers and Rob Dibble (Cincinnati)

WORLD SERIES

Cincinnati Reds 4 Oakland A's 0

Game 1 (at Cincinnati) Cincinnati 7 Oakland 0

Game 2 (at Cincinnati) Cincinnati 5 Oakland 4

Game 3 (at Oakland) Cincinnati 8 Oakland 3

Game 4 (at Oakland) Cincinnati 2 Oakland 1

MVP Jose Rijo (Cincinnati)

COLLEGE BASEBALL

COLLEGE WORLD SERIES

Georgia 2 Oklahoma State 1

Division II Champion Jacksonville State

Division III Champion Eastern Connecticut State

LITTLE LEAGUE WORLD SERIES

Taiwan 9 Shippensburg (PA) 0

BASKETBALL

NATIONAL BASKETBALL ASSOCIATION (NBA)

NBA 1989–90 FINAL STANDINGS

EASTERN CONFERENCE

Team	W	L	Pct
Detroit	59	23	.720
Chicago	55	27	.671
Philadelphia	53	29	.646
Boston	52	30	.634
New York	45	37	.549
Milwaukee	44	38	.537
Cleveland	42	40	.512
Indiana	42	40	.512
Atlanta	41	41	.500
Washington	31	51	.378
Miami	18	64	.220
Orlando	18	64	.220
New Jersey	17	65	.207

WESTERN CONFERENCE

Team	W	L	Pct
L.A. Lakers	63	19	.768
Portland	59	23	.720
San Antonio	56	26	.683
Utah	55	27	.671
Phoenix	54	28	.659
Dallas	47	35	.573
Denver	43	39	.524
Houston	41	41	.500
Seattle	41	41	.500
Golden State	37	45	.451
L.A. Clippers	30	52	.356
Sacramento	23	59	.280
Minnesota	22	60	.268
Charlotte	19	63	.232

NBA AWARDS

MVP Magic Johnson (Los Angeles Lakers)

Rookie of the Year David Robinson (San Antonio Spurs)

Sixth Man Ricky Pierce (Milwaukee Bucks)

Defensive Player of the Year Dennis Rodman (Detroit Pistons)

NBA 1989–90 STATISTICAL LEADERS

Points (average) 33.6 Michael Jordan (Chicago Bulls)

Rebounds (average) 14.0 Akeem Olajuwon (Houston Rockets)

Assists (average) 14.5 John Stockton (Utah Jazz)

NBA PLAYOFFS

Western Conference

First Round Results (Series)

LA Lakers 3 Houston Rockets 1

Phoenix Suns 3 Utah Jazz 2

San Antonio Spurs 3 Denver Nuggets 0

Portland Trail Blazers 3 Dallas Mavericks 0

Semifinals (Series)

Phoenix Suns 4 LA Lakers 1

Portland Trail Blazers 4 San Antonio Spurs 3

Finals (Series)

Portland Trail Blazers 4 Phoenix Suns 2

Eastern Conference

First Round (Series)

Detroit Pistons 3 Indiana Pacers 0

New York Knicks 3 Boston Celtics 2

Philadelphia 76ers 3 Cleveland Cavaliers 2

Chicago Bulls 3 Milwaukee Bucks 1

Semifinals (Series)

Detroit Pistons 4 New York Knicks 1

Chicago Bulls 4 Philadelphia 76ers 1

Finals (Series)

Detroit Pistons 4 Chicago Bulls 3

NBA CHAMPIONSHIP

Detroit Pistons 4 Portland Trail Blazers 1

Game 1 (at Detroit) Detroit 105 Portland 99

Game 2 (at Detroit) Portland 106 Detroit 105 (OT)

Game 3 (at Portland) Detroit 121 Portland 106

Game 4 (at Portland) Detroit 112 Portland 109

Game 5 (at Portland) Detroit 92 Portland 90

MVP Isiah Thomas (Detroit)

COLLEGE BASKETBALL

NCAA REGULAR SEASON CONFERENCE CHAMPIONS

American South Lousiana Tech, New Orleans (tie)
Atlantic Coast Clemson
Atlantic 10 Temple
Big East Syracuse, Connecticut (tie)
Big Eight Missouri
Big Sky Idaho
Big South Coastal Carolina
Big Ten Michigan State
Big West New Mexico State, UNLV (tie)
Colonial James Madison
East Coast Hofstra, Towson State (tie)
Ivy League Princeton
Metro Atlantic Holy Cross (north), La Salle (south)
Metro Louisville
Mid-American Ball State
Mid-Continent S.W. Missouri State
Mid-Eastern Coppin State
Midwestern Collegiate Xavier
Missouri Valley Southern Illinois
North Atlantic Boston U., Northeastern (tie)
Northeast Robert Morris
Ohio Valley Murray State
Pacific 10 Oregon State
Southeastern Georgia
Southern East Tennessee State
Southland N.E. Louisiana
Southwest Arkansas
Southwestern Southern
Sun Belt Alabama-Birmingham
Trans-America Centenary
West Coast Loyola Marymount
Western Athletic Colorado State

NCAA DIVISION I MEN'S BASKETBALL TOURNAMENT

East Regional
First Round
U. Conn 76 Boston U. 52
California 65 Indiana 63
Clemson 49 BYU 47
La Salle 79 S. Mississippi 63
St. John's 81 Temple 65
Duke 81 Richmond 46
UCLA 68 UAB 56
Kansas 79 Robert Morris 71

Second Round
U. Conn 74 California 54
Clemson 79 La Salle 75
Duke 76 St. John's 72
UCLA 71 Kansas 70

Regionals
U. Conn 71 Clemson 70
Duke 90 UCLA 81

Semifinals
Duke 79 U. Conn 78 (OT)

East Regional Final Four Qualifier Duke

Midwest Regional
First Round
Oklahoma 77 Towson State 68
UNC 83 S.W. Missouri State 70
Dayton 88 Illinois 86
Arkansas 68 Princeton 64
Xavier 87 Kansas State 79
Georgetown 70 Texas Southern 52
Texas 100 Georgia 88
Purdue 75 N.E. Louisiana 63

Second Round
UNC 79 Oklahoma 77
Arkansas 86 Dayton 84
Xavier 74 Georgetown 71
Texas 73 Purdue 72

Regionals
Arkansas 96 UNC 73
Texas 102 Xavier 89

Semifinals
Arkansas 88 Texas 85

Midwest Regional Final Four Qualifier
Arkansas

Southeast Regionals

First Round

Michigan State 75 Murray State 71 (OT)

UCSB 70 Houston 66

LSU 70 Villanova 63

Georgia Tech 99 E. Tennessee State 83

Minnesota 64 UTEP 61

N. Iowa 74 Missouri 71

Virginia 75 Notre Dame 67

Syracuse 70 Coppin State 48

Second Round

Michigan State 62 UCSB 58

Georgia Tech 94 LSU 91

Minnesota 81 N. Iowa 78

Syracuse 63 Virginia 61

Regionals

Georgia Tech 81 Michigan State 80 (OT)

Minnesota 82 Syracuse 75

Semifinals

Georgia Tech 93 Minnesota 91

Southeast Regional Final Four Qualifier

Georgia Tech

West Regionals

First Round

UNLV 102 Arkansas-Little Rock 72

Ohio State 84 Providence 83 (OT)

Ball State 54 Oregon State 53

Louisville 78 Idaho 59

Loyola Marymount 111 New Mexico State 92

Michigan 76 Illinois State 70

Alabama 71 Colorado State 54

Arizona 79 South Florida 67

Second Round

UNLV 76 Ohio State 65

Ball State 62 Louisville 60

Loyola Marymount 149 Michigan 115

Alabama 77 Arizona 55

Regionals

UNLV 69 Ball State 67

Loyola Marymount 62 Alabama 60

Semifinals

UNLV 131 Loyola Marymount 101

West Regional Final Four Qualifier UNLV

NCAA FINAL FOUR
(site: McNicholls Sports Arena, Denver, CO)

Semifinals

Duke 97 Arkansas 83

UNLV 90 Georgia Tech 81

Championship Game

UNLV 103 Duke 73

Final Four MVP Anderson Hunt (UNLV)

Other Championships

Division II Kentucky Wesleyan 93 Bakersfield State 79

Division III Rochester 43 DePauw 42

WOMEN'S NCAA DIVISION I CHAMPIONSHIPS

Final Four
(site: Thompson-Boling Arena, Knoxville, TN)

Semifinals

Auburn 81 Louisiana Tech 69

Stanford 75 Virginia 66

Championship Game

Stanford 88 Auburn 81

Final Four MVP Jennifer Azzi (Stanford)

Other Championships

Division II Delta State 77 Bentley 43

Division III Hope College 65 St. John Fisher 63

BOBSLED AND LUGE

BOBSLED

WORLD CHAMPIONSHIPS
(AT ST. MORITZ, SWITZERLAND)

Two-Man Bobsled Switzerland (Gustav Weder and Bruno Gerber)

Four-Man Bobsled Switzerland (Gustav Weder, driver)

LUGE

World Championships (at Calgary, Canada)

Singles (Men) Marcus Prock (Austria)

Doubles (Men) Hansjorg Raffl and Norbert Hubert (Italy)

Singles (Women) Gabi Kohlisch (East Germany)

BOWLING

P.B.A. Tour

Triple Crown Events

Seagram's Coolers U.S. Open Ron Palombi

Firestone Tournament of Champions Dave Ferraro

PBA National Championship Jim Pencak

Leading Money Winner $204,775, Amleto Monacelli (Venezuela)

P.B.A. Player of the Year Amleto Monacelli

BOXING

World Champions
(as of 30 December 1990)

Heavyweight

Evander Holyfield (US); W.B.A., W.B.C., I.B.F.

Cruiserweight

Robert Daniels (US), W.B.A.

Massimiliano Duran (Italy), W.B.C.

Jeff Lampkin (US), I.B.F.

Light Heavyweight

Virgil Hill (US), W.B.A.

Dennis Andries (UK), W.B.C.

Charles Williams (US), I.B.F.

Super Middleweight

Christopher Tiozzo (France), W.B.A.

Mauro Galvano (Italy), W.B.C.

Lindell Holmes (US), I.B.F.

Middleweight

Mike McCallum (US), W.B.A.

Julian Jackson (US), W.B.C.

Michael Nunn (US), I.B.F.

Junior Middleweight

Terry Norris (US), W.B.C.

Gianfranco Rossi (Italy), I.B.F.

W.B.A. title vacant

Welterweight

Aaron Davis (US), W.B.A.

Maurice Blocker (US), W.B.C.

Simon Brown (US), I.B.F.

Junior Welterweight

Loreto Garza (US), W.B.A.

Julio Cesar Chavez (Mexico), W.B.C., I.B.F.

Lightweight

Pernell Whitaker (US), W.B.A., W.B.C., I.B.F.

Junior Lightweight

Brian Mitchell (South Africa), W.B.A.

Azumah Nelson (Ghana), W.B.C.

Tony Lopez (US), I.B.F.

Featherweight

Antonio Esparragoza (Venezuela), W.B.A.

Marcos Villasana (Mexico), W.B.C.

Jorge Paez (Mexico), I.B.F.

Junior Featherweight

Luis Mendoza (Colombia), W.B.A

Pedro Decima (Argentina), W.B.C.

Welcome Ncita (South Africa), I.B.F.

Bantamweight

Lusita Espinosa (Philippines), W.B.A.

Raul Perez (Mexico), W.B.C.

Orlando Canizales (US), I.B.F.

Junior Bantamweight

Kaosai Galaxy (Thailand), W.B.A.

Sunkil Moon (South Korea), W.B.C.

Robert Quiroga (US), I.B.F.

Flyweight

Leopard Tamakuma (Japan), W.B.A.

Sot Chitalada (Thailand), W.B.C.

Dave McCauley (Ireland), I.B.F.

Junior Flyweight

Myung Woo-Yuh (South Korea), W.B.A.

Humberto Gonzalez (Mexico), W.B.C.

Michael Carbajal (US), I.B.F.

Mini-Flyweight

Bong-jun Kim (South Korea), W.B.A.

Ricardo Lopez (Mexico), W.B.C.

Far-Lan Lookmingkwan (Thailand), I.B.F.

CYCLING

TOUR DE FRANCE Greg LeMond (US)

WORLD CHAMPIONSHIPS (at Maebashi, Japan)

Men's Pro Road Rudy Dhaenene (Belgium)

Men's Pro Sprint Michael Hubner (East Germany)

Women's Road Catherine Marsal (France)

Women's Sprint Connie Paraskevin Young (US)

MISCELLANEOUS RACES

U.S. Pro Road Kurt Stockton (US)

Tour de Trump Raul Alcala (Mexico)

Tour of Italy Gianni Bugno (Italy)

U.S. Pro Championships Paolo Cimini (Italy)

Tour de Suisse Sean Kelly (Ireland)

FOOTBALL

NATIONAL FOOTBALL LEAGUE (NFL)

NFL 1990 FINAL STANDINGS
AMERICAN CONFERENCE
Eastern Division

Team	W	L	T	Pct.
Buffalo	13	3	0	.813
Miami	12	4	0	.750
Indianapolis	7	9	0	.438
N.Y. Jets	6	10	0	.375
New England	1	15	0	.063
Central Division				
Cincinnati	9	7	0	.563
Houston	9	7	0	.563
Pittsburgh	9	7	0	.563
Cleveland	3	13	0	.188
Western Division				
L.A. Raiders	12	4	0	.750
Kansas City	11	5	0	.688
Seattle	9	7	0	.563
San Diego	6	10	0	.375
Denver	5	11	0	.313

NFL 1990 FINAL STANDINGS (Continued)
NATIONAL CONFERENCE
Eastern Division

Team	W	L	T	Pct.
N.Y. Giants	13	3	0	.813
Philadelphia	10	6	0	.625
Washington	10	6	0	.625
Dallas	7	9	0	.438
Phoenix	5	11	0	.313
Central Division				
Chicago	11	5	0	.688
Tampa Bay	6	10	0	.375
Green Bay	6	10	0	.375
Detroit	6	10	0	.375
Minnesota	6	10	0	.375
Western Division				
San Francisco	14	2	0	.875
New Orleans	8	8	0	.500
L.A. Rams	5	11	0	.313
Atlanta	5	11	0	.313

NFL 1990 STATISTICAL LEADERS

Passing Yardage 4,689 yds Warren Moon (Houston Oilers)

Rushing 1,304 yds Barry Sanders (Detroit Lions)

Receptions 100 Jerry Rice (San Francisco 49ers)

Touchdowns 16 Barry Sanders (Detroit Lions)

Sacks 20 Derrick Thomas (Kansas City Chiefs)

Interceptions 10 Mark Carrier (Chicago Bears)

NFL PLAYOFFS

American Conference

Wildcard Games

Miami Dolphins 17 Kansas City Chiefs 16

Cincinnati Bengals 41 Houston Oilers 14

Second Round

Buffalo Bills 44 Miami Dolphins 34

L.A. Raiders 20 Cincinnati Bengals 10

A.F.C. Championship Game

Buffalo Bills 51 L.A. Raiders 3

National Conference

Wildcard Games

Chicago Bears 16 New Orleans Saints 6

Philadelphia Eagles 6 Washington Redskins 20

Second Round

New York Giants 31 Chicago Bears 3

San Francisco 49ers 28 Washington Redskins 10

N.F.C. CHAMPIONSHIP GAME

San Francisco 49ers 13 New York Giants 15

SUPER BOWL XXV (SITE: TAMPA STADIUM, TAMPA, FL)

New York Giants 21 Buffalo Bills 20

MVP O.J. Anderson (New York Giants)

NCAA COLLEGE FOOTBALL 1990

1990 NATIONAL CHAMPIONS Colorado (AP), Georgia Tech (UPI)

1990 NATIONAL POLLS	
Associated Press (Top Five)	
Team	Record
Colorado	11-1-1
Georgia Tech	11-0-1
Miami (FL)	10-2-0
Florida State	10-2-0
Washington	10-2-0
United Press International (Top Five)	
Team	Record
Georgia Tech	11-0-1
Colorado	11-1-1
Miami (FL)	10-2-0
Florida State	10-2-0
Washington	10-2-0

BIG FOUR BOWL GAMES (Played 1 January 1991)

ORANGE BOWL Colorado 10 Notre Dame 9

ROSE BOWL Washington 46 Iowa 34

COTTON BOWL Miami 46 Texas 3

SUGAR BOWL Tennessee 23 Virginia 22

OTHER BOWL GAMES

CALIFORNIA BOWL San Jose 48 Central Michigan 24

INDEPENDENCE BOWL Maryland 34 Lousiana Tech 34

ALOHA BOWL Syracuse 28 Arizona 0

LIBERTY BOWL Air Force 23 Ohio State 11

ALL-AMERICAN BOWL North Carolina State 31 Southern Mississippi 27

BLOCKBUSTER BOWL Florida State 24 Penn State 17

PEACH BOWL Auburn 27 Indiana 23

FREEDOM BOWL Colorado State 32 Oregon 31

HOLIDAY BOWL Texas A&M 65 BYU 14

JOHN HANCOCK BOWL Michigan State 17 Southern Cal 16

COPPER BOWL California 17 Wyoming 15

CITRUS BOWL Georgia Tech 45 Nebraska 21

FIESTA BOWL Louisville 34 Alabama 7

GATOR BOWL Michigan 35 Mississippi 3

HALL OF FAME BOWL Clemson 30 Illinois 0

NCAA DIVISION CHAMPIONS

Division I-AA Georgia Southern 36 Nevada 13

Division II North Dakota State 51 Indiana (PA) 11

Division III Allegheny College 21 Lycoming 14

NCAA AWARDS

Heisman Trophy Winner Ty Detmer (BYU)

Outland Trophy Russell Maryland (Miami [FL])

Butkus Award Alfred Williams (Colorado)

GOLF

GRAND SLAM EVENTS (MEN)

THE MASTERS Nick Faldo (UK)*

U.S OPEN Hale Irwin*

BRITISH OPEN Nick Faldo (UK)

P.G.A. CHAMPIONSHIP Wayne Grady (Australia)

GRAND SLAM (WOMEN)

NABISCO DINAH SHORE Betsy King

DU MAURIER CLASSIC Cathy Johnston

U.S. WOMAN'S OPEN Betsy King

MAZDA LPGA CHAMPIONSHIP Beth Daniel

1990 PGA TOURNAMENT WINNERS

MONY TOURNAMENT OF CHAMPIONS Paul Azinger

NORTHERN TELECOM TUCSON OPEN Robert Gamez

BOB HOPE CHRYSLER CLASSIC Peter Jacobsen

PHOENIX OPEN Tommy Armour III

AT&T PEBBLE BEACH NATIONAL PRO-AM Mark O'Meara

HAWAIIAN OPEN David Ishii

*Playoff Winner

SHEARSON LEHMAN HUTTON OPEN Dan Forsman

NISSAN LOS ANGELES OPEN Fred Couples

DORAL RYDER OPEN Greg Norman (Australia)*

HONDA CLASSIC John Huston

THE PLAYERS CHAMPIONSHIP Jodie Mudd

THE NESTLÉ INVITATIONAL Robert Gamez

INDEPENDENT INSURANCE AGENT OPEN Tony Sills*

THE MASTERS Nick Faldo (UK)*

DEPOSIT GUARANTEE GOLF CLASSIC Gene Sauers

MCI HERITAGE CLASSIC Payne Stewart*

K MART GREATER GREENSBORO CLASSIC Steve Elkington

USF&G CLASSIC David Frost (South Africa)

GTE BYRON NELSON GOLF CLASSIC Payne Stewart

MEMORIAL TOURNAMENT Greg Norman (Australia)

SOUTHWESTERN BELL COLONIAL Ben Crenshaw

BELLSOUTH ATLANTA CLASSIC Wayne Levi

KEMPER OPEN Gil Morgan

CENTEL WESTERN OPEN Wayne Levi

US OPEN Hale Irwin*

BUICK CLASSIC Hale Irwin

CANON GREATER HARTFORD OPEN Wayne Levi

ANHEUSER-BUSCH GOLF CLASSIC Lanny Wadkins

BANK OF BOSTON CLASSIC Morris Hatalsky

BUICK OPEN Chip Beck

FEDERAL EXPRESS ST. JUDE CLASSIC Tom Kite*

PGA CHAMPIONSHIP Wayne Grady (Australia)

THE INTERNATIONAL Davis Love III

NEC WORLD SERIES OF GOLF José Marie Olazabal

CHATTANOOGA CLASSIC Peter Persons

GREATER MILWAUKEE OPEN Jim Gallagher Jr.*

HARDEE'S GOLF CLASSIC Joey Sindelar*

CANADIAN OPEN Wayne Levi

B.C. OPEN Nolan Henke

BUICK SOUTHERN OPEN Kenny Knox*

H.E.B. TEXAS OPEN Mark O'Meara

LAS VEGAS INVITATIONAL Bob Tway*

WALT DISNEY WORLD/OLDSMOBILE CLASSIC Tim Simpson

NABISCO CHAMPIONSHIPS Jodie Mudd*

Skins Game Curtis Strange

*Playoff winner

1990 Leading Money Winner $1,165,477 Greg Norman (Australia)

Player of the Year Nick Faldo (UK)

Rookie of the Year Robert Gamez

1990 SENIOR PGA TOURNAMENT WINNERS

MONY SENIOR PGA TOURNAMENT OF CHAMPIONS George Archer

SENIOR SKINS GAME Arnold Palmer

ROYAL CARIBBEAN CLASSIC Lee Trevino

GTE SUNCOAST CLASSIC Mike Hill

AETNA CHALLENGE Lee Trevino

VINTAGE CHRYSLER INTERNATIONAL Lee Trevino

VANTAGE AT THE DOMINION Jim Dent

FUJI ELECTRIC GRAND SLAM Bob Charles

THE TRADITION AT DESERT MOUNTAIN Jack Nicklaus

PGA SENIORS CHAMPIONSHIP Gary Player

LIBERTY MUTUAL LEGENDS OF GOLF Charles Coody and Dale Douglass

MURATA REUNION PRO-AM Frank Beard

LAS VEGAS SENIOR CLASSIC Chi Chi Rodriguez

SOUTHWESTERN BELL CLASSIC Jimmy Powell

DOUG SANDERS KINGWOOD CELEBRITY CLASSIC Lee Trevino

BELL ATLANTIC CLASSIC Dale Douglass*

THE NYNEX COMMEMORATIVE Lee Trevino*

MAZDA SENIOR TPC Jack Nicklaus

MONY SYRACUSE SENIOR CLASSIC Jim Dent

DIGITAL SENIORS CLASSIC Bob Charles

USGA SENIOR OPEN Lee Trevino

NORTHVILLE LONG ISLAND CLASSIC George Archer

KROGER SENIOR CLASSIC Jim Dent

AMERITECH SENIOR OPEN Chi Chi Rodriguez

NEWPORT CUP Al Kelley

PAINEWEBBER INVITATIONAL Bruce Crampton

SUNWEST BANK/CHARLES PRIDE SENIOR GOLF CLASSIC Chi Chi Rodriguez

SHOWDOWN CLASSIC Rives McBee

GTE NORTHWEST CLASSIC George Archer

GTE NORTH CLASSIC Mike Hill*

VANTAGE BANK ONE CLASSIC Rives McBee

*Playoff winner

GREATER GRAND RAPIDS OPEN Don Massengale

CRESTAR CLASSIC Jim Dent

FAIRFIELD BARNETT SPACE COAST CLASSIC Mike Hill*

VANTAGE CHAMPIONSHIP Charles Coody

GATLIN BROTHERS SOUTHWEST GOLF CLASSIC Bruce Crampton

TRANSAMERICA SENIOR GOLF CHAMPIONSHIP Lee Trevino

GOLD RUSH AT RANCHO MURIETA George Archer

SECURITY PACIFIC SENIOR CLASSIC Mike Hill

GTE KAANAPALI CLASSIC Bob Charles

THE NEW YORK LIFE CHAMPIONS Mike Hill*

1990 Leading Money Winner $1,190,518 Lee Trevino

1990 LPGA TOURNAMENT WINNERS

THE JAMAICA CLASSIC Patty Sheehan

OLDSMOBILE LPGA CLASSIC Pat Bradley*

THE PHAR-MOR AT INVERRARY Jane Crafter

ORIX HAWAIIAN LADIES OPEN Beth Daniel

WOMAN'S KEMPER OPEN Beth Daniel

DESERT INN LPGA INTERNATIONAL Maggie Will

CIRCLE K LPGA TUCSON OPEN Colleen Walker

STANDARD REGISTER TURQUOISE CLASSIC Pat Bradley

NABISCO DINAH SHORE Betsy King

RED ROBIN KYOCERA INAMORI CLASSIC Kris Monaghan

SARA LEE CLASSIC Ayako Okamoto

CRESTAR CLASSIC Dottie Mochrie

PLANTERS PAT BRADLEY INTERNATIONAL Cindy Rarick

LPGA CORNING CLASSIC Pat Bradley

JC PENNEY LPGA SKINS GAME Jan Stephenson

LADY KEYSTONE OPEN Cathy Gerring

MCDONALD'S CHAMPIONSHIP Patty Sheehan

ATLANTIC CITY LPGA CLASSIC Chris Johnson

ROCHESTER INTERNATIONAL Patty Sheehan

DU MAURIER CLASSIC Cathy Johnston

JAMIE FARR TOLEDO CLASSIC Tina Purtzer

U.S. WOMEN'S OPEN Betsy King

THE PHAR-MOR IN YOUNGSTOWN Beth Daniel*

*Playoff Winner

MAZDA LPGA CHAMPIONSHIP Beth Daniel

BOSTON FIVE CLASSIC Barb Mucha*

STRATTON MOUNTAIN LPGA CLASSIC Cathy Gerring*

THE JAL BIG APPLE CLASSIC Betsy King

NORTHGATE LPGA CLASSIC Beth Daniel

RAIL CHARITY GOLD CLASSIC Beth Daniel

PING-CELLULAR ONE LPGA GOLD CHAMPIONSHIP Patty Sheehan

SAFECO CLASSIC Patty Sheehan

MBS LPGA CLASSIC Nancy Lopez*

CENTEL CLASSIC Beth Daniel

1990 Leading Money Winner $863,578 Beth Daniel

Player of the Year Beth Daniel

Rookie of the Year Hiromi Kobayashi (Japan)

U.S. AMATEUR CHAMPIONSHIP

Men Phil Mickelson

Women Pat Hurst

NCAA CHAMPIONSHIPS

MEN

Division I (individual) Phil Mickelson (Arizona State)

Division I (team) Arizona State

WOMEN

Division I (individual) Susan Slaughter (Arizona

Division I (team) Arizona State

HARNESS RACING

TRIPLE CROWN WINNERS

TROTTERS

Yonkers Trot Royal Troubador

Hambletonian Harmonious

Kentucky Futurity Star Music

PACERS

Cane Pace Jake and Elwood

Little Brown Jug Beach Towel

Messenger Stakes Jake and Elwood

HORSE RACING

Triple Crown Winners

Kentucky Derby Unbridled (Craig Perret)

Preakness Stakes Summer Squall (Pat Day)

Belmont Stakes Go and Go (Michael Kinane)

The Breeders' Cup

Sprint Safety Kept (Craig Perret)

Juvenile Fillies Meadow Star (José Santos)

Distaff Bayakoa (Laffit Pincay Jr.)

Mile Royal Academy (Lester Piggott)

Juvenile Fly So Free (José Santos)

Turf In the Wings (Gary Stevens)

Classic Unbridled (Pat Day)

International Races

Prix de l'Arc de Triomphe, France Sumarez (Gerald Mosse)

Epsom Derby, England Quest for Fame (Pat Eddery)

Irish Derby, Ireland Salsabil (Willie Carson)

Grand National, England Mr. Frisk (Marcus Armatyge)

1990 Eclipse Awards

Horse of the Year Criminal Type

Jockey Craig Perret

Trainer Carl Nafzger

Breeder Calumet Farm

Owner Frances Genter

ICE HOCKEY

NHL 1989-90 FINAL STANDINGS
WALES CONFERENCE
Patrick Division

Team	W	L	T	Pts
N.Y. Rangers	36	31	13	85
New Jersey	37	34	9	83
Washington	36	38	6	78
N.Y. Islanders	31	38	11	73
Pittsburgh	32	40	8	72
Philadelphia	30	39	11	71

NHL 1989-90 FINAL STANDINGS
(Continued)
WALES CONFERENCE
Adams Division

Team	W	L	T	Pts
Boston	46	25	9	101
Buffalo	45	27	8	98
Montreal	41	28	11	93
Hartford	38	33	9	85
Quebec	12	61	7	31

CAMPBELL CONFERENCE
Norris Division

Team	W	L	T	Pts
Chicago	41	33	6	88
St. Louis	37	34	9	83
Toronto	38	38	4	80
Minnesota	36	40	4	76
Detroit	28	38	14	70

Smythe Division

Team	W	L	T	Pts
Calgary	42	23	15	99
Edmonton	38	28	14	90
Winnipeg	37	32	11	85
Los Angeles	34	39	7	75
Vancouver	25	41	14	64

NHL 1989-90 Statistical Leaders

Points 142 Wayne Gretzky (Los Angeles Kings)

Goals 72 Brett Hull (St. Louis Blues)

Assists 102 Wayne Gretzky (Los Angeles Kings)

NHL Awards 1989-90

Hart Trophy (MVP) Mark Messier (Edmonton Oilers)

Art Ross Trophy (scoring champion) Wayne Gretzky (Los Angeles Kings)

Vezina Trophy (top goalie) Patrick Roy (Montreal Canadiens)

Calder Trophy (top rookie) Sergei Makarov (Calgary Flames)

NHL Playoffs 1989-90

WALES CONFERENCE

Adams Division

First Round

Boston Bruins 4 Hartford Whalers 3

Montreal Canadiens 4 Buffalo Sabres 2

Semifinals

Boston Bruins 4 Montreal Canadiens 1

Adams Division Champion Boston Bruins

Patrick Division

First Round

New York Rangers 4 New York Islanders 1

Washington Capitals 4 New Jersey 2

Semifinals

Washington Capitals 4 New York Rangers 1

Patrick Division Champions Washington Capitals

Wales Conference Final

Boston Bruins 4 Washington Capitals 0

CAMPBELL CONFERENCE

Norris Division

First Round

Chicago Blackhawks 4 Minnesota North Stars 3

St. Louis Blues 4 Toronto Maple Leafs 1

Semifinals

Chicago Blackhawks 4 St. Louis Blues 1

Norris Division Champion Chicago Blackhawks

SMYTHE DIVISION

First Round

Los Angeles Kings 4 Calgary Flames 2

Edmonton Oilers 4 Winnipeg Jets 3

Semifinals

Edmonton Oilers 4 Los Angeles Kings 0

Smythe Division Champions Edmonton Oilers

Campbell Conference Final

Edmonton Oilers 4 Chicago Blackhawks 2

Stanley Cup Final 1989-90

Edmonton Oilers 4 Boston Bruins 1

MVP Bill Ranford (Edmonton Oilers)

ICE SKATING

FIGURE SKATING

**WORLD CHAMPIONSHIPS
(at Halifax, Nova Scotia, Canada)**

Men's Champion Kurt Browning (Canada)

Women's Champion Jill Trenary (US)

Pairs Champions Ekaterina Gordeeva and Sergei Grinkov (USSR)

Dance Champions Marina Klimova and Sergei Ponomarenko (USSR)

MOTORCYCLE RACING

WORLD CHAMPIONS

125 cc Loris Capirossi (Italy)

250 cc John Kocinski (US)

500 cc Wayne Rainey (US)

RODEO

PRCA All-Around World Champion Ty Murray (US)

SKIING

ALPINE WORLD CUP CHAMPIONS

Overall

Men Pirmin Zurbriggen (Switzerland)

Women Petra Kronberger (Austria)

INDIVIDUAL CHAMPIONS (MEN)

Downhill Helmut Hoeflehner (Austria)

Slalom Armin Bittner (West Germany)

Giant Slalom Ole-Kristian Furuseth (Norway), Guenther Mader (Austria) (tie)

Super Giant Slalom Pirmin Zurbriggen (Switzerland)

INDIVIDUAL CHAMPIONS (WOMEN)

Downhill Katrin Gutensohn-Knoph (West Germany)

Slalom Vreni Schneider (Switzerland)

Giant Slalom Anita Wachter (Austria)

Super Giant Slalom Carole Merle (France)

SLED DOG RACING

The Iditarod Susan Butcher, 11 days 53 mins 23 sec

SNOOKER

WORLD CHAMPIONSHIPS
(at Sheffield, England)

Winner Stephen Hendry (Scotland)

SOCCER

1990 WORLD CUP (at Italy)				
Group A Final Standings				
Team	W	L	T	Pts
Italy	3	0	0	6*
Czechoslovakia	2	1	0	4*
Austria	1	2	0	2
USA	0	3	0	0
Group B Final Standings				
Cameroon	2	1	0	4*
Romania	1	1	1	3*
Argentina	1	1	1	3*
USSR	1	0	2	2
Group C Final Standings				
Brazil	3	0	0	6*
Costa Rica	2	1	0	4*
Scotland	1	2	0	2
Sweden	0	3	0	0
Group D Final Standings				
West Germany	2	0	1	5*
Yugoslavia	2	1	0	4*
Colombia	1	1	1	3*
United Arab Emirates	0	3	0	0
Group E Final Standings				
Spain	2	0	1	5*
Belgium	2	1	0	4*
Uruguay	1	1	1	3*
South Korea	0	3	0	0
Group F Final Standings				
England	1	0	2	4*
Ireland	0	3	0	3*
Netherlands	0	3	0	3*
Egypt	0	1	2	2

* Second round qualifiers

Second Round

Italy 2 Uruguay 0

Ireland* 0 Romania 0

Brazil 0 Argentina 1

Spain 1 Yugoslavia 2

Cameroon 2 Colombia 1

England 1 Belgium 0

Czechoslovakia 4 Costa Rica 1

West Germany 2 Netherlands 1

Quarterfinals

Italy 1 Ireland 0

Argentina* 0 Yugoslavia 0

Cameroon 2 England 3

Czechoslovakia 0 West Germany 1

Semifinals

Italy 1 Argentina* 1

West Germany* 1 England 1

Third Place Game

Italy 2 England 1

World Cup Final

West Germany 1 Argentina 0

Leading Scorer 6 Salvatore Schillaci (Italy)

MAJOR INDOOR SOCCER LEAGUE (MISL)

CHAMPIONSHIP SERIES 1989-90

San Diego Sockers 4 Baltimore Blast 2

NCAA DIVISION I CHAMPIONSHIP

UCLA* 0 Rutgers 0

INTERNATIONAL CLUB CHAMPIONSHIPS

World Club Championship (at Tokyo, Japan)

A.C. Milan (Italy) 3 Olimpia (Paraguay) 0

European Champions Cup (at Vienna, Austria)

A.C. Milan (Italy) 1 Benfica (Portugal) 0

European Cup Winners' Cup (at Gothenberg, Sweden)

Sampdoria (Italy) 2 Anderlecht (Belgium) 0

* Won penalty kick shootout

U.E.F.A. Cup (two-game aggregate score final)

Juventus (Italy) 3 Fiorentina (Italy) 1

Fiorentina (Italy) 0 Juventus (Italy) 0

Juventus won 3-1 on aggregate

TENNIS

GRAND SLAM CHAMPIONSHIPS (1990)

AUSTRALIAN OPEN

Men's Singles Ivan Lendl (Czechoslovakia)

Women's Singles Steffi Graf (West Germany)

Men's Doubles Pieter Aldrich/Danie Visser (South Africa)

Women's Doubles Jana Novotna/Helena Sukova (Czechoslovakia)

Mixed Doubles Jim Pugh (US)/Natalya Zvereva (USSR)

FRENCH OPEN

Men's Singles Andres Gomez (Ecuador)

Women's Singles Monica Seles (Yugoslavia)

Men's Doubles Sergio Casal/Emilio Sanchez (Spain)

Women's Doubles Jana Novotna/Helena Sukova (Czechoslovakia)

Mixed Doubles Aranxta Sanchez Vicario/Jorge Lozano (Spain)

WIMBLEDON

Gentlemen's Singles Stefan Edberg (Sweden)

Ladies' Singles Martina Navrátilová (US)

Gentlemen's Doubles Rick Leach/Jim Pugh (US)

Ladies' Doubles Jana Novotna/Helena Sukova (Czechoslovakia)

Mixed Doubles Zina Garrison/Rick Leach (US)

US OPEN

Men's Singles Pete Sampras (US)

Women's Singles Gabriela Sabatini (Argentina)

Men's Doubles Pieter Aldrich/Danie Visser (South Africa)

Women's Doubles Martina Navrátilová/Gigi Fernandez (US)

Mixed Doubles Elizabeth Smylie/Todd Woodbridge (Australia)

ASSOCIATION OF TENNIS PROFESSIONALS (ATP) TOURNAMENT WINNERS 1990

B.P. NATIONAL (WELLINGTON, NZ) Emilio Sanchez (Spain)

AUSTRALIAN MEN'S HARDCOURTS (ADELAIDE) Thomas Muster (Austria)

NEW SOUTH WALES OPEN (SYDNEY) Yannick Noah (France)

NEW ZEALAND OPEN (AUCKLAND) Scott Davis (US)

AUSTRALIAN OPEN (MELBOURNE) Ivan Lendl (Czechoslovakia)

STELLA ARTOIS INDOOR (MILAN) Ivan Lendl (Czechoslovakia)

VOLVO TENNIS (SAN FRANCISCO) Andre Agassi (US)

SKYDOME WORLD TENNIS (TORONTO) Ivan Lendl (Czechoslovakia)

BELGIAN INDOOR CHAMPIONSHIP (BRUSSELS) Boris Becker (West Germany)

US PRO INDOOR TENNIS CHAMPIONSHIPS (PHILADELPHIA) Pete Sampras (US)

STUTTGART CLASSIC Boris Becker (West Germany)

VOLVO TENNIS INDOOR (MEMPHIS) Michael Stitch (West Germany)

ABN WORLD (ROTTERDAM) Brad Gilbert (US)

NEWSWEEK CHAMPIONS CUP (INDIAN WELLS) Stefan Edberg (Sweden)

LIPTON INT'L PLAYERS (KEY BISCAYNE) Andre Agassi (US)

PRUDENTIAL-BACHE SECURITIES CLASSIC (ORLANDO) Brad Gilbert (US)

JAPAN OPEN (TOKYO) Stefan Edberg (Sweden)

PHILIPS OPEN (NICE) Juan Aguilera (Spain)

MONTE CARLO OPEN Andrei Chesnokov (USSR)

MADRID GRAND PRIX Andres Gomez (Ecuador)

BMW OPEN (MUNICH) Karel Novacek (Czechoslovakia)

GERMAN OPEN (HAMBURG) Juan Aguilera (Spain)

US MEN'S CLAY COURTS (KIAWAH ISLAND) David Wheaton (US)

ITALIAN OPEN (ROME) Thomas Muster (Australia)

FRENCH OPEN (PARIS) Andres Gomez (Ecuador)

STELLA ARTOIS GRASS COURT (LONDON) Ivan Lendl (Czechoslovakia)

MANCHESTER OPEN Pete Sampras (US)

WIMBLEDON CHAMPIONSHIPS Stefan Edberg (Sweden)

SWISS OPEN (GSTAAD) Martin Jaite (Argentina)

SWEDISH OPEN (BASTAD) Richard Fromberg (Australia)

HALL OF FAME (NEWPORT) Pieter Aldrich (South Africa)

MERCEDES CUP (STUTTGART) Goran Ivanisevic (Yugoslavia)

SOVRAN BANK CLASSIC (WASHINGTON DC) Andre Agassi (US)

PLAYER'S INTERNATIONAL (TORONTO) Michael Chang (US)

VOLVO TENNIS (LOS ANGELES) Stefan Edberg (Sweden)

ATP CHAMPIONSHIP (CINCINNATI) Stefan Edberg (Sweden)

US HARDCOURTS (INDIANAPOLIS) Boris Becker (West Germany)

HAMLET CHALLENGE CUP (LONG ISLAND) Stefan Edberg (Sweden)

US OPEN (FLUSHING MEADOW) Pete Sampras (US)

GRAND PRIX PASSING SHOT (BORDEAUX) Guy Forget (France)

SWISS INDOORS (BASEL) John McEnroe (US)

QUEENSLAND OPEN (BRISBANE) Brad Gilbert (US)

AUSTRALIAN INDOOR TENNIS CHAMPIONSHIPS (SYDNEY) Boris Becker (West Germany)

SEIKO SUPER TENNIS (TOKYO) Ivan Lendl (Czechoslovakia)

STOCKHOLM OPEN Boris Becker (West Germany)

PARIS OPEN Stefan Edberg (Sweden)

DIET PEPSI INDOOR CHALLENGE (LONDON) Boris Becker (West Germany)

KREMLIN CUP (MOSCOW) Andre Cherkasov (USSR)

ATP WORLD CHAMPIONSHIPS (FRANKFURT) Andre Agassi (US)

1990 ATP Tour Leading Money Winner
$1,995,901 Stefan Edberg (Sweden)

KRAFT GENERAL FOODS WORLD TOUR TOURNAMENT WINNERS 1990

DANNON OPEN (BRISBANE) Natalya Zvereva (USSR)

NEW SOUTH WALES OPEN (SYDNEY) Natalya Zvereva (USSR)

AUSTRALIAN OPEN (MELBOURNE) Steffi Graf (West Germany)

PAN PACIFIC OPEN (TOKYO) Steffi Graf (West Germany)

VIRGINIA SLIMS OF CHICAGO Martina Navrátilová (US)

VIRGINIA SLIMS OF WASHINGTON Martina Navrátilová (US)

VIRGINIA SLIMS OF INDIAN WELLS Martina Navrátilová (US)

VIRGINIA SLIMS OF FLORIDA (BOCA RATON) Gabriela Sabatini (Argentina)

LIPTON PLAYERS INTERNATIONAL (KEY BISCAYNE) Monica Seles (Yugoslavia)

VIRGINIA SLIMS OF HOUSTON Katerina Maleeva (Bulgaria)

US HARDCOURTS (SAN ANTONIO) Monica Seles (Yugoslavia)

FAMILY CIRCLE MAGAZINE CUP (HILTON HEAD ISLAND) Martina Navrátilová (US)

BAUSCH & LOMB CHAMPIONSHIPS (AMELIA ISLAND) Steffi Graf (West Germany)

JAPAN OPEN (TOKYO) Catarina Lindqvist (Sweden)

ECKERD TENNIS OPEN (TAMPA) Monica Seles (Yugoslavia)

INT'L CHAMPIONSHIPS OF SPAIN (BARCELONA) Arantxa Sanchez Vicario (Spain)

CITIZEN CUP (HAMBURG) Steffi Graf (West Germany)

ITALIAN OPEN (ROME) Monica Seles (Yugoslavia)

GERMAN OPEN (BERLIN) Monica Seles (Yugoslavia)

EUROPEAN OPEN (GENEVA) Barbara Paulus (Austria)

FRENCH OPEN (PARIS) Monica Seles (Yugoslavia)

DOW CLASSIC (BIRMINGHAM) Zina Garrison (US)

PILKINGTON GLASS CHAMPIONSHIPS (EASTBOURNE) Martina Navrátilová (US)

WIMBLEDON CHAMPIONSHIPS Martina Navrátilová (US)

VIRGINIA SLIMS OF NEWPORT Arantxa Sanchez Vicario (Spain)

CANADIAN OPEN (MONTREAL) Steffi Graf (West Germany)

GREAT AMERICAN BANK CLASSIC (SAN DIEGO) Steffi Graf (West Germany)

VIRGINIA SLIMS OF ALBUQUERQUE Jana Novotna (Czechoslovakia)

VIRGINIA SLIMS OF LOS ANGELES Monica Seles (Yugoslavia)

US Open (Flushing Meadow) Gabriela Sabatini (Argentina)

Volkswagen Grand Prix (Leipzig) Steffi Graf (West Germany)

Moscow Open Leila Meskhi (USSR)

European Indoors (Zurich) Steffi Graf (West Germany)

Porsche Tennis Grand Prix (Fildenstadt, W. Ger.) Mary Joe Fernandez (US)

Midland Bank Championships (Brighton) Steffi Graf (West Germany)

Puerto Rico Open Jennifer Capriati (US)

Virginia Slims of Oakland Monica Seles (Yugoslavia)

Virginia Slims of New England Steffi Graf (West Germany)

Virginia Slims Championship New York Monica Seles (Yugoslavia)

1990 Leading Money Winner $1,921,853 Steffi Graf (West Germany)

TRACK AND FIELD

Mobil Grand Prix 1990 Final Standings

Men

Leroy Burrell (US) 63 points

Nourredine Morceli (Algeria) 61 points

Danny Harris (US) 59 points

Women

Merlene Ottey (Jamaica) 63 points

Heike Drechsler (East Germany) 63 points

Petra Felke (East Germany) 63 points

Ilke Wyludda (East Germany) 63 points

Ana Quirot (Cuba) 63 points

Patti-Sue Plumer (US) 63 points

Marathons

Race Winners

New York City (Men) Douglas Wakiihuri (Kenya)

New York City (Women) Wanda Panfil (Poland)

Boston (Men) Gelindo Bordin (Italy)

Boston (Women) Rosa Mota (Portugal)

European Championships (Men) Gelindo Bordin (Italy)

European Championships (Women) Rosa Mota (Portugal)

NCAA Championships

Outdoors

Team Champions (Men) Lousiana State

Team Champions (Women) Lousiana State

Indoors

Team Champions (Men) Arkansas

Team Champions (Women) Texas

Cross Country

World Championships (at Aix-les-Bains, France)

Men's Champion Khalid Skah (Morocco)

Women's Champion Lynn Jennings (US)

WRESTLING

NCAA Championships

Team Champions Oklahoma State

118 lbs Jack Griffin (Northwestern)

126 lbs Terry Brands (Iowa)

134 lbs Tom Brands (Iowa)

142 lbs Joe Reynolds (Oklahoma)

150 lbs Brian Dolph (Indiana)

158 lbs Dan St. John (Arizona State)

167 lbs Dan St. John (Arizona State)

177 lbs Chris Barnes (Oklahoma State)

190 lbs Matt Ruppell (Lehigh)

Heavyweight Kurt Angle (Clarion)

YACHTING

Whitbread Round the World Race *Steinlager 2*, Peter Blake (New Zealand)

Vendée Globe Challenge *Ecureuil d'Aquitaine*, Titouan Lamazou (France)

I would like to thank Andrew C. Young, the British Broadcasting Corporation's 1987 "Brain of Sport" champion, for his help in compiling this review. —M.Y.

ILLUSTRATION CREDITS

William S. Romano, Jr.: 107   Dale Williams: all other illustrations

PHOTOGRAPH CREDITS

t=top b=bottom m=middle l=left r=right

Abilene-Christian University: 86t
Allsport: 59t, 59b, 132t, 139t, 141bl, 141tr, 145tl, 145tr, 145bl, 147t, 158t, 165t, 191ml, 191br
America's Cup Organizing Committee: 206b, 207tl, 207tr

Allsport/Robert Beck: 24b
Bruce Bennett: 122b, 123b, 129tr, 129br, 130b, 131tl
Bruce Bennett/Scott A. Levy: 121b
The Blood-Horse: 116b
Brigham Young University: 87ml
Allsport/Simon Bruty: 104b, 105b, 163b, 203b

California Angels: 15bl
Allsport/David Cannon: 102br
Chicago Bears: 72br
Chicago White Sox: 15br, 16t
Clemson University; 41bl
Bob Coglianese: 112tr, 114b, 118b, 119t

Allsport/Tim DeFrisco: 31br
Allsport/Tony Duffy: 108bl, 108mr, 145br, 169t, 197t

Edmonton Eskimos: 90t
Edmonton Oilers: 129tl

James Fain: 152t, 153b, 153t

Golden Bear International: 96 (all), 97 (all)
Grambling State University: 87tr
Allsport/Otto Greule: 27br

Ken Haldeman: 57b
Allsport/Scott Hallesan: 189b
Hamilton Tiger-Cats: 91m
University of Houston: 35br
Richard Howard: 19b

University of Illinois: 78mr
Indianapolis Colts: 72tr
International Tennis Hall of Fame and Tennis Museum: 175t, 175b, 176b, 176t, 180t, 183t, 188b

Keeneland Library: 112tl
Allsport/Pascal Kondeau: 8t

Ladies' Professional Golf Association: 100t, 101b, 103ml, 103tr, 103br
Allsport/Ken Levine: 5t, 5b, 31bl
Allsport/Robert Levine: 30t
Bruce Bennett/Scott A. Levy: 121b
Los Angeles Dodgers: 15tm
Los Angeles Raiders: 78tl
Los Angeles Rams: 67bl
Lousiana State University: 38bl

Allsport/Bob Martin: 180b
Miami Dolphins: 67br, 75t
University of Michigan: 88t
Allsport/Adrian Murrell: 52b, 156t

University of Nevada, Las Vegas: 38br
New York Giants: 72bl
New York Yankees: 14bl, 15tr, 22t, 23b
University of Notre Dame: 35bl, 79b

Oakland Athletics: 14br
Orienteering North America: 148bl, 148br

Philadelphia Phillies: 14tr
Allsport/Mike Powell: 6b, 48b, 50t, 144, 172t
Allsport/Steve Powell: 43b, 146tr, 194b
Professional Bowlers Association: 44b, 45tl, 45bl, 45tr

Seattle Mariners: 15bm, 18b
Allsport/Rick Stewart: 184t
Bud Somerville: 53b
Syracuse University: 39b

Allsport/Oli Tennent: 201b
University of Texas 41br
Texas Rangers: 14tl
Toronto Blue Jays: 15tl

United States Fencing Association: 61t
United States Field Hockey Association: 62t
United States International Speedskating Association: 134bl, 134br, 146tl
United States Modern Pentathlon Association: 137tr, 137br
Utah Jazz 27bl

Allsport/Van Drystadt: 56t, 56b, 146b, 158b, 159b, 209tl, 209tr

Allsport/Steve Wade: 102bl
University of Washington: 83t
Washington Capitals: 130t
Women's International Bowling Congress: 46b, 47t

INDEX